KU-301-631

INVESTMENT & SAVINGS HANDBOOK

1997/98

General Editor:

David Ballance

Investment Director

PITMAN PUBLISHING
128 Long Acre, London WC2E 9AN
Tel: +44 (0) 171 447 2000
Fax: +44 (0) 171 240 5771

A Division of Pearson Professional Limited

First published in Great Britain by Pitman Publishing in 1996

© Allied Dunbar Assurance plc 1997

The right of David Ballance to be identified as author of
this work has been asserted by him in accordance with the
Copyright, Designs and Patents Act 1988.

ISBN 0 273 62805 4

British Library Cataloguing in Publication Data
A CIP catalogue record for this book can be obtained
from the British Library

All rights reserved; no part of this publication may be reproduced,
stored in a retrieval system, or transmitted in any form or by any means,
electronic, mechanical, photocopying, recording, or otherwise without either
the prior written permission of the Publishers or a licence permitting restricted
copying in the United Kingdom issued by the Copyright Licensing Agency Ltd,
90 Tottenham Court Road, London W1P 9HE. This book may not be lent,
resold, hired out or otherwise disposed of by way of trade in any form
of binding or cover other than that in which it is published,
without the prior consent of the Publishers.

Typeset by M Rules
Printed and bound in Great Britain by Biddles Ltd, Guildford and King's Lynn

*The Publishers' policy is to use paper manufactured
from sustainable forests.*

No responsibility for loss occasioned to any person acting or refraining
from action as a result of the material in this publication can be
accepted by Allied Dunbar, the author or publishers.

The views and opinions of Allied Dunbar may not necessarily coincide
with some of the views and opinions expressed in this book which
are solely those of the author and no endorsement of them by
Allied Dunbar should be inferred.

CONTENTS

PREFACE

The Allied Dunbar Investment and Savings Handbook is now in its eighteenth year of publication. This year's edition covers, as usual, all the major areas and aspects of investment. Of the 21 chapters in the Handbook, 19 are devoted to specific investment areas and the remaining two, the first and the last, are the Introduction and a chapter on Investor Protection. All the chapters have been fully revised and updated.

Where investment decisions lead the reader into other specialised areas, eg inheritance tax, the making of wills etc, reference should be made to other products in the Allied Dunbar Library.

It is important to note that Scottish law varies from English law on many subjects, but in most aspects of tax, trusts and domicile, the two systems coincide.

The Law is stated as at 31 December 1996; in compiling this year's book we have endeavoured to include any changes caused by the General Election, but given the date of the new Government's Budget it is possible that there are some omissions. Not the least because of this I should like to record my grateful thanks to all this years' contributors for their hard work and their punctuality.

David Ballance
June 1997

Some favourite investment maxims from our authors

'Buy low, sell high.'   (Anon)

'If it's obvious, it's obviously wrong.'   (Joe Granville)

'Market dogmatists frequently bark up the wrong trees.'
(David Fuller)

'Beware of company chairmen who either:
  a) wear more gold than is in the balance sheet
  b) have an all-year-round sun tan.'   (David Ballance)

'Endeavour to chain-link decisions. Before dealing in a stock look back at what has happened (if anything) since your previous transaction in that stock, and relate this to the change in the share price.'   (idem)

'Test the extremes. Suppose you are tempted to buy for a 20 per cent gain, but fear a 20 per cent fall. Ask yourself a different question – which is more likely, a doubling or a halving of the share price?'   (idem)

'If it sounds too good to be true – it is.'   (Jeremy Burnett Rae)

'All markets are cyclical and short-term performance is more about timing of investment and sale decisions than anything else.'   (Geoff Abbott)

'When all advisers and commentators are in agreement be warned — the market is approaching the top or the bottom of its current cycle.'   (idem)

'When property values fall below the cost of the bricks and mortar on site – start buying.'   (idem)

'In depressed markets lenders will always try to support you through into the recovery phase – so as to be sure of getting all their money back.' (idem)

'When you observe a strong consensus, take the opposite view.' (David Fuller)

'Trust in a sufficiency of wealth as the by-product of a good life.' (John Train)

'Soar not too high to fall; but stoop to rise.' (Philip Massinger 1583–1640, from *The Duke of Milan*)

'When choosing an investment for tax reasons follow the "Yellow Box Principle". Do not enter the box unless your exit is clear.' (Stuart Reynolds)

'Learning from your own mistakes is all very well, but learning from the mistakes of others is cheaper.' (Oscar Wilde)

'Experience is the name everyone gives to his mistakes.' (idem)

'An economist is an expert who will know tomorrow why the things he predicted yesterday didn't happen today.' (Prof L J Peter)

'The riskiest place to leave one's long-term investments is in a deposit account.' (D W Adams)

'The best time to invest is when you have the cash.' (Sir John Templeton)

'The closest you can come to safety in investing is to buy shares in many countries and many industries.' (Sir John Templeton)

CONTRIBUTORS

Geoffrey Abbott, Dip FBA (Lon) FRICS, is Agricultural Investment Partner and Head of Purchases & Sales Department in Smiths Gore (Chartered Surveyors) based in their London Office. He was assisted by a number of his partners in their sixteen offices throughout England & Scotland.

Douglas W Adams, MA, MBA, is Business Planning Director at Templeton Investment Management Ltd, the UK subsidiary of the world-wide Franklin Templeton Group. Templeton manage over £7.0bn in emerging markets portfolios. Mr Adams is an economist by profession.

William Adams is Head of Metals Research at Rudolf Wolff & Co Ltd; the company was one of the founding members of the London Metal Exchange in 1876. He is involved in fundamental and technical analysis of the markets and in the operation of technical trading systems.

David Ballance, MA (Oxon), is Director of the European Investment Department at Threadneedle Investment Managers Ltd, and also has previous experience in UK equities.

William Bourne, MA (Oxon) is a Director of Threadneedle Investment Managers Ltd with responsibility for Strategic Research.

Andrew Bull, ARICS, is a Partner at Jones Lang Wootton, the world's largest independent property consultants with specific responsibilities for the investment strategy and implementation of two UK pension funds.

Peter Howe, LLB, Barrister, is Company Secretary and a Divisional Director in the legal department of Allied Dunbar Assurance plc. The legal department provides a complete legal and technical service to companies in the Allied Dunbar Group. Financial Services legislation is his principal area of specialisation.

Vince Jerrard, LLB, ACII, Solicitor, is the Legal Director of Allied Dunbar Assurance plc. Mr Jerrard has contributed chapters to other Allied Dunbar publications, including the *Tax Handbook*, *Capital Taxes Guide* and the *Business Tax and Law Handbook*.

Michael Kemp is the Director in charge of derivatives and quantitative research at Threadneedle Investment Managers Ltd. He gained a first class Honours Degree from Cambridge University in 1981, qualified as an Actuary in 1987 and was a partner in the investment consulting practice of Bacon & Woodrow, Consulting Actuaries, before joining Threadneedle in early 1996.

Ross MacLean, LLB, is Assistant Company Secretary of Threadneedle Investment Managers Ltd and the IMRO Compliance Officer of Eagle Star Unit Managers Ltd.

Paul Manduca, MA (Oxon), is the founding Chief Executive of Threadneedle Asset Management Ltd, having joined from Henderson Touche where he was previously Group Deputy Managing Director. He also sits on the Executive Committee of the Institutional Fund Managers' Association and sits as an investment adviser on the Universities' Superannuation Scheme and the Lord Chancellor's Public Trustee Investment Committee.

John Myers and Ian Somerville are from Solon Consultants, a specialised research firm that focuses on property and alternative investments. John Myers is also a visiting professor at Strathclyde Business School and has been a contributor to the *Allied Dunbar Investment and Savings Handbook* since it was first published in 1980.

Stuart Reynolds, LLB, is a Divisional Director in the Legal Department of Allied Dunbar Assurance plc where his primary responsibility is in relation to the development of new life assurance and pension products for the Company.

John Smithard, LLB, formerly a Member of The Stock Exchange and now a Member of the Securities Institute, is with stockbrokers James Capel Investment Management, a division of HSBC Investment Bank.

Mike Wilkes is a Senior Tax Manager with Pannell Kerr Forster, an international firm of chartered accountants. He specialises in the taxation of Lloyd's underwriters and foreign domiciled individuals, but also deals with the general taxation affairs of a number of other personal clients.

INTRODUCTION

PAUL MANDUCA

Threadneedle Asset Management Ltd

This book, which was first published in 1980, is aimed primarily at the investment adviser and is designed to give an annual update on the various types of investment. Most chapters include a section designed to cover highlights of the previous year, a preview of the coming year and a view on the next year or two based on current thinking.

This chapter covers the following topics:

- the investment adviser;
- types of investor;
- ways of arranging and holding investments;
- the nature of an investment;
- investment policy;
- trustees; and
- overseas investors.

1.1 INTRODUCTION

The basic principles of investment do not change. It is only the influences on investment policy that are likely to alter over the years. These influences are primarily of a political and economic nature, that is to say, the world economic climate and, for the UK investor, the economic and taxation policies of the government of the day.

The investment adviser's task is always to ensure that the client's asset portfolio is well balanced and robust in the face of changing investment conditions. When interest rates are exceptionally high, as they have been from time to time over the last two decades, the appeal of short-term deposits can be hard to resist. However, as we have seen more recently, interest rates can fall sharply, leaving clients with the twin problems of declining real value and declining income. The adviser must always be prepared if necessary to lean against the winds of investment fashion to ensure that his clients achieve the right balance of risk and reward to suit their personal circumstances through a portfolio which can deliver a satisfactory result regardless of fashion.

1.2 THE INVESTMENT ADVISER

Today's investment adviser has the unenviable burden of coping with more and more information about an increasing choice of investments. Nowadays, more investment media exist than ever before, described in an ever growing mass of literature, commented on by experts of varying experience and qualifications in an environment of proliferating legislation.

Against that background, the investment adviser — solicitor, accountant, stockbroker, insurance broker, bank manager or anyone else — has five main responsibilities:

(1) He needs to know which investment media are available and to establish which are suitable for his individual clients (particularly so following the passing of the Financial Services Act 1986).
(2) He needs to know which questions to ask about which investment medium and where to find the answers.
(3) He needs to be able to support his decision and, if necessary, show that his advice is not influenced by the method of remuneration.
(4) He must be able to make arrangements for a particular investment (or disinvestment) to be made on behalf of his clients.
(5) He will need to be kept up to date on a fast-changing regulatory framework which applies to all those in the business of providing investment advice.

Most important of all, he has to recognise his own limitations and to look for advice himself. That is the purpose of this book, which identifies the main investment media, identifies the investor for whom they are suitable or unsuitable (posing the main questions which should be asked about each medium) and provides signposts to the specialist consultants or dealers and to the legal, fiscal and other technicalities.

1.3 TYPES OF INVESTOR

This book is concerned with people advising individual investors (including trustees and family investment companies). It is essential that the adviser identifies the particular category of investor to which his client belongs. It would be impossible to devise a precise categorisation which is exhaustive and so it follows that the adviser must take into account a number of personal factors in appraising both the investor and also the investment and disinvestment situations with which he is concerned. These factors will include the investor's age and health, his intention with regard to his place of residence and/or domicile, his willingness to accept risk, his willingness to participate in the choice of investments and his capacity to delegate.

1.4 WAYS OF ARRANGING AND HOLDING INVESTMENTS

All the foregoing assumes considerable sophistication on the part of the investment adviser and also a willingness to give his time, for which he will obviously expect to be remunerated. The fact that investors of moderate means are usually unwilling to pay for this level of individual attention has meant that collective investment media have developed hand-in-hand with the relative decline of individually tailored investment portfolios. A corollary of this development is that an ever-growing body of legislation and regulation (see Chapter 21) has had to be developed to protect the small saver against fraud or against unscrupulous salesmanship.

In respect of many of the specific investments, comment is made on methods of arranging and holding those investments, although a number of such methods are common to many investment media. It is beyond the scope of this book to give detailed explanations or advice on either the mechanics of establishing and conducting the particular 'vehicle' or its taxation implications. The investment adviser will be aware that the principal ways in which investments can be arranged and held are:

(1) by personal direct investment by the individual;
(2) through a trust or settlement (including a will trust);
(3) in partnership with others;
(4) through a family investment company.

1.5 THE NATURE OF AN INVESTMENT

1.5.1 Capital and income

The two basic elements of investment are capital and income. At one end of the scale, the capital remains constant while the income produced may vary (eg bank and building society deposits); at the other end, there are non-income-producing assets (such as commodities and works of art) where no income is produced but the capital value fluctuates.

Between the two extremes, there are many variations. Gilt-edged securities can produce a constant level of income and a known repayment value at maturity. Short dated securities will have more certainty over the rise (or fall) in capital values to maturity whereas values of long-dated gilts will vary considerably as interest rates rise and fall. Investments in property or equities will produce variations in both capital value and income. Life assurances, such as single premium bonds, in theory produce no income while they are held as an investment, but in practice this disadvantage can be overcome by the various withdrawal plans which are available (see Chapter 14).

1.5.2 Inflation

An essential third element in evaluating investments is inflation. The need for a hedge against inflation has had a strong influence on investment policy since the 1960s. As inflation rates fluctuate, opinions will vary widely on what represents an effective hedge; inflation has different consequences for different people. Commodities, works of art or tangible assets may turn out to be a good hedge against inflation, but the same hope of finding a good hedge often underlies investment in land, buildings and shares in companies, both domestic and overseas. The list is endless; and the investor must take his pick, according to his own philosophy or judgement.

This is also an area where fashion can play a part. The current view is that inflation provides only a modest threat to markets which, on analysis would seem to mean that it has been below 4 per cent for just over three years. People with not particularly long memories will recall inflation at five times that level and everybody has to take account of the fact that the reduction in inflation has brought other ills in its wake such as unemployment and slower growth. A future administration might feel that unemployment is not a 'price worth paying' and the long-term investor has to be ready for this.

1.5.3 Time

A fourth investment dimension is the time factor. In most, if not all, of the following chapters, references are made to fluctuations, trends and fashions affecting the various markets. Within a long-term trend, there are likely to be many short-term fluctuations, caused by a myriad of factors. When to buy and when to sell are therefore difficult decisions for the investor. He can be guided by professional advisers who have knowledge of the technical factors affecting a particular market, but who can only express an opinion on political factors and the general state of the economy, and who can therefore make only intelligent general forecasts not amounting to precise predictions. For those who invest overseas, fluctuations in exchange rates form a further element in the evaluation of investments.

1.6 INVESTMENT POLICY – GENERAL PRINCIPLES AND SPECIAL FACTORS

1.6.1 Diversification

The first maxim for practically every investor should be diversification (indeed, for trustees the Trustee Investments Act 1961 prescribes diversification, although its provisions can be excluded when a trust is created). Diversification can be achieved by investing in varying kinds of investments but can also be achieved within a particular class of investment.

There will always, of course, be the investor who has to commit, or to leave committed, a substantial part of his capital in one particular way (eg the man who has built up a substantial business). It might also be thought that the small investor with little money to invest would have little scope for diversification, but unit trusts (see Chapter 8) or bonds (see Chapter 3) indirectly provide diversification.

1.6.2 Balance

The investor should as far as possible have a balanced portfolio. A part of his capital should be earmarked for security and invested in, for example, building society or bank deposits. However, every investor should also look for a measure of capital appreciation as a hedge against inflation, so a part of his capital should be invested in equity-type investments. The precise balance will depend on the individual circumstances and inclinations of the particular investor.

1.6.3 Advice of specialists

The investor should be guided by the advice of the various specialists in the markets discussed in this book. They all provide a service which, if well performed, is a valuable one, for which they quite properly charge fees. However, they all wish to sell their wares and another reason for diversification is to avoid total dependence on the judgement and integrity of any one particular specialist.

Any investor investing overseas should pay particularly close regard to the advice of specialists familiar with the markets in the countries concerned. The additional advice required will cover such things as marketability, banking arrangements and (particularly in the case of purchase of property) legal advice to ensure that the investor obtains a good title.

1.6.4 Taxation

The general rule is that, whilst full account should be taken of likely tax implications, investment policy should not be dictated by tax. It is often the case, for example, that decisions tend to be unduly influenced by capital gains tax considerations. The investor has to balance the right time to sell an investment which is showing a profit against a loss of use of the money required to pay the tax. In general terms, investors should not be deterred from realising investments simply by capital gains tax considerations alone.

Investments with favourable tax treatment include national savings certificates (see Chapter 2) and life assurances (see Chapter 14) which continue to have capital gains tax benefits and, in the case of certain trust policies, inheritance tax benefits as well. Other tax-efficient investments include TESSAs and PEPs (see Chapter 20).

These tax benefits are a good reason for investing in this way. However, there is no guarantee that, over a given period, they will necessarily produce a better return than investments which have no tax benefits at all. Not only may these other investments have compensating benefits (eg better capital appreciation), future tax legislation could alter or even nullify tax benefits that are now available – yet another reason for a policy of diversification.

1.6.5 Commission and expenses of buying and selling

At one end of the scale, there is no explicit cost at all in investing money in a building society or bank deposit. Commission on the purchase of gilt-edged securities is small, while for equities it is reasonable, although *ad valorem* stamp duty on purchases will also be payable (see Chapter 3). Commissions on equities vary from broker to broker following the abolition of fixed commissions in 1986.

At the top end of the scale comes the art market where the total commission can be as high as 20 per cent + VAT (see Chapter 18). The investor hoping to make an eventual gain must realise that, immediately after purchase, the item may be worth only around 80 per cent of the amount paid (or even less, where VAT is taken into account).

1.6.6 Buying and selling prices

On The Stock Exchange, separate buying and selling prices are quoted, the difference between these prices being the market-maker's turn or potential profit. The same principle can apply to other markets and, with certain assets (eg jewellery), the fact that the asset has only second-hand value the moment it has been purchased must be taken into account.

1.6.7 Other benefits

Investments should not be considered only by reference to pure investment criteria. Property may be purchased as a home or, eg if it is a farm, to provide a livelihood. Life assurance brings with it the element of family protection. Works of art (unless stored away in a safe deposit) bring pleasure to the owner and collector.

1.6.8 Methods of investment

The normal method of investment is for the investor, either personally or through an agent, to buy and sell individual investments (and he could give his agent discretionary power to buy and sell on his behalf). The investor can either buy the investment outright or acquire options to buy at some time in the future. Alternatively, he may be able to buy a future, which effectively gives full exposure to fluctuations in the value of the underlying asset, but at a much lower cost.

The same type of investment can sometimes be acquired through different means. For example, investment in property can be by direct purchase of property (see Chapters 9–12), shares in a property company (see Chapter 3) or property bonds (see Chapter 3). Overseas investment can be through investment trusts or unit trusts (either based in the UK or offshore) holding overseas investments, or in UK companies with substantial overseas activities.

1.6.9 Gearing

For the smaller investor, borrowing can only be a sensible strategy if tax relief is available on the loan interest. Under the present law, tax relief for loan interest is available for loans for the purchase of a house as a principal residence (the ceiling being £30,000) but this relief has fallen in value as the rate of tax relief was reduced to 20 per cent in the 1994/95 tax year and 15 per cent for the 1995/96 tax year.

Such borrowing, however, will only appeal to an investor with free assets who thinks he can invest these assets so as to produce greater capital appreciation. It would be pointless, for example, for the cautious investor to borrow from a building society and then reinvest the amount borrowed in a building society (or other equally safe investment) because the interest paid would exceed the interest received and the only beneficiary would be the building society itself.

For the wealthy investor, borrowing is less a question of tax relief than of altering the shape of the asset portfolio. For example, consider an investor with £250,000 who buys a house for £150,000. If he buys the property without a mortgage, he will have a £150,000 stake in the property market and £100,000 invested elsewhere. If he takes a £100,000 mortgage, he will have an unchanged stake in the property market but £200,000 invested elsewhere.

1.7 TRUSTEES

Trustees are usually appointed by a settlement or a will. They can, however, be bare trustees, nominees or attorneys for others (under a power of attorney) who might well be infants or persons under some disability. They also include anyone who owes a fiduciary duty of care to others.

For investment purposes their 'bible' is the Trustee Investments Act 1961, although its provisions are often expressly varied by the trust instrument itself. The principles that the Act lays down are discussed below.

1.7.1 Suitability of investments for the trust

Normally the question of what investments are suitable for a particular trust involves considering the interests of the beneficiaries under that trust. If there is a life tenant and remaindermen, then the trustees must ensure that the income produced for the life tenant is reasonable, but at the same time they must consider security of capital and possible capital appreciation for the remaindermen. Where there are infant beneficiaries, a special duty of care is required.

1.7.2 Diversification

In a normal trust, the trustees could be in breach of trust if they do not diversify the trust investments. In a small trust, diversification can be achieved through the medium of, for example, unit trusts or investment trusts. However, diversification can be a problem in the fairly common case where a settlor has built up a business through a company and settled shares in that company upon trust for his children. In this case the trust instrument should include the appropriate authority for the trustees to continue to hold that investment even though that approach does not lead to diversification.

1.7.3 Expert advice

Trustees must obtain and consider proper advice from a specialist in the relevant field of investment. This principle is seldom expressly excluded. Unless there is a specific provision in the trust instrument to the contrary, trustees must make investment decisions personally (and cannot delegate this to the expert adviser).

1.7.4 Authorised investments

The Act specifies the kinds of investment in which trustees are authorised to invest and states that at least half the trust fund should be invested in the 'narrower range' and that the balance can be invested in the 'wider range'. Investments in the 'narrower range' include deposits with approved banks and building societies, gilt-edged securities, mortgages on property and debentures of companies that, first, have an issued and paid-up share capital of at least £1m and, secondly, have paid dividends (however small) on the whole of their ordinary share capital in each of the previous five years. The 'wider range' includes unit trusts and ordinary shares in companies satisfying the conditions stated above for debentures in the narrower range.

It is fairly general practice nowadays for trust instruments to confer express powers of investment, overriding the provisions of the Trustee Investments Act 1961 in this respect, and it is quite usual for the trustees to be given very wide powers in the interests of flexibility. The investment clause will always require close examination because, either by design or as a consequence of bad drafting, the powers actually given may not be so wide as appears at first sight. An investment in its narrow legal sense is an income-producing instrument. Consequently, if trustees are to be given powers to buy houses as residences for beneficiaries or to use capital for improving or repairing them, specific powers must be included. Again, if trustees are to be permitted to invest in assets such as capital shares with no participation in the profits of the company or chattels or commodities or currency, specific powers must be given. Specific powers must also be given in respect of insurances and assurances.

1.7.5 Caution

In their own interests trustees should tend to be cautious and adopt a conservative policy. They must act within the principles laid down in the trust or settlement deed and the 1961 Act. Their first duty is to familiarise themselves with the powers of investment that they have been given and whether these are restricted as specified in the Act or whether, as is often the case, they are given the powers of an absolute owner, but even then they must ensure that they are given *all* the powers of an absolute owner.

If a known liability arises (and this commonly occurs on the death of a testator, where a liability to inheritance tax may arise), the trustees or the personal representatives should set about covering that liability, if necessary by realising investments and placing the money on deposit with a bank or with building societies or even by investing in short-dated gilts. A prudent trustee who does this cannot be criticised if the market in those realised investments then goes up, but, conversely, a trustee who does not do this is open to criticism if the market goes down.

1.8 OVERSEAS INVESTORS

1.8.1 Exchange control

A UK investor can invest in any country in the world without restriction, although he will be subject to whatever restrictions the country in which he plans to invest may impose. Conversely, an overseas investor can freely invest in the UK but he may be subject to exchange control provisions imposed by his country of residence.

1.8.2 Taxation

Detailed advice on taxation is outside the scope of this book and so the comments made below are necessarily only in very general terms. Overseas investors (and also immigrants and emigrants) have to be particularly aware of taxation considerations, which for them depend on domicile and residence.

For tax purposes, a person is regarded as resident in the UK if he is physically present in there for 183 days or more in any tax year, or, if over a period of four such years, he is present there for an average of three months or more in each tax year.

He will be regarded as 'ordinarily resident' if he is habitually resident in the UK year after year and will continue to be regarded as ordinarily resident if he usually lives there but is in fact physically absent (eg on a long holiday) for even the whole of any tax year.

Inheritance tax

Liability to UK inheritance tax depends basically on domicile. The investor domiciled in the UK will be subject to inheritance tax on his worldwide assets, whereas an investor not domiciled in the UK will be subject to inheritance tax on his UK property or investments only.

Domicile is a concept of general law and is determined by a range of factors. Broadly speaking, domicile is where the individual has his permanent home. It is distinct from nationality or residence and an individual can have only one domicile at a time.

An individual would normally acquire a domicile of origin from his father when he was born, though this may change if the person on whom the individual was dependent at the time changed his domicile before the individual was aged 16.

Married women who married before 1974 automatically acquired their husband's domicile, though they may now change it to a domicile of their choice.

Anyone over the age of 16 has the legal power to apply for a new domicile of choice. However, it is not at all easy to do and will usually require proof that the individual has severed all connections with his existing country and intends to settle permanently in a new country.

Capital gains tax

Liability to capital gains tax depends on UK residence or 'ordinary residence' for tax purposes. The general rule is that the investor ordinarily resident in the UK is subject to capital gains tax and the investor not ordinarily resident in the UK is exempt from it. Investors immigrating to or emigrating from the UK should take advice on the timing of the sale of assets so as to avoid any liability to capital gains tax.

Income tax

Liability to income tax depends on residence, but there are certain concessions for people not domiciled in the UK. Many factors, including the provisions of double taxation agreements, are relevant and the investor must take professional advice.

1.8.3 Other restrictions

Normally, an overseas investor can invest in any form of UK investment without problems. However, difficulties might arise where the investor ultimately wanted to export the investment (particularly where it is a work of art) or where the investment involves a liability in the UK (which could arise with, say, an investment in leasehold property as the landlord might require a UK-resident guarantor).

1.9 CONCLUSION

If there is any conclusion to be drawn for the investor and the investment adviser from the foregoing analysis, it is that nothing is constant and that continual review and permanent vigilance are essential. The investment strategies appropriate to one investor may not be right for another and those suitable for one particular generation of investor may be wholly inappropriate for the next generation, when the investment climate and the law may have changed. Even a strategy appropriate now may be inappropriate in the future by which time the investor will have aged and his needs and his family circumstances will have changed.

1.10 INCOME TAX RATES, ALLOWANCES, AND NATIONAL INSURANCE RATES FROM 6 APRIL 1996

Table 1.1 Income tax rates 1997/98

Bands of taxable income £	Rate %	Tax on band £
0–4,100	20	820
4,101–26,100	23	5,880
Over 26,100	40	–

Table 1.2 Personal allowances

(1) Personal and married couple's allowances
The rates which will apply for 1997/98 (equivalent figures for 1996/97 in italics) are:

Age	Personal allowance £		Married couple's allowance £	
Under 65	4,045	*3,765*	1,830	*1,790*
65 to 74	5,220	*4,910*	3,185	*3,115*
75 and over	5,400	*5,090*	3,225	*3,115*

Note: The income limit for persons aged 65 and over is £15,600. Where the taxpayer's total income exceeds this limit, the age-related allowances are reduced by £1 for every £2 of income over the limit. The allowances are not reduced below the level of the basic personal or married couple's allowances.

(2) Additional allowance and widow's bereavement allowance – £1,830.

(3) Blind person's allowance – £1,280.

National Insurance contributions 1997/98

Table 1.3 Contracted-in

Employer contributions		Employee contributions		
Earnings £pw	% of all earnings	Earnings £pw	% on first £62	% on remainder
0–61.99	0	0–61.99	0	0
62–109.99	3.0	62–465	2	10
110–154.99	5.0	Over 465	2	10% up to £465
155–209.99	7.0			
210–465.00	10.0			
Over 465	10.0			

Table 1.4 Contracted-out

Employer contributions			Employee contributions		
Earnings £pw	COSR Schemes %	COMP Schemes %	Earnings £pw	% on first £62	% on remainder
0–61.99	0	0	0–61.99	0	0
62–109.99	0	1.5	62–465	2	8.4
110–154.99	2.0	3.5	Over 465	2	8.4% up to £465
155–209.99	4.0	5.5			
210–465.00	7.0	8.5			
Over 465	10.0	10.0			

Self-employed contributions
Class 2 Contributions: where profits are over £3,480, flat weekly rate increased from £6.05 per week to £6.15 per week.
Class 4 Contributions: 6 per cent on profits between £7,010 and £24,180 per annum.

These rates take effect from 6 April 1996.

1.11 CAPITAL GAINS TAX

Capital gains tax is charged on real capital gains. A person who makes a gain is allowed to deduct not only his actual acquisition value (in addition to the costs of acquisition and disposal) but also a proportion of the acquisition value which represents the increase in the RPI between the month of acquisition and the month of disposal.

Up until the November 1993 Budget, it was permissible to use indexation relief to create or increase a capital loss. From 30 November 1993, indexation relief may only be used in this way for transactions prior to 30 November 1993.

The intention of the new rules was that, in all future transactions, indexation relief should only be used to reduce or extinguish a gain, not create or increase a loss. The rule was relaxed as the Finance Bill made its way through the committee stages; indexation may continue to be used in this way but only for the 1993/94 and 1994/95 tax years and only up to an overall limit of £10,000.

2

UNLISTED INVESTMENTS

JOHN SMITHARD

James Capel Investment Management

2.1 TYPES OF UNLISTED SECURITY

This chapter deals with the most commonly available forms of investment which do not have an official quotation or market price. It includes
investments issued by the government through National Savings, by
local authorities, by building societies and by other financial institutions
wishing to raise money, and in general can only be redeemed by the
borrower.

With some exceptions, these securities provide the investor with interest
until they mature, whereupon he receives the return of his original capital. Although the rates of return on some of these investments might not
always compare favourably with returns on other forms of investment,
some have taxation advantages up to a specific amount, particularly for
the higher rate taxpayer. Other investments covered in this chapter may
produce no income in the course of their lives, but give a guaranteed
improvement in capital value on maturity. Premium bonds give no guarantee of income or capital appreciation but offer the holder a chance in
draws for tax-free prizes. A comparison of rates of return, the limitations
on amounts invested, and conditions of withdrawal are set out in Table
2.1 on pp 18 and 19.

2.2 REVIEW OF 1996

National Savings passed its targeted net sales figure of £4.5bn for
1996/97 in January this year, two months before the end of its accounting period; this was a very creditable performance. With the PSBR for
the year to end-March 1997 to the order of £27bn, the National Savings
movement needed to pull in its fair share of public savings, and by the
end of January the figure for the net addition to National Savings was 23
per cent higher than at the corresponding time in 1996.

With interest rates starting again to move upwards, it was understandable that fixed interest products would begin to suffer in terms of sales, especially the standard National Savings Certificates. However, perhaps the greatest growth in sales was seen in pensioners' bonds with their fixed 7 per cent return over five years. This could indicate that the worries of at least one sector of the public over a return to a high inflation rate/high interest rate economy were broadly over, and as the rate of growth in sales of index-linked NSCs was showing no real signs of accelerating, inflation might generally be seen to be less of a problem than before. But it is noticeable that the outstanding balance of index-linked certificates at the end of 1996 was only slightly lower than that of fixed NSCs; many holders of the latter, of course, are locked in through to 2001, being holders of earlier issues at lower rates.

Sales of premium bonds grew sharply again in 1996, benefiting from the constant newspaper promotion of National Savings and the public's continuing lottery-induced enchantment with gambling.

2.3 TYPES OF UNLISTED INVESTMENT

2.3.1 National Savings Bank accounts

The National Savings Bank is guaranteed by the government and is operated by the Post Office as agent. Two types of account – ordinary accounts and investment accounts – are available.

Anyone aged seven years or over can open an account in his or her own name, and an account can be opened on behalf of a younger child by his parent or legal guardian although withdrawals and encashments are not allowed until the child is seven. Friendly societies and other classes of investor can also open accounts.

Interest on both types of account is credited annually on 31 December. In the case of ordinary accounts, this is for each complete calendar month. For investment accounts, interest is calculated from the day funds are deposited until the day prior to withdrawal. There is a maximum amount which can be withdrawn daily from an ordinary account, and all withdrawals from an investment account require one month's notice.

Interest is paid gross (ie without deduction of tax at source). In the case of ordinary accounts an individual is given exemption from basic and higher rate income tax for the first £70 interest. If a husband and wife each have an account, they can each claim exemption up to this level, although if they hold a joint account the exemption is £140. However, there is no such exemption for the higher gross interest earned on investment accounts.

Although the limit on income tax exemption for ordinary accounts is relatively low, a holding up to this level may be attractive for higher rate taxpayers.

Accounts can be opened by completing a simple form available from almost any branch of the Post Office. The account holder receives a pass book in which all deposits and withdrawals are entered. The minimum for each deposit is £10 (ordinary account) and £20 (investment account) and the maximum holding is £100,000 (investment account).

The pass book no longer needs to be sent in once a year for the adding of interest, as this will be done on the next occasion that it is received by the National Savings Bank.

2.3.2 National savings certificates

National savings certificates are guaranteed by the government. They cannot be sold to third parties. A number of different issues of certificates have been made over the years.

A maximum individual holding is specified for each issue of national savings certificates. Trustees and registered friendly societies and charities approved by the director of savings can also buy certificates.

No interest is paid, but after a stated period of time the certificates can be redeemed at a higher value than the original purchase price. The total rate at which the value appreciates during this period is indicated on the certificate and in the prospectus. However, the value builds up by the addition of increments at the end of the first year and each subsequent period of three months. The full table, showing how the value rises more steeply towards the end of the period and levels off after the end of the period, is available from the details issued by the Department of National Savings. Certificates from the seventh issue earn interest at the general extension rate after maturity. The general extension rate is a variable rate of interest for matured certificates when they have completed their fixed period terms and is currently only 3.51 per cent gross.

The capital appreciation is free from both income tax and capital gains tax. The minimum holding is £100 and the maximum £10,000 in the current issue, but holders may have a further £20,000 worth of certificates if these arise from reinvestment of a holding in an earlier issue.

The certificates can be a suitable form of savings for children, although parents and children should also consider children's bonus bonds (see **2.3.7**). For the pure investor they are not suitable for non-taxpayers or for short-term savings; but for the investor paying tax at the higher rate, the certificates may be attractive. Application forms are available from most post offices.

Table 2.1 Current rates of return and conditions (May 1997)

Investment	Return (% pa)		Amount invested		Withdrawal notice (days)	Notes
	Gross*	Net*	Min	Max		
1 National Savings Bank:						
Ordinary accounts	1.5–2.5	1.2–1.9	£10	£10,000	£100 on demand	Depending on balance, first £70 free of tax
Investment accounts	4.8–5.5	3.7–4.2	£20	£100,000	30	
2 National savings certificates (44th issue)	5.35[1] (tax free)		£100	£10,000	8	[1]Equivalent to 7.7% to basic-rate taxpayers: further £10,000 if from re-investment of expired NSC
3 National savings index-linked certificates (10th issue)	Increase in RPI[2] (tax free)		£100	£10,000	8	[2]Paid on withdrawal if after one year, with tax-free interest. Further £10,000 if from matured NSC
4 National savings children's bonus bonds	6.8 (tax free)		£25	£1,000	8	If held for 5 years
5 National savings income bonds	6.0–6.3	4.6–5.0	£2,000	£250,000	3 months	
6 National savings capital bonds	6.7	5.1	£100	£250,000	8	
7 National savings FIRST option bonds	6.0–6.3	4.6–5.0	£1,000	£250,000	8	
8 National savings pensioner's guaranteed income bonds	7.0	5.4				

Table 2.1 cont

	Chance of prize (tax free)		£100	£20,000		
9 Premium savings bond	Chance of prize (tax free)				8	Monthly prize fund; one month's interest at 5.2% on each bond eligible for draw
10 Local authority mortgage bonds: 1 year	6.9	5.3				Other terms available
11 Commercial banks: Deposit accounts (7 day)	1	0.8	25p	None	7[3]	[3]But may be withdrawn on demand subject to deduction of 7 days' interest from balance
High Interest cheque	4.5–5.9	3.5–4.5	£1,000	None	None	
Certificates of deposit	6.4[4]	5.0	£50,000	None	Marketable security	[4]3-month term and 6-month term
12 Building societies: Share accounts	5.8–6.4	4.5–4.9	£1		On demand[5]	[5]Up to £300 in cash or £5,000 by cheque; above £5,000 branch refers to head office
Premium accounts	5.8–7.0[6]	4.5–5.6[6]	£500	None	0–12 months	[6]Rates vary according to size
13 Certificates of tax deposit	2.5–5.5[7] / 1.3[8]	1.9–4.2[7] / 1.0[8]	£2,000	None	0–12 months	[7]If withdrawn for payment of tax [7]If withdrawn in cash
14 Treasury bills	6.2	4.7	£5,000	None	Marketable security	

*Based on tax at the basic rate of 23%

Holdings should be reviewed from time to time, particularly since new issues may carry more attractive rates of capital appreciation than those already held. A review of holdings should certainly be made at the end of the specified period as the general extension rate is usually unattractive.

Any number of certificates can be cashed at one time, on at least eight working days' notice, and repayment forms are available at most post offices and banks.

2.3.3 National savings index-linked certificates

As with national savings certificates, these certificates are guaranteed by the government. They cannot be sold to third parties.

There is no lower age limit for holding these certificates, although encashment is not allowed until a child reaches the age of seven, except in special circumstances. No more than 400 certificates of £25, ie £10,000 at initial purchase price can be held in the current issue unless they came from a reinvestment of mature certificates in which case the limit is increased by £20,000. The minimum holding is four certificates, costing £100.

If a certificate is encashed within the first year, the purchase price only is repaid, unless it is a reinvestment certificate. If the certificates are held for more than a year, the redemption value is equal to the original purchase price, increased in proportion to the rise in the RPI between the month of purchase and the month of redemption. In the event of a fall in the RPI, the certificates can be encashed for the original purchase price in the first year, and not less than their value at the previous anniversary otherwise. After the death of a holder, indexation can continue for a maximum of 12 months.

The latest issue guarantees a return above the rate of inflation for a five-year term by offering extra tax-free interest as well as indexation. The amount of extra interest credited to the holding rises in each year of the certificate's life after its second anniversary and is itself inflation-proofed. Details of these calculations are shown in the prospectus available at post offices.

After the fifth anniversary, certificates continue to earn interest and index-linking, but on such terms as the Treasury may decide. As with national savings certificates, capital appreciation is exempt from income tax and capital gains tax.

Certificates are suitable for individuals who do not need immediate income but are seeking protection in real terms for the amount invested. Higher rate taxpayers in this category will find the certificates particularly attractive. Application forms are obtainable from most post offices.

2.3.4 National savings income bonds

As with national savings certificates, these bonds are guaranteed by the government. Anyone aged seven years or over can buy income bonds and they may be bought for children under seven, but there are two special conditions:

(1) interest is normally credited to a national savings bank account in the child's name;
(2) the bond is not normally repayable until the child reaches seven.

Friendly societies and other classes of investor can also buy these bonds.

Gross interest is paid on a monthly basis but the interest is subject to tax. Investors may cash in part of their holding in multiples of £1,000, but they must keep a minimum balance of £2,000. Investors should be aware of the following terms of repayment:

(1) for repayments in the first year, interest is credited at half the rate from the date of purchase to the date of repayment on the amount repaid;
(2) for repayments after the first year, interest is paid in full.

Three months' notice of repayment is required. The maximum holding is £250,000. If the investor dies, the money can be withdrawn without any formal period of notice and with interest paid in full up to the date of repayment.

A slightly higher interest rate is given for amounts exceeding £25,000. Rates of interest are variable.

The bonds are particularly suitable for investors who require high regular income, who can afford to tie up at least £2,000 for a minimum period of 12 months and are not subject to tax. Income is paid monthly, on the fifth of each month. The first payment is made on the next interest date after the bonds have been held for six weeks. Application forms are obtainable from post offices. Investors aged 60 or over should also compare the rates with those available on pensioner's guaranteed income bonds.

2.3.5 National savings capital bonds

The bonds are guaranteed by the government. They may be held by individuals, by children and by trustees of a sole individual.

Bonds are bought with a £100 minimum and a £250,000 maximum and give a rate of return fixed at the date of purchase. Although called capital bonds, they accrue interest which is capitalised on each anniversary of the purchase date, and this accrued interest must be notified to the Inland Revenue on the individual's tax return (and income tax paid, if necessary, before actual receipt of the capitalised interest at the date of maturity). An annual statement of value, showing the capitalised interest, is sent to the bondholder shortly after the end of each tax year.

The capitalised interest accrues at an increasing rate during the bond's life and the full advertised compound rate is received only if held to maturity. This occurs on the fifth anniversary of the purchase date, before which the bondholder will have been reminded by the bond office of the imminence of maturity.

Repayment can be requested at any time for a minimum amount of £100, provided this leaves at least the minimum holding. No capitalised interest accrues before the first anniversary.

Depending on the level of interest rates available elsewhere, capital bonds may prove an excellent investment for an individual who pays little or no income tax and who can tie up his funds for five years, assuming that interest rates will move downwards in the intervening period.

2.3.6 FIRST option bonds

FIRST option bonds are a means of lump sum saving in a government security, the returns on which are guaranteed for one year at a time. The interest rate for the first year is set at the time of purchase and the interest, net of basic rate tax, is capitalised within the bond on the first anniversary. At the same time, holders are notified of the next year's interest rate and this accrues, again net of basic rate income tax, on the value of the bond, being added to the capital at subsequent anniversaries.

The amount held in the FIRST option bond must not be reduced by subsequent withdrawals to below the minimum holding of £1,000, but up to £250,000 may be held in total in one or any number of bonds.

FIRST is an acronym for Fixed Interest Rate Savings, Tax-paid. Interest accrues daily but is added only on the anniversary; an improved rate is given on a bond exceeding £20,000, although an amalgamation of a number of bonds to make £20,000 or over would not qualify. Bonds may be purchased and held by anyone aged 16 or over, and by trustees.

Withdrawals should be made only on anniversary dates for, if not, only half the stated interest rate accrues since the last anniversary on the capitalised interest at that date. No interest is given on a withdrawal in the first year.

FIRST option bonds have been designed for basic rate taxpayers looking for a competitive return who can make lump sum payments which they intend to hold for at least one year. Non-taxpayers, who would need to reclaim tax deducted at source, might find other national savings instruments paying gross interest more convenient. Higher rate taxpayers, who will need to find a further tax payment, might consider tax-free investments.

Applications for bonds are made to National Savings on prospectus forms available from post offices.

2.3.7 Children's bonus bonds

These bonds are guaranteed by the government and are designed to encourage children to save. They can be bought to a maximum of £1,000 by or for children under 16, although they can be held to the age of 21. The minimum holding is £25 and the bonds are available in multiples of £25. After five years, holders receive a bonus payment and the bonds then attract interest at extension terms yet to be announced.

All interest, and the bonus, is exempt from income tax and need not be declared to the Inland Revenue. The proposed return should be in excess of that available on normal five-year fixed rate certificates. Repayment is normally made to a parent or guardian only if the holder is then still below the age of 16.

They may prove attractive to parents wishing to give capital to children, for there is no liability to income tax on the interest which in most other circumstances is deemed still to belong to the parent if it exceeds a token level of £100.

2.3.8 Pensioners' guaranteed income bonds

This National Savings product has been designed to produce a competitive income return for older investors who wish to fix a monthly return for a period of five years despite any change in the level of interest rates during that period.

Interest is paid without deduction of income tax, although it is subject to income tax. This will be of certain benefit to non-taxpayers, who need not make a reclaim of tax already deducted at source. Interest is paid monthly on the 19th of each month, but only to a bank or building society account.

The bonds can only be bought by individuals of 60 years of age or older, or held in trust for a beneficiary who has reached that age. The minimum limit for each purchase is £500, but any amount above this level can be bought, up to a maximum of £50,000 for each individual. Application forms are available at post offices, with applications being made to National Savings.

Interest is earned on each day that the bonds are held. Repayment is subject to 60 days' notice, although no interest is paid for the notice period. However, there is no loss of interest on the repayment of the bonds on their fifth anniversary, or on a holder's death. The amount of each repayment must be at least £500, and there must be at least a £500 minimum holding retained after any withdrawal. Applications for repayment are also made direct to National Savings.

At the time of the bond's fifth anniversary a holder should receive a reminder notifying him of the rate of interest for the next five-year period. The holder then needs to make a decision whether to leave the bonds in place or to have them redeemed and reinvest in an alternative investment. This depends on the bondholder's needs at that time and the prevailing level of interest rates, although it is the intention to offer pensioners a competitive return for their savings.

2.3.9 Premium bonds

Premium bonds are guaranteed by the government. They cannot be sold to third parties.

Any person aged 16 or over can buy the bonds, and a parent, grandparent or legal guardian may buy bonds on behalf of a child under 16. A bond cannot be held in the name of more than one person or of a corporate body, society, club or other association of persons. Prizes won by bonds registered in the name of a child under the age of 16 are paid on behalf of the child to the parent or legal guardian.

Bonds are sold in units of £1 and purchases must then be in multiples of £10 subject to a minimum purchase at any time of £100 up to a maximum of £20,000 per person.

No interest is paid, but a bond which has been held for one full calendar month is eligible for inclusion in the regular draw for prizes of various amounts. The size of the monthly prize fund is determined by applying one month's interest at a predetermined rate to the total value of the eligible bonds at that time. This rate is reviewed from time to time. Bonds can be encashed at any time. All prizes are free of income tax and capital gains tax. Every month 350,000 prizes are paid, ranging from £50 to £1m.

Premium bonds are suitable for higher rate taxpayers who do not wish to receive income and can set aside some savings with no guaranteed return but with the chance of receiving a tax-free prize. They are also a 'fun' investment for any investor who wishes to take the chance of a prize, knowing he can always have the return of his cash investment, and so can be favourably compared to the National Lottery. The odds against winning any prize are 15,000 to 1 for each unit.

Application forms are available at post offices. Winning bondholders are notified in writing at their last recorded address and lists of winning numbers are advertised in newspapers. Repayment forms are also available at post offices.

2.3.10 Government stock

Gilts, gilt-edged or government stock represent a loan to the Bank of England, repayable on a fixed future date and, with the exception of index-linked gilts, on which a fixed rate of annual interest is payable to the holder. By far the largest active market for gilts is through The Stock Exchange, but they can also be bought and sold across post office counters through National Savings. There are certain benefits to individuals in doing so, although transactions take slightly longer to process.

The full range of gilt-edged stock is now available through National Savings. Potential investors must decide whether to buy stock which has a high income return with perhaps restricted capital growth prospects, or even a guaranteed fall in value if held to redemption; a low income return and a guaranteed rise in value until maturity; or a balance between the two. In the majority of cases, investment in index-linked stock will protect the capital against inflation until redemption, while providing a low, but inflation-proofed, income.

Gilts can also be bought when offered by the Bank of England through application forms published in the national newspapers.

Interest on gilts bought on the National Savings register is paid without deduction of income tax and so gilts can certainly be considered by non-taxpayers and, depending on their return, by others who normally pay tax. Basic rate and higher rate taxpayers must account for the tax due on the interest at their marginal rate. There is no liability to capital gains tax on profits made on the redemption or sale of gilts.

The main characteristics of gilts are described in **3.5.1**.

Application forms are available from post offices. Investors can buy either a fixed nominal amount of stock, or they can invest a certain amount of cash. The maximum that can be invested on any one day is £25,000, but there is no maximum holding in one or any stock. When buying or selling through National Savings, the delay between sending the application and the purchase or sale of the stock means that no guarantee can be given to the price paid or received as the market value of gilts fluctuates throughout the day. Sales are made by sending in the appropriate completed application form and the stock certificate. Commission charges are often considerably lower than those charged by stockbrokers.

2.3.11 Local authority mortgage bonds

These borrowings are secured on the revenues of local authorities, which have the power to levy the council tax. It is generally assumed that the government would stand behind such borrowings, although it has no legal commitment to do so.

A minimum investment is usually specified: this varies between authorities but is smaller than for local authority negotiable bonds (ie less than £1,000).

Local authority mortgage bonds are issued for a fixed term, usually between two and seven years. Unlike local authority negotiable bonds, in which there is a market on The Stock Exchange, they cannot normally be sold to third parties.

Interest is subject to income tax and is paid after deduction of basic rate tax. Non-taxpayers therefore have to claim a rebate of tax, while higher rate taxpayers are assessed for the balance of tax due.

Deposits are suitable for the investor who is seeking a competitive rate of interest and is prepared to tie up his capital for a fixed term. An investor who may require to realise his investment more quickly should explore the possibility of negotiable bonds.

Authorities seeking deposits advertise in the national press, stating the period, rate of interest paid and details of where applications should be made. Deposits are acknowledged by the issue to the holder of mortgage bonds.

2.3.12 Commercial banks – current, deposit and savings accounts and certificates of deposit

Deposits with banks carry no government guarantee and their security therefore lies in the reputation and viability of the bank concerned. Certificates of deposit (CDs) are bearer documents and can be sold to third parties, whereas deposit and savings accounts represent a non-assignable debt from the bank to the holder.

There are normally no pre-conditions to opening a deposit or savings account with a commercial bank. However, the minimum sum for an investment in CDs is usually fairly high.

Interest, which is paid at regular intervals on accounts, can be varied by the bank as the general level of interest rates and the bank's own base rate change. Seven days' notice of withdrawal is required for deposit accounts. The interest on CDs is fixed for the duration of the certificates – normally between three months and five years.

Interest on deposit and savings accounts is paid net of basic rate tax which may be reclaimed if tax deducted at source exceeds the total tax due. Higher rate taxpayers are given credit for the tax at basic rate.

Deposit and savings accounts are useful means of investing funds which may be needed at short notice. CDs are suitable for large deposits and consequently earn a higher return than deposit or savings accounts. Since 1 January 1991, banks have been able to offer tax exempt special savings accounts (TESSAs) – see **2.3.14** and Chapter 20.

Deposit and savings accounts may be opened, and CDs purchased, by instruction and transfer of cash to the bank concerned. Bank account statements should be kept for reference. Since CDs are bearer documents, they should be held in safe custody.

2.3.13 Building society accounts

Building societies offer share accounts, various higher interest accounts, term bonds and save-as-you-earn (SAYE) contracts. None of these investments can be sold to third parties. Security lies in the reputation and viability of the building society concerned. Since 1 January 1991 building societies have been able to offer tax exempt special savings accounts (TESSAs) – see **2.3.14** and Chapter 20.

The minimum age for entering into an SAYE contract is 16, but any of the other forms of savings may be undertaken by children aged seven or over. For younger children an account may be opened in the name of trustees (normally the child's parents). SAYE contracts are open only to individuals and cannot be undertaken on joint accounts.

Building societies compete for deposits not only with banks but also with each other (their offices are often open to the public for longer hours than the banks during the week and are also open on Saturday mornings). On lump sum investments, interest is usually paid every six months, although in some cases monthly. On SAYE contracts the bonus is fixed at the outset and paid at the end of the fifth and the seventh years, but other savings plans bear interest rates which, although specified at the time of investment, vary from time to time with the general level of interest rates. A period of notice is specified for withdrawals from share accounts but is in practice seldom required except for large sums. There may be penalties for early withdrawal from term bonds.

Since April 1991 basic rate tax is deducted from gross interest, but this can be reclaimed if tax deducted at source exceeds the total tax due. Higher rate taxpayers are liable for the balance of tax at those rates on the gross amount.

Since February 1989 building societies have been able to pay interest gross to depositors in certain instances.

The simplicity of building society deposit and share accounts and the ease with which small withdrawals can be made on demand, coupled with the sound record of building societies, make them attractive for basic or higher rate taxpayers. Application forms are available from local branches of the building societies. Passbooks are issued for most types of investment, although certificates are issued in some cases for fixed term contracts.

2.3.14 Tax exempt special savings accounts (TESSAs)

TESSAs were announced in the 1990 Budget and were introduced on 1 January 1991. They provide a means of longer-term saving, tax free, and are operated on a commercial basis by banks and building societies.

Each individual over 18 is allowed one TESSA lasting for five years, following which a new TESSA can be opened under the regulations then in force. A total of £9,000 can be placed in a TESSA, either by monthly deposits of £150, or by lump sum payments of up to £3,000 at the start of the first year, followed by annual payments of up to £1,800 in the three succeeding years and up to £600 in the final year.

On the maturity of a TESSA on its fifth anniversary the full capital amount – a maximum of £9,000 – can be transferred into a new TESSA. The accrued interest cannot be reinvested if it brings the total above the £9,000 limit.

Interest accrues during the five-year period and is credited net of basic rate tax. At the end of the five years a bonus of the basic rate tax is credited to the account so that in effect the deposit interest is tax free. During the life of the TESSA up to the full amount of the net income can be withdrawn but any repayment of capital will bring the account to an end, without the bonus. Interest on a TESSA does not need to be declared on tax returns.

Any investor with cash savings, and especially the higher rate taxpayer, should consider a TESSA in combination with his or her other deposits. Although there is a five-year life to the account, he can withdraw his capital and net accrued income at any time (but losing the right to the tax bonus), so the position is not dissimilar to an ordinary deposit account. However, except in cases where the accrued income has been continually withdrawn, an investor thinking of closing his account early should give consideration to the fact that all accrued income will be deemed to have been paid at the time of closure and may increase that year's income tax liability (see **20.2.1**).

2.3.15 Certificates of tax deposit

Certificates of tax deposit are not strictly speaking a form of investment but a scheme operated by the Inland Revenue whereby future tax liabilities can be provided for in advance. The deposits are therefore guaranteed by the government.

Certificates are available to any taxpayer – individual, trustee or corporate – and can be surrendered to meet tax liabilities of any kind, except PAYE income tax or income tax deducted from payments to subcontractors. Different rates apply to deposits below £100,000; there is no maximum deposit.

Interest is paid for a fixed maximum period at a rate specified by HM Treasury when purchased, but the rate varies in line with money market rates. If the deposit is not used to meet tax liabilities but is instead withdrawn for cash, interest is paid at a much lower rate. Interest is paid gross and is subject to income tax.

These certificates are suitable only for taxpayers facing known future tax liabilities, although such taxpayers should consider whether a better return could be obtained by investing elsewhere until such time as the liability has to be met.

Deposits are made by applying to any Collector of Taxes, who issues a certificate specifying the date of receipt and the amount of the deposit. Any request for a deposit to be withdrawn for cash should be made to the Collector, accompanied by the relevant certificates.

2.3.16 Treasury bills

Treasury bills are bearer documents issued by the Bank of England and guaranteed by the government. There is a £5,000 minimum holding.

A Treasury bill is initially a 91-day loan to the Bank of England. No interest is paid but bills are issued at a discount. The difference between the discounted price and £100, the redemption price, is the capital gain accruing to the investor, and the annual rate of discount which it represents is called the Treasury bill rate. Although the holder may not encash the bills at the Bank of England before the due date, they can be sold through the discount market at any time at the prevailing market price.

The difference between the discounted price and the price at which the bills are redeemed at the Bank of England or sold in the market is subject to tax. In the unlikely event of a private investor holding a Treasury bill, the gain would be liable to income tax. Treasury bills are suitable for companies rather than individuals and confer total security on short-term deposits.

Tenders for Treasury bills must be made on printed forms (available from the Chief Cashier's Office, Bank of England) and must be submitted through a London clearing bank, discount house or stockbroker. The value of bills tendered for and the price at which the investor is prepared to buy them must be specified. On the day tenders are received the Bank notifies persons whose tenders have been accepted in whole or in part. Since Treasury bills are bearer documents, they should be held in safe custody.

2.4 COMPARING DIFFERENT TYPES OF SECURITY

The investor, in making a choice between different types of security, should take into account not only the relative importance to him of income and of capital gain but also:

(1) the degree of security against default;
(2) the expected rate of return;
(3) the tax advantages or disadvantages attaching to the security (see also Chapter 20);
(4) the convenience and cost of dealing in the particular security;
(5) the ability to realise the investment; and
(6) the prevailing rate of inflation.

2.4.1 Security against default

The British government has the power to levy taxes and to print money and it is in the highest degree unlikely that it would ever default on any of its borrowings, which include national savings certificates, National Savings Bank deposits, premium bonds and government guaranteed fixed interest stocks. It is generally assumed that the government would stand behind borrowings of local authorities, which in any event have the power to levy local charges. All these securities, therefore, have an intrinsic safety which the private sector cannot emulate.

2.4.2 Rate of return

The rate of return on securities may be specified and fixed, as it is for conventional national savings certificates, local authority deposits, Treasury bills and fixed interest stocks issued by public and private sector organisations. In most other cases the rate of return is specified initially but may be subject to variation to reflect the general movement of interest rates. Returns on some investments may be linked to the prevailing rate of inflation.

2.4.3 Tax advantages

Certain securities carry tax advantages, which may be of particular benefit to higher rate taxpayers. Examples are National Savings Bank ordinary accounts (up to a specified limit), national savings certificates, index-linked national savings certificates and prizes on premium bonds. British government guaranteed stocks are free of capital gains tax (see also Chapter 20).

2.4.4 Convenience and cost of dealing

The securities described in this chapter can (with the exception of certificates of tax deposit and Treasury bills) be negotiated conveniently through high street outlets such as post offices, banks and building societies. In many cases no commission or other dealing costs are incurred.

2.4.5 Ability to realise the investment

With the exception of Treasury bills and certificates of deposit, the securities covered in this chapter cannot be sold to third parties. Thus the investment can be realised only by withdrawing the money from the borrowing organisation. This can be done on demand or at fairly short notice in the case of National Savings Bank accounts and certificates, national savings index-linked certificates (after one year if indexation is required), premium bonds, government stock, and bank, Girobank and building society accounts. In other cases the capital initially invested is tied up for a particular period: this applies to local authority deposits and building society term investments as well as national savings income bonds. If certificates of tax deposit are encashed instead of being used to meet tax liabilities, a lower rate of interest is paid. Early withdrawal in these cases will either be impossible or entail a financial penalty. This disadvantage also applies to commitments to save regular amounts through yearly plan schemes.

2.4.6 Maintenance

The investor should retain safely all documents (particularly bearer documents) relating to the investments covered in this chapter. If the investor changes his address he should notify the appropriate body.

2.5 PREVIEW OF 1997

The expected figure for the Public Sector Borrowing Requirement in the year to March 1998 is likely to be of the order of £15bn, a huge figure but a far cry from the £36bn needed only two years ago. As always, National Savings will be expected to bring in its share of the funding.

Age-old worries about Labour and inflation – although perhaps no longer merited – are bound to influence savers towards greater investment in inflation-proofed products, so we shall probably see a further acceleration of sales of Index-Linked NSCs, which were beginning to pick up again in the 1996/97 year. Most analysts were expecting base rates to rise during 1997 from the 6 per cent figure at the turn of the year to the $6\frac{1}{2}$–7 per cent range by the end, but competition for National Savings against the building societies might prove more relaxed from the second half of 1997; much of the latter industry will be turning into shareholder-owned businesses during the year and so will have dividend payments to fund, as well as deposit interest.

Some useful addresses can be found at the end of Chapter 3.

3

LISTED INVESTMENTS

JOHN SMITHARD

James Capel Investment Management

3.1 INTRODUCTION

This chapter is concerned with securities created when bodies such as the government and individual companies wish to raise money. These securities can be traded on The Stock Exchange, where they are listed. However, this chapter does not deal with shares in private companies. Unlisted securities are covered in Chapter 2.

This chapter contains an introduction to The Stock Exchange and also deals with the distinction between market-makers and agency dealers, the mechanics of dealing in listed UK and overseas securities, as well as those traded on the Alternative Investment Market, and sources of information.

Sections **3.5** and **3.6** cover fixed interest borrowings ('stocks'); section **3.5** deals with those issued by the public sector and which are traded on The Stock Exchange, and section **3.6** with analogous private sector stocks. The purchaser of either kind of stock knows precisely what interest payments he will receive during the life of the stock, since, with very few exceptions, these are fixed. He also knows what he will receive if he retains the stock until redemption, and since this amount is normally more than the purchase price, he will realise a known capital gain. He also has the option of selling in the market before redemption, although the price obtainable in the market fluctuates from day to day.

Section **3.7** covers companies' ordinary shares traded on The Stock Exchange. Shareholders normally receive dividends the total of which may vary from year to year, reflecting the company's changing profitability. In addition, the market price of shares may also fluctuate from day to day. There is thus no certainty of the level either of income return or of capital gain, although the hope is that over a period of years the general level of share prices will rise to reflect inflation and growth in the economy.

3.2 REVIEW OF 1996

A year of quite reasonable economic growth in the UK helped push the equity market – measured by the FTSE All Share Index – up by 11.6 per cent in capital terms. The outperformance of the FTSE 100 larger capitalised stocks was only marginally higher, implying that smaller companies had a better year in 1996 than for some time. Gilts were down slightly over the year, falling by just over 1 per cent in capital terms on the FT Government Securities Index. Overseas investment, measured in Sterling terms by the FT World Index, fell by 0.6 per cent, although this disguised the continued excellent performance on Wall Street.

As always, the performance of individual sectors diverged greatly. The rising oil price – which had dipped to nearly $16 in late January and ended the year around the $24 level – was the force behind the strength of the oil exploration sector, led by Enterprise Oil, so long one of the market's dull stocks. The integrated oils, BP and Shell, were not all that far behind. The support services sector received an early boost from the Rentokil takeover of BET, and was helped very much by the performance of the shares of some of the smaller companies involved in computer personnel services; they became much in demand in anticipation of the effect the year 2000 will have on many office systems. The leisure and hotels sector pushed along smartly with Ladbroke bouncing from depressed levels and Granada's bid for Forte giving the grouping an early boost.

The second half of the year was notable for the performance of the financials. Restructuring and cost cutting proposals, together with the paying back to shareholders of excess cash balances no longer required in the business, helped the retail banks to put in a solid performance, while shares in the life assurance companies were buoyed both by takeover activity and hopes that shareholders would be able to benefit from the assets in the long-term investment funds over and above those deemed needed for likely future claims. Even the utility sectors picked up in the final quarter after a difficult first nine months, as some of the fears of increased regulation and windfall taxes under a new administration began to diminish.

The worst performing sector, and one where there seems to have been no respite for years, was textiles, which remained friendless and may do so for some time. Tobacco, which meant BAT for most of the year and Imperial for just three months, suffered from adverse rulings in the US courts over the liability of companies for smoking-related diseases. The spirits companies, Allied Domecq, Guinness and especially Matthew Clark, had a very challenging year with demand falling, while the diversified industrials fell out of favour due to the huge costs of restructuring in their attempt to focus more on smaller areas of excellence. The strength of Sterling in the latter part of the year also increased concern for the prospects for companies seeking to compete in the export sector. Hanson was a case in point, trying to increase shareholder value by splitting itself up into its four remaining component parts; unfortunately, the process was seen by some only as a thinly disguised means to cut its overall dividend and the shares performed poorly.

Although not as high as the figure for 1995, the total value of public bids and deals in 1996 was over £24bn. The year saw consolidation in many industries where lack of organic sales growth was forcing a restructuring process through the pooling together of resources and the subsequent cost savings. However, the year started with Granada's £3.6bn takeover of the Forte hotel business, where determined new management was the key to success, and ended with the potential of huge changes in the UK telecommunications industry through the expected merger in 1997 of the businesses of British Telecom and MCI Communications of the US to form Concert, and the linking of Cable & Wireless' Mercury telecoms business with Nynex, Bell Cable and Videotron to provide telecoms services to roughly 5 million UK households. Earlier in the year there had been intense merger discussions between BT and C&W – the joint company would have had a market capitalisation of around £35bn – but these floundered on price and the difficulty of jumping worldwide regulatory hurdles. During 1996, Trafalgar House shareholders were at last put out of their misery by the £900m bid from Kvaerner – which had just failed to win Amec – and many of the remaining regional electricity companies (RECs) were bought up, mostly by US companies seemingly unworried by the strict regulation of the UK electricity sector and determined to expand overseas. Scottish Power was allowed to buy Southern Water to go with its MANWEB electricity acquisition in 1995, but National Power and PowerGen were barred by the government from buying RECs, against the advice of the Monopolies Commission.

Mergers were dominated by the formation of Royal & Sun Alliance, which created a major force in the insurance industry, and a company with a market capitalisation at the end of the year of nearly £7bn, a third of the listed composite insurance sector. Among the life assurance companies, Refuge and United Friendly merged to form United Assurance, the third largest listed life company by the end of the year. And at the end of 1996, the Lloyds TSB Group acquired the 38 per cent of Lloyds Abbey Life not already in its hands.

Flotations raised about £10bn in 1996, with privatisations raising another £1bn. The corresponding figure for non-privatisation flotations in 1995 was only £2.6bn. Both Railtrack and AEA Technology – part of the Atomic Energy Authority – were sold off by the state, as was British Energy, formed through the merger of Nuclear Electric and Scottish

Nuclear. Among the largest issues were the mobile telecommunications company Orange (which raised £700m for its vendors in a part sale and which had a market capitalisation at the end of the year of over £2.2bn), the upmarket retailer Harvey Nicholls, the chemicals concern Brunner Mond, the old Gateway food retailer Somerfield and the Thistle Hotels chain.

Gilts had a rather lacklustre time over the year as a whole, with the rise in the bond market from early May insufficient to recover all the lost ground in the first three months of the year. Yields on longer-dated stocks started and ended the year on roughly the same figure of $7^3/_4$ per cent. The rise in prices and consequent fall in yields was not just a UK phenomenon; bond yields fell in tandem in all the world's major economies in the second half of 1996 as steady, non-inflationary growth continued to come through.

Looking overseas, the world's equity markets showed good growth in general, and most of them outperformed the UK in local currency terms. Sterling's strength reduced the returns quite sharply for domestic holders of overseas equities, held either direct, or through managed funds. The US rose by 22 per cent in the presidential election year with interest rates, inflation and overall economic growth staying fairly low; Canada, however, was better at 29 per cent. Many of the European markets performed well; that of Spain was up by 43 per cent, those of Sweden and Finland by 39 per cent, the Netherlands 33 per cent, and France and Germany by 27 per cent and 25 per cent respectively. The Far East had a more difficult time. While the Pacific Basin index – excluding Japan – rose by 16 per cent, this masked a quite savage fall of 42 per cent in Thailand. However, the changes affecting Hong Kong in June 1997 did not cause much concern on the stockmarket as it grew by 31 per cent. Japan itself was down 6 per cent following a poor final quarter.

Back home, July saw the introduction of the new CREST settlement system, designed to reduce risk and speed up the process of settling transactions through the stockmarket. Following the failure of TAURUS, the new system had to work well, and while initial teething troubles and processing delays produced some grinding of teeth in brokers' offices, the new system seems to be coping so far. The big test comes this year with the massive Halifax issue. AIM, the Alternative Investment Market, settled down well and is growing in quite an encouraging manner following the ending of the USM.

The graphs on pages 38–40 illustrate:

(1) the performance of ordinary shares measured by the FTSE 100 Share Index;

(2) the performance of government securities (gilt-edged stocks), measured by the FT Actuaries All Stocks Index;

(3) the movement in UK interest rates and the inflation rate;
(4) the movement of sterling on a trade-weighted basis;
(5) the sterling-adjusted performance of New York, Tokyo and continental European equities.

3.3 COMPARING DIFFERENT TYPES OF SECURITY

The investor, in making a choice between different types of security, should take into account not only the relative importance to him of income and of capital gain but also:

(1) the degree of security against default;
(2) the expected rate of return;
(3) the tax advantages or disadvantages attaching to the security;
(4) the convenience and cost of dealing in the particular security; and
(5) the ability to realise the investment.

3.3.1 Security against default

The British government has the power to levy taxes and to print money and it is in the highest degree unlikely that it would ever default on its borrowings whether as National Savings (see Chapter 2), gilt-edged securities or Treasury bonds. It is generally assumed that the government would stand behind borrowings of local authorities, which in any event have the power to levy rates and the council tax. All these securities, therefore, have an intrinsic safety which the private sector cannot emulate. The safety of private sector borrowing lies in the reputation, integrity, viability and good management of the body concerned.

3.3.2 Rate of return

The rate of return on securities may be specified and fixed, as it is for fixed interest stocks issued by the government and by public and private sector bodies. In many other cases the return is specified initially but may be subject to variation to reflect the general movement of interest rates. Returns on some investments may be linked to the prevailing rate of inflation. Finally, the return may be dependent, as in the case of ordinary shares, on confidence in and the performance of the company. The more uncertain the return, the more attractive it has to be to compensate for the risk of underperformance. On the other hand, the investor should beware of overvaluing the certainty of return in money terms, since the real value of such returns can be eroded by inflation.

Figure 3.1   FTSE 100 index

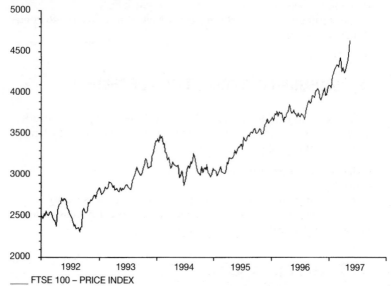

____ FTSE 100 – PRICE INDEX

HIGH 4630.9 9/5/97, LOW 2312.6 28/8/92, LAST 4630.9 9/5/97

Source: *Datastream*

Figure 3.2   London FTA Government all stocks index

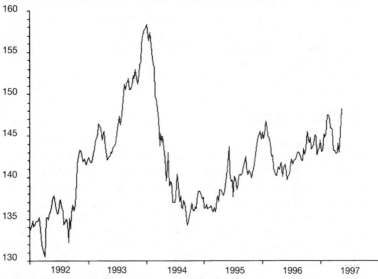

____ FTA GOVERNMENT ALL STOCKS – PRICE INDEX

HIGH 158.37 31/12/93, LOW 130.53 3/4/92, LAST 148.27 9/5/97

Source: *Datastream*

Figure 3.3   London clearing banks base rate and UK inflation rate

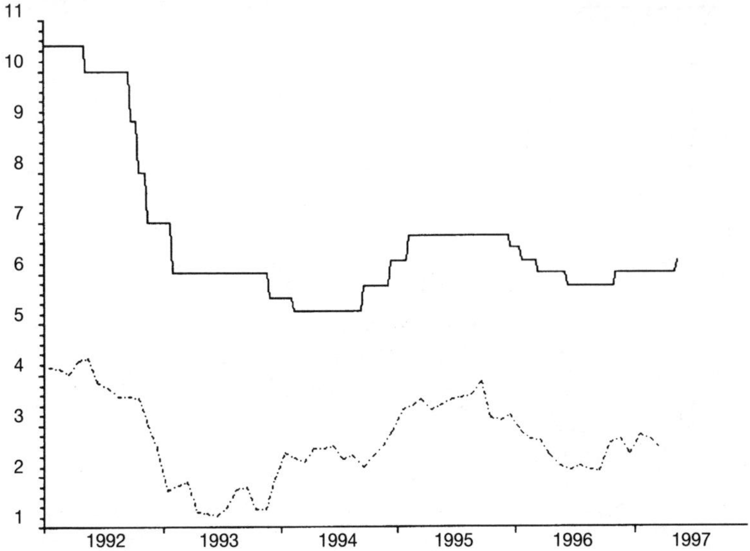

UK CLEARING BANKS BASE RATE – MIDDLE RATE
UK INFLATION RATE

Source: *Datastream*

Figure 3.4   Bank of England trade weighted sterling index

UK £ INDEX 90=100 (BOE) – TRADE WEIGHTED
HIGH 102.11 26/6/92, LOW 82.30 17/11/95, LAST 98.00 9/5/97

Source: *Datastream*

Figure 3.5   New York, Tokyo and Continental indices in sterling (rebased to 100)

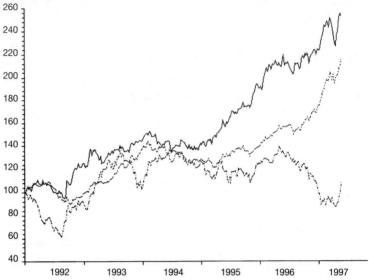

_____ DOW JONES INDUSTRIALS – PRICE INDEX (˜£)
.... NIKKEI 225 STOCK AVERAGE – PRICE INDEX (˜£)
----- FT/S&P WORLD EUROPE EX-UK – PRICE INDEX

Source: _Datastream_

3.3.3 Tax advantages

The basic rate income tax payer is likely to find little tax advantage in individual forms of listed security and he must choose whether the emphasis in his portfolio is to be on high income, the prospect of capital gain, or a balance between the two. Naturally, both among fixed interest stocks and ordinary shares, the investor will find a range of income yield from which to choose, and a stock which offers a good net return to a basic rate investor may not appeal so much to an investor who pays the higher rate. In terms of capital gains tax, British government stocks are exempt, no matter how long they have been held, and individuals will find that they have an exemption also for the first £6,500 of capital gains on disposals in the 1997/98 tax year, after the indexation of book cost. Now that separate taxation of married couples has been introduced, each spouse has his or her individual capital gains tax allowance. Most trusts have an exemption of the first £3,250 of indexed capital gains on disposals in this tax year. An individual can also take advantage of a personal equity plan, in which dividend income is free of all income tax and capital gains are exempt from capital gains tax, by investing up to £9,000 a year in equities, including unit and investment trusts, and some qualifying corporate bonds.

3.3.4 Convenience and cost of dealing

In general, investments listed on The Stock Exchange are liquid within reason and no investor should feel tied into any holding unless it is of unmarketable size. Dealing on The Stock Exchange, whether direct through a stockbroker, or indirect through an agent, will generally involve the payment of commission and other expenses (see pp 44 and 46).

3.4 THE STOCK EXCHANGE

3.4.1 Constitution and regulatory role

Historically, the burden of supervision of the securities industry has lain with The Stock Exchange. However, under the Financial Services Act 1986, Stock Exchange member firms must now be monitored by a self-regulatory organisation (SRO) which, in turn, is approved by the Securities and Investments Board (SIB). In the SIB's hands rests the responsibility, delegated by the Department of Trade and Industry, for the entire securities industry – this includes Stock Exchange business, life assurance, unit trusts and commodities – both to regulate and to defend standards. Rules of any SRO must be equivalent in effect to those of the SIB and the remainder of the industry.

From its earliest origins in the coffee houses, through the establishment of an elected membership at the beginning of the nineteenth century, practice and regulation have developed together. The rules had evolved to meet changing circumstances and to deal with abuses. Under the Financial Services Act 1986, the position has now changed in that the Securities and Futures Authority (as SRO) has taken over a number of the regulatory roles, such as the authorisation of members, their conduct of business with clients and compliance matters. The Stock Exchange (as the Recognised Investment Exchange) remains responsible for the dealing rules, the listing of new securities and the provision of market related information services amongst many other matters. There is a close working relationship between the two bodies.

3.4.2 **The primary and secondary markets**

The Stock Exchange provides the main securities market in the UK, representing both a new issue and a trading market. The new issue, or primary, market provides the mechanism for the raising of capital by means of the issue of securities. Users of capital, be they government, local authorities or public companies, all seek funds of a long-term nature, and a large part of these funds is obtained by the issue of securities through the primary market.

Suppliers of capital, whether they are institutional or individual savers, need to invest their money in such a way that it is readily realisable – hence the existence of the secondary, or trading, market in which it is possible to deal in several thousand securities listed on The Stock Exchange. It is also possible to deal in traded options (see **3.7.2**). The overall market capitalisation of securities listed on The Stock Exchange at 31 December 1996 was £4,087bn, of which gilts accounted for £292bn and UK equities for £1,012bn. The balance was made up by overseas stock with a London listing and eurobonds.

3.4.3 **Alternative Investment Market**

The Alternative Investment Market (AIM) was launched in February 1995 as a means by which small unlisted companies could raise capital in a relatively inexpensive manner and investors become involved in expansion-minded and growth-orientated companies in their infancy. Regulation is much lighter in this market with much of the work falling on the shoulders of the sponsoring intermediary, and with costs much lower than for a full London listing, many companies on the former Unlisted Securities Market have moved to AIM, with some smaller companies even moving down from full listing. There has also been a progression of companies whose shares were formerly traded on rule 4.2. With reporting levels less onerous, and with companies on the market often much younger – not even requiring a trading record on entry – potential investors must not lose sight of the risks of the market, but its arrival has certainly been welcomed.

3.4.4 **Overseas securities**

This chapter is primarily concerned with UK securities, but British investors should remember that they can also deal in foreign securities, not only those listed on The Stock Exchange in London, but also those listed on foreign exchanges (see Chapters 4 and 5).

Residents of the UK are no longer required to deposit all foreign currency securities with an authorised bank or other authorised depositary in the UK, although on grounds of security and to protect the investor's interests on dividends and stock issues, it is still advisable for some foreign stocks, in particular those which are in bearer form, to be held by a bank or agent, either in the UK or overseas. Neither should investors overlook the withholding tax of the country in which they invest, since this is not always allowable against UK tax. Should bearer bonds be lost, the expenses incurred and work involved in obtaining duplicates can be considerable.

3.4.5 Dealing on The Stock Exchange

Following Big Bang in October 1986, the distinction between firms acting as stockbrokers and stockjobbers became blurred. Formerly, a member firm of The Stock Exchange would deal only as one or the other: as a broker it would advise and transact business for its clients, either individuals (private clients) or institutional, with a jobbing firm whose role was to buy and to sell securities owned by it for its own profit. Investors could not deal direct with a jobber, but were obliged to deal through a stockbroker who would charge a commission for this (the amount being laid down by The Stock Exchange). This commission also covered ancillary services such as advice, valuations and tax calculations.

The current position is that broking and jobbing (now called market-making) subsidiaries can belong to the same parent. Institutional investors can now deal direct with market-makers. However, many institutions, and all private clients, continue to use the broking arm of a firm exercising both roles, or a firm which concentrates solely on broking. Broking continues in the same manner as before: advice, recommendations, dealing at best price, settlement and protection of benefits accruing to the investment until registration.

The minimum rates of commission (formerly set by The Stock Exchange) have been abandoned and firms have been left to charge their own rates. For the private client, it may be that the commission charge has changed very little, and firms are now moving towards charging for ancillary services to keep dealing commissions competitive.

Generally, the method of dealing in stocks and shares is as shown in Figure 3.6, overleaf. The client will speak or write to the stockbroker looking after his affairs and is likely to discuss what he wishes to do. The initial contact might alternatively have been made by the stockbroker. At this stage, if a sale is intended, it may be necessary for the broker to estimate potential tax liabilities as this may have some bearing on the discussions – many brokers will keep a running record of earlier

Figure 3.6 Dealing on The Stock Exchange

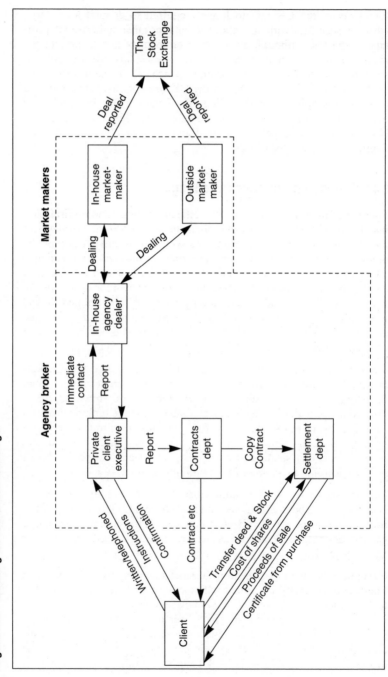

transactions for the client to help them. By referring to sources of information to hand, primarily the screen-based price service, the broker will be able to give some indication of the current trading price. If an order is given by the client, it will be attempted immediately unless an unobtainable price limit has been set.

The broker then contacts his dealing staff whose function is to deal with the market-maker in that share who is offering or bidding the best price in the size (number of shares) required by the client. The change from face-to-face encounters on The Stock Exchange floor to a screen-based system means that the agency dealer needs only to look at his monitor to find the best price available in the most frequently traded stocks where market-makers' two-way quotes are firm; but those shown for the smaller-capitalised stocks are often indicative only and are not necessarily true dealing prices. The dealer will complete the order, occasionally with reference to the private client executive if there is some difficulty in dealing, with one or more market-makers including, in many cases, the in-house market-making side. The dealer should always try to improve on the prices quoted by the market.

With investor protection being of paramount importance, any deal for a client transacted through the in-house market-maker has to be done at the best price available in the market at that time, whether made by the in-house team or others. It will often be the case that the in-house team will match the best available price elsewhere, when they are not making it themselves, as the private client order is on average relatively small set against the size of institutional orders.

The dealer, having completed the bargain, will report to the private client broker who in turn, if requested, will contact the client with oral confirmation. The time of dealing will appear on the contract note so that no confusion will arise as to price, especially important in shares whose prices are volatile. The contract note, which will indicate whether the bargain has been made with a connected party, will then be produced together with any other documentation required to cover a sale. An example of a bought contract note appears overleaf (Figure 3.7) – a sold contract note would not include stamp duty, and the costs would be deducted from the sale consideration, rather than being added.

The settlement date appears on the contract note. Generally, settlement for a gilt is made on the next working day although delayed settlement can be agreed in advance.

Rolling settlement for equities, the greatest change in Stock Exchange settlement practice in 200 years, was introduced on 18 July 1994. The settlement date was set for a ten working-day basis (T+10). Since June 1995, the settlement period has been shortened further to 5 days (T+5). The cost of purchases, and the proceeds from sales, should then be

Figure 3.7   Contract note

Name and address of stockbrokers	

Bargain ref:

Bargain date:
Time of deal:

As agents we have bought for Mr J Smith

20,000 United Sprockets ord 25p at 56p

£11,200.00

Commission at 1.5%   £168.00
Stamp duty   56.00
PTM levy   0.25
                        ─────────
                          224.25
                        ─────────
                       £11,424.25
                       ═════════

Bargain effected with connected company

Settlement date:

Subject to the rules, customs, usages and
interpretations of The Stock Exchange

(Signature of stockbrokers)
Members of The Stock Exchange

available on this fixed date after dealing (sales, of course, only if the paperwork has been returned to the broker).

Special provisions will be available for settlement for any date between T+2 and T+30 to tie in with clients' requirements, although the dealing price may reflect this change to the normal pattern. This will help investors wishing to close a position already opened just a few days earlier.

When selling, a client can expect to receive immediately in the post the contract note, which should be kept for tax purposes, and a transfer form. The transfer must be signed by the registered holder of the investment and returned to the brokers (together with the certificate representing the holding). The transfer form for sales of gilts eventually shows both seller and purchaser, although only the seller's name appears initially. Sales of unit trusts are covered by the same type of form, or through endorsing the reverse of the certificate.

The transfer form needed for UK shares and corporate loan stocks depends on whether the investment has yet passed from the TALISMAN to the CREST settlement systems. TALISMAN should be phased out by the end of 1997.

Transfer of bearer shares – mostly overseas companies – passes on good delivery. North American shares are in bearer form once the registered holder has signed the pre-printed form on the reverse of the certificate.

The buying client will not see a transfer form but will immediately receive a contract note. This should be kept for taxation purposes. If so arranged, he may also be sent a dividend mandate form, to be signed and passed to his bank, which will authorise the company (or the Bank of England for a gilt) to pay all dividends direct to his bank account instead of his registered address. There is little more for him to do, except to arrange payment to his broker on settlement day. Depending on the speed of registration (usually out of the broker's hands) he would expect to see a certificate for his new holding within eight weeks of purchase. The company's registrars must be informed of any change of the investor's address.

CREST

Following the abandonment of TAURUS owing to its cost over-runs and huge delays in its implementation timetable, market participants and the Bank of England still felt it necessary to produce a system of settlement of Stock Exchange trades which reduced the risk of the financial failure of one of the parties to the transaction. CREST provides a highly secure system for the simultaneous exchange of securities and irrevocable payment obligations: it will provide delivery of stock against payment (DVP), with registration and full legal title being provided within two hours of settlement. This should do away with much of the counterparty risk in settlement, and will revolutionise the entire market process by removing paper from settlement and improving its efficiency and cost.

The efficiency of holding certificates in a private individual client's own name is gradually being whittled away. There is undoubtedly a move towards the use of brokers' nominees – most brokers will be direct or sponsored members of the CREST operation – so as to eradicate what is perceived as the weakest link in the system, the delivery of share certificates and signed transfers by the client, or the provision of funds for value on the correct date to cover purchases. A two-tier system will be developed to allow clients to retain certificates in their own names if they wish, although the cost of transacting business through their brokers may reflect the extra work involved in settling paper-based transactions.

Dividends

When a company intends paying a dividend, it must temporarily halt the registration of new shareholders in order to produce dividend warrants and tax vouchers in time for the dividend date. The registration process for that dividend stops on the 'record' or 'books-closing' date. Dealings in cum-dividend form include the right to the forthcoming dividend; dealings in ex-dividend form do not include the right to the dividend and it belongs, when paid, to the seller. Even under the TALISMAN or CREST systems, shares bought cum-dividend are occasionally not able to be re-registered in time for the record date and the company is obliged to pay the seller, as his name still appears on its books. It is then for the seller's broker to claim the dividend from his client and for the buyer's broker to pay the dividend to his client. The dividend will be passed from selling broker to buying broker.

Capitalisation and rights issues

If a company makes a capitalisation issue (often called a scrip, bonus or free issue) or a rights issue, a record date is used once again, although The Stock Exchange will not usually mark the shares ex-entitlement until the working day immediately after new certificates or documents of title are posted. It is the buying broker's duty to claim from the selling broker any entitlement received by the seller which belongs to the buying broker's client. Where a seller is unable to produce documents of title for a rights issue by the time that new shares have to be accepted, then his broker must protect the buyer's entitlement so that those new shares do not lapse.

Stamp duty

Stamp duty is payable on purchases of shares, warrants and convertible loan stocks: it is collected by the buying broker and accounted for on the bought contract note. With CREST settlement, the present rate is 0.5 per cent of the consideration. There is no stamp duty payable on purchases of gilts or corporate loan stocks. For unit trust purchases, the stamp duty is covered by the initial charge. Stamp duty at differing rates may be charged on purchases of overseas shares. In certain transactions, eg purchase and sale by an investor of the same shares for the same settlement date or purchase of renounceable letters of acceptance or allotment, stamp duty reserve tax is payable at the rate of 0.5 per cent on the amount or value of the consideration.

Commission

The scale of minimum commissions set by The Stock Exchange has now been abolished and brokers are able to charge competitive rates. A new client should ensure that he knows what rate of commission will be charged on his dealings; firms have started to charge non-advisory clients, requiring only a dealing service, different rates from those charged to clients needing advice and periodic valuations.

PTM levy

Deals showing consideration of £10,000 or more also attract a flat 25p levy to help fund the costs of the Panel on Take-overs and Mergers. This is only charged on dealings in UK equities and UK registered convertibles.

3.4.6 Stockbroker services

Stockbrokers, market-makers, licensed dealers in securities and all others in the industry are subject to regulation by self-regulatory organisations, answerable to the Securities and Investments Board with wide-ranging powers.

Stockbrokers provide a variety of services in addition to buying and selling on behalf of clients. Brokers act on the specific instructions of their clients and give advice when called on to do so. They can also provide valuations of a portfolio at regular intervals and make recommendations. Alternatively a client may choose to give his broker discretion to manage his investments on his behalf, buying and selling when the broker considers it to be advantageous and reporting his actions to his client. Charges, if any, for these services (over and above the commission that they charge for dealing) vary from firm to firm.

The stockbroker, with access to economic and analytical material, often produced by his own firm's research department, is able to advise on investment policy and help in the choice of securities which best match his client's objectives. The investor can approach a firm of stockbrokers direct, or can instruct his bank, accountant, solicitor or other financial adviser to approach a stockbroker on his behalf.

3.4.7 Sources of information

Every weekday the previous day's dealing prices and closing quotations of listed securities are published in The Stock Exchange Daily Official List. The last recorded marks are also shown for securities traded in the USM and the AIM. The *Financial Times* and other newspapers also give a list of closing prices – generally the middle market price of each (ie the average of the buying and selling prices).

A number of indices are published, of which the FTSE 100 Share Index is the best known: it is widely quoted in the press and used as a barometer of price movement of shares. More sophisticated indices are published for government securities, fixed interest and gold mining shares. The FTSE 100 Share Index is an arithmetically weighted index of 100 leading UK shares, revalued each minute, giving an immediate picture of market movements. The companies appearing in the index are, in general, the largest in market capitalisation terms and account for almost 70 per cent of the total capitalisation of the UK equity market.

The most representative indices for ordinary shares are the FTSE Actuaries Share Indices, covering at present around 900 shares and 36 different sections of the market. These are compiled daily. To give a broader picture of equity price movements the *Financial Times* and the Institute of Actuaries also produce daily indices for the next 250 highest capitalised companies after the components of the 100 Share Index, an index for the top 350 companies, a Small Cap index and a Fledgling Index.

Daily indices of government securities, corporate fixed interest securities and gold mining shares are published in the financial press, together with indices of overseas markets.

Apart from primary sources of information such as political and economic news and statements, and annual accounts and other reports and circulars issued by companies, a wide range of information and comment is available from financial columns in newspapers, financial journals and newsletters. In addition, the results of stockbrokers' research covering both individual companies (most of which have been visited by the stockbroker) and sectors of the market are published together with economic forecasts, and various publicly available statistical services provide immediate access to relevant information. All this information provides the raw material for what is termed 'fundamental analysis'.

Technical analysis – the use of charts – provides data expressed in three forms: line, bar and point-and-figure charts. It is not the purpose of this chapter to explain these three forms of chart in detail, still less to comment on methods of interpreting them. However, charts are often a useful source of further information: for instance, apart from displaying the levels of the main markets, they can also be used to show a price level of a particular share or stock in relation to an appropriate index and how the performance of the particular investment has changed over a period of time in relation to the market generally.

Information issued by The Stock Exchange, such as the total number of daily bargains and the volume of equity turnover, has for some time been used as a measure of the current level of activity in the market. Other more sophisticated charts, such as confidence and over-bought/over-sold indicators, are now increasingly used and from these and many others the technical analyst tries to assess what is likely to happen in the future. In essence, chartists use technical analysis as a tool for demonstrating the existence of complex interrelationships between events and expectations, with a view to determining from established trends and patterns the direction in which the market generally, or a particular share, will move.

3.5 LISTED PUBLIC SECTOR SECURITIES

3.5.1 British government stocks

Legal nature

British government stocks (also called 'British funds' or 'gilt-edged securities' or simply 'gilts') represent borrowings by the British government or borrowings of certain nationalised industries which are guaranteed by the government. The investor can be entirely confident that interest will be paid and the principal repaid in accordance with the terms of the loan. A number of names are used for specific stocks – Treasury, Exchequer, etc – but these have no practical significance for the investor.

Pre-conditions

Gilt-edged securities listed on The Stock Exchange may be held by all categories of UK investor – governmental, personal, corporate or trustee.

However, friendly societies or trustees acting without specific investment powers in their trust deeds must observe the Trustee Investments Act 1961.

Characteristics

British government stocks, with certain limited exceptions, carry a fixed rate of interest (the 'coupon') which is expressed as an annual rate on £100 nominal of the stock. Thus the holder of £100 nominal of Treasury $8\frac{1}{2}$ per cent 2007 will receive £8.50 per year until that date (subject to deduction of income tax at the basic rate), irrespective of the price which he may have paid or of the market price from time to time. In March 1981 the first issue of an index-linked gilt-edged stock was launched on which both capital and interest were linked to the RPI and currently stocks are available with redemption dates ranging to 2030. With the exception of Consols $2\frac{1}{2}$ per cent, on which interest is paid quarterly, interest on all British government stocks is paid at six-monthly intervals.

In addition to paying interest during the lifetime of the stock, the government has an obligation to redeem its stock, ie to repay each loan at the nominal, or par, value of £100. The precise nature of this obligation is different for different stocks: it may be to redeem either:

(1) on a fixed date (eg Treasury $8\frac{3}{4}$ per cent 1997 must be redeemed on 1 September 1997); or
(2) within a specified range of dates (eg Treasury 8 per cent stock 2002/06 must be redeemed at some time between 5 October 2002 and 5 October 2006); or
(3) on a small number of low coupon stocks (eg Consols $2\frac{1}{2}$ per cent, Treasury 3 per cent and War Loan $3\frac{1}{2}$ per cent) at any time chosen by the government.

The government is unlikely ever to redeem the stocks in the last category unless the general level of interest rates falls below the coupon. They are purchased mainly for the interest payments, which give a high level of fixed income; but capital growth on them depends on interest rates falling rather than on the passage of time to a certain redemption date. The government is also unlikely to redeem a stock in category (2) above before the last date for redemption if the general level of interest rates remains higher than the coupon.

The period still unexpired before redemption is used to classify government stocks, as follows:

(1) Short-dated stocks ('shorts') are defined as stocks with less than five years until redemption.
(2) Medium-dated stocks ('mediums') are stocks with between five and 15 years still to run to redemption.

(3) Long-dated stocks ('longs') are stocks with over 15 years until redemption.

(4) Undated or irredeemable stocks are those with no final date specified for redemption.

Although all the irredeemable stocks have low coupons, there is a wide choice of different coupons in the other categories, ranging from 3½ per cent to 15 per cent. The investor should therefore be able to find a stock which combines the redemption date which he is seeking with his preferred rate of coupon.

The two benefits of buying gilt-edged stocks are (1) the interest received and (2) the capital profit which can be made when a stock bought below par is repaid at par or when a stock is sold through The Stock Exchange at more than the purchase price. Two kinds of yield can be calculated to help in assessing the benefits: running yield and redemption yield.

The running, flat, or interest yield ignores the possibility of capital profit and takes into account only the interest. It is calculated by dividing the coupon by the price paid by the investor, ignoring any accrued interest, and multiplying by 100 to produce a percentage.

The redemption yield takes account of both the interest and the capital gain (or, in some cases, loss) which would occur if the stock was held until redemption. The most common form of redemption yield is the gross redemption yield, which ignores the effect of income tax. Redemption yields cannot of course be calculated for undated stocks, since there is no realistic prospect of redemption.

The price of gilts is determined by such factors as the amount of new stock which the government might have to issue to fund its borrowing requirement, the amount of new money flowing into the institutional investors (such as pension funds), and the attractiveness of gilts compared with other investment opportunities. Thus, if the general interest rates and yields on other investments rise, the yields on gilts will also rise, ie the price of gilts will fall. With the probable exception of index-linked stocks, gilt prices will also fall if inflationary expectations rise. Any kind of political, economic, financial or industrial news may affect gilt prices, in so far as it affects the market's expectations about inflation, interest rates or the government borrowing requirement.

Although gilt prices do not tend to fluctuate as much as those of ordinary shares, the timing of both purchases and sales still requires careful consideration.

Accrued interest

Following the introduction of new rules in February 1985 designed to prevent 'bond-washing' or the substitution by investors of tax-free capital gain for taxable income, the market price of all gilts excludes the interest which has accrued since the last interest date and a separate payment is made in respect of this. In a 'cum-dividend' transaction (one where the purchaser will receive the next dividend payment) the purchaser pays to the seller the amount of interest which has accrued to the date of sale since the last interest payment, as the purchaser will later be receiving interest for the full six-month period. In an 'ex-dividend' transaction (where the seller will receive the next dividend payment) the seller pays to the purchaser the amount of interest which will accrue between the date of sale and the next interest date.

Index-linked gilts

In March 1981, the government made its first issue of an index-linked gilt, whose redemption value and annual income return were linked to the change in the RPI in order to compensate the holder to maturity for the effects of inflation. Since this date, and with inflation at lower levels, these stocks have been a cheaper method of finance for the government than conventional higher-coupon fixed interest gilts and a number of further issues have been made.

Income from index-linked stocks is relatively low as the main advantage to a holder is through the inflation proofing afforded to the invested capital. The income payments increase every six months to reflect changes in the RPI.

The timing of market purchases and sales requires consideration since dealing prices do not necessarily reflect the underlying value of the stock. A comparison might here be made with index-linked national savings certificates which increase in value each month in line with the change in the RPI (see **2.3.3**).

As with conventional gilt-edged stocks, the market price of index-linked stocks will not include interest which has accrued since the last payment date.

Taxation

Interest is paid net of basic rate income tax, except in the case of War Loan 3½ per cent and any stock bought through branches of the Post Office. Interest received by individuals is treated as investment income and is subject to higher rate income tax, where appropriate.

With some exceptions, overseas holders of gilts who are both resident and ordinarily resident outside the UK are exempt from all UK taxes on a large number of British government securities.

For transfers of certain interest-bearing securities made on or after 28

February 1986, the provisions of the accrued income scheme, introduced by the Finance Act 1985, apply. The securities affected include any loan stock or similar security (but not shares in a company) whether of the UK government, any other government, any public or local authority in the UK or elsewhere, or of any company.

Where such securities are transferred, the scheme provides for apportionment of interest on a daily basis with the result that, for tax purposes, the seller is treated as having received interest accruing up to and including the settlement day and the purchaser is treated as having received the interest accruing thereafter. Interest is therefore deemed to have been received by the seller on a sale 'cum div' and by the purchaser on a sale 'ex div' and, in each case, there is a corresponding rebate for the other party to the transaction. The charge to tax is calculated by reference to interest periods which usually end on each normal interest payment date. If deemed interest exceeds rebates for a given interest period, the difference is chargeable to income tax under Schedule D, Case VI (or, where the securities are non-UK securities, Schedule D, Case V).

No charge arises if the taxpayer concerned is an individual and at no time in the year of assessment in which an interest period ends, or the previous year of assessment, does the nominal value of securities held by him exceed £5,000. Husband and wife are treated separately for this purpose.

Stamp duty is not payable on purchases of British government stock.

Suitability

Investment in British government stocks is a convenient way of providing for future commitments, the timing and size in money terms of which are known or can be confidently predicted. On the other hand, if the size of the commitment is uncertain because of the impact of inflation in the intervening period, the investor should consider a portfolio comprising both fixed interest stocks, index-linked stocks and ordinary shares.

Because default is virtually inconceivable and interest and redemption value are both fixed, with the exception of the irredeemable issues and the index-linked stocks, gilts are also ideal for the investor for whom security is paramount. Most investors through The Stock Exchange will place some value on security and are therefore well advised to include a proportion of such stocks in their portfolios. Trustees, if they have not been given express powers by their particular trust deed, are obliged by the Trustee Investments Act 1961 to invest a proportion of the trust funds either in this sector of the market or in other fixed interest stocks carrying 'trustee' status.

Further, the advantages of ready marketability and reasonably high yields should not be overlooked.

Mechanics

There are four ways of dealing in gilt-edged stocks:

(1) by a direct approach to a stockbroker;
(2) by an indirect approach to a stockbroker;
(3) through the Post Office; or
(4) by application for newly issued stock direct to the Bank of England.

Direct approach to a stockbroker

An investor may place his order to buy or sell with a stockbroker who will execute the transaction on The Stock Exchange for a commission. For information on dealing see **3.4.6**.

Indirect approach to a stockbroker

The investor can instruct his solicitor, accountant, bank or other financial adviser to place the order to buy or sell on his behalf with a stockbroker. The stockbroker may share the commission earned from an agent's client with that agent.

Dealing through the Post Office

Members of the public can buy all stocks (on the National Savings Stock Register) through branches of the Post Office, from which application forms can be obtained, or by direct application to the National Savings Stocks and Bonds Office in Blackpool. Interest on stocks purchased in this way is paid gross. The maximum amount that may be invested in any one stock on any one day is £25,000, but there is no limit to the total amount of stock which may be held. Execution of orders takes longer than if they are placed direct with the stockbroker, leaving the price paid or received more open to chance. Moreover, the Post Office, unlike stockbrokers, will accept orders to buy or sell only at the best price obtainable, and it cannot give advice, manage portfolios or take orders to buy and sell when prices reach particular levels. On the other hand, fees charged by the Post Office on both purchases and sales may be considerably lower than Stock Exchange commissions. See also **2.3.10**.

The Post Office maintains a separate register from the Bank of England Register. Any stock on the National Savings Stock Register may be transferred to the Bank of England Register, but only £5,000 nominal of a particular stock may be transferred by any one investor from the Bank of England Register in a calendar year.

Purchase of newly issued stocks

The above methods of dealing in stocks concern those already issued and trading on The Stock Exchange. When a new stock is first issued by the Bank of England, application forms (obtainable from the Bank of England, banks or stockbrokers or cut out from newspaper advertisements) must be sent to the New Issue Department of the Bank of England.

The names of holders (other than those who bought through branches of the Post Office) are registered with the Bank of England, and holders receive certificates which are evidence of registration.

The direct cost of dealing is limited to the commission charged by the stockbroker, the Post Office or other agents. For dealing on The Stock Exchange see **3.4.6**.

As a rule, prices per £100 nominal of stock are quoted in multiples of $£^{1}/_{32}$. Three months before redemption, prices are quoted in pounds and pence.

Safe custody

The contract note, which constitutes evidence of a sale or purchase, is relevant, *inter alia*, for taxation purposes and should be kept in a safe place. For stocks where a register is maintained, certificates are evidence of title and should also be kept in a safe place. If certificates are lost, duplicates can be obtained only against an appropriate form of indemnity.

3.5.2 Other public sector stocks

Certain public boards are entitled by Act of Parliament to borrow on the security of their revenues without government guarantees, stated or implied. Examples are the Agricultural Mortgage Corporation, the Metropolitan Water Authority and the Port of London Authority.

Commonwealth stocks carry no British government guarantee and are the obligation of the issuing authority.

Commission on both public board stocks and Commonwealth and overseas government stocks is likely to be charged by the stockbroker. In most respects they are similar to debenture stocks (see **3.6.1**). For dealing on The Stock Exchange see **3.4.6**.

3.6 LISTED COMPANY FIXED INTEREST SECURITIES

3.6.1 Legal nature

Fixed interest stocks issued by companies are a form of borrowing. There are three basic types of security:

(1) debenture stocks;
(2) loan stocks; and
(3) preference shares (which are not borrowings).

Debenture stocks

These are either mortgage debentures, secured by a fixed charge on the company's properties, or debentures secured by a floating charge on some or all of the company's assets.

For all debenture stocks (and, nowadays also, all listed unsecured loan stocks), a trustee is appointed to supervise the performance of the company's obligations and to act for the holders in the event of default. The trust deed sets out the rights of the lenders, including limitations on the company's freedom to act in ways which might undermine their security (eg borrowing limits are imposed and changes in the nature of the business and substantial disposals of assets are restricted).

Loan stocks

Loan stocks are unsecured obligations. If the borrowing company fails to meet its obligations, loan stockholders are in the same position as other unsecured creditors: they can sue for their money, but if the company's assets remaining after creditors ranking ahead of the unsecured creditors have been paid off are insufficient to meet the claims of all unsecured creditors, stockholders receive only that proportion of the remaining assets which the outstanding principal amount of the loan stock bears to the company's total unsecured debts.

An important variant is convertible loan stock, which carries the right of conversion into the company's ordinary shares (see further **3.6.3**).

Preference shares

Preference shares are not debts but are part of the share capital of the company, issued on terms which are usually set out in the company's articles of association. Before any dividend is paid to ordinary shareholders, preference shareholders are normally entitled to receive a fixed dividend, provided that sufficient profits are available to cover it. If the company is wound up, preference shareholders rank ahead of ordinary shareholders up to the nominal value of their capital, but have no further rights unless expressly provided for in the articles.

An important variant is convertible preference shares, which carry the right of conversion into the company's ordinary shares (see **3.6.3**).

3.6.2 Pre-conditions

Fixed interest stocks listed on The Stock Exchange may be held by most categories of UK investor, although friendly societies and trustees acting without specific investment powers in their trust deeds must observe the Trustee Investments Act 1961.

3.6.3 Characteristics

Like dated government stocks, dated debentures, dated loan stocks and redeemable preference shares carry a fixed rate of interest for a specified number of years, at the end of which the principal amount becomes due for repayment. However, unlike the government, the company may have the right to repay before the stated redemption date and may do so if general interest rates fall substantially below the coupon. Thus the actual life of the investment may prove to be shorter than the originally stated term.

Private sector securities are less easily marketable than gilt-edged stocks and, with the exception of most convertible stocks, can normally be purchased on higher yields than government securities paying the same rate of interest over the same number of years. This yield differential also reflects the value given by the market to the weaker level of security offered by the loan stock.

Convertible stocks

Convertible stocks, sometimes referred to as 'deferred equities', have certain additional characteristics. Essentially they are securities issued with a fixed interest payment and fixed redemption date, but conferring the right to convert on a certain date or dates into a stated number of ordinary shares of the company.

Convertible stock usually provides a much higher running yield than the ordinary shares of the company concerned, in addition to being slightly more secure, although an investor who exercises his conversion right will not share in any capital gain achieved up to that point by an investor who had originally invested in the ordinary shares. Until the first conversion date, the market price of convertible stock tends to maintain a fairly steady relationship to the market price of a corresponding block of ordinary shares. However, the price of the convertible stock will not fluctuate to the same extent as the share price, since it will also be influenced by the general level of yields on non-convertible fixed interest securities.

Holders of convertible stocks will receive notification of the conversion option and advice should be sought at that time. It is most important to take action by the final conversion date, either exercising the conversion option or selling the convertible stock. Once the right to convert is lost, the stock will then be valued as a straightforward fixed interest security, which often results in a sharp drop in value.

The decision to exercise the right to convert on one of the conversion dates will largely depend on whether the income on the stock is likely to be less than the prospective return, in the form of dividends, on the holding of ordinary shares into which the stock can be converted.

The majority of the convertible securities in issue are convertible loan stocks, but some convertible debenture stocks and some convertible preference shares exist (see **3.6.1**).

3.6.4 Taxation

Stamp duty is not payable on transfer of debentures and non-convertible debenture or loan stocks, but it is payable (by the purchaser) on transfer of convertible stocks and on preference shares, whether convertible or not.

Fixed interest non-convertible stocks bought after 13 March 1984 and fulfilling the requirements for 'qualifying corporate bonds' in s 64 of the Finance Act 1984 are treated in a similar way to government securities (see **3.5.1**) and disposal or redemption gains are exempt from capital gains tax. Losses are not offsettable.

Gains on disposals of convertible stocks and on disposals of shares received following conversion of convertible stocks are subject to capital gains tax.

Interest on loan stocks is paid after deducting income tax at the basic rate. Holders not liable to tax may reclaim it, while those liable at the higher rate will be assessed on the gross amount of the interest, credit being given for the tax already deducted at source. The provisions of the accrued income scheme described in **3.5.1** may apply to the transfer of loan stocks.

In the case of preference shares, the 'imputation system' results in a slightly different treatment. The dividend paid is not subject to deduction of tax; instead it carries a 'tax credit'. The recipient's tax liability is calculated on the total of the dividend and the tax credit, with the result that for a basic rate taxpayer there will be no further liability to tax after allowing for the credit. Those not liable to tax may claim back the tax credit, while higher rate taxpayers will be liable to tax on the total of the dividend and the tax credit, the credit satisfying the basic rate part of their liability.

3.6.5 Suitability

Fixed interest stocks are suitable for investors who have known future commitments to meet or who want to maximise the return on their invested capital through a mixed portfolio of stocks and ordinary shares. Private sector debentures or loan stocks may represent a cheaper route to these goals than gilts if the investor is prepared to forgo the additional security offered by gilts.

Convertible stocks are a means of keeping the investor's options open as between investing in ordinary shares or in fixed interest stocks.

3.6.6 Mechanics

The method of dealing is shown at **3.4.6**.

3.6.7 Safe custody

The contract note, which constitutes evidence of the sale or purchase, is relevant, *inter alia*, for taxation purposes and should be kept in a safe place. Certificates are evidence of title and should also be kept in a safe place, although if certificates are lost, duplicates can usually be obtained against an appropriate form of indemnity.

3.7 ORDINARY SHARES

3.7.1 General

Legal nature

A company is a legal person, capable of perpetual succession and distinct from its proprietors, namely the persons who contributed the original capital, or their successors. Ownership of a company takes the form of 'shares' in the capital of the company. All companies listed on The Stock

Exchange, or the subject of trading in the USM and the AIM, are limited liability companies, and the shareholders usually have no liability to creditors if the company defaults on its obligations.

Shareholders are the proprietors (or members) of the company. Subject to a company's memorandum and articles of association, and to whatever dividends the company in fact pays, ordinary shareholders have the right to all profits after payment of prior charges on the company's revenue, such as interest, wages, other running expenses, taxes and dividends on preference shares. In the same way, if the company is wound up they are entitled to all assets remaining when prior claims have been met. Thus they own the residual assets or 'equity' of the company – hence the term 'equities' to describe ordinary shares.

Ownership of most shares listed on The Stock Exchange is established by registration; the owner's name is entered on a share register by the company's registrars (sometimes an agent office of the company and sometimes a bank or other specialist organisation), which then issue share certificates.

Extensive and up-to-date information is required from companies when they seek an initial listing on The Stock Exchange, issue new shares or other securities for cash, make a take-over offer, or seek to effect a merger or reconstruction. Such information requirements may be prescribed by legislation, by The Stock Exchange or by the Panel on Take-overs and Mergers.

Pre-conditions

Shares listed on The Stock Exchange can be held by most categories of UK investor, although friendly societies and trustees acting without specific investment powers in their trust deeds must observe the Trustee Investments Act 1961.

Characteristics

Ordinary shares are a company's risk capital; the investor expects a reasonable and rising level of dividend income and a rise in the share price, but there can be no certainty about this. If his expectations are fulfilled or exceeded, he is rewarded for taking the risks that dividends might have been low or non-existent and that the share price might have fallen.

Dividends are paid out of profits, normally following the recommendation of the directors.

The market price of a company's shares will fluctuate from day to day and will in part reflect objective data such as its past records on profits and dividends and its assets; but prices will also be affected by subjective judgements about the company's probable future performance. News about the company (including its regular profit announcements) will influence the price, but so too will news concerning the sector or sectors in which the company operates and, indeed, news affecting the political situation and/or economy as a whole. Prices are also influenced by the amount of new money which the institutional investors, in particular, have to invest, some of which is likely to find its way into company shares, the proportion depending on how attractive shares are considered by comparison with other investments.

Scrip dividends

In order to conserve cash flow and to give shareholders a method of accumulating more shares, many companies now allow their shareholders to elect to take dividends in the form of shares in lieu of cash. This is commonly known as a scrip dividend. As the company is issuing new capital direct to its shareholders there are no brokers' costs nor stamp duty, but there are no tax savings for the recipient. Although the individual is treated as having received gross dividend income of an amount which, when reduced by basic rate income tax, is equivalent to the 'cash equivalent', this latter figure (the net dividend on his holding) only is used to acquire new shares at a pre-ordained pricing formula. The tax credit on the dividend cannot be reclaimed where a shareholder does not have sufficient annual income to pay income tax at the basic rate. A higher rate taxpayer must also eventually find the difference between the tax credit deemed to be his and the tax liability on the dividend's gross equivalent out of cash from other sources as he will have received no cash from the company, save perhaps for a small balancing item. The active share investor ought also to bear in mind before accepting scrip dividends that records will need to be kept completely up to date for the purposes of capital gains tax as each new allotment of shares requires an updated book cost.

Some companies now offer enhanced scrip dividends, to a value greater than the underlying cash dividend, and may offer a cheap broker option for selling the dividend shares at a premium value to the underlying cash dividend.

Taxation of income and capital gains

Ordinary shareholders in receipt of dividends also receive a tax credit (corresponding to the advance corporation tax paid by the company in respect of the dividend). Non-taxpayers may claim repayment of the tax credit, while the liability of basic rate taxpayers is satisfied by the credit. For those liable to tax at the higher rate, tax is calculated on the total of the dividend and the tax credit, and the tax payable is reduced by the amount of the credit.

Capital gains realised from the sale of shares may be liable to capital gains tax, and capital losses can be used to offset other gains. As a general rule capital losses can only be carried forward, but they may be used to offset earlier capital gains where they all occur in the same fiscal year.

Capital gains tax considerations are important and investors should try to make full use of the annual exemption for capital gains tax available in each tax year to individuals. This implies that an investor should endeavour either to switch from investments where the income or growth potential has run its course to others where the return is likely to be greater, or to increase the base costs of his shares (within the capital gains tax exemption) by the action widely known as 'bed and breakfasting'. This entails a sale of shares one afternoon and their repurchase the next morning in the expectation that the share price has not moved. As these transactions are completed for the same settlement date and as the investor's name need not have to be deleted from the company's share register, it is not necessary for him to provide a share certificate to the broker or to sign a transfer deed. However, the Inland Revenue has the ability to see through transactions made purely for the avoidance of tax, and the nervous investor wishing to take a capital gains tax advantage in this way should consider selling the shares and repurchasing them for a later settlement date so that he comes off the company's register of shareholders. He will run the risk of market movements between the sale and purchase. The costs of 'bed and breakfasting' are relatively low, limited only to the stockbroker's commission and the market-maker's 'turn' (the difference between the selling and the repurchase price) together with stamp duty. Not only can an investor 'bed and breakfast' a gain which would be covered by the annual exemption but he could also 'bed and breakfast' a loss to offset chargeable gains made elsewhere during the tax year.

The Finance Act 1982 provides for indexation relief on capital gains from the 'appointed date'. The 'appointed date' is 6 April 1982 in all cases with the exception of companies, for which it is 1 April 1982. The calculation of the indexation relief, where there has been a single purchase of shares, is straightforward. For shares bought after March 1982, their historic cost is increased by a factor equal to the change in the RPI from the month of acquisition to the month of disposal. For those bought before April 1982, the Finance Act 1988 brings forward the deemed acquisition date to 31 March 1982 and the deemed book value of the holding to the value on that date, as adjusted by capital issues made by the company in the intervening period, provided an election to do this has been made to the Inland Revenue. Some sales will produce indexed gains under the new system where these would have been losses under the old, and *vice versa*, and these will be treated as 'no gain, no loss' situations. Naturally, at the time of disposal, it is impossible to calculate the indexation relief exactly as the RPI figure for that month is not issued until the following month, but an estimated figure can be given by financial advisers or a certain amount of leeway can be left to cover this unknown element. Indexation relief can only be used to reduce a gain, and cannot increase a loss nor turn a gain into a loss.

Where a shareholding has been built up in a company over a period, the calculation of the capital gains tax position on disposal including any indexation relief can be extremely complicated, and accurate records of dates of purchase should be kept by all investors. This is especially the case where scrip dividends have been taken in lieu of cash.

Suitability

Ordinary shares are suitable for the investor who is able to accept an element of risk and is looking for rising income and a hedge against inflation, particularly if he follows attentively the fortunes of companies in which he invests.

For the investor who needs to estimate with a degree of confidence the timing and size in money terms of his future commitments, shares are not as suitable as fixed interest stocks.

Unlike some of the fixed term savings schemes described in **2.3**, most ordinary shares in public listed companies are readily marketable at a moment's notice. However, since share prices are subject to a considerable degree of fluctuation (greater than that in fixed interest stocks), an investor who is likely to be faced suddenly with unexpected commitments should endeavour not to rely on ordinary shares to meet such commitments.

Mechanics

For the mechanics of dealing see **3.4.5**.

Safe custody and maintenance

The contract note, which constitutes evidence of the sale or purchase, is relevant, inter alia, for capital gains tax purposes and should be kept in a safe place. Share certificates are evidence of title and should also be kept in a safe place, although if certificates are lost, duplicates can usually be obtained against an appropriate indemnity. Company registrars are likely to make a small administration charge in replacing lost certificates and a bank or insurance company will also charge a fee for 'joining in' the indemnity.

In the case of bearer shares no register is maintained and possession is evidence of title. Bearer shares should therefore be held in safe custody.

The investor is well advised to keep his portfolio under review, either continuously or periodically. Some stockbrokers and other agents automatically review and revalue the portfolios of their private clients at regular intervals and are prepared to offer advice. Between these reviews they may also contact their clients to make recommendations affecting individual holdings or the balance of the portfolio between the main investment areas.

In addition to regular reviews, which are essential, the investor who follows the economic, industrial and financial news and who is prepared to buy when a good investment opportunity arises at a reasonable price or to sell a share when its prospects have dimmed or its price is high, will do better than a more passive investor, provided of course that his judgement and the advice that he receives are good.

All registered shareholders will receive the annual report and accounts of the company in which they hold shares. Companies listed on The Stock Exchange or the subject of trading on AIM also have to make an interim report, normally containing profit figures for the first six months of the company's financial year and reporting any interim dividends declared. The interim dividend, which is paid at the board's discretion, and the final dividend which is recommended by the directors at the company's year end (subject to the approval of its shareholders at the annual general meeting), normally make up the total dividend for the year. Some major international companies issue interim statements every quarter.

Although annual and interim reports provide natural occasions on which to consider increasing or reducing shareholdings, such action should not necessarily be taken straight away, since the impact of the report will immediately be reflected in the share price. Few tactics can be worse than trying to sell when others are selling and the price is low, or trying to buy when the price is high. Having formed a judgement on whether to buy, sell or merely retain an existing holding, the prudent investor will await a suitable opportunity before acting.

Nominees

Most stockbroking firms offer the use of a nominee facility to their clients. When bought, shares and other Stock Exchange investments (as well as unit trusts) are registered into the name of a nominee company instead of the client's own name. This makes for administrative ease both on the part of the stockbroking firm – which does not then have to chase clients for paperwork following a sale of investments, merely producing a contract note as proof of the transaction – but, more importantly, for the client. Using a firm's nominee company does not mean giving the firm discretion over one's investments; a client will often retain an advisory relationship, although in most cases firms will require the use of their nominee services if handling clients' investments on a discretionary basis.

The benefits to the client are numerous. No longer responsible for the safe-keeping of certificates, nor expected to pay the bank for holding them, the investor also does not need to sign transfer forms when completing sales. This becomes very important under rolling settlement, especially with the settlement period now at five working days. It becomes the broker's responsibility to advise on rights issues and other corporate actions relating to the client's holdings, for which the documentation is handled by the nominee company. Dividend income can be mandated direct to the investor's bank, either straight from the investment company if 'designated' nominees are used or, at intervals, from the stockbroking firm when investments are held in 'undesignated' nominees. Brokers can produce a composite tax voucher, acceptable to the Inland Revenue, at the end of each tax year, listing all dividends received by the nominee company on behalf of the investor during that year, and can provide capital gains tax calculations.

It is important, however, to ensure that the security of the nominee company is of the highest order and, especially, that the company has adequate backing over and above any investors' protection schemes in case of fraud within the nominee company.

Personal equity plans (PEPs)

PEPs were introduced in the 1986 Budget and allow investors to commit in 1997/98 up to £9,000 in a tax-efficient form of saving.

A new plan can be entered into each tax year. Investment changes within the plan are allowed. The tax advantages continue until the investor ends the plan.

UK registered shares listed on The Stock Exchange or dealt on AIM may be included in the plan as direct equity holdings, but the full £6,000 of a general PEP may be initially invested in investment trusts or authorised unit trusts which themselves are at least 50 per cent invested in UK and EU equities. To reflect the advent of the single European market, the PEP rules are in the process of being changed to allow direct investment of up to £6,000 in equities of EU companies. Certain preference shares and convertible preference shares are included as acceptable investments, allowing an element of fixed 'interest' into PEPs. Cash may be held in a PEP and interest is credited net of basic rate tax, which is reclaimable by the PEP manager to produce a gross figure, provided the cash is eventually invested in qualifying shares or unit trusts.

Since January 1992, individuals have also been able to invest £3,000 in a single company PEP issued either by a listed UK company (in which case only shares in that company are acceptable) or by a recognised Plan Manager (allowing switches from time to time between shares of differing companies).

Shares arising from new issues, including privatisations, can be transferred into a PEP within 42 days of the announcement of allocation, at the issue price. This issue value will count towards the annual investment limit. There is no liability to income tax at basic rate or higher rate on dividends on shares held in the PEP, nor is there any liability to capital gains tax on any disposal in the duration, or at the end of the plan. PEPs are therefore an advantageous method of saving through risk investment for all equity investors, but especially so for those on the higher rate of income tax or who generally have an annual capital gains tax liability. The advantages to basic rate or non-taxpayers who do not pay capital gains tax are not so obvious, especially if management charges are high.

PEPs can be held by anyone aged 18 or over who is resident and ordinarily resident in the UK or, though non-resident, is a Crown employee serving overseas.

Each plan must be managed by an investment adviser, authorised under the Financial Services Act 1986, and registered with the Inland Revenue. The manager may arrange for investors to receive annual reports of each investment, although often charging a fee for this service, and ensure that all rights of that shareholder are made available to him. All records, dealing and other paperwork would be the responsibility of the manager, who should liaise on the investor's behalf with the tax authorities (see also Chapter 20).

3.7.2 Warrants and options

Legal nature

An alternative to buying a security outright is to purchase the right to buy a security (see also Chapter 6). There are three ways of doing this:

(1) Warrants give holders the right to buy a particular company's ordinary shares at a fixed price. The right can normally only be exercised between two specific dates in the future.

(2) Conventional options confer the right to deal in a specified number of company's shares at a fixed price (the 'striking price') at any time during the option period (normally three months). To obtain an option the investor pays a price ('option money' or 'premium'), often expressed in pence per share. A 'call' option confers the right

to buy at the striking price. A 'put' option confers the right to sell at the striking price. A 'double' option entitles the investor either to buy or to sell at the striking price.

(3) Traded options – 'calls' or 'puts' – are available in a limited but increasing number of leading companies, the FTSE Index and the Euro-FTSE Index, and, in the case of company shares, take a standardised form, each unit normally representing 1,000 shares in the underlying equity. At any time before the expiry date (either three, six or nine months after the commencement of the option), the holder can exercise the option. Alternatively, he can sell the option on The Stock Exchange, where another investor can buy it.

Pre-conditions

Before dealing in traded options it is essential for the investor to have read the brochures prepared by The Stock Exchange which cover in detail this specialist area of the market. The investor will also need expressly to authorise the stockbroking firm in writing before it can transact traded options business on his behalf. There are no other special pre-conditions to investment in warrants or conventional options over and above those applying to ordinary shares. However, such investment would not ordinarily qualify under the Trustee Investments Act 1961.

Characteristics

There are clearly two sides to any option transaction. On the one hand, the purchaser of the option is paying a premium in the hope that the underlying share price will rise or fall depending on the type of option. Since the premium will be low relative to the share price, the investor is able to obtain gearing (buy the option to acquire or sell more shares than if he dealt in the underlying shares). At the same time, should the share price decline substantially, his risk is limited to the option money (which can be lost entirely).

On the other hand, there must be a writer of such an option, who will take the option money and any dividends on the underlying shares (if he is a covered writer and already holds the stock) in exchange for an agreement to supply to, or take up, the shares from the option buyer if the price rises or falls sufficiently. This role will appeal to the shareholder who wishes to hedge.

Taxation

The short-term nature of transactions in traded options may involve their being treated for taxation purposes as trading rather than capital transactions or even possibly as transactions falling within Schedule D Case VI.

The full cost of acquisition is taken into account in the capital gains tax computation. The abandonment of a traded option is treated as a disposal.

Suitability

Options are suited to the active investor, prepared to risk a small premium on his judgement about likely movements in share prices over the short-term. If he has little capital to invest, he might well consider traded options. The longer-term investor wishing to back a judgement that a particular company's shares will improve might consider purchasing warrants, although the number of companies with warrants is limited.

Mechanics

The mechanics of investing in options are similar to those applicable to private sector stocks (see **3.4.6**), except that for traded options the London Clearing House supervises the registration and settlement of transactions.

Safe custody

Warrant or option contract notes should be kept for tax purposes and certificates for warrants should be kept in a safe place.

3.7.3 Offers from companies

Whereas earlier sections were concerned with dealings by an investor in the market on his own initiative, this section is for the most part concerned with opportunities which may arise suddenly and may require an investor to respond rapidly to them. However, an application for shares under an offer for sale has often, though not always, to be actively sought out by an investor, and a take-over offer comes not from the company in which the investor has invested but from some other company.

It is a common feature of all the transactions referred to below that strict time limits are laid down for the taking of decisions by the investor, who should therefore allow adequate time for taking advice.

Offers for sale

Although there are several ways in which a company may obtain an initial listing of its shares, only one of them, the 'offer for sale', normally involves the private investor, although very occasionally the private investor is given an opportunity to participate in a private placing of shares on an initial listing or on entry to the AIM.

In the most normal type of offer for sale, an unlisted company seeks an initial listing (or permission for trading to take place on the AIM) for all its shares and makes a substantial proportion of its issued share capital (normally not less than 25 per cent) available to the general public. The shares may be made available either by means of a sale by existing shareholders of part of their holding or by the offer of subscription for new shares, the subscription moneys being paid into the company. Sometimes an offer for sale combines a sale and a subscription.

The offer is made by means of a prospectus, usually prepared by the company in conjunction with an issuing house or a firm of stockbrokers and with the help of professional advisers. The prospectus and accompanying application form are available from the issuing house, the stockbrokers acting for the company and selected branches of banks, and are also advertised in newspapers. If members of the public wish to participate in the offer, they must take steps to obtain a copy of the prospectus and complete and lodge the application form, with the application moneys, within the (very short) period prescribed by the prospectus.

Occasionally investors receive an opportunity to participate in an offer for sale by reason of a holding of shares in another company which is 'floating off' a subsidiary.

Rights issues

A company wishing, subsequent to obtaining its initial listing or permission to enter the AIM, to raise capital by the issue of new shares or of securities convertible into shares will normally have to do so by means of an issue by way of rights to its existing shareholders. If it wishes to issue shares to third parties for subscription in cash, it will normally, in accordance with the requirements of The Stock Exchange, have to seek the prior approval of shareholders.

An issue by way of rights will almost invariably be made on terms considered to be favourable to the shareholders, with a view to persuading them to take up the offer. Generally, a shareholder who does not wish to take up the whole of the offer (whether because he does not have available funds or for some other reason) may sell, prior to the payment of subscription monies (ie nil paid), the rights subscribed, either through the market or privately, or simply fail to accept the offer, leaving it to the company to sell the rights on his behalf and account to him for any premium. He may, if he wishes, accept the offer in part.

However, there has been a discernible move towards a form of disguised rights issue, known as a placing with clawback, where a company making an acquisition will raise sufficient funds, subject to agreement by its shareholders in general meeting, by placing new shares with institutions while allowing current shareholders to apply for these shares in proportion to their present holdings. Entitlements not taken up by shareholders may be transferred but cannot be sold through the stock market in nil paid form. The higher the level of acceptance shown by shareholders, the greater the clawback from the institutional placees.

A rights issue is made by means of a prospectus, which typically consists of a provisional allotment letter and an accompanying, or earlier, circular. The provisional allotment letter is a temporary bearer document of title, which is negotiable for the period during which the offer is open for acceptance (a minimum of three weeks) and for a further period of weeks when the shares are dealt in on these documents. Thereafter, the shares become registered.

Capitalisation issues

From time to time companies also make capitalisation issues – from the company's viewpoint, merely a book-keeping exercise, reflecting the incidence of accumulated and undistributed profits and/or the effects of inflation. Although shareholders receive 'free' shares, which can be dealt in on a temporary bearer document of title (either a fully paid renounceable allotment letter or a renounceable certificate) for a period of weeks, the issue of these shares represents no more than a rearrangement of existing shareholdings and any disposal of the new shares may give rise to a liability to capital gains tax. Special rules apply for arriving at the acquisition cost for capital gains tax purposes, depending on whether all or part of the underlying holding was acquired before 5 April 1982.

Demergers

The growth of companies through acquisition is occasionally reversed by demerger, allowing a subsidiary to be managed more effectively without centralised control. In terms of shareholder value, it is probable that the sum of the demerged parts initially will be more than the consolidated holding prior to the demerger. The separated companies will subsequently pay to their shareholders (who on demerger will be the same) dividends recommended by their own boards. Dealings on The Stock Exchange in the demerged companies will commence, with the share price of the parent company adjusted downwards to take into account the distribution of assets. The book cost of the original holding is apportioned between that holding and the demerged company in accordance with their first day values so that the book cost of the demerged company is equivalent to the reduction in cost in the original holding. It is deemed to have been acquired at the same date or dates as the original holding for capital gains tax indexation purposes.

Take-over offers

From time to time shareholders in a particular company may receive offers from another company wishing to acquire their shares in exchange for cash and/or shares and/or other securities of the other company. Most take-over bids are conditional upon a reference not being made to the Monopolies and Mergers Commission. Under the Fair Trading Act 1973, the Director General of Fair Trading has the power to recommend to the Secretary of State for Trade and Industry that a proposed merger be referred to the Monopolies and Mergers Commission if, *inter alia*, (1) the value of the assets being taken over exceeds £70m, or (2) he believes that the merger involves the national or public interest, usually due to the combined enterprise having more than 25 per cent market share of a defined class of goods or services. Whether the take-over proposal has or has not been agreed with the directors of the target company, the directors of that company will have to give to shareholders a recommendation as to whether to accept the offer. Shareholders can expect to receive not only that recommendation, but also offer documents and (particularly in the case of a contested take-over offer) a flood of circulars. The prudent course for the shareholder is to take careful note of the timetable for accepting the offer prescribed in the offer document and to delay taking any decision or action until a day or two before the closing date under the offer, in the hope that a higher offer may be forthcoming either from the original offeror or from a counter-bidder. If a higher offer is made by the original offeror, an earlier acceptance of the offer at the lower level will not preclude the shareholder from accepting the higher offer, and if a competing offer is made by a third party, an earlier acceptance of an offer can be withdrawn in certain circumstances.

Maintenance

The investor should retain safely all documents (particularly bearer documents) relating to the investments covered in this chapter. Each time he changes his address the investor should notify the appropriate body.

3.8 PREVIEW OF 1997

The outlook for the UK equity market seems dependent on at least three factors: the state of the economy, the new labour administration and the performance of Wall Street.

As to the first, UK economic growth should continue through 1997, led by a rise in consumer expenditure. The reduction in the basic rate of income tax to 23 per cent from April, the increase in average net incomes above the still low inflation rate, and the huge amount of wealth passed in the way of shares and cash pay-outs to investors from the building society demutualisations, will continue to encourage consumer spending. Fortunately, Sterling's strength will have reduced the costs of the imports that consumers tend to crave, and reduce the overall damage to the trade balance at a time when our export markets are being hit both by the level of our currency, and by some weakness in important overseas economies.

Most commentators predict a rise in base rates over 1997, perhaps moving to $6\frac{1}{2}$ per cent by the end of the year from the 6 per cent figure in January. Headline retail price inflation may stubbornly stay above the $2\frac{1}{2}$ per cent target, slap in the middle of the long-held 1–4 per cent range. The underlying rate of earnings growth should still be above this figure, helping consumer expenditure to rise. Unemployment will continue to fall, mainly through the creation of more fixed contract or part-time service industry jobs. Overall growth in the economy may turn out to be around $3\frac{1}{2}$ per cent, quite a reasonable improvement over 1996's figure.

The election of a Labour government should not scare markets. With a disappearing Conservative majority, a change in administration was on the cards for so long that markets expected – and prices reflected – this likelihood. After all, it was noticeable that although equities were up by around 11 per cent in a growing economy in 1996, they underperformed most other markets and gilts hardly moved on balance; perhaps this was in anticipation of a change to Labour. The overall financial policies of both parties seem not dissimilar, with Labour now having fully accepted the market forces theory, but the government is saddled from the start with a huge borrowing requirement somehow left by the Conservatives, even after three years of reasonable economic growth and falling unemployment costs. The likely figure for the PSBR in 1997/98 is around £15bn, limiting Labour's actions. The huge Labour majority might unnerve the market a little, bringing back worries of economic mismanagement of the past, but many see Labour as more committed to fighting Britain's corner from the centre of Europe than on the periphery. A growing realisation that EMU is a goal – however long-term – rather than something to sneer at will allow longer-term interest rates to fall closer to core European averages, boosting domestic fixed interest markets and helping equities in turn.

The summer months will be dominated by the huge flotations of the building societies as they turn themselves into listed banks. Halifax, certainly, will have automatic entry into the FTSE 100 index, bringing the weighting of banks in the index to around 18 per cent. Alliance & Leicester, the Woolwich and Northern Rock will also see their shares listed, but some in the sector may not retain their independence too long. Norwich Union also proposes a flotation during 1997.

After its initial teething troubles the CREST system should have taken over almost completely from TALISMAN, bringing a more secure environment for the settlement of equity trades on the market.

But so much still depends on the health of the US markets. There is no merit in pretending that other markets can go it alone when Wall Street starts to decline. The US still leads the world in the great growth areas of microchip technology and biotechnology and will continue to attract money for this, let alone the continuing growth of the world's largest open economy. The chairman of the Federal Reserve Board has made his feelings known about the high prices that equities command, and has stated that shorter-term interest rates may need to rise again in a pre-emptive strike to choke off any return of inflation. But there still seems to be cautious optimism on Wall Street and that must be good for worldwide equity markets, including the UK's.

3.9 CONCLUSION

Historically, listed investments have presented a good means of saving with the flexibility of choice between income or growth, or a balance of the two. However, potential investors must give full regard to the detrimental effect that inflation can have on the return on fixed interest securities, and the damage to capital values that a decline in the general level of a stock market can create even to a quality list of blue chip equities. Most investment is on a long-term basis, regard being given to the real economic growth potential of the chosen investment area, and provided that the individual can accept the risks involved in this form of investment, balanced against the twin benefits of the potential for reward and the ease of encashment, if necessary, listed investments would seem an excellent place for savings over and above more immediate cash requirements. The spate of privatisations during the 1980s has done a lot to draw back the veil of mystery over equities in particular; they can now be accepted as part of the savings of all individuals as, especially in the case of personal equity plans, the level of entry is now within the reach of so many more people. No longer can equity investment be thought to be limited to the very rich.

SOURCES OF FURTHER INFORMATION

Bibliography

Admission of Securities to Listing (looseleaf), The Stock Exchange

The City Code on Take-overs and Mergers, and the Rules Governing Substantial Acquisitions of Shares (looseleaf), The Panel on Take-overs and Mergers, 1985

Self-defence for Investors, Securities and Investments Board, 1986

Financial Services – A Guide to the New Regulatory System, Securities and Investments Board, 1986

An Introduction to The Stock Market, The Stock Exchange, 1986

An Introduction to Buying and Selling Shares, The Stock Exchange

Introduction to Traded Options, The Stock Exchange

What's the Form?, The Stock Exchange, 1990

The International Stock Exchange Official Yearbook, The Stock Exchange, 1995

Investing in Gilts, Bank of England, 1993

Allied Dunbar Tax Handbook 1997–98, Pitman Publishing

Professional and Impartial Investment Advice, APCIMS, 1993

Useful addresses

The Public Relations Department
The Stock Exchange
Old Broad Street
London
EC2N 1HP

Tel: (0171) 588 2355

Director of Savings
National Savings Bank
Boydstone Road
Glasgow
G58 1SB

Tel: (0141) 649 4555

The Director
Department of National Savings
Bonds and Stock Office
Preston New Road
Blackpool
FY3 9XR

Tel: (01253) 766151

The Director of Savings
Savings Certificate and SAYE
    Office
Milburngate House
Durham
DH99 1NS

Tel: (0191) 386 4900

National Girobank
Bridle Road
Bootle
Merseyside
G1R 0AA

Tel: (0151) 928 8181

The Securities and Investments
  Board
Gavrelle House
2–14 Bunhill Row
London
EC1Y 8RA

Tel: (0171) 638 1240

Inland Revenue
Public Enquiry Room
West Wing
Room 62
Somerset House
London
WC2R 1LB

Tel: (0171) 438 6622

The Building Societies Association
3 Savile Row
London
W1X 1AF

Tel: (0171) 437 0655

Finance Houses Association
18 Upper Grosvenor Street
London
W1X 9PB

Tel: (0171) 491 2783

Bank of England
Threadneedle Street
London
EC2R 8AH

Tel: (0171) 601 4444

The Association of Investment
  Trust Companies
8–13 Chiswell Street
London
EC1Y 4YY

Tel: (0171) 588 5347

The Securities and Futures
  Authority
Cottons Centre
Cottons Lane
London
SE1 2QB

Tel: (0171) 378 9000

The Panel on Take-overs and
  Mergers
PO Box 226
The Stock Exchange Building
Old Broad Street
London
EC2P 2JX

Tel: (0171) 382 9026

Association of Unit Trusts and
  Investment Funds
65 Kingsway
London
WC2B 6TD

Tel: (0171) 831 0898

Association of Private Client
  Investment Managers and
  Stockbrokers
112 Middlesex Street
London
E1 7HY

Tel: (0171) 247 7080

4

MAJOR OVERSEAS MARKETS

WILLIAM BOURNE

Threadneedle Investment Managers Ltd

4.1 INTRODUCTION

One of the earliest acts of the first Thatcher government, in October 1979, was to suspend exchange controls. Investing overseas, hitherto a cumbersome operation, suddenly became much easier, leading to a substantial growth in London's investment management and broking activities.

This rapid growth is illustrated overleaf: Figure 4.1 shows the amounts invested each year by banks, by financial institutions such as insurance companies and by other residents, usually individuals. A typical pension fund will now hold possibly 35 per cent of its assets in foreign securities whereas this figure would have been perhaps only 5 per cent in 1979.

It is possible to distinguish two motives for this surge in overseas investment. One, which might be called the 'passive' reason – though this is not to decry it in any way – is the desire to further diversify the risk in a portfolio by reducing its dependency on one country's market alone. The other motive, the 'active' one, is quite simply the belief that overseas assets are going to do better than those in the UK.

4.2 OPPORTUNITIES OVERSEAS

The range of possibilities when investing overseas is wide, from the large, well developed markets of the US to the fledging entities of what used to be the Soviet Union and its satellite nations. Excluding the 'emerging markets' (for which see Chapter 5) the UK-based investor can divide the world into five main areas. The relative size of each of these markets within the 'global' stock market at the end of 1996 was as follows: the US 49 per cent; Japan 15 per cent; Continental Europe 17 per cent; the UK 10 per cent; and other Far Eastern markets 6 per cent.

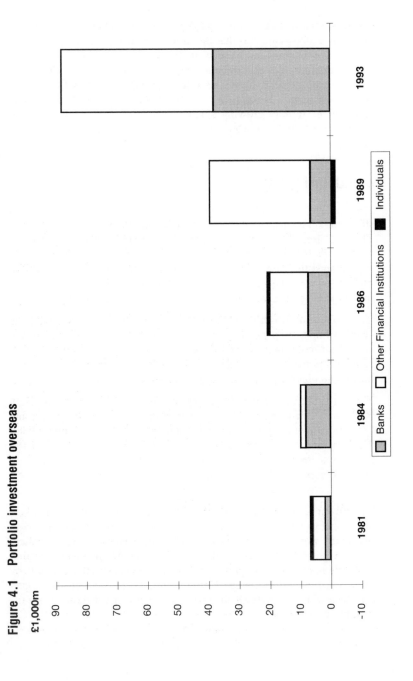

Figure 4.1 Portfolio investment overseas

£1,000m

It can be seen that the US market dominates in terms of size, though it was only a few years ago that this title went to Japan. The percentage taken up by Continental Europe might seem surprisingly small, given that it contains several economies larger than or as large as the UK: a similar point might be made about the other Far Eastern markets which comprise not only Hong Kong and Singapore, but also Australia and some of the rapidly growing smaller economies such as Taiwan and Korea. Below, the characteristics of each of these main areas are considered.

4.2.1 United States

The thin line in Figure 4.2 opposite shows the performance of the US stock market as measured by the Standard and Poors Composite Index. The thick line shows the performance of the US market in percentage terms with 100 as the base, adjusted for the sterling/dollar exchange rate, against the British market; it gives an accurate picture of what an investor would have gained (rising trend) or lost (falling trend) by investing in the US rather than the UK.

Until 1994 there was little to choose between the two markets, though the swings of up to 30 per cent during the period show how important it is to get one's timing right. In the last year, however, the US has done better, as investors have been attracted by signs of renewed vitality. This has been particularly true in the new technology industries.

There are in fact a number of exchanges in the US. In the case of the New York Stock Exchange (NYSE), companies quoted are generally large and to obtain a quotation they must have sound finances and a good record. The American Exchange and the over-the-counter market exist primarily for companies not qualified for the NYSE, but many large and good quality companies choose to remain on one or the other, finding the service perfectly adequate.

Apart from being the largest stock markets in the world, the US markets are probably the most sophisticated. Companies are closely analysed and many portfolios are run on an extremely rigorous mathematical basis. A great deal of company information is published and is readily available in printed form or on screens. Business is strictly regulated by the Securities and Exchange Commission. There are well developed options and futures markets, though these are principally designed for the institutional investor.

Figure 4.2   United States

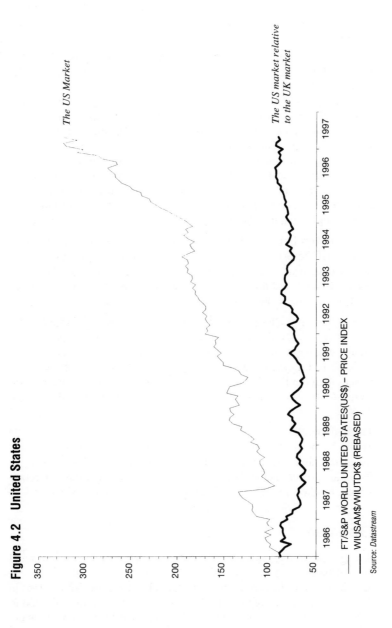

FT/S&P WORLD UNITED STATES(US$) – PRICE INDEX
WIUSAM$/WIUTDK$ (REBASED)

Source: *Datastream*

4.2.2 Continental Europe

In Figure 4.3 opposite, the thin line shows the actual performance of the European markets, while the thick line tracks their performance relative to the UK.

The European stock markets performed extremely well in the mid-1980s, a result of their 'discovery' by international investors after a long period of somnolence. There then followed a period of under-performance as economic growth began to slow and, following the crash of 1987, international investors drew in their horns. Another sharp upward movement was precipitated by the fall of the Berlin Wall in November 1989 and the subsequent reappraisal of growth prospects for Europe. In the event, this vision was interrupted by the Gulf War and more particularly by the global recession which began to bite in Europe in 1991, against a background of high interest rates. European markets performed relatively badly during this period and it was not until 1993, when interest rates fell convincingly, that they began to do better.

Stock markets in Europe have traditionally played a less important part in national life than in the UK or the US. Historically, companies have turned to the banks rather than to a country's stock exchange when looking for finance and this goes some way to explaining why their stock markets are smaller and less developed than elsewhere.

Although changes have occurred in the last ten years, and particularly in the last two years, the managers of European companies tend to place greater emphasis on the well-being of employees and customers than is the case in English speaking countries. Shareholders, therefore, come lower down the list of priority, with the result that they are treated less well than in some other markets and information is more difficult to obtain.

The main markets, in terms of size, are France and Germany, followed by the Netherlands and Switzerland. Among the Mediterranean countries, Italy and Spain figure largest though there are also bourses in Portugal, Greece and Turkey. All the Scandinavian countries are represented. Markets in the former Eastern Bloc are covered in Chapter 5.

4.2.3 Japan

Strong economic growth and financial deregulation created a substantial pool of liquidity in the mid-1980s. Much of this money found its way into the property market, though substantial sums were also invested in the stock market, giving rise to the now notorious 'bubble' of 1986 to 1989. The bubble finally burst when the authorities began to worry about asset inflation feeding through into more general price increases and,

Figure 4.3   Continental Eruope

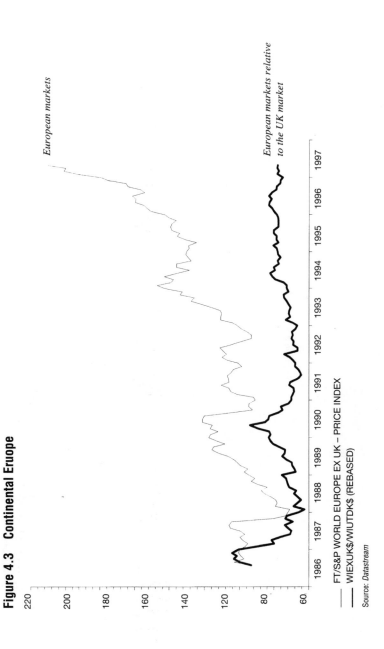

European markets

European markets relative to the UK market

—— FT/S&P WORLD EUROPE EX UK – PRICE INDEX
—— WIEXUK$/WIUTDK$ (REBASED)

Source: *Datastream*

Figure 4.4   Japan

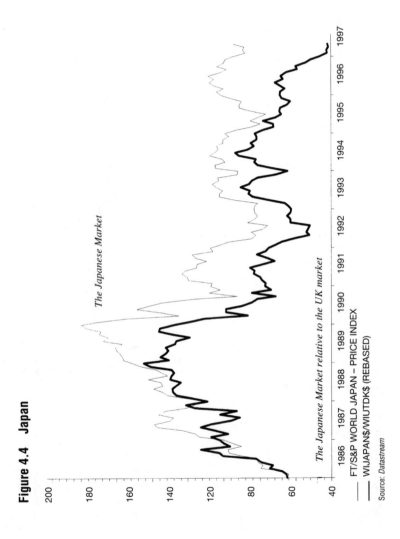

Source: *Datastream*

indeed, the stability of the whole financial system. The ensuing period of monetary retrenchment was followed by a sharp slowdown in the rate of economic activity: both of these factors lay behind the significant under-performance by the Japanese market between 1989 and 1995.

The Bank of Japan's efforts to stimulate the economy led to a recovery in the stock market in the second half of 1995, but renewed concerns over the future returned in 1996. The market is still standing at under half its level at the top of the bubble.

There are eight stock exchanges in Japan, although only the ones in Tokyo, Osaka and Nagoya handle large volumes of transactions. There are over 2,500 listed companies and these are split into three categories. The first category comprises nearly 1,300 large companies; the second, some 760 smaller companies; and the over-the-counter market, around 450 recently listed entities. In general, companies graduate from the over-the-counter market to the second category and then to the first category as their sales and profits reach the appropriate levels.

Japanese companies report business results every six months and the degree of information disclosed to investors is improving year by year, although sometimes falls short of standards experienced in the West.

An unusual feature of the Japanese stock market has been the presence of large 'cross shareholdings' in which one company will hold shares in a selection of other companies with which it has business or other relation-ships. In the past this has accounted for as much as 30 per cent of the market. There are some signs that some of these cross shareholdings are now being unwound.

The poor performance of Japanese pension fund managers in the early 1990s has spurned deregulation, so that foreign managers are gaining market share. This in turn has led to a shift in the way individual shares are appraised by fund managers, from which some companies have gen-erally benefited.

4.2.4 Other Far Eastern markets

The performance of the Far Eastern markets in relation to the British market has been mixed, as shown in Figure 4.5 overleaf. Between 1986 and 1990 the record was dull, though this had much to do with the weak-ness in the US dollar which is the key currency for many of these markets. From 1991 onwards performance was much better, as investors began to recognise the potential in the region. This culminated in late 1993 when interest from America and Japan in particular drove markets to unsustainable levels. Since then, although the economic development in the region has continued, markets have fallen back.

Figure 4.5 Pacific Basin – excluding Japan

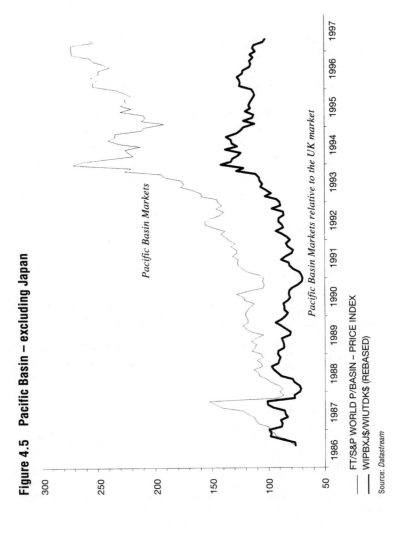

FT/S&P WORLD P/BASIN – PRICE INDEX

WIPBXJ$/WIUTDK$ (REBASED)

Source: *Datastream*

The Far Eastern markets include, by convention, Australia and New Zealand in the south, Hong Kong, Malaysia, Singapore and the smaller but fast growing areas such as Indonesia, Thailand, as well as Taiwan and Korea, and the Philippines. Increasingly China, with its own stock markets in Shanghai and Shenzhen, is attracting direct investment; India is expected to become a major market in the region. The smaller markets are covered more fully in Chapter 5.

While Australia and New Zealand are relatively mature economies, the rest of the area is seeing rapid expansion. As an example, national income in Thailand, Indonesia and Taiwan has grown in real terms by between 5 and 10 per cent over each of the last five years. (In Europe, 3 per cent growth is thought to be good.) These economies benefit from well-trained, low cost labour forces and good connections with the huge consumer markets of the US and Japan. In addition to traditional commodity-based industries, these countries are seeing rapid growth in manufacturing and tourism.

Stock markets are echoing the economy in terms of rapid development. However, local investors tend still to dominate activity and these markets are more prone to speculative excess than is the case elsewhere. This volatility is exaggerated by the fragility of the political regimes in some areas.

While Australia and Hong Kong offer a broad range of investments, the other markets tend to consist of a limited number of blue chip stocks, particularly banks, and a large number of small stocks that are not so easily traded.

4.2.5 Emerging markets

In addition to these well established homes for international investors, there are the emerging markets such as Mexico, Turkey, or India. These are covered in Chapter 5.

4.3 CHOOSING A MARKET

4.3.1 Economic activity

It would seem common sense to argue that, since stock markets have something to do with the creation of wealth, choosing a market is a matter of picking the country with the best economic prospects. In the long term, this is generally true. However, it is not an infallible guide. For example, between 1975 and 1985, at a time when the German economy was growing substantially faster than that of the UK, the German stock market rose at an annualised rate of 10.4 per cent, while the British market went up by an annualised 15.6 per cent. Over a shorter-term horizon, it is generally true that the stock market of a country that is about to emerge from a recession is more likely to perform well than one where the economy is beginning to cool down.

4.3.2 Interest rates

Interest rates are important too, and these will generally shadow the rate of inflation. As a rule of thumb, a market where interest rates are falling should generally do better than one where interest rates are rising, as the cost of financing an equity investment will be falling at the same time as interest rates do.

4.3.3 Valuation

We now come to the vexed question of valuation. In the UK market, stocks can be evaluated against their earnings or their asset backing or their dividend yield, and the same thing can be done for individual stock markets. However, varying accounting standards in different countries, as well as the different roles stock markets are perceived to play, make international comparisons of this sort dubious. What may be useful is to look at each individual market against its own historical averages, but even here there are so many different measures that may be used that the results are often contradictory.

4.3.4 Currency

One of the most important considerations in investing overseas is that the investor is not only buying into the shares or bonds of a foreign country, but also its currency, and currencies can fluctuate substantially against one another. It is perfectly possible for the gains made by investing in one market in preference to another to be wiped out by adverse currency movements. For instance, between June 1991 and August 1992, the US market rose by around 12 per cent, far outstripping that of the UK, which fell by 5 per cent. However, during that period the dollar fell by over 20 per cent against sterling so that for a UK-based investor the overall return from the US market would have been a fall of 9 per cent, in other words worse than if the investor had left his money at home. Hence it is absolutely vital to take the effects of likely movements in currencies into account.

To summarise, then, the major factors that should be considered when choosing where to invest are:

(1) the likely performance of the economy;
(2) the level of interest rates and likely changes in their direction;
(3) the valuation of stock markets; and
(4) the likely movements in the foreign exchange rate.

The correct choice of stock market involves a thorough command of these factors, judgement and, let it be said, a certain degree of luck. No-one – not even the most experienced professional – expects to get it right all the time. If all this seems too intimidating, bear in mind that later in this chapter we discuss how to gain the advantages of investing overseas without having to make these choices.

4.4 THE MECHANICS OF INVESTING OVERSEAS

4.4.1 Direct investment

Despite the seemingly cumbersome arrangements for transferring stock, running a portfolio invested in British shares is not a particularly daunting task. Investing directly overseas can be different.

Consider, first, the information needed to make a decision about which shares to buy. Aside from the obvious language difficulties, companies in many overseas markets place little emphasis on their shareholders, so that even the annual accounts may yield significantly less information than would be the case for a British company. In addition, the accounts are likely to have been prepared under different accounting conventions, which further complicates analysis.

Then comes the question of buying, selling and holding stock. Stock may still be held in bearer form, so that the share certificates are the only evidence of title. In this case, dividends are not paid out automatically by the company, but have to be claimed by the shareholder. The same applies to capital issues. Hence the administrative work starts to build up and this can only be avoided by employing a custodian bank to hold the shares on the investors' behalf. At this stage the costs of owning shares begin to rise quite considerably. By extension, the whole process can be made much simpler by dealing through a British bank or broker who will look after the administration, but in this case a fee will be payable to the British company in addition to any local custodian or brokerage charges.

On top of this comes the question of local taxation which, even when a double taxation agreement is in operation, involves substantial extra work or administrative fees.

It is apparent, then, that investing directly in overseas assets is not an attractive route for most. It is therefore necessary to think about the various types of collective investment schemes which are available.

4.4.2 Collective investment schemes

A major advantage of any collective investment scheme run by a well resourced, professionally run investment management house is that the investor gets access to a broadly diversified pool of assets that are under continual review. However, in the arena of overseas investment, collective schemes funds offer further advantages.

Administration

The complexities of the mechanics of investing overseas have been outlined above; by investing through a collective investment scheme, the burden of all this administration is borne by the managers. Buying and selling overseas investments through a collective scheme is as simple as buying domestic funds.

Flexibility

The complexities surrounding the decision of which market to invest in were discussed earlier. The great advantage of a collective investment scheme is that it offers two different approaches to international investment – the global route and the country specialist.

Global funds

In general these funds will invest all around the world, changing their exposure to different markets as the managers see fit. The difficult decision about which markets to invest in is taken by the fund managers rather than the individual. The investor can therefore gain exposure to overseas markets with none of the agonising involved in the country allocation decision.

Specialist geographical funds

These funds are limited to investing in one specific area, generally one of those in **4.2** above. These are for investors who want to make their own decisions about country allocation, but want all the other advantages of collective schemes.

Whichever route is chosen, the international fund or the country specialist, the investor has a substantial array of vehicles to choose from. Most of the funds quoted will be general funds, in the sense that they will tend to invest in the larger stocks in each market. However, as in the UK, there are a number of specialist funds, invested in smaller companies, asset-backed stocks or particular sectors such as commodities.

The characteristics of each type of collective scheme – unit trust, offshore fund or investment trust – are discussed in Chapters 7 and 8. However, there are a few points to make about each of them in the context of international investment.

4.4.3 Unit trusts

These are probably the most accessible category of collective scheme for the overseas investor; most trusts tend to be generalist funds offering either particular regions or a wholly global portfolio (see Chapter 8).

4.4.4 Offshore funds

These are broadly similar to unit trusts, except that income is received gross of tax. From the perspective of an overseas investor, the offshore fund sector tends to offer more specialist investment vehicles as well as the 'bread and butter' funds found elsewhere. For instance, one management house has no less than six funds specialising in different aspects of the US stock market.

One obstacle to an understanding of investment in offshore funds is that the fund may be valued in a currency that is neither the investor's own currency nor that in which the investments were originally denominated. For instance, the price of many offshore funds will be quoted in US dollars, even though the fund may have sterling-based investors and may itself be invested in the Tokyo stock market. A common mistake in this case would be to assume that, since the fund is denominated in US dollars, movements in the dollar will affect the value of the investments to the sterling-based investor. Not so; what affects the value of the investments in this case is the level of the stock market and the yen/sterling exchange rate – nothing else.

4.4.5 Investment trusts

The stock market value of an investment trust will usually be at a discount or, more rarely, a premium to the value of the underlying assets. This discount to net asset value is a very useful indicator of investors' sentiment towards a particular stock market; the discount will tend to narrow as the market becomes more popular and conversely will widen as it falls from favour. For the contrarian investor who likes to invest in areas that are out of favour in the belief that sentiment will improve at some point, the level of the discount is a useful indicator; in other words the contrarian buys when the discount is large and sells when it narrows. The advantage of investment trusts is that the investor not only benefits from the rise in the value of the underlying assets but also from the narrowing discount to net asset value. For those who fancy their ability to pick the winners among global stock markets this is an attractively geared way of backing their judgement.

4.5 CONCLUSION

To summarise, investing overseas is most easily done through one or other of the collective schemes. Those looking to diversify their portfolios may feel attracted towards a global fund, where all the country allocation decisions are taken by the fund managers. Those going abroad because they feel that prospects are better than in the UK may well have more specific ideas and are more likely to be tempted by a fund specialising in a particular region or country. A key factor to remember is that returns on investments overseas can be significantly affected by fluctuations in exchange rates.

5

EMERGING MARKETS

DOUGLAS W ADAMS

Marketing Director, Templeton Investment Management Ltd

5.1 INTRODUCTION

Do you ever look at where things are made? If you do, you may have
noticed the growing number of products that have their origin outside the
major Western economies. This is just one aspect of the changing nature
of the world economy. Companies in many developing nations now
compete successfully with the best in the world, combining skilled, but
low cost, labour with up-to-date technology. In turn, these trends are
opening up opportunities for investors to participate in the development
process and spread of prosperity.

Are these opportunities only for professional investors or should anyone
constructing a portfolio to meet long-term objectives include emerging
markets in their range of possibilities? As the arguments set out below
show, there are good reasons to include a degree of emerging market
exposure in most equity portfolios. With young, ambitious populations
the probabilities are that a number of emerging economies in Asia, Latin
America and Southern and Eastern Europe will become economic
powerhouses in the next 10 to 20 years.

5.2 WHAT ARE EMERGING MARKETS?

'Emerging markets' is the term commonly applied to financial markets
in the developing nations of the world. This definition includes most of
Asia (with the exception of Japan), all of Central and South America,
parts of Southern and Eastern Europe, and all of Africa. Not all countries
covered by this definition possess equity markets, and some that do will
not permit investment by foreigners. Prominent among emerging markets
that have attracted substantial funds from Western investors in recent
years are countries as diverse as Egypt, Morocco and Russia; and states
better known for economic success, such as Hong Kong, Singapore and
Korea also often feature in emerging market portfolios.

5.3 WORLD OF CHANGE

Thoughts of developing nations often conjure images from television news bulletins of famines, civil wars, coups and deprivation. Problems do exist, but an exclusive focus on the problem areas blinds us to the more generalised, if less newsworthy, progress that most countries are making. A number of factors contribute to this progress. Improving standards of nutrition and education, the application of technology and the liberalisation of economies are judged by many to provide the real driving force for improvement.

Better nutrition

The world has never before enjoyed such an abundance of food. This growth in food supply provides a much more nutritious diet for the fast growing populations of the developing world. In November last year, the World Food Summit in Rome was told that per capita food supplies in the developing world would rise from 2,500 calories in 1990/92 to more than 2,700 by 2010. Indeed, per capita daily calorie supply in the Near East/North Africa and Latin America/Caribbean is expected to be near or above 3,000, close to developed world levels.

Improved healthcare

At the same time, the quality and availability of medical care shows substantial gains, even if it does lag the standards the UK enjoys. The number of doctors per 1,000 of population in Brazil rose from an average of 0.4 in 1950 to 1.5 in 1995 – a 275 per cent increase. In Turkey, over the same period, the number rose from 1.4 doctors per 100 to 3.1 – a 121 per cent rise.

Increased life expectancy

Putting better nutrition and healthcare together results in dramatic increases in life expectancy. A child born in a lower-income country in 1960 had a life expectancy at birth of just 54 years. By 1993, this had grown to 69 years. Since the years from 16 to 65 tend to be the most economically productive, this increase in life expectancy boosts the economic potential of the developing nations. By contrast, in the developed economies, slowing population growth and an increase in the retired population will act as a damper on growth potential as we enter the 21st century.

More education

Learning and experience are further aspects of longer life spans. An individual finds it more worthwhile to learn skills the longer expected life is, and he also becomes much more productive through work experience. Moreover, educational standards have been rising in many of the developing nations. For example, in 1950 under 50 per cent of Brazilian adults were literate. By 1994 this proportion stood at over 83 per cent.

Technology transfer

Better standards of education give greater capacity to absorb and adapt new techniques and ideas. And as technology advances so it becomes more transportable. Thus it is now commonplace for companies in emerging economies to apply the state-of-the-art techniques to their businesses.

Faster growth

Taken together, these socio-economic changes have helped to boost growth in the developing nations as a group, leading to improved living standards for their populations. Annual growth in developing nations has been outstripping that of the developed economies over an extended period, and as shown in Figure 5.1 overleaf, the World Bank predicts that this outperformance will continue well into the next century.

This fast growth translates into an opportunity for investors only if there are accessible equity and fixed interest markets where transactions can be carried out cost effectively, preferably without intervening taxes and exchange controls. Moreover, the extent to which shares or bonds represent good value for the future must be considered. If the enthusiasm of other investors has bid up the price of shares, then faster economic growth may already be discounted in the marketplace. In this sense emerging market investment has direct parallels with investment disciplines in the major markets.

Liberalisation

While many shares in emerging markets have shown exceptional gains in recent years, the trend towards economic liberalisation and privatisation has provided a dramatic increase in the number, width and depth of those markets which are open. Increasingly the governments of developing nations view investment by foreign portfolio investors as a means of attracting much needed capital to fund growth. Experience shows that these inflows tend to speed up considerably following the introduction of open market policies. In addition, removing government control in many areas of developing economies often acts as a spur to growth, with Latin

Figure 5.1 Higher economic growth over the longer term – forecast growth in real GDP 1995–2004 (% per annum)

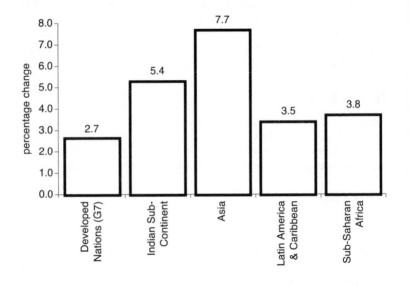

Source: *World Bank*

American countries providing an excellent example. Thus a virtuous circle develops with investment flows raising the sustainable growth rate, which in turn adds to the attractiveness of the country to further investment.

Volatility spells opportunity

Often the euphoria that accompanies this process carries share prices to levels of extreme overvaluation, making them vulnerable to any bad news or shock and, as is typical in all markets, periods of excess optimism are usually followed by bouts of excess pessimism. Thus individual emerging markets may prove highly volatile. This is both the danger and the opportunity of emerging markets. Astute investors prepared to sell at times of extreme optimism, but then to buy again when pessimism reigns, can reap handsome rewards from the long-term progress of developing countries.

Figure 5.2 Emerging markets, UK and World share index movements compared 1989–1996 (£)

Source: *Datastream*

Figure 5.3

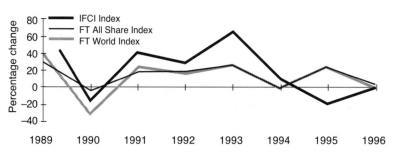

Source: *Datastream*

Markets in context

One way of putting these developments in context is to compare the overall size of the emerging markets with those of the developed world. At the end of December 1996 the International Finance Corporation (IFC) calculated that emerging markets were capitalised at £1,250bn. This compares with the Morgan Stanley Capital International (MSCI) estimate of developed market capital capitalisation of £10,163bn, and a figure of £1,017bn for the London market.

Market catch-up

A striking example of the growth of emerging markets is given by the near 22 fold expansion of the total value of emerging market shares over the last 13 years. The December 1996 figure of £1,250bn contrasts with a figure of only £57bn in 1983. Put another way, in 1983 emerging markets as a group were only equivalent to around one-third of the total value of the UK market. At the end of December, they were over 27 per cent bigger than London – the world's third biggest equity market.

5.4 PERFORMANCE

The IFC, an arm of the World Bank, has been at the forefront of encouraging institutional investment in developing nations, and provides a series of indices which show the performance record of emerging markets individually and as a group. Of particular use are the series of investible indices tracking the performance of those markets and shares that are available to foreign investors. As Figure 5.2 overleaf shows, the IFC Investible Composite rose by 281 per cent in sterling terms in the period from its first calculation at the end of 1988 to December 1996. This compares with rises of 212 per cent for the FT All Share Index (an average of UK share prices) and 91 per cent for the FTA World Index (a measure of average share price movements worldwide) over the same period.

Variation

As shown in Figure 5.4 opposite, this average picture masks much variation in terms of both year-to-year movements and individual markets. For example Argentina, the best- performing market according to the IFC, shows a rise of 851 per cent since the end of 1988. This compares with a rise of only 47 per cent in Portugal, the poorest performer in the IFC Database.

Big swings

Breaking down the longer-term picture into annual slices shows that the progress of individual markets is anything but smooth. Table 5.1 opposite gives the year-by-year movements in sterling for some typical examples. There may be strong long-term returns, but the ups and downs can be severe in comparison to the developed markets.

Figure 5.4 Eight-year index price performance to December 1996 % (£)

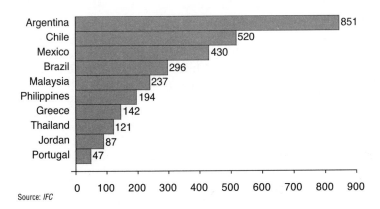

Argentina	851
Chile	520
Mexico	430
Brazil	296
Malaysia	237
Philippines	194
Greece	142
Thailand	121
Jordan	87
Portugal	47

Source: *IFC*

Diversification gives stability

Another feature of emerging markets suggested by Table 5.1 below is a tendency for them to move out of sync. Analysis of the correlation between these markets does confirm that their month-to-month movements are much more out of step than is the case for the developed markets. This is an extremely important attribute. As a consequence, a portfolio exposed to a wide range of emerging markets will suffer from much less volatility than a portfolio invested in one market. In other words, in a diversified emerging market portfolio, losses in one area are likely to be offset by gains in another. This may not give the spectacular returns available when a portfolio is concentrated in a sharply rising market, but it does provide a much more stable route to long-term gains.

Table 5.1 Share price movements by country by year (£%)

	1990	1991	1992	1993	1994	1995	1996
Korea	−37.6	−13.2	28.0	23.8	9.5	−7.3	−44.4
India	−0.8	22.1	51.9	21.5	0.3	−38.8	−11.1
Philippines	−61.5	63.9	46.2	140.4	−16.3	−15.9	2.6
Argentina	−47.0	412.6	−9.2	76.3	−30.2	−10.7	7.7
Mexico	5.7	119.2	33.3	37.6	1.2	−50.4	6.0
Greece	70.6	−16.7	−9.8	24.8	−6.3	9.2	−9.0
Turkey	−18.8	−39.9	−41.6	242.1	−45.8	−13.5	29.1
UK	−14.3	15.1	14.8	23.4	−9.6	18.8	11.7

Source: *IFC & Datastream*

5.5 INDIVIDUAL MARKETS

As would be expected with such a diverse set of economies there is considerable variation among emerging markets in terms of size, whether measured by market capitalisation (total value of shares quoted on a market) or number of shares listed. India has by far the greatest number of shares quoted, 5,999, roughly four times the next largest market Czech Republic, which has 1,588. But the capitalisation of the Indian market is relatively modest at £72bn (end December 1996). This is just 40 per cent the size of Malaysia (£180bn) (end December 1996), the largest market in terms of value. Yet there were only 621 Malaysian shares listed at the end of December 1996. Pakistan has slightly more listed shares than Malaysia, but its market capitalisation is only £6.2bn (December 1996).

While the situation shows great improvement in recent years, the degree of openness of markets varies too. For example Chile, India and Korea still impose administrative or fiscal barriers of varying degrees of severity to foreign portfolio investors.

The data in Table 5.2 opposite shows that 1996 was a mixed year for emerging markets and followed on from a disappointing 1995. Among the major emerging markets regions only Latin America showed a modest positive return as the recovery from the Mexican financial crisis in 1995 began. But these poor results in 1995 and 1996 have to be seen in the context of very strong returns early in the 1990s that still leave the IFC Investible Index ahead of the Developed Markets indices over the medium term. Moreover, economic growth in the developing world has continued apace, so this recent underperformance has done much to restore attractive valuation levels in emerging markets.

Table 5.2   Market statistics

Latin America	Market Capitalisation £bn (December 1996)	Number of Issues (December 1996)	Five year price performance (to December 1996) %	1996 %
Argentina	26.1	149	31.3	7.7
Brazil	126.8	550	244.2	17.8
Chile	38.5	291	84.5	−24.8
Colombia	10.0	189	122.6	−4.0
Mexico	62.3	193	−0.6	6.0
Peru	8.1	240	n/a	−9.5
Venezuela	5.9	87	−25.2	97.5
Total	277.7	1,699	44.8	3.5

Asia	Market Capitalisation £bn (December 1996)	Number of Issues (December 1996)	Five year price performance (to December 1996) %	1996 %
China	66.5	540	n/a	23.6
Korea	81.1	760	n/a	−44.4
Philippines	47.1	216	187.5	2.6
Taiwan	159.9	382	64.4	23.3
India	71.6	5,999	n/a	−11.1
Indonesia	53.2	253	143.0	5.6
Malaysia	179.5	621	170.9	12.6
Pakistan	6.2	782	−29.6	−26.8
Sri Lanka	1.1	235	n/a	−17.1
Thailand	58.3	454	41.0	−46.6
Total	724.5	10,242	113.0	−1.2

Europe, Middle East & Africa	Market Capitalisation £bn (December 1996)	Number of Issues (December 1996)	Five year price performance (to December 1996) %	1996 %
Czech Republic	10.6	1,588	n/a	6.1
Egypt	8.3	646	n/a	n/a
Greece	14.1	224	−8.2	−9.0
Hungary	3.1	45	n/a	81.4
Jordan	2.7	98	104.3	−8.3
Morocco	5.1	47	n/a	n/a
Nigeria	2.1	183	n/a	n/a
Poland	4.9	83	n/a	55.9
Portugal	14.4	158	74.9	14.9
Russia	21.8	73	n/a	n/a
South Africa	141.2	626	n/a	−26.7
Turkey	17.5	229	12.0	−29.1
Zimbabwe	2.1	64	n/a	56.4
Total	247.9	4,064	16.5	−14.0

Total emerging markets	Market Capitalisation £bn (December 1996)	Number of Issues (December 1996)	Five year price performance (to December 1996) %	1996 %
Total	1,250.1	16,005	60.8	−2.9

Source: *IFC and Datastream*

5.6 WHERE NEXT?

In the mid-1980s, when diversified emerging market funds first began to appear, it was commonplace for the portfolio to hold shares from as few as five or six countries, including Hong Kong and Singapore. And even then, portfolio managers would often include shares quoted on the major markets, where the choice could be justified by the companies' trading or business links with the developing world. Now as many as 25 to 30 countries can be represented in a diversified portfolio. This increase in diversity should, in the long term, help to lower the risk of global emerging market funds.

Changing attitudes

The sharp increase in interest in emerging markets by Western investors, and the resulting flow of capital, provides a tempting example to governments of countries short of capital and where equity markets either do not exist or where restrictions keep out foreign investors. It is hardly surprising therefore that a new wave of developing nations are now seeking ways in which they can overcome these hurdles to attract their share of this capital flow.

At the same time investment managers faced with the challenge of maintaining strong performance records strive to be first to invest in a new market where shares may still be bought very cheaply. These mutually supportive forces will see a growing list of markets appearing in portfolios in the years to come.

New markets

For example, in 1993 the potential of China held the focus, while in 1994 possibilities for investment in Russia and Vietnam began to emerge. More managers are now talking about the potential to be found in some African countries, largely because of the cheapness of shares, rather than the anticipation of an economic miracle. Kenya, Zimbabwe, Botswana and Ghana all probably fall into this category, while the transition to democracy in South Africa provides the possibility of investing in a relatively developed market. The Arab nations of northern Africa – Morocco, Tunisia and Egypt – all possess small equity markets which could become popular in time.

In Eastern Europe, Poland, Hungary and the Czech Republic have attracted most interest to date. Equity markets are also developing in Russia and the Baltic States. And the privatisation process is moving at a whirlwind pace compared with that undergone in the UK – according to *The Economist* by late 1994 14,000 big and middle-sized enterprises, employing 86 per cent of Russia's industrial workforce, had been privatised. This gives Russia a smaller state-owned sector than Italy.

More than anything, it is this potential for new markets to blossom that adds credibility to the view that emerging markets will be a long running theme rather than a fad of the early 1990s.

5.7 FACTORS TO CONSIDER

If you feel that you wish to take advantage of the opportunities available in emerging markets, how should you go about it?

5.7.1 Direct investment

Direct investment in emerging markets will not prove straightforward for the private individual or even for smaller institutions. Apart from Hong Kong, and perhaps Malaysia, Singapore and Mexico, it would probably prove difficult to find a private client stockbroker with the experience and inclination to deal directly in emerging markets. Thus direct dealing requires either purchase of those emerging market shares that are listed on developed markets or contact with a broker operating in the markets chosen. Then difficulties of time zone, language, currency, settlement, delivery of share certificates and cost of contact all arise. For example in Turkey settlement the day after dealing is required, hardly sufficient time for the paperwork to have reached the UK even by fax. Tracking direct investments in emerging markets would also prove difficult for the intrepid private investor. Coverage of individual shares in emerging markets is almost non-existent in the daily press, and even reporting of market movements is patchy. A final consideration is the risk inherent in investing in a single share in these new markets. If the markets themselves are volatile the movements at the level of individual shares can be extreme.

5.7.2 Funds

As a result of the recent popularity and strong track record of emerging markets a wide range of funds suitable for the private investor now exists. These fall into a number of categories. Both closed-ended and open-ended funds are available, and in each case global, regional and country-specific varieties can be found.

Investment trusts

In the UK closed-ended funds are more usually known as investment trusts, and have a fixed number of shares in issue. This means that the fund manager has a given amount of assets to manage and if new investors buy the trust the fund manager receives no additional assets to manage, rather the share price rises reflecting the buying pressure (see Chapter 7).

Unit trusts

Open-ended funds are typically unit trusts, although very similar vehicles called Sicavs, usually registered in Luxembourg or Dublin, have appeared in recent years. As the name implies, these funds are open to new assets, and new buying of the fund results in new assets for the fund manager to look after, but has no direct impact on the valuation of units (see Chapter 8).

57 Varieties

Global emerging market funds enjoy the freedom to invest in developing nations worldwide and so may move assets between countries as conditions dictate. Regional funds are more constrained in their investment scope, and are limited to a particular geographical area of the world, such as South East Asia or Latin America. Country funds limit their exposure to a specific economy.

5.7.3 Open versus closed-ended

As with many investment decisions, there is no right or wrong answer on which is the best route to take. It all depends on circumstances. Broadly speaking, open-ended funds allow an investor to purchase units at a price equivalent to his share of the net assets of the fund, after initial charges. And in most open-ended funds currently available in the UK no charge is made for the sale of units back to the manager. Thus an investor in an open-ended fund knows that units may be sold at any time at a price that is based on the value of the assets in the trust.

Watch the premium

The price paid for shares in an investment trust depends on the balance of supply and demand in the marketplace at a given point of time. Typically, investment trusts trade at a price per share which is below the net assets attributable to a share. This gap is termed 'discount to net asset value'. The opposite phenomenon of a premium to net asset value is much less common. In 1993 and 1994 the popularity of emerging market investment trusts drove many on to a premium. In other words, even taking dealing costs out of the calculation, investors seem prepared to pay more than the value of their share of the trust's assets when making purchases of the investment trust.

The Mexican crisis at the beginning of 1995 saw these premiums evaporate, illustrating the argument that investors who paid a premium run the risk of facing a discount when they come to sell.

In such a case the return realised is below the underlying return on the trust's assets. An investor paying £1.10 for shares with an underlying net asset value of £1 and selling them later for £1.80, at a time when the net asset value per share stands at £2, realises a profit of 63.6 per cent. However, the assets in the trust have risen by 100 per cent over the same period. An investor in an equivalent open-ended fund would have achieved a return of around 95 per cent, even taking account of typical initial charges. And it is interesting to note that a number of emerging market specialists offer both open and closed-ended versions of their funds, utilising the same investment team, disciplines and shares. When a premium exists on a closed-ended fund and an open-ended alternative is available it may prove beneficial for the investor to sell shares in the investment trust and buy units in the open-ended fund. Of course the opposite can also occur, giving a distinct advantage to investment trust purchasers in depressed market conditions.

Long-term advantages

Proponents of closed-ended funds point out that in the case of volatile markets like those of the developing world, investment trusts possess a clear advantage for the long-term investor. The manager of a closed fund does not have to worry that an inflow of new cash will appear at times of optimism, forcing him to buy shares that may have already risen to unattractive price levels from a long-term perspective. Nor does he face sudden calls for cash to meet the liquidations that often accompany a market setback, forcing the manager to sell shares that offer sound long-term prospects. Thus, it is argued that an investment trust manager can take a more objective long-term view, buying and selling shares according to his own judgements, rather than finding that investment decisions are driven, at least in part, by the money flows that the fund experiences.

Micropal, the performance measurement service, provides comprehensive data on all the emerging markets funds available in the UK. An examination of these performance tables, an extract of which is shown in Table 5.3 overleaf, suggests that for the short period during which both open and closed-ended emerging markets funds have co-existed no category of fund has a clear upper hand. Variations in performance driven by other factors remain more important.

Table 5.3 Global funds available in the UK: performance by type

Global Funds	5 year performance to December 1996	Type *
Templeton Emerging Markets Investment Trust	130.2%	CE
Genesis Emerging Markets Limited	90.8%	CE
Foreign & Colonial Emerging Markets Investment Trust	49.8%	CE
Beta Global Emerging Markets Investment Trust	57.3%	CE
Fleming Emerging Markets Investment Trust	33.8%	CE
City of London Emerging Markets	166.9%	OE
Invesco Global Emerging Markets	50.7%	OE
Abtrust Emerging Markets	74.9%	OE
Martin Currie Emerging Markets	67.4%	OE
Gartmore Emerging Markets Fund	34.3%	OE
IFCI Composite Index	63.5%	–

* Open Ended (OE) or closed ended (CE)

Source: *Micropal Emerging Markets Fund Monitor*
Data Source Micropal Ltd. Tel 0181 741 4100 http/www/micropal.com

5.8 COUNTRY VERSUS GEOGRAPHICALLY DIVERSIFIED FUNDS

Among the emerging market funds available to UK investors, some have the freedom to invest in all the emerging markets of the world, some focus on particular regions such as South East Asia, or Latin America, while yet others concentrate on single countries. Generally the more specific a fund, the more risky it will be.

Choosing a fund investing in the next market to enjoy popularity from domestic and international investors alike can give spectacular returns. But being sucked into a fund in a market that has already risen a long way can prove an expensive mistake. As illustrated by events in Mexico in 1995, falls of 50 per cent or more can occur rapidly in these markets, with little that the fund manager can do if the objective of the fund requires the assets to be invested in that country. For most investors a more diversified approach is appropriate.

Diversity equals safety

The main advantage of more widely spread funds is the safety that comes from diversification among economies with different structures, business environments, and political conditions. These differences mean that a change that affects one market adversely may have no effect, or even a beneficial impact elsewhere. This is most true for those funds that have the freedom to invest in any emerging market in the world. While regional funds do have an advantage over individual country funds, there is a tendency for markets within regions to move in step, reflecting the similarities often found among neighbouring countries and their degree of economic integration from trading links. This message was driven home to investors in Latin American Funds in early 1995 as the markets in Brazil and Argentina tumbled on the back of problems in Mexico.

5.9 CHOOSING A FUND MANAGER

For emerging markets the criteria for choosing a fund management group are no different from those that apply for choosing managers for the developed markets. First, does the manager's literature demonstrate a coherent strategy to the challenge of investing in emerging markets? Many different approaches exist – some focusing on individual shares, others on economic and political fundamentals, and yet others on a mixture of the two. A good manager will be able to articulate clearly the approach adopted. A poorer manager will be less capable of explaining how the task is carried out.

Resources

Secondly, can a manager show that the resources are available in terms of experience, people, technology and contacts to put the chosen strategy to work? For example, even professionals find good information on emerging market companies harder to find. Therefore if a manager professes a stock-by-stock approach then a global team will be required to carry out the necessary research.

Consistent success

Thirdly, can the manager demonstrate a consistent record of success in emerging markets? While performance in isolation provides an unreliable guide to the future, when examined in conjunction with other criteria it can provide greater insights. A good record but no clear strategy may just reflect good luck in the past which may not be repeatable in the future.

Diversify managers

Do not just look for one manager. Except for the smallest portfolios it makes sense to choose two or more managers with contrasting approaches. This adds to your overall diversification, as the pitfalls of one strategy are likely to be avoided by another.

5.10 TIMING

As with all equity investment there is no certain means of knowing the best time to invest.

Many who committed money to emerging markets in early 1994, following the strong performances in 1993, bitterly regretted their decision a year later. But to sell on short-term disappointments flies in the face of equity market experience. All equity markets can be volatile in the short-term, but the long-term rewards usually outstrip the returns available from other forms of investment and saving. Remember that the arguments in favour of emerging markets rely on the long-term structural changes that are under way in the world economy. Patient investors who let these powerful trends work for them over an extended period of time are likely to reap the greatest benefits and, as in developed markets, regular investment through one of the many savings schemes linked to emerging market funds provides an excellent means of reducing the risk of committing funds at a short-term market peak.

5.11 CONCLUSION

Emerging economies will exert a major influence over the rest of our lives, with a strong probability that they will provide the most dynamic economic performance in terms of growth and progress in living standards. For investors they will provide the potential for strong long-term returns. However, the path will not be smooth and any investor in these markets must be prepared for the ups and downs. Do not invest money that you may need in the short or medium-term in these markets, ie money you might want to call on in the next five to seven years to meet living and other expenses. As a general rule, the younger or wealthier you are the greater the exposure you can afford to have in these markets, but it is probably wise to place an upper limit of 20 per cent of an equity portfolio in these markets. Also remember to include in your decision the exposure you may have to emerging markets via more generalist international unit or investment trusts. Finally remember to update your thoughts on what markets are in the emerging category. Japan was an emerging market 25 years ago. Perhaps Mexico, South Korea and Turkey will count as developed markets in 2020, replaced by nations such as Peru, Cambodia and Ukraine in the truly emerging markets portfolios.

6

DERIVATIVES DE-MYSTIFIED

MALCOLM KEMP

Threadneedle Investment Managers Ltd

6.1 INTRODUCTION

The aim of this chapter is to set out what futures, options and swaps are, indicate how they are priced and give a few examples of when they are used. Derivatives enable asset management decisions to be undertaken cheaply and quickly. They offer fund managers the ability to tailor the risk/return profile of a fund in many different ways.

6.2 'SURELY DERIVATIVES ARE VERY RISKY?'

Derivatives have acquired a reputation for being risky, and have been blamed for some large losses, eg at Barings. However, this reputation is often misguided. The important thing is to consider the derivatives not in isolation, but *in conjunction with other assets in the fund*. Some derivatives will still add risk to the portfolio, but many can actually reduce the risk being run.

For example, a fund invested in equities might buy put options, which give the fund the right (but not the obligation) to sell the equities for a fixed floor, even if the equities have fallen further than this floor. These effectively provide insurance against large falls in the values of these equities. Viewed in isolation, they have speculative characteristics because they will rise in value very substantially if the market falls. Buying a put option in isolation is no more sensible than an individual buying insurance on a property he does not own. But viewed in conjunction with the rest of the portfolio the options make a lot more sense. In the above example, the rise in the value of the option compensates the fund for the fall in the value of the equities it owns, just like any sensible sort of insurance.

The key way to control any risks derivatives might introduce is to avoid *gearing*. It is gearing that could cause a modest market movement to lead to insolvency. It is gearing that is dangerous, not derivatives *per se*. This was vividly displayed by the collapse of Barings Bank in February 1995. It had two large positions relating to the Japanese equity market which doubled up on each other, rather than cancelling out each other. This introduced massive gearing, which went badly wrong when the market moved adversely. However, it is important to bear in mind that gearing is not specific to derivatives. Dangerous gearing can be entered into by borrowing and investing in blue chips or gilts, without going anywhere near an option or a future.

6.3 WHAT IS A CONTRACT, AND HOW DOES IT WORK?

Futures contracts are quick and efficient ways of increasing (or reducing) exposure to a particular market. There are many different exchanges on which they are traded, the largest three being the Chicago Mercantile Exchange (CME), Chicago Board of Trade (CBoT) and the London Financial Futures and Options Exchange (LIFFE). Futures are based on or derived from (hence *derivatives*) an underlying asset. When futures began in 1848 at the CBoT, these underlying assets were agricultural produce as farmers were wanting to fix now a selling price for a specified quantity for a specified date in the future. More recently, however, these contracts have been eclipsed by financial futures in which the futures contract is linked to some underlying financial asset or variable, eg stock market indices, bonds, currencies or interest rates.

Perhaps the most important future for a UK investment manager is the FTSE futures contract traded on LIFFE. It is a contract based on the FTSE 100 share index of 100 leading UK equities. It is by far the most liquid futures contract relating to the UK equity market (indeed the amount of equity exposure traded using FTSE futures contracts usually exceeds the amount traded on the underlying stock market!). Similar contracts for other global equity markets are traded on other exchanges around the world.

The exposure to the equity market represented by one FTSE futures contract is £25 times the price paid. Thus with the FTSE around 4,200, the value of the market exposure represented by one futures contract would be around £105,000. This is the amount that would be lost by a buyer of one futures contract if the equity market fell to zero, the same as for an investor who bought actual stocks for £105,000 (in the proportions that make up the FTSE index). Similarly if the market doubled, any investor who had bought/sold one contract would gain/lose £105,000.

A *buyer* of one FTSE futures contract will therefore gain/lose £25 for every point that the FTSE 100 index moves above/below the price paid until the contract expires. At any point in time there are three separate futures contracts potentially tradable, with expiries in March, June, September or December. Most of the trading actually takes place in the month with the nearest expiry, which is known as the *front month* contract.

Conversely a *seller* of one FTSE futures contract would lose/gain £25 for every point that the FTSE 100 index moved above/below the price received. It is possible to sell a future without holding the underlying stocks (indeed it is easier to do this than to short sell the stocks themselves), but it would of course be very risky to do this, since it introduces a form of gearing.

Every FTSE futures contract will have a buyer and seller. However, when a futures contract is effected, no cash or stocks are transferred between the two parties. Instead the futures contract behaves as if the buyer and the seller commit to buy/sell equities at expiry date. Perhaps a good analogy is the exchange of contracts prior to purchase of a property. Once contracts are exchanged the investor becomes exposed to the implications of owning the property (for example, if the house burns down, the investor will on completion pay a large sum to acquire a worthless asset, which is why it is important to insure a property from exchange of contract and not just from completion). Legal ownership however only transfers on completion.

In any sort of contract in which two parties commit to do something in the future each becomes exposed to the risk that the other will default on the contract. This is why a deposit is paid on exchange of contracts in a property transaction. Most of the complexities of futures arise from the need to introduce a procedure protecting either side from default of the other. Derivatives exchanges try to limit these exposures by use of a *central clearing house* and a *margining system*.

When a futures contract is entered into, both parties put up merely a returnable good faith deposit, called *initial margin*, to the clearing house. The current level of margin per contract is £3,000, but this figure is increased in periods of high volatility. The clearing house for LIFFE is the London Clearing House, owned by several of the leading Clearing Banks. The clearing house then interposes itself between the two parties by replacing the original contract with two separate equal and opposite contracts, one between itself and the first party and one between itself and the second party. To avoid additional credit exposures arising as the FTSE index moves up or down, the contracts are *marked to market* at the end of each day, with any capital gain or loss being paid from or to the clearing house. These payments are called *variation margin*.

When the contract matures the initial margin is returned to each party. At expiry the FTSE future is *cash settled*, ie the seller transfers only the cash value of the shares rather than the shares themselves to the buyer. This means that the contract is legally classified as a *contract for differences*.

6.4 DEALING IN FUTURES AND STOCKS COMPARED

Futures contracts enable exposures to be bought and sold much more cheaply, quickly and efficiently than dealing in the underlying shares.

If FTSE futures did not exist, an institutional fund manager moving in and then subsequently out of the UK equity market would typically incur the following expenses:

(a) on buying
middle price to offer spread	0.2%
commission	0.2%
stamp duty	0.5%

(b) on selling
bid price to middle price	0.2%
commission	0.2%
Total	**1.3%**

Thus if FTSE were about 4,200, it would need to move by nearly 55 points merely to compensate for the expenses incurred in such a 'round trip'.

In contrast, with FTSE futures, the bid-offer spread is around one index point, plus slightly less for the total round-trip commission. Also no stamp duty is payable. Hence for each £105,000 that is 'round-tripped', dealing in futures might cost roughly £40 compared with approximately £1,400 – a vast reduction in cost!

In addition, consider what would need to happen if the fund manager wished to change exposure quickly. With futures the trade could be done in a few minutes, with just one deal ticket. Effectively all the stocks would be dealt in at the same time. In contrast, the problems posed by dealing in 100 individual stocks at times of rapidly changing prices – plus the effort of booking, checking and settling all these trades, registering and perhaps claiming dividends, scrip issues etc – are obvious.

Moreover the required change in UK equity exposure might involve a compensating change in exposure to gilts or some specified overseas equity market(s). Appropriate futures contracts can also be used for the other side of such asset allocation switches.

6.5 PRICING FUTURES CONTRACTS

An investor who buys FTSE futures will make or lose money depending on market movements in much the same fashion as an investor who buys actual stock. However, the purchaser of the futures will be able to earn interest on the cash he does not need to use to invest in the market, although he will not receive the dividend yield that holding the shares would generate. If the interest on cash is 6 per cent per annum and the dividend yield is 4 per cent per annum then the use of futures saves what is known as the *cost of carry* of:

$$6\% - 4\% = 2\% \text{ p.a.}$$

For FTSE futures with, say, three months before they expire, the cost of carry is 2 per cent divided by four, ie 0.5 per cent. So if FTSE were, say 4,200 then the *fair value* of the futures contract, allowing for this cost of carry, would be 4,221. The futures contract will in general trade at a price which differs from this fair value, but not normally by very much, because otherwise arbitrageurs would become active bringing the actual price back closer to the contract's fair value.

6.6 WHAT IS AN OPTION?

Options are more versatile than futures contracts, but this also makes them more complicated.

There are two main types of options, called *calls* and *puts*. Again, it is possible to both buy and sell either sort of option – indeed for every buyer there must also be a seller of the relevant option.

A *buyer* of a call option has the *right*, but *not the obligation*, for a specified term to buy an agreed quantity of a particular asset at a stipulated price (from the option seller, otherwise known as the option *writer*). The stipulated price is called the *exercise* price or the *strike* price.

A *buyer* of a put option has the *right*, but *not the obligation*, for a specified term to sell an agreed quantity of a particular asset at a stipulated price.

An investor who buys an option, whether a call or a put, will not lose more than the option premium paid because he or she does not need to *exercise* the option if the asset price moves in the opposite direction from that anticipated. Potential profit from the option in isolation is virtually unlimited.

Conversely, an option writer will not make more profit than the option premium received, unless the option buyer behaves irrationally. Potential profits from the option in isolation can, however, be virtually unlimited. At first sight writing options would appear to be a very risky strategy. However, if the option is covered (see **6.1**) then losses from the written option are compensated for by profits in the stock used to cover the option. For example, if an investor holds stock and writes a call option on that stock then if the market rises a loss arises from the option, but it is counteracted by a gain on the stock held by the option writer. In effect the writer has foregone market upside (since the option buyer can buy the stocks off him at a fixed price even if the stocks rise above this level in value). In return, the option writer receives some premium income.

Two principal classes of options are recognised: so-called *American-style* options which can be exercised at any time up to the expiry date of the option, and so-called *European-style* options which can be exercised *only* at the expiry date. These terms no longer have any relationship to the geographic area to which the options relate or from which they originate.

6.7 PRICING OPTIONS CONTRACTS

Calculating a fair value for an option is a lot more difficult than calculating a fair value for a futures contract. The reason is that the value of an option depends in part on how likely it is for the option to be exercised. The price of an option also depends, inter alia, on the time to expiry, interest rates, volatility of the stock to which the option relates and the current stock price in relation to the exercise price of the option.

By far the most important tool used to value and price options is the *Black-Scholes option pricing formula*. This provides a theoretical fair value, C, for a European-style call option which depends on the sorts of factors described above. The formula is:

$$C = S.N(d_1) - X.\exp(-rT).N(d_2)$$

$$where: \quad d_1 = \frac{\ln(S/X) + (r + \sigma^2/2)T}{\sigma\sqrt{T}}$$

$$d_2 = d_1 - \sigma\sqrt{T}$$

S = current stock price

X = exercise price of option

T = time to expiry of option

r = risk-free interest rate (ie return on cash)

σ = standard deviation of stock price (measuring how volatile the stock is)

exp(x) = exponential function
ln(x) = natural logarithm function
$N(x)$ = cumulative probability density function for a standardised normal distribution (as might be expected,
given the dependence on the probability of the
option to be exercised)

Although these mathematical functions look complicated, they are all available within modern spreadsheet packages, such as Microsoft Excel. It is therefore very simple to calculate the Black-Scholes price within such a package, as long as suitable estimates of the parameters on which it depends are available, eg the rate of return available on risk-free investments and the volatility of the underlying stock price. The formula requires the stock not to be dividend paying, but there are relatively simple adjustments that can be made if the stock does provide dividends.

There is a similar formula for the fair value, P, of a European-style put option, but it can more easily be found using a relationship called put-call parity, ie:

$$S + P = C + X.\exp(-rT)$$

Put-call parity recognises the equivalence between buying a stock and a put now, and buying a call now to be exercised at some specified future date. The ultimate *pay-off* from either strategy at expiry is the same, and therefore the two should also have the same value.

Although the Black-Scholes formula provides the basis for nearly all option pricing approaches, it is widely accepted within the market that it does not in isolation provide a complete explanation of actual market prices. For example, call options which are *out-of-the-money* (ie would not be exercised immediately, ie $S<X$), tend to trade at prices which require a higher volatility assumption (*implied volatility*) than call options which are at-the-money ($S=X$) or in-the-money ($S>X$). Also, the Black-Scholes formula only applies to European-style options and not to American-style options. For more complicated options it is nearly always necessary to modify the formula in some way, usually increasing the complexity of the mathematics involved. Indeed, derivative pricing experts are often jokingly called rocket scientists by others in the investment field, because of the high level of mathematical skills they often possess.

6.8 OVER-THE-COUNTER OPTIONS

Options traded on recognised exchanges are restricted to specified assets, strike prices and expiry dates. The sorts of assets on which options are available range from specific shares such as B.A.T. or market indices, such as FTSE. Usually there will be a range of strike prices and expiry dates available for any given asset, but most of the liquidity, ie dealing, would be concentrated in contracts which have the shortest period to expiry and have strike prices quite close to current market levels.

Options which are not traded on recognised exchanges are called *over-the-counter* – colloquially OTC. These permit much greater flexibility in contract design, including the ability to incorporate more complicated pay-off characteristics, and thus permit the option to be tailored to the precise requirements of the investor.

If the option is being used purely as a way of implementing an investment view then it is worth bearing in mind that the more restrictions and caveats are placed on the pay-off, the less will be the cost of the option.

However, option activity may be driven more by concerns over liabilities than assets. For example, a fund manager may launch a retail guaranteed equity bond which provides to the investor a guarantee of no capital loss, but also promises to give the investor a set percentage of any rise in the market over, say, a 5-year period. The fund management house can then match this liability (and thus avoid the risk of not being able to provide the stated guarantee) by buying a suitable option from an investment bank.

6.9 WHAT IS A SWAP, AND HOW IS IT PRICED?

The most common equity derivatives are futures and options. The exposures bought and sold via equity derivatives often exceed those bought and sold via transactions in the underlying equities. However, even these volumes are relatively small compared to the volumes transacted in the swaps markets.

In a swap one party agrees to pay the other one sort of cash flow stream, receiving a different sort of cash flow stream in return. The most common sort of swap is a fixed for floating rate swap. In this contract, there will be some agreed principal sum, eg £100m. The first party will then agree to pay the interest receipts receivable were this sum to be invested in cash, which for large sums will vary up and down in line with what is known as LIBOR, the London Interbank Offered Rate. In return the second party will pay a fixed rate, eg 7 per cent per annum (ie £7m per annum) for the lifetime of the swap, which might be up to 25 years, say.

A corporation might for example be willing to enter into this sort of transaction in order to help it fix more precisely its likely borrowing costs. It might, for example, borrow money at today's variable interest rate, but avoid the risk of this interest rate rising substantially by swapping fixed payments in return for the floating rates it needs to service this debt. Fixed for floating rate swaps are also used extensively by building societies and the like if they are offering fixed rate mortgages to their customers (since they will generally need to pay floating rates to their depositors).

Practically any sort of cash flow can be swapped in this sort of fashion. For example, the swap could involve paying away the return achieved on the FTSE index in return for the (floating) return available from cash. By entering into such a swap, the investor would shed exposure to the UK equity market gaining exposure to cash instead, much like the result of selling a FTSE futures contract.

Not surprisingly, the fair price of such a swap can thus be calculated in a manner which is similar to that used for futures contracts. Swap contracts that contain *optionality*, ie some element of option-like behaviour, are more complicated to value and require techniques of the sort mentioned in **6.7**.

6.10 CONCLUSION

The difficulties of Barings, Sumitomo and Orange County amongst others have shown what can happen when the fundamental principles of trading in derivatives are forgotten by operators. However, when sensibly used, derivatives are a useful investment management tool, providing quick, cheap and efficient ways of shifting between different asset categories and managing risk exposures.

SOURCES OF FURTHER INFORMATION

Exchanges

The London International Financial Futures and Options Exchange (LIFFE)
Cannon Bridge
London EC4R 3XX.
Tel: (0171) 623 0444
Fax: (0171) 588 3624
Internet: http://www.liffe.com

Books

Options, Futures and Other Derivatives (3rd edn), John Hull, Prentice-Hall, 1997

Academic Papers

Actuaries and Derivatives, Malcolm Kemp, Institute of Actuaries, 1996

7

INVESTMENT TRUSTS

DAVID BALLANCE
Investment Director,
Threadneedle Investment Managers Ltd

7.1 INTRODUCTION

Collective investment media enable investors to pool their resources to create a common fund for investment by professional managers. The two great benefits of this collective approach to investment are (1) more efficient and economical investment management; and (2) greater security through the spreading of risk over a diverse range of investments.

To meet these needs, various different media, such as investment trusts, unit trusts and offshore funds (see Chapter 8) and insurance bonds (see Chapter 14) have evolved from separate legal and financial origins, subject to varying regulation and tax treatment. The choice between the different media in practice may depend on the investor's convenience as much as the features of the collective media, which are increasingly given a 'level playing field' by regulations. Nevertheless there are still some marked differences in the ways these investments are marketed, priced and taxed, quite apart from the management of the underlying assets.

The most straightforward and flexible of these media is the investment trust, which is actually not really a trust, but simply a limited company in which investors buy shares and other securities so as to benefit indirectly from its assets and income. An investment trust is constrained by its authorised capital, which cannot readily be changed or repaid to shareholders, and the shares are generally bought and sold by investors on The Stock Exchange at market prices determined only by supply and demand.

7.2 HISTORICAL BACKGROUND

The first investment trust to be established in England was the Foreign and Colonial Government Trust, which was created as a trust in 1868 and in 1879, owing to doubts concerning the legality of its original structure, was reorganised as a public limited liability company under the Companies Act 1862. The original objective of this trust was, in the words of its initial prospectus, to provide '. . . the investor of moderate means the same advantage as the large capitalists in diminishing risk in foreign and colonial stocks by spreading the investment over a number of stocks'. By the early 20the century a number of other investment trust companies had been incorporated in England and Scotland and the investment trust had become firmly established in the UK as an investment medium. Some of these early trusts (including 'The Foreign and Colonial Investment Trust plc') still exist today despite two World Wars and many serious economic crises. During the last 100 years, investment trust companies have provided much new capital for UK businesses by underwriting or subscribing for public issues of securities and accepting private placings, thus giving important support to capital investment in the UK.

Investment trusts are probably the most flexible of the collective media, free to invest in any kind of assets, and the individual companies and the securities that they issue vary widely. In comparison with the other media, two distinctive characteristics are their ability to 'gear up' their sensitivity to the markets by borrowing, and the fact that the shares are generally priced by supply and demand in the market at significantly less than the value of the underlying assets of the investment trust. Both these factors tend to make investment trusts more sensitive to movements in the markets as a whole, while still spreading the specific risks of investments in individual stocks.

As explained in **7.7**, certain capital gains tax concessions are given to those investment trusts which have been approved by the Inland Revenue. In order to obtain approval the investment trust must, among other requirements, be resident for tax purposes in the UK and have its ordinary share capital listed on The Stock Exchange. This chapter deals primarily with investment trusts which have been so approved for tax purposes and which have been incorporated in the UK. Unapproved investment trusts can generally be treated like any other company.

7.3 RECENT DEVELOPMENTS

Investment trusts (ITs) constantly attract innovative uses and developments in the best traditions of the City. As well as around 400 existing investment trusts available in the stock market, a continual stream of new issues and additional tranches provides opportunities for both general and specialist investment of all kinds. Investment trusts are particularly attractive to private investors in the form of personal equity plan holdings, (although regrettably they remain ineligible for single company PEPs), and new issues are often made in the 'PEP season' before 6 April each year.

The venture capital trusts (VCT) announced in the previous budget eventually got off to rather a slow start, currently looking unlikely to meet the Treasury's three-year target. VCTs are not really typical of ITs generally, but merely happen to use the flexible form of an IT for a special purpose vehicle. A VCT, like any IT, is exempt from capital gains tax, so that VCTs themselves will be broadly tax neutral. However, in addition, investment in a VCT is free of income tax and capital gains tax, like a PEP; investors will receive income tax relief on subscriptions into new VCTs, and capital gains on other investments which would otherwise be chargeable to tax can be rolled over into a VCT investment within six months before or after realisation. It should always be realised that CGT rollover is a deferral, not a cancellation of the tax liability. The limit of £100,000 investment per annum is far more generous than for PEPs.

A VCT, like an IT, is a listed public company specially approved by the Inland Revenue, which must derive its income 'wholly or mainly' (in practice, at least 70 per cent) from securities; but which must also within three years of approval invest at least 70 per cent of its assets in 'qualifying holdings' in unquoted UK trading companies. At least 30 per cent of a VCT's investments overall must be in ordinary shares, with the balance in other share capital or long-term debt. A VCT may invest a maximum of £1m per year in any one trading company, which may not be larger than £11m immediately after the investment, and must not be controlled by the VCT or anyone else. No holding may exceed 15 per cent of the VCT. The detailed requirements for the trading companies are comparable to those for the Enterprise Investment Scheme, such as the requirement for the investment to be used in trading within 12 months.

All the VCT's investments must be new, ie initial subscription of shares or debt, and no securities of the trading company may be listed or quoted on the USM at the time (although listing on the AIM is allowed, as is subsequent admission to listing). Like an approved investment trust, a VCT must retain 15 per cent of its income, but it may also choose to distribute capital profits (see **7.7.1**).

The most significant general development during the year was the publication by the Accounting Standards Board of a new Statement of Recommended Practice (SORP), which will standardise accounting practice for the special needs of ITs, allowing better comparisons between companies, and clarifying the rights of IT securities which can be directly affected by the directors' accounting practice. Income will be recognised on an accrual basis, and if subsequently not considered collectable then provided for as an expense; and financing costs and management fees can in future be allocated between capital and income accounts according to the expected returns of the investments. Thus income distributions could increase, and perhaps there could be some relevant consequential increase in the overall tax change.

The November 1995 Budget made unusually few changes affecting ITs, primarily a technical change on taxation of gilts and bonds, and a proposal for housing investment trusts (see **7.12**).

7.4 LEGAL NATURE

7.4.1 Constitution

An investment trust is a limited liability company with a share capital, and is a legal entity separate from its shareholders or managers. In practice the trusts are often promoted and managed by fund management groups who run a number of investment trusts and other funds which, in some cases, own the management group. All trusts must now have a majority of non-executive directors, according to AITC guidelines. However, the shareholders are always entitled to vote to replace the management, and there has been much take-over activity in the industry.

Like any limited company, an investment trust company is constituted by the contract with its shareholders contained in its memorandum and articles of association. The memoranda of investment trusts usually contain wide powers to invest the company's funds in securities and property and to borrow, but, for tax reasons, commonly prohibit trading (as opposed to investing) in securities or property; and their articles of association normally contain a provision prohibiting the distribution of capital profits by way of dividend. However, approved status for tax purposes (see **7.7**) requires certain practical limitations on the exercise of these wide investment powers.

An investment trust, like any limited company, itself is not permitted to advertise its shares for sale except by reference to Listing Particulars, registered with the Registrar of Companies and complying with the Financial Services Act. However, managers will eagerly respond to enquiries, and increasingly advertise schemes to facilitate investment. Further advice and information are available from stockbrokers, through whom the shares are often bought, and from the Association of Investment Trust Companies (see 'Sources of further information' at the end of this chapter).

7.4.2 Investment trust securities

Investments are made by buying stocks, shares and warrants of the trusts. Apart from ordinary shares, a trust may issue debenture stock (secured by a charge on its assets), unsecured loan stock, preference shares or warrants. The holders of such securities are entitled to receive interest or preference dividends at the applicable rate before any dividends are paid to the ordinary shareholders. These securities may, in the long run, prove less profitable, but are more secure since, on a winding-up of the company, the ordinary shareholders are entitled only to any surplus assets remaining after payment of all other liabilities, including the repayment of principal and income due to holders of loan capital or preference shares. If an investment trust has a high proportion of its capital in the form of loan capital and preference shares, major fluctuations in the value of the underlying assets attributable to the holders of its equity share capital can result. This topic is discussed in more detail at **7.6.5**. (Debenture stocks, loan stocks and preference shares are discussed at **3.6**.)

Warrants are securities which give the holder the right (without obligation) to subscribe for shares subsequently on fixed terms: in the meantime the warrants are themselves listed investments whose market price will change rapidly according to the prices of the underlying shares, but in most cases without yielding an income. For example, suppose a warrant entitles the holder to subscribe for certain investment trust shares at 95 pence each. If the shares are currently worth £1, the warrant will trade at about 5 pence. In practice the majority of warrants will trade at a premium to their intrinsic value, because of time value. If the shares rise by 10 per cent to £1.10, the warrants should rise 200 per cent to 15 pence; conversely if the shares fall by 10 per cent to 90 pence, the warrants would be practically worthless. Warrants clearly offer a more volatile capital investment in the success of an investment trust than its ordinary shares (see also **3.7.2**).

7.4.3 Split capital trusts

As well as issuing all the usual company securities, investment trusts can also go further and, instead of ordinary shares, issue their capital split into different issues tailor-made for different kinds of investors.

In most ordinary companies, directors generally have considerable freedom as to how much dividend to distribute out of profits, and are only expected to manage their dividend policy to provide growing dividends indefinitely; such companies are not expected to be wound up, and shareholders' rights in a liquidation are largely academic. Investment trusts must distribute most of their income and none of their capital profits for tax reasons, although to some extent they can manage what proportion of profits are receivable as income.

However, some 60 split capital trusts are constituted with separate classes of shares which will be repaid (or at the least, the question will be put to a vote of shareholders) at a fixed date. Each class of share capital has specified entitlements to dividends in the meanwhile and to capital distributions, in a stated order of priority between the classes of shares, and the directors have very little discretion as to the application of whatever profits they make. While the total performance of the investment trust will always depend on the success of its investment managers, each class of shares will have relatively more or less predictable expectations, designed to be particularly valuable to certain kinds of investors. These benefits can make the total value of the trust's securities higher than if it simply issued one class of ordinary shares.

The earliest split capital trusts have capital shares, which provide no dividend income at all but the right at liquidation to all capital gains within the trust, and income shares, which distribute the entire trust's net income, but will be repaid at the liquidation date normally at their issue price. The prices of each share will reflect the demand from investors, taking account of the specified rights of *all* prior classes of shares and other securities. Thus, the income shares offer a very high running yield, suitable for PEPs or for trustees paying a widow's annuity, while the capital shares would attract a higher rate taxpayer approaching retirement, or anyone who has not used his valuable tax-free capital gains tax allowance.

7.4.4 Specialised split capital investment trust securities

Investment trusts are free to create any kind of securities for their investors, and the principle has been used to design shares with sophisticated characteristics, which require individual analysis of exactly what is offered and the security that will be obtained. These securities can be superbly efficient investments, but it is quite inadequate and highly dangerous merely to rely on the names of such specialised securities, and investors must consider the rights of both their own intended shares and all other securities which will have priority in any situation, together with current circumstances which change after the securities are issued. Some kinds of income shares have little or no capital entitlement, and other preference shares can have index-linked or other formula based income. Each class of security will have its own profile of risk and reward, ranging from a preferred stock many times covered by assets, to highly speculative zero coupon shares. The latter should not be confused with zero dividend preference shares or zero coupon debentures, which are actually very 'safe' (see below). Needless to say, the value of these securities will ultimately depend on the success of the managers' investment policy, but to very differing extents. The only real rule is that, inevitably, the sum of the rights of all classes of issued capital is equal to the total net capital and income of the trust. Thus, at the end of the queue on each distribution, one class of shares will have the most uncertain outcome, in effect securing all the prior entitlements; and naturally such risky securities will be priced to earn, on average, the highest expected rewards.

Amongst these more sophisticated securities are:

Zero dividend preference shares

This is a low risk investment suitable for financing future capital sums without income tax liability in the meanwhile, such as school fees. The risk can be assessed by measuring how many times the capital repayment is covered by net assets, or in other words how much the managers can lose without affecting the repayment at all.

Capital entitlements: a fixed capital return payable on liquidation.
Income: nil.

Income shares and annuity shares

It is essential to check exactly what type of share is being considered. These shares can be particularly appropriate for non-taxpayers, in PEPs, or for non-working spouses. In many cases, a gross redemption yield can be calculated and compared with that on the nearest equivalent gilt-edged securities, taking account of the different levels of risk.

Capital entitlements:

(1) the original split capital trusts repay a fixed amount on liquidation, and their income share price will fall towards this value as this date approaches; for example, traditional income shares that are issued at £1 and repaid at £1 would normally see their share price increase in the early years, as dividend growth increases the yield, before falling towards their final value in the latter years;
(2) some more recent issues are also entitled to part of any capital appreciation, after prior classes of shares are satisfied;
(3) a very different type, sometimes called annuity shares, have little capital entitlement which may be as low as 1p, or even less.

Income: these shares have exceptionally high running yields, benefiting from the income gearing probably by other classes of capital such as zero coupon shares and capital shares that do not rank for dividends.

Stepped preference shares

Another low risk security having priority over ordinary shares and most other classes, giving a known growing income and capital return if held to redemption (hence redemption yields can be calculated and compared with government securities).

Capital entitlements: a fixed capital return payable on liquidation.
Income: a predetermined dividend rising at a specified rate such as 5 per cent per annum.

Geared income shares

Otherwise known as highly geared ordinary shares, or income and residual capital shares. These shares are typically in structures with zero dividend preference shares or RPI-linked debentures. They are, effectively, a combination of income shares and capital shares and offer a high level of running yield and geared capital exposure.

7.5 CONDITIONS FOR PURCHASE

There are in general no limitations on the purchase of UK investment trust shares. Investors must of course satisfy any restrictions imposed by their own powers (eg as trustees), or any foreign laws to which they are subject. Investment trusts are normally a wider-range investment under the Trustee Investments Act, and collective investment media generally help to satisfy trustees' duty of diversification.

Personal Equity Plans can invest freely only in qualifying investment trusts, which are those that keep at least half of their portfolio in EU ordinary shares. PEPs can invest only up to a limit of £1,500 in 1996/97 (instead of the standard £6,000) in non-qualifying investment and unit trusts.

7.6 CHARACTERISTICS

All investment trusts have the same legal structure in common, but its flexibility gives an enormous range of very different investment vehicles, both as to the underlying investment management of the trust and the interests that investors can take. As well as traditional general trusts directly comparable with conservatively regulated unit trusts and insurance bonds, there are highly specialised issues tailor-made for particular purposes and suitable only for sophisticated or expertly advised investors of the appropriate type (see **7.4.4**).

7.6.1 Spread of risk and flexibility

An important feature of investment trust shares, like other collective investments, is the spread of risk which can be achieved by the investor. Investment trust shares represent an indirect interest in all the underlying assets of the trust, which can give the small investor a well balanced portfolio with a good spread of risk which would be too expensive and impracticable to obtain and manage by direct investment. But larger investors (personal or corporate) also invest through investment trusts in order to obtain professional or specialised investment management, currency management or gearing, and their attention to the trust's management of their interests may benefit all shareholders.

The wide investment powers of most investment trusts enable them, subject to the limitations acceptable for tax purposes, to follow a reasonably flexible investment policy. In response to changes in investment or fiscal conditions, they can adjust the emphasis in their portfolios on income or capital appreciation or on a particular sector of the market or geographical location. In addition, they are able, within limits, to invest in real property (although usually through the securities of listed property companies), in shares of unlisted companies and in other assets and, although they do not trade in securities themselves for tax reasons, they may establish dealing subsidiaries to take short-term positions in securities. Owing to SIB regulations, an authorised unit trust must necessarily have a less flexible investment policy than that of an investment trust.

The basic investment characteristics of any investment trust are stated in its prospectus and may be indicated in its name. However, since investment trusts are flexible vehicles and investment conditions are constantly changing, a better indication of an investment trust's current policy can be obtained from its latest report and accounts.

As well as its investment objectives and financial record, another vital characteristic of an investment trust is its size. A small investment trust may be able to out-perform a larger one by adopting a more flexible investment policy, but its shares could be less marketable than those of a bigger trust, with a greater spread between buying and selling prices.

7.6.2 Income and capital gains

The total returns from an investment are traditionally assessed as income and capital gains, but in an age where the marginal rates of tax on income and capital gains are similar the distinction is rather artificial, and the balance between the two can be deliberately adjusted (eg by selling securities cum- or ex-dividend). However, in general, dividend income is usually more predictable than capital performance, not least because it is often actively managed for consistency. Income and capital gains from investments are taxed differently and may be separately owned, so the balance between the two is very significant to many investors. Some markets, for example in the Far East and continental Europe, offer negligible dividend yields and correspondingly greater expectations of gains, but investment trusts may be chosen with a wide range of dividend policies.

As previously mentioned, the majority of warrants yield no income at all, which can be useful for instance to parents who would otherwise be liable to income tax on investments given to their children.

Most investors are free to adjust the 'income' they draw from their investments, either by reinvesting surplus net dividends, or by regularly selling shares to supplement the dividend yield. So far from being improvident, this is often a very sound strategy: up to £6,300 capital gains per year can be taken free of tax, in addition to the income tax allowances. Provided that the withdrawals do not exceed the capital gains (often profits retained within the trusts), the value of the investment will not be eroded. Note that if one sells discounted assets to realise a capital gain and provide a running income, then one can erode one's capital base markedly.

7.6.3 Investment overseas and currency management

Although most investment trusts adopt a flexible investment policy and are not rigidly committed to maintaining a particular proportion of their investments in any one geographical area, some of them specialise in one or more overseas areas in which they maintain special knowledge and investment expertise. These trusts provide a useful medium for overseas investment which often presents practical difficulties for direct investors.

Many trusts use foreign currency loans for overseas investment, so that the exposure of the trusts to the foreign exchange markets can be managed independently of the investments made in any country. At the same time the trust may be geared-up (see **7.6.5**), but whenever the managers choose to reduce the exposure of the trust to the market they can simply make a sterling deposit to remove the gearing.

For example, a foreign investment which gains by 20 per cent in local currency terms would still show a 20 per cent sterling loss if the exchange rate fell by a third. However, if the managers borrow the amount of the investment locally and the exchange rate falls, the liability to repay is reduced along with the assets. At the same time the trust's original capital remains intact, and could also be invested in any market.

Another, sometimes cheaper, way of hedging against exchange rate exposure is the 'currency swap' under which a UK investment trust swaps an amount in sterling with, say, a US company for an equivalent amount of US dollars. The US dollars received by the investment trust are used for portfolio investment. At the end of the agreed period the investment trust simply hands back the same amount of dollars to the US company in return for the sterling amount agreed at the outset. The risk of a default by the other party is limited to the possible exchange loss and attributable expenses, and both companies avoid the expenses of using a bank as intermediary.

The investment trust has always been a useful medium for overseas investment by UK residents because such investment is a difficult matter for most private investors, having regard to the distances involved, foreign market and settlement practices and the taxation and other problems which may arise in the overseas territories concerned. The average UK investor does not have sufficient resources to manage his UK investments effectively, let alone a portfolio of overseas investments.

7.6.4 Stock market price and underlying net asset value

An investment trust incorporated in the UK in general cannot usually purchase or redeem its own shares. Consequently, investment trust shareholders can normally only realise their investment by selling their shares through the stock market to other investors, or if the trust is wound up or taken over. The market prices of investment trust shares are dictated by supply and demand and for many years have generally stood at a discount to the value of their underlying net assets. These discounts and valuations are regularly published for most trusts. Investment trusts still often stand at a price in the stock market which is 15 or 25 per cent lower than the estimated amount per share which would be paid to shareholders on a liquidation of the company. The obvious explanation for these substantial discounts is a lack of demand for investment trust shares in the market. It is due, in part, to lack of publicity, competition from pension and insurance funds and unit trusts (whose managers are free to advertise their units for sale and to offer commissions to selling agents), and the fact that investment trust shares are often held by long-term investors. All these factors have contributed towards a comparatively low level of regular dealing activity in investment trust shares and so reduced their marketability. It also seems that as institutional fund management has become more sophisticated, it also seems that their appetite for investment trust shares has diminished.

To realise the profit inherent in the discount on net asset value, a number of investment trust companies have been reconstructed by their managers, taken over by other companies, placed in voluntary liquidation or 'unitised'. Unitisation is a scheme under which the shareholders pass a special resolution to wind up the investment trust and transfer its investments to an authorised unit trust in exchange for units of the unit trust. Subject to Inland Revenue clearance, unitisation does not of itself involve the investment trust shareholders in any liability to capital gains tax and on a subsequent disposal of units in the authorised unit trust, the acquisition cost of those units for capital gains tax purposes is the original acquisition cost of the shares in the investment trust from which the units arose. Following the unitisation, the former shareholders in the investment trust can sell their new units in the authorised unit trust at a price based on the underlying assets of the unit trust (see Chapter 8) and so the discount will have been effectively eliminated, although one needs to be aware of dealing costs and the bid/offer spreads.

The discount on net asset value has also been eliminated for some investment trust shareholders by take-over offers being made for their shares at prices near their underlying net asset value. Some of these take-over offers have been made by predator companies, while others have been made by institutions, such as pension funds, which see the acquisition of an investment trust company as an inexpensive means of acquiring a 'ready-made' investment portfolio and perhaps eliminating a competitor. However, a take-over, unlike a unitisation, may unexpectedly crystallise a liability to capital gains tax, though most will offer a tax efficient rollover.

If the discount is eliminated in one of these ways, or simply narrows as a result of increased market demand, it will be beneficial to holders who bought their shares at a discount and can sell at a price nearer to the net asset value. When the investor comes to sell his shares, so long as the discount is not larger than when he bought them, he should not suffer loss solely by reason of its existence, and in the meantime will have benefited from the income on the undiscounted or gross assets.

Another factor which will affect the stock market price of investment trust shares is the market-maker's turn, ie the difference between the higher offer price (at which the market-maker is prepared to sell to the investor) and the lower bid price (at which the market-maker is prepared to buy from the investor). The spread between the market-maker's bid and offer price will usually be wider in the case of shares of the smaller, less marketable trusts. It should be emphasised though that spreads are actually very narrow, and much narrower than bid/offer spreads on unit trusts.

This assumes that there is a sufficient market for the shares to enable them to be sold at all. In practice, a small investor in most of the larger investment trusts should not experience any difficulty in disposing of his shares at close to current market prices.

7.6.5 **Gearing**

In addition to its equity share capital, an investment trust may raise further capital by issuing debenture or loan stocks or preference shares and borrow money in sterling and foreign currencies. On a liquidation of the investment trust, holders of such stocks or preference shares and lenders of funds to the investment trust are entitled to repayment of fixed amounts of capital or principal from the assets of the trust in priority to equity shareholders. Only the surplus assets remaining, after discharge by the investment trust of all its other liabilities, are distributable to the equity shareholders. In effect, any increase or decrease in the value of the assets of the investment trust is primarily attributable to one or more classes of its equity share capital. An overall increase or decrease has a greater effect on the underlying value of its equity share capital in the case of a trust which has raised most of its capital in the form of loans or preference shares than in the case of a trust which has raised most of its capital by issues of equity shares. In UK securities terminology, if the proportion of a company's capital which has been raised in the form of loans and preference shares is large in relation to its equity capital, the company is described as 'highly geared' and, if small, the company's 'gearing' is said to be low; the US term is 'leverage'. Gearing levels of 10–15 per cent would normally be regarded as moderate for an investment trust. For conventionally structured trusts (ie excluding geared ordinary or capital shares in splits) gearing in excess of 30 per cent would be considered high.

The following examples illustrate the consequences of gearing; taxation and other factors have been ignored in the interests of simplicity.

Example 1: **Ungeared trust**

A new ungeared investment trust raises £1m by an issue of equity shares and invests the proceeds of the share issue in a portfolio of securities. If the value of the portfolio doubles to £2m, the assets of the trust attributable to the equity shareholders will increase 100 per cent. If the portfolio halves, the net value for ordinary shareholders will, likewise, decrease by 50 per cent.

Example 2: **Geared trust**

Suppose a new geared investment trust raises £1m by (a) issuing 500,000 preference shares at £1 each and (b) issuing equity shares at an aggregate price of £0.5m, and then invests the total proceeds of £1m in a portfolio of securities. If the portfolio doubles in value to £2m, on liquidation the investment trust will have to pay £0.5m to the preference shareholders; but, after this payment, the amount attributable to the trust's equity shares will have increased by 200 per cent from £0.5m to £1.5m. On the other hand, if the value of the portfolio halves, the preference shareholders will be repaid £0.5m, leaving nothing for the ordinary shareholders – a 100 per cent loss.

The ability of investment trusts to gear their portfolios in this manner is one of the principal differences between investment trusts and unit trusts. The latter have only very limited powers to borrow money without gearing up.

The examples given above illustrate the effect of gearing on the capital assets of an investment trust, but, if the lenders of money to an investment trust or its preference shareholders are entitled to payment of interest or dividends at a fixed rate, gearing will also have an effect on the income of the trust from its investments which is distributable to its equity shareholders. An increase (or decrease) in the income arising from a geared trust's investments will have a greater impact on the amount of income available for distribution to equity shareholders of the trust by way of dividend than will a similar fluctuation in the income of an ungeared trust.

Equity shareholders of investment trusts will benefit from investing in highly geared investment trusts when the assets in which those trusts have invested are rising in value, but they are at greater risk when such assets are falling in value. One of the more difficult tasks of a professional investment manager is to utilise gearing successfully. The investment manager must decide when to gear up the trust and when to undertake a rapid 'de-gearing' exercise by repaying borrowings or turning substantial portions of the investment portfolio into cash or assets which are not likely to fluctuate significantly in value.

7.7 TAXATION

7.7.1 Approval of investment trusts

This chapter deals with 'approved' investment trusts as opposed to 'unapproved' investment companies. Only approved investment trusts (and authorised unit trusts) attract the capital gains tax exemption outlined below. An approved investment trust is one which is not a 'close company' and which, in respect of an accounting period, has been approved by the Board of Inland Revenue. The Inland Revenue appears to have discretion to withhold approval, even in the case of an investment trust which would otherwise qualify, but it will approve a company that can show that:

(1) it is resident for taxation purposes in the UK;

(2) its income is derived wholly or mainly (which in practice means approximately 70 per cent or more) from shares or securities, or from eligible rental income (see **7.12**), or from any combination of the two;

(3) no holding in a company (other than another approved investment trust or a company which would qualify as such but for the fact that its shares are not listed as required by (4) below) represents more than 15 per cent by value of its investments;

(4) all its ordinary share capital is listed on The Stock Exchange;

(5) the distribution as dividend of capital profits on the sale of its investments is prohibited by its memorandum or articles of association; and

(6) not more than 15 per cent of its income from securities is retained unless legally required.

It is expressly provided that an increase in the value of a holding after it has been acquired will not result in an infringement of the 15 per cent limit referred to in (3) above. However, the holdings of an investment trust in its subsidiary companies are treated as a single holding for the purposes of this limit, as are its holdings in other companies which are members of the same group of companies. In addition, any loans made by the trust to its subsidiaries are treated as part of its investment in the subsidiaries for the purposes of ascertaining whether the limit has been infringed.

7.7.2 Approved investment trusts – capital gains

Investment trusts are corporations and their income is subject to corporation tax in the same manner and at the same rates as other corporations, but capital gains accruing to approved investment trusts are wholly exempt from capital gains tax in the hands of the trust. Thus active management of the trust's investments need not be constrained by tax on realising gains and the investor may only be subject to tax on disposing of his investment trust shares.

7.7.3 Approved investment trusts – income

The taxation of the trust's own income, and of the income and gains of investors in the trust, is exactly the same as for other limited companies (see Chapter 3). The corporation tax system is complicated and a detailed explanation of it is outside the scope of this handbook, but a brief summary may help.

Income

Franked income

This is income received by a trust in the form of dividends paid by a UK company in respect of which that company has paid advance corporation tax (ACT). ACT is effectively a payment by a UK company on account of its own corporation tax liability and is made in respect of dividends paid by it. The rate of ACT is expressed as a fraction of the dividend paid. The current fraction is 20/80, which means that if a company pays a dividend of £80 to a shareholder it must pay £20 ACT in respect of that dividend; the shareholder will receive a tax credit of £20. The amount of the dividend plus the ACT is known as a 'franked payment'. A trust is itself liable to pay ACT on paying dividends to its own shareholders, but franked income received by a trust can be passed on by way of dividend to its own shareholders without any payment of ACT by the trust. Further, the franked income is not liable to corporation tax in the hands of the trust.

Unfranked income

This is all other income (such as interest on gilt-edged securities, bank deposit interest and dividends paid by foreign companies) which does not carry a tax credit indicating that ACT has been paid in respect of it. Unfranked income is less favourably treated, being subject to corporation tax. However, interest paid by the trust and the fees paid to its investment managers are set primarily against unfranked income, reducing the amount liable to tax.

7.8 UNAPPROVED INVESTMENT COMPANIES

Unless an investment company has the status of an approved investment trust (see **7.7.1**), it is subject to ordinary forms of corporate taxation and will not qualify for the capital gains tax exemption mentioned in **7.7.2**. Thus both the investment income and capital gains made by such a company will be taxed, under the terms of the Finance Act 1987, at the corporation tax rate. Under the Taxes Act 1988, a close investment holding company does not qualify for the small companies' rate. In addition, if an investment company disposes of its assets and is then liquidated there is effectively a double capital gains tax charge, because (1) the company will be liable to corporation tax on capital gains realised by it on the disposal, and (2) its shareholders will be liable to capital gains tax for any capital gains realised by them on the disposal of their shares in the investment company, which will occur by reason of the distribution of cash proceeds to them in the liquidation. (Considerations affecting investment in a private investment company are discussed in **13.4**.)

Having regard to these disadvantages and to the fact that, so long as the investment company continues in existence, profits on the sale of investments may only be distributed to its shareholders by way of comparatively highly taxed dividends, the investment company has become unpopular as an investment medium. In fact, in order to mitigate this unsatisfactory taxation position, many unapproved investment companies have been 'unitised' (see **7.6.4**). The advantage of unitisation is that it defers the capital gains liability on the company shares until the ultimate disposal of the units issued on unitisation, which may be spread over several years to take full advantage of the annual CGT exemptions.

7.9 SUITABILITY

Investment trusts are a suitable investment medium for small and large investors who are resident in the UK for tax purposes, who wish to spread their investment risk and who do not have the expertise or the resources to make direct investments. However, the investor in investment trusts should be aware of the possible advantages and disadvantages which may result from the existence of the discount on net asset value (see **7.6.4**) and from the ability of investment trusts to gear their portfolios (see **7.6.5**). If the investor is unwilling to accept the risk involved for the sake of the possible greater rewards, the unit trust is probably a more suitable investment medium. On the other hand, investment trusts have frequently shown better long-term returns. Split capital trusts are highly suitable for the investors for whom they are designed, but more care must be taken accordingly.

7.10 MECHANICS

Investment trust shares may be bought in new issues or acquired on The Stock Exchange through stockbrokers, banks and other investment advisers. A number of stockbroking firms specialise in the investment trust sector and will be able to provide detailed information relating to individual trusts, including analyses of past performance, level of discount on underlying net asset value and investment policy. The Association of Investment Trust Companies freely offers excellent literature on investment trusts generally, and its members in particular. Information on individual trusts can be obtained from Extel cards (available in large public libraries), or directly from the managers, who may also offer shares for sale through 'savings schemes'.

Investment trust savings schemes are operated by managers to avoid some of the restrictions on marketing shares. Typically they offer lump sum, regular savings and dividend reinvestment options. The contributions are pooled by the managers and used to buy shares on The Stock Exchange, and the saving in transaction costs may reduce the investor's brokerage as low as 0.2 per cent, although some schemes provide for the payment of substantial commissions to intermediaries, the cost of which is ultimately borne by the investor.

Costs of both acquisition and disposal on The Stock Exchange will normally include stockbrokers' commission, which is subject to negotiation, but for a private investor is likely to be something between 1 and 1.65 per cent, depending on the extent of the service the client requires from the broker; there will usually be a minimum, perhaps £25, and a lower rate for large deals. On purchases, there will also be stamp duty at 0.5 per cent and the spread between bid and offered prices may be around 1.5 per cent, though it will usually be less on the freely traded shares of large companies. There is no initial charge payable to the managers, but further brokerage will be payable on final realisation of the shares by sale.

7.11 MAINTENANCE

Running costs vary from one investment trust to another, but management fees, often in the region of 0.5 per cent per annum on the value of the portfolio, are usually payable by the trust at half-yearly intervals in addition to its day-to-day operating expenses. New and converted specialist trusts, such as those involved in providing venture capital, often pay higher fees, perhaps 1.5 per cent. Economies can often be achieved in cases where the managers act as managers for several investment trusts and are therefore able to spread the burden of management and administrative expenses among a number of different trusts. These management fees and expenses are normally deductible from the trust's income for corporation tax purposes, whereas the management fee of a private portfolio manager generally has to be found out of his client's after-tax income. In the case of investment trusts, the level of management fees and the extent to which operating expenses may be charged to the trust are not controlled by any external regulation and generally trusts are lightly regulated without the expensive compliance arrangements required of unit trusts.

Like any other investment, holdings in investment trusts should be periodically reviewed by the investor or his adviser. Performance of the investment trust may be monitored by observing its quoted stock exchange price in the daily newspapers and the changes in its underlying net asset value, and by reading the half-yearly financial statements and annual directors' reports and audited accounts, which will be sent to registered shareholders and are generally available free on request. The annual report and accounts will contain detailed financial and other information relating to the trust and will usually include details of its investment portfolio as at the date of its balance sheet. The trust will also convene an annual general meeting of shareholders to adopt the annual report and accounts and to conduct other business. Any registered shareholder may attend and vote on the resolutions proposed at these meetings or, if he does not wish to attend, he may appoint a proxy to vote on his behalf.

7.12 PREVIEW OF THE YEAR AHEAD

The flexibility of an IT as a collective investment vehicle always offers a good starting point both for continual development, and other innovations. The previous budget initiative to launch venture capital trusts has been one example of this (see **7.3**), and this year's budget announcement was of housing investment trusts (HITs), designed to increase the supply of housing for rent by allowing listed investment trusts to invest in suitable property. On Royal Assent to the Finance Act 1996 an IT's income may then be derived wholly or mainly from shares and securities, or from eligible rental income, or any combination of the two. The property must be acquired after March 1996 on specified freehold and leasehold interests, and let on assured tenancies, and there are rather low limits to individual purchase or construction costs, at £125,000 in Greater London and £85,000 elsewhere.

The establishment of open-ended investment companies is still waiting for tax regulations from HM Treasury. Although they will have in investment terms more in common with units trusts than with ITs, the publicity may perhaps distract some investment which would otherwise have contributed demand for ITs.

7.13 CONCLUSION

While the market prices of investment trust shares are below their underlying asset values, investors can take the opportunity to profit from this discount, either on a reconstruction, take-over or winding-up of the trust, or if rule changes or market conditions increase demand for (and so prices of) investment trusts. Predators continue to give every incentive for good performance to trust managers, who have started to respond with increased emphasis on advertising and developing retail demand through savings schemes and PEPs, combined with a greater emphasis on performance and providing enhanced shareholder value through structural change. The freedom of investment trusts to issue innovative securities using sophisticated financial structures, and to invest with new techniques and instruments which are largely denied to other collective media, is of increasing importance as other differences are reduced. For example, because investment trusts do not have to contend with fluctuating capital flows, they are particularly suitable for index-matching investment policies: the first conversion of a trust into a fully indexed fund was not a success, but other trusts may do better. The flexibility of investment trusts in the hands of their professional managers will ensure they remain efficient and attractive investment vehicles for small and large investors alike.

SOURCES OF FURTHER INFORMATION

Useful addresses

Association of Investment Trust
  Companies
8–13 Chiswell Street
London
EC1Y 4YY

Tel: (0171) 431 5222

SBC Warburg
1 Finsbury Avenue
London EC2M 2PP

(This firm does not deal directly with private investors, but publishes an annual *Private Investor Guide to Investment Trusts*, which includes a list of some suitable brokers.)

8

UNIT TRUSTS AND OFFSHORE FUNDS

ROSS MACLEAN
LLB Hons
Assistant Secretary, Threadneedle Investment Managers Ltd

8.1 INTRODUCTION

Another form of collective investment medium (see Chapter 7) is that of unit trusts. A unit trust is a trust fund in which the investors hold direct beneficial interests. It is normally open-ended, meaning that units are created or redeemed at the current fair prices, and so the managers buy and sell units as required by investors (see **8.7**).

Obviously the honesty and competence of the managers of such trusts is of fundamental importance, and the constitution, management and marketing of trusts are all regulated in the UK, primarily under the Financial Services Act 1986. These powers are exercised by the Securities and Investments Board (SIB) and a number of self-regulatory organisations with delegated powers over member firms. Only authorised persons may conduct investment business. The European Community Directive on Undertakings for Collective Investment in Transferable Securities (the UCITS Directive) requires all member states to assimilate their regulations for certain collective schemes, which may then be sold throughout the European Economic Area.

8.2 HISTORICAL BACKGROUND

Units in the first unit trust in the UK were offered to the public in April 1931 by the M&G Group, which still exists today as one of the leaders of the industry. Allied Investors Ltd, now Allied Dunbar Unit Trusts plc, followed in 1934 and remains one of the largest unit trust groups in the UK. The first trusts were 'fixed' trusts and offered virtually no flexibility in investment policy once the trust deed had been executed. Each new subscription was invested in the fixed portfolio and each unit was thus unchanged in its composition. Each unit was normally divided into sub-units for sale to the public.

The first 'flexible' trust (the type of trust which is marketed today) was not offered to the public until 1936. When the Prevention of Fraud (Investments) Act 1939 came into force, supervision of the new industry was made the responsibility of the (then) Board of Trade. Under that Act, revised and re-enacted as the Prevention of Fraud (Investments) Act 1958, the Department of Trade and Industry (DTI) laid down regulations for the conduct of unit trusts, supervised charges and 'authorised' unit trusts complying with its requirements until 1988. The power of authorisation for new unit trust schemes then passed from the DTI to the SIB.

8.3 AUTHORISATION

The main requirement for authorisation of a unit trust by the SIB is that a trust deed conforming with the Board's regulations is executed between a company performing all management functions for the trust (the managers) and an independent trust corporation (the trustee) to hold the trust's investments and supervise the managers. Both the managers and the trustee must be incorporated under the law of, or of some part of, the UK or any other EU member state, must maintain a place of business in Great Britain and must be authorised persons to conduct investment business and so subject to the regulators' rules for conduct of business. The persons who are to be directors of a unit trust management company must be approved by the SIB. The trust deed and regulations must provide for, *inter alia*:

(1) managers' investment and borrowing powers and limits on investment of the trust's assets;
(2) determining the manner in which prices and yields are calculated and the obligation of managers to repurchase units at the 'bid' price;
(3) setting up a register of unitholders, with procedures for issuing certificates and dealing with transfers;
(4) remuneration of the managers and trustees;
(5) periodic audits of the trust and the issue of financial statements to unitholders, with reports by the managers, trustees and auditors;
(6) meetings of unitholders under certain circumstances.

Authorisation makes it possible for unit trust managers to advertise units for sale to the public and carries with it tax privileges for the trust. Here we deal only with unit trusts which have been authorised by the SIB; 'unit trust' here means an authorised unit trust unless otherwise indicated. (For discussion on unauthorised unit trusts, see **8.12**.)

8.4 HIGHLIGHTS OF THE PREVIOUS YEAR

Sales of unit trusts in 1996, compared with the previous two years, were as follows:

	1994 £m	1995 £m	1996 £m
Industry sales	19,722	18,333	25,766
Industry repurchases	11,378	11,435	15,762
Net new investment	8,344	6,898	10,004

Source: AUTIF.

At 31 December 1996 the total funds invested in authorised unit trusts were £131.9bn.

One hundred and fifty-five new trusts were launched in the year making a total of 1,633, operated by 160 management companies, the same as at the end of 1995, and compared with 162 at the end of 1994. There was another significant rise in the number of unitholders. At the end of 1996 there were 8.14 million unitholders, compared with 6.63 million in 1995 and 6.11 million in 1994.

During the first half of 1996 global bond and equities markets followed the lead of the US, falling in the wake of strong employment data which raised fears of renewed inflationary pressures.

In the second half of the year bond markets strengthened as signs suggested that the US, European and Japanese economies were weaker than anticipated. Strong corporate earnings in the US caused the equity market to strengthen and the rest of the world followed this lead. A series of market all time highs in the UK saw the FTSE 100 finish the year above the 4,000 point level.

8.5 PRICING OF UNITS

Since 1 July 1988, unit trust managers have been free to choose whether to deal on 'forward prices', ie at the next price to be calculated, or at prices already calculated and published, as had been the norm. Most management companies have availed themselves of this opportunity. With forward pricing, a buyer does not know exactly how many units he will receive, but he does know that he will deal at a fair, up-to-date price. If, on the other hand, a management company is dealing on historic prices and the value of a trust is believed to have changed by more than 2 per cent since the valuation on which the company is offering to deal, a new price must be calculated, and indeed a forward price must be given to any customer who requests it.

The bid and offer (or selling and buying) prices can be found in the newspapers with additional information available if the customer asks the management company for it.

The Financial Services Act 1986 became effective in 1988, superseding the Prevention of Fraud (Investments) Act 1958. As a result, much of the regulation of unit trusts, including authorisation, was transferred from the DTI to other bodies. The regulation of borrowing powers and permitted investment remains with the DTI, and the constitution of unit trusts is regulated by the DTI and the SIB, but the management of trusts is regulated by the Investment Management Regulatory Organisation (IMRO) and the marketing by the Personal Investment Authority (PIA).

8.6 LEGAL NATURE

A unit trust scheme is constituted by a trust deed which is made between the managers, who are the promoters of the scheme and who will subsequently be responsible for the conduct of the investment and for administration, and the trustee (usually one of the clearing banks or major insurance companies), which is responsible for ensuring that the managers act in accordance with the provisions laid down in the trust deed and which holds the trust's assets on trust for the unitholders. Regulations determine the content of the trust deed and other binding requirements, and both the trustee and the management company are subject to the IMRO Conduct of Business Rules.

The underlying securities are registered in the trustee's name or, if in bearer form, held in the custody of the trustee, which also holds any cash forming part of the fund. The trustee, as the legal owner of the underlying assets for the unitholders, receives on their behalf all income and other distributions made in respect of such assets.

The trust deed and regulations also lay down a formula for valuing the trust to determine the prices at which units may be sold to the public by the managers and at which units must be bought back by the managers from the public (see below). Additional units may be created to meet demand from the public or existing units may be cancelled as a result of the subsequent repurchase of units from the public. A unit trust is thus 'open-ended' and can expand or contract depending on whether there is a preponderance of buyers or sellers of its units.

Three prices are quoted for unit trusts. These are the 'offer' price, at which units are offered for sale to or subscription by the public, and the 'bid' price, at which the managers buy back units, and the cancellation price, at which the managers may arrange for units to be redeemed out of the trust's assets. These prices are, broadly speaking, ascertained in the following manner:

(1) the offer price is calculated by reference to the notional amount which would have to be paid to acquire the underlying assets held by the trust, to which are added the notional acquisition costs (such as brokers' commission and stamp duty) and the preliminary management charges (see **8.11.1**);

(2) the bid price is calculated by reference to the amount which would be received on a disposal of the assets held by the trust, from which are deducted the notional costs of the disposal, ie brokers' commission and contract stamp.

An investor must never be required to pay more for his units than the offer price as calculated under the trust deed, nor may the unitholder on a sale of his units be paid less than the bid price as so calculated. When an investor buys units, the managers may either create them or sell units that they have previously repurchased and are holding in the manager's 'box'. The spread between the offered and bid prices under the DTI rules is normally between 8 and 11 per cent, but in practice most unit trust managers quote spreads for their own dealings in units between 5.5 and 7.5 per cent, which may be positioned anywhere between the maximum offered and minimum bid prices applicable on subscription for new units and cancellation of existing units.

Managers normally base their buying price for units in a particular trust on the full bid valuation if they are buying back more units than they are selling, since this is the price at which units must be cancelled. Conversely, if the managers are selling more units than they are buying, their selling price is normally based on the full offer price, at which units must be created.

A unit trust cannot 'gear' its portfolio by borrowings, either unsecured or secured on the trust's assets. The only circumstances in which borrowing is permitted are to anticipate known cash flows (such as dividends due).

The trust deed, which takes effect subject to any regulations under the Financial Services Act, may make provision for the trust to be terminated and also specifies circumstances in which the approval of unitholders at a general meeting needs to be sought. Such approval is required, among other things, for proposals to vary the provisions of the trust deed, to change the investment objectives of the trust or to amalgamate it with another trust. Unitholders' interests are thus protected despite the fact that no annual general meeting is held, since certain material changes affecting their interests may be effected only with their approval in general meeting.

8.7 CONDITIONS FOR PURCHASE

Any individual, corporate body or trustee may acquire and hold unit trusts without any condition or restriction, subject to any limitation which may be imposed on its own investment powers.

Unit trusts are specifically mentioned as approved 'wider range' investments under the Trustee Investments Act 1961. Unit trusts whose portfolios consist exclusively of investments suitable for 'narrow range' investments under the same Act may themselves be included in the narrow range investments. Trustees should, however, satisfy themselves of their powers to invest in unit trusts by reference to their trust instrument.

Nearly all unit trust managers specify a minimum investment, usually in the range of £250–£1,000. Certain specialist funds have higher minima. These minima do not apply to monthly saving schemes, where amounts from £10 per month may be invested on a regular basis.

Since a unit trust is open-ended, there is no maximum holding, though a corporate or trustee unitholder may be restricted by his own investment limitations.

Persons resident outside the UK may acquire and hold unit trust units, subject to the local exchange control rules in their country of residence or domicile. However, for reasons of taxation, it is usually preferable for such people to invest in 'offshore' funds.

8.8 CHARACTERISTICS

Unit trusts must invest the greater part of their portfolios in securities listed on recognised stock exchanges. Each manager, with the trustees' approval, will determine a list of 'eligible markets' for each trust. These will be markets which are considered to meet basic criteria of investor protection such as having regulatory authorities, high accounting standards and no restrictions on the repatriation of funds. Up to 10 per cent of the trust's property may be held in 'non-eligible markets'. Note that the determination of eligibility is not made by the SIB.

The investments of the majority of unit trusts are usually in equity shares.

Traditional authorised unit trusts may, in general, invest only in securities, although newer classes of unit trusts are now authorised to invest in other financial instruments, such as futures and options, warrants or property. These new schemes have separate regulations of investment and borrowing powers, and may have a separate tax regime. All trusts may use derivatives within the constraints of Efficient Portfolio

Management for hedging purposes. With the exception of GFOFs (Geared Futures and Options Funds) all derivatives must be fully covered by cash, stock or other derivatives.

The specific investment characteristics of unit trusts will vary depending on the stated objective of any particular trust. However, all unit trusts share certain general characteristics.

8.8.1 General characteristics

Spread of risk

By acquiring an interest in a portion of all the investments in the underlying portfolio of a unit trust, an investor can achieve a much wider spread of risk than he could himself achieve economically with limited resources. By spreading his investment across a large number of companies in a wide variety of industries in a number of different countries, the investor can much reduce the risks inherent in a holding of shares in only one company or a small number of companies. The result is likely to be a much more even progression of capital and income growth. Regulations covering the maximum investment of a trust's assets in a single company or issue ensure that a wide spread of risk is achieved. In practice, unit trusts usually hold something between 30 and 100 investments, considerably more than the required minimum.

Professional management

By committing his investment funds to the purchase of a holding in a unit trust the investor is in effect delegating the day-to-day management of his portfolio to the trust's managers. Virtually all unit trust management companies employ a team of investment specialists whose aim is to maximise capital and/or income performance, and who are given a wide discretion within the limitations imposed by the trust deed to increase or decrease the trust's liquidity or to switch investments as they consider appropriate. The advantage to the investor is that his investments are under the continuous supervision of people whose business it is to keep abreast of economic, political and corporate developments at home and abroad.

Simplicity and convenience

The sometimes tedious paperwork associated with owning a portfolio of securities is largely eliminated. Day-to-day decisions on such matters as rights and scrip issues, mergers and take-overs are all taken by the managers. Dividends are received by the trustee and distributions of the trust's income are made, usually twice a year, to unitholders together with a report on the progress of their trust during the preceding accounting period.

Marketability

In view of their open-ended nature, as a result of which units can be created or cancelled to meet investors' requirements, unit trust units can be regarded as an almost totally liquid investment, with none of the constraints on marketability sometimes encountered in connection with investment in some of the smaller listed companies. As a result of the pricing structure, referred to in **8.6**, purchases and sales of units take place at prices which reflect the underlying value of the trust's assets.

8.8.2 Types of unit trust

While all unit trusts share the investment characteristics listed above, there are a very wide range of trusts which offer different investment objectives designed to suit different categories of investors. The main types are described below.

Balanced trusts

These invest in a portfolio which is usually composed of leading 'blue chip' shares with the aim of achieving a steady growth of both capital and income. These trusts are designed for the investor who wishes to invest in a wide spread of ordinary shares. They are suitable for the first-time investor in equities, who wishes to hold the units for longer term investment or saving.

Income trusts

These aim to achieve an above-average yield to the investor whose primary need is for a high and growing income. Normally, such trusts give a yield between 1.2 and 1.5 times that available on shares generally. These trusts are most suitable for retired people, widows, or others who depend on investment income. Such trusts may purchase convertible shares as a way of achieving their yield objectives.

Capital trusts

These are designed to seek maximum capital growth. The income from such trusts is usually low. These characteristics make them particularly suitable for those who want to build up a nest-egg.

Fixed interest trusts

These generally invest in a portfolio of government bonds, corporate bonds and convertible shares and may be either income or capital trusts. Such trusts may be suitable for those requiring a high income, although prospects for income growth are unlikely to be as good as in equity trusts.

Overseas trusts

These aim to provide the investor with an opportunity to invest through stock markets in other countries. Investment overseas is a particularly complex and difficult task for the private person, but can be rewarding in times when sterling is weak against other currencies or when economic conditions in a region overseas are particularly buoyant. The sharp depreciation of sterling in 1992 proved again the merits of investing in these trusts, as a hedge against devaluation.

Specialist trusts

Certain trusts, sometimes referred to as 'specialist trusts', are promoted to invest in particular sectors of the securities market (eg commodities or smaller companies). These trusts are suitable for the larger or more sophisticated investor who wishes to concentrate on a particular sector while still achieving a spread of risk. The specialist nature of such trusts means that the investor may be somewhat more at the whim of fashion; UK smaller companies' unit trusts, for example, after many years of above-average returns, markedly underperformed their more balanced counterparts from 1989 to 1991.

Accumulation trusts

Certain trusts within all the categories referred to above are structured and promoted on the basis that they will accumulate the net income within the trust rather than distribute it to unitholders. This income is nonetheless subject to taxation as if it had been received by unitholders.

'Tracker' trusts

Certain trusts are structured to imitate a stock market index and so achieve a performance matching that market. Because of their essentially passive nature, with investment managers taking fewer active decisions, such trusts normally have lower management charges. These trusts are also referred to as indexed trusts.

147

8.9 TAXATION

Most trusts are authorised unit trust schemes and accordingly not liable to corporation tax on capital gains on the disposal of any of the trust property. Income derived from the property of each of the trusts is liable to corporation tax. From 1994–95 onwards unit trusts which hold less than 60 per cent in qualifying investments are able to claim for a 20 per cent corporation tax rate. Funds invested in more than 60 per cent of qualifying investments are chargeable to tax at 25 per cent (20 per cent for 1996–97). Qualifying investments include cash and loan stock or similar securities issued by the Government, a public or local authority, or a company and shares in building societies, or in other trusts.

Funds may distribute dividends (dividend distributions) and will account to the Inland Revenue for an amount of Advance Corporation Tax (ACT). For individual unitholders resident in the UK a tax credit will be available on dividend distributions equal to the amount of ACT, which they may set off against their total income tax liability and in appropriate cases reclaim in cash. The tax credit will satisfy the total tax liability of basic and lower rate payers. Higher rate taxpayers may be liable to an additional tax liability.

The amount of distribution received by a unitholder subject to corporation tax (and not dual resident) will be separated into franked and unfranked components of the dividend distribution. The unfranked component will be deemed an annual payment received after a deduction of tax at the lower rate of 20 per cent and the franked component will be treated as a dividend, with a tax credit equal to the amount of ACT.

Whether unitholders who are resident in countries other than the UK are entitled to payment from the Inland Revenue of a proportion of the tax credit depends in general upon the provision of any double tax convention or agreement which exists between the relevant country and the UK.

For distribution periods commencing on or after 1 April 1994 trusts which receive foreign income or foreign income dividends (FIDs) from UK companies may pay an FID either on its own or together with a dividend distribution. If the unitholder receives an FID, lower and basic rate taxpayers have no further tax liability. Higher rate taxpayers have further tax to pay but receive credit for the notional tax deducted from the FID. The notional tax on the FID is not repayable. A unitholder that is subject to corporation tax will receive an FID distribution separated into franked and unfranked components. The unfranked component is received as an annual payment received after deduction of tax at the lower rate. The franked component is received as a dividend with a notional tax credit which is non-repayable.

For distribution periods commencing on or after 1 April 1994, funds can make interest distributions (but not at the same time as FIDs or dividend distributions). It is likely that only trusts suffering the 25 per cent tax rate will take this option. An interest distribution will have income tax deducted at the basic rate on the payment of the interest distribution. For distribution on or after 6 April 1996 tax will be deducted at the lower rate. The total interest payment including the income tax credit will be subject to income or corporation tax. In appropriate cases, both corporate and individual unitholders will be able to reclaim the income tax credit in cash.

Non-resident unitholders may be eligible for interest distributions to be made gross. When they are not paid gross, all or some of the income tax credit may be recoverable from the Inland Revenue. This depends upon the provisions of any tax convention or agreement which exists between the relevant country and the UK.

No taxation will be withheld from payment made to unitholders on redemption of units. However, the redemption, sale or transfer of units may constitute a disposal (or part disposal) for the purposes of UK taxation of capital gains.

8.10 SUITABILITY

Unit trusts are suitable for investors, large or small, whether trustees, corporations or private individuals who wish to invest in a portfolio of either general or specialist securities in the UK or overseas, but who do not wish, or are not investing sufficient sums, to run their own investments.

Because the income from and the value of all securities can fluctuate, investors should understand that unit trusts are risk investments. 'The value of the units as well as the income from them may go down as well as up' is the caveat which must appear in all unit trust advertisements and literature soliciting purchases of units issued by managers. However, the fact that unit trusts cannot, generally, gear up, that present regulation ensures a reasonable level of diversification within the trust, and the overseeing function of the trustee, considerably reduces the inherent risk of the investment.

8.11 MECHANICS AND MAINTENANCE

8.11.1 Mechanics

Unit trust units may be acquired through any professional adviser (stockbroker, bank, accountant, solicitor or insurance broker). Many have departments specialising in advice on the selection of unit trusts. There are also several firms which offer unit trust portfolio management and advisory services. If there is any doubt about the suitability of unit trusts to the investor's needs, professional advice may be desirable in any case.

Alternatively, unit trusts' units may be acquired directly from the managers on either telephoned or written instructions. The disposal of units can be achieved in exactly the same way.

The names, addresses and telephone numbers of unit trust managers are given in many leading newspapers, together with a list of the current prices of the trusts they manage. All managers supply more comprehensive information and copies of recent reports on particular trusts on request.

The Association of Unit Trusts and Investment Funds can supply a comprehensive list of members and other general information about unit trusts on request. (See end of chapter for details.)

When units are purchased, an initial charge payable to the managers is usually included in the unit price. There is no restriction on the initial charge, but the trust deed must contain a figure for the maximum permissible charge and all advertisements or literature must give details of the actual current charge. Initial charges are normally in the region of 5 to 6 per cent.

Most managers pay commission to accredited agents. This is borne by the managers from the permitted initial charge.

The unitholder receives a contract note giving details of this purchase and subsequently receives a certificate showing the number of units of which he is the registered holder. Payment of the proceeds of sale is normally made by the managers within a few days of their receiving the certificate signed on the reverse by the unitholder.

8.11.2 Maintenance

Annual management fees based on the trust's value are deducted by the managers from the trust's income. As in the case of investment trusts, these fees are deductible from the trust's income for tax purposes. From the annual charge the managers must meet the costs of trustees' fees, audit fees, administration and investment management. The maximum permitted level of annual management fees must be laid down in the trust deed and the actual level charged set out in all advertisements and literature. If managers wish to increase the fees to a level not exceeding the maximum figure, unitholders must be given three months' notice in writing. Increases in the maximum figure must be approved by unitholders at an extraordinary meeting. Fees charged usually vary between 0.75 and

1.5 per cent per annum, although management charges for certain indexed trusts may be as low as 0.5 per cent.

Certain other costs, including agents' fees for holding investments in safe custody overseas and the cost of collecting foreign dividends, may be charged to the trust's income. These costs are usually small in relation to the total income.

The stamp duty and brokerage on the purchase and sale of underlying investments are borne by the trust but are reflected in the pricing structure (see **8.6**).

Like any other investment, unit trust holdings should be periodically reviewed by the investor or his adviser. The investor should be able to monitor the performance of the managers by reading the half-yearly (or sometimes annual) reports which they are required to send him. These reports should contain:

(1) a statement of the trust's capital and income performance during the period, compared with appropriate indices;
(2) an assessment of portfolio changes during the period or any change in investment philosophy;
(3) the managers' view of the forthcoming period;
(4) a list of the current investment holdings;
(5) the figures for the income distribution; and
(6) a ten-year capital and income record.

8.12 UNAUTHORISED UNIT TRUSTS

Unauthorised unit trusts are unit trusts which have not been authorised by the SIB (see **8.3**). In some circumstances, authorised status for a unit trust may, for somewhat technical reasons, carry with it certain taxation disadvantages. In particular, if an authorised unit trust (other than one established specially to invest in UK government securities) is to receive a substantial proportion of its income other than by way of distributions from companies which are tax-resident in the UK (ie in unfranked form), it will have income which is liable to corporation tax because of the rule deeming an authorised unit trust to be a company for taxation purposes. In these circumstances an authorised unit trust would have to pay corporation tax on a substantial proportion of its income, thus reducing the amount of income available for distribution to unitholders. This may be contrasted with the position where an authorised unit trust is in receipt solely of dividends from UK companies, in which case all the income which it receives will be 'franked investment income' and thus not liable to corporation tax. Accordingly, in cases where a material proportion of foreign income or other income liable to corporation tax is to be received, a unit trust may be established in unauthorised form to ensure that its income is liable only to ordinary income tax at the basic rate (presently 25 per cent), the payment of which is reflected in distributions to the unit-holders. The treatment for income tax purposes of an unauthorised trust which receives a high proportion of its income in unfranked form is more favourable than that of an authorised unit trust which receives a like proportion of unfranked income. But usually the advantage is small compared with the disadvantage relating to capital gains (see **8.9**), and it was negated, from 1 January 1991, by changes announced in the 1990 budget (see **8.9**).

An unauthorised unit trust does not benefit from the capital gains tax exemption of authorised unit trusts. Capital gains tax is therefore payable in full, putting such a trust at a disadvantage in comparison with an authorised trust so far as capital gains tax is concerned, unless the unauthorised trust is an exempt trust.

8.13 EXEMPT UNIT TRUSTS

Exempt unit trusts are unit trusts designed for particular types of unit-holders. While many such funds exist, their rationale was destroyed by the exemption of unit trusts from tax on chargeable gains in the Finance Act 1980. Exempt unit trusts may be in authorised or unauthorised form.

8.14 PREVIEW OF THE YEAR AHEAD

Last year the advent of the open ended investment company (OEIC) was being heralded. In retrospect the enthusiasm was premature as the necessary legislation was not passed in time. Interest, at least from the product providers, remains high and the final pieces are virtually in place.

Although very similar in many respects to existing unit trusts OEICs will be corporate vehicles rather than trusts, under a code separate from that of the existing Companies Acts, so that a 'unitholder' will in fact be a share-holder. There will be prospectuses issued, reports and accounts, and annual general meetings where shareholders can make their voices heard.

To an existing or potential unit trust investor there will still be easy access and egress, there will be a manager (technically known as a 'des-ignated corporate director') and a 'trustee' function, carried out by an entity known as a depositary.

Unit trust managers have a window of opportunity until 30 June 1999; up to that date the conversion of two or more unit trusts into an OEIC will qualify for stamp duty and stamp duty reserve tax relief.

8.15 CONCLUSION

For the private investor who wishes to participate in the historically greater returns available from investment in the world's stock markets as compared to deposits or savings accounts, the unit trust is an ideal vehicle to mitigate some of the inherent risks. Prime examples of this include the role of the trustees who will protect the customer assets in the event of the manager's default, and the ability to gain the skill of an entire investment team of professionals for as little as £10 a month. Having decided on the vehicle the choice of manager and fund type, although initially daunting, should be enough to satisfy the requirements of almost every private investor.

If not, one can be sure that product development teams are already working on the next evolution in the market.

SOURCES OF FURTHER INFORMATION

Legislation

Capital Gains Tax Act 1979
Companies Act 1985
Finance Act 1980
Finance Act 1982
Finance Act 1984
Finance Act 1985
Finance Act 1986
Finance Act 1987
Finance Act 1988
Finance Act 1989
Finance Act 1990
Finance Act 1991
Finance (No1) Act 1992
Finance (No2) Act 1992
Finance Act 1993
Finance Act 1994
Finance Act 1995
Finance Act 1996

Financial Services Act 1986
Income and Corporation Taxes Act 1988
Prevention of Fraud (Investments) Act 1958

Useful addresses

Association of Unit Trusts and
   Investment Funds
65 Kingsway
London
WC2B 6TD

Tel: (0171) 831 0898

Association of Investment Trust
   Companies
8–13 Chiswell Street
London
EC1Y 4YY

Tel: (0171) 588 5347

Department of Trade and Industry
Companies Division
10–18 Victoria Street
London
SW1H 0NN

Tel: (0171) 215 5000

The Association of Corporate
   Trustees
43 Surrey Road
Bournemouth
BH4 9HR

Tel: (01202) 761112

Tel: (0171) 378 9000

Securities and Investments Board
Gavrelle House
2–14 Bunhill Row
London
EC1Y 8RA

Tel: (0171) 638 1240

REAL PROPERTY

GEOFFREY J ABBOTT
Dip FBA (Lon) FRICS

Head of Sales and Purchases Department
and Investment Partner of Smiths Gore (Chartered Surveyors)

9.1 INTRODUCTION TO REAL PROPERTY

This chapter is a general introduction to the subject of real property and to Chapters 10 (dealing with residential property), 11 (agricultural land and woods) and 12 (commercial property). Readers should appreciate that the subjects covered are vast and complex. All matters referred to have been condensed and investors must take independent professional advice.

Real property is a legal interest in land and/or buildings of four principal types:

(1) residential;
(2) commercial;
(3) farmland;
(4) woodlands.

In the case of vacant farmland and woodland it may also include growing crops as well.

Investment in property falls into two main categories:

(1) Direct investment: by purchase of an interest in a property.
(2) Indirect investment: by purchase of units in property bonds and other unit linked schemes, or by the purchase of shares in a property company.

These chapters deal with direct investment.

Property is generally considered one of the most secure forms of investment as it is almost totally indestructible and immovable (it cannot be lost or stolen) and usually produces an income. However, an investment in property is complicated and a thorough understanding of all its implications is necessary to ensure optimum results are obtained from the investment selected.

Today, ownership of land and property is in many hands. The principal types of owner are:

(1) private individuals;
(2) trust funds;
(3) public and private investment and trading companies;
(4) institutions; and
(5) national and local government and various bodies under them.

The property owner, or the freeholder (superior in Scotland), may have others with lesser interests in the whole or parts of his property. The owner of these lesser interests is normally either a lessee, a tenant or a licensee (vassels/feuers) depending on the nature of their interests. There can also be third party rights over property. These may vary from a right of the general public to use a footpath for instance, or a statutory undertaking to lay a water pipe or electricity on, under or over the owner's or lessee's land, or a personal right to cross another person's land.

An interest in property may satisfy three separate needs: enjoyment, investment and security. Enjoyment in its broadest sense might be considered as the actual use of that land, whether agricultural, a place to live, a place to manufacture, a place from which to extract minerals or a place of employment or entertainment. Enjoyment and investment are commonly combined, eg owner-occupiers of residential property rarely consider their home as an investment, although for the great majority it is the largest single investment that they will ever make.

Many forms of ownership of an interest subject to a letting do not entitle the investor to any direct enjoyment of the land but simply to participate in an agreed share of the income or produce obtained from it, usually in the form of a cash rent.

All readers must appreciate, however, that where investments are made for maximum financial gain the most important factor is timing. All markets are cyclical. Whatever the care in initial selection and subsequent management, if a purchase is made at the top of a market cycle short-term performance will inevitably be disappointing. Alternatively, almost all purchases made at the bottom of a cycle will ultimately perform well. Investment based on this strategy is known as counter-cyclical.

9.2 LEGAL, TAXATION AND COST FACTORS OF REAL PROPERTY

9.2.1 Legal

The legal root of English and Welsh property law is fundamentally different from that in Scotland. Whilst legislation is commonly drafted to give similar effects, it does not always do so in practice. Historically, the main purpose of property laws and legislation was to establish ground rules by which owners, landlords and tenants should behave to each other and their neighbours. However, recent legislation to protect the wider community's interests with planning and other legislation has tended to restrict the owner or tenant's right to do what he likes with his property. The body of law is substantial but its application to any individual property varies. An experienced property lawyer is therefore an essential member of any property investor's team.

9.2.2 Taxation

As with all forms of investment, owners of real estate are liable to pay revenue, capital gains and inheritance taxes in one way or another. The impact of these taxes on the owners of different types of property varies significantly and may determine the type of property invested in and even whether to choose property or non-property investments. Finally, business rates apply on occupation of most commercial property, and council tax on residential property.

The body of taxation law is again substantial, detailed and complex. An experienced property tax adviser should be consulted.

9.2.3 Costs

The purchase, ownership and the eventual sale of any interest in real estate will normally incur costs. When property is held for investment they will affect the net yield achieved. The level of costs will reflect the particular nature and circumstances of the property or portfolio held and will typically be in the form of acquisition, management or disposal costs.

Acquisition costs

The purchaser of any real estate should be prepared for costs of 2.5 to 3 per cent on top of the purchase price (costs associated with a lease may be substantially different). These costs are made up of 1 per cent stamp duty on properties having a value of £60,000 or more, 1 per cent for agents' fees and 0.5 per cent for solicitors' fees. There may be an additional charge on the solicitors' account for search fees and VAT is payable on both agents' and solicitors' fees. The VAT status of many forms of property investment should also be checked out before an offer is made.

Investors should consider certain other additional costs, eg a structural survey on older buildings or a planning appraisal for potential development situations. The investment may also involve a mortgage or other form of borrowing and the associated valuation and commitment fees are normally paid by the borrower/purchaser.

Finally, the purchase of vacant farmland usually also involves the purchase of growing crops and the payment of tenant right. Professional fees for the valuation and negotiation of agreement on these will normally be in the 2.5 to 5 per cent range.

Management costs

Stocks and shares are essentially a passive investment, whereas most forms of property investment call for active management. Property management costs are very variable. Over the years most property will need to be repaired, insured, altered, re-let, improved or perhaps redeveloped. It is only by good management that the asset can maximise its rental and capital value in a changing marketplace.

Examples of typical management costs are:

(1) Fully let office on full repairing and insuring (FRI) lease – 2 to 3 per cent of gross rent.
(2) Small market town shop on standard repairing lease – 5 per cent of gross rent.
(3) Substantial arable farm on FRI lease – 7 per cent of gross rent.
(4) Complex traditional let estate – 10 per cent of gross rent.
(5) Short-term furnished residential letting – 20 per cent of gross rent.

Agents' property management fees are usually agreed at the outset, as a package to reflect the range of services needed, and paid out of rental income when received. Fees for farm and forestry management services depend on whether the agent is merely used on a consultancy basis or is responsible for the day-to-day running of a trading business. Where a surveyor is instructed to negotiate or advise on a rent review, lease renewal or re-letting, fees range from 7.5 to 10 per cent of either the first year's rental obtained, or of the increase over the previous rent, depending on the circumstances of each case, plus VAT and expenses.

Disposal costs

The costs of selling are as variable as the types of property involved. Agents' fees vary from 1 per cent of the price achieved for a large commercial property investment up to 2.5 per cent for a smaller residential property, with the associated solicitors' fees normally in the 0.5 to 0.75 per cent range. VAT is also payable on professional fees.

Local advertising costs at the lower end of the residential markets are normally borne by the agent. National advertising and higher quality particulars, professionally printed, are usually met by the vendor, who also carries the cost of all advertising and printing for most other forms of property sale.

An owner may wish to dispose of just part of his property interest for a certain period. This would normally be dealt with by granting a lease, tenancy or licence. Agents' fees are typically up to 10 per cent of the first year's rent plus VAT and direct expenses, including marketing costs. Solicitors' fees depend on whether a standard lease/agreement is used or whether a document has to be specially drafted to meet the circumstances.

9.3 PROPERTY VALUATION

The diversity of property types and reasons for ownership produce a wide range of approaches to property valuations. The location, accessibility and setting of a property will always influence its value.

The capital value of a vacant house is an equation of demand and supply in the relevant market at the time. Reference to sales of comparable properties is the only guide. However, a specific purchaser may pay a premium for a particular property for no better reason than that he wants to live in it.

In other sectors, such as sporting estates, the market seeks to quantify a purchaser's potential pleasure of ownership by relating value to past bag or catch records. Similarly the value of amenity woodlands is linked to the purchaser's anticipated pleasure in ownership. In commercial woodlands, however, the value is based on capitalisation of future income flows from timber sales, perhaps many decades ahead.

It is only in the markets for let properties that value is linked to the capitalisation of rent passing. Indeed in many sectors of the commercial property markets a well-let property is worth significantly more than its vacant equivalent.

In most commercial property markets the rental income is capitalised over a term of years or in perpetuity (depending on whether the property is leasehold or freehold) at an investment rate set by the market. This reflects the risks associated with that property (security of income, obsolescence of the building, economic factors and the cost/inconvenience of management). The capitalisation rate also reflects the expectation of future rental growth. Most forms of professional valuation today are covered by the *Royal Institution of Chartered Surveyors Appraisal and Valuation Manual* (the Red Book).

9.4 ROLE OF ADVISERS

Real property should never be acquired, sold or developed without the investor first obtaining competent professional advice. For most investors the advisers will comprise:

(1) A chartered surveyor: for his knowledge of the relevant market, his ability to appreciate and value potential properties, his negotiating skills and finally his ability to manage the property over the years and maximise its end value.

(2) A solicitor: with appropriate property experience to advise on legal matters generally, convey properties on purchase and sale and draw up leases and other legal documents throughout the life of the investment.

(3) A chartered accountant/financial adviser: to advise generally on funding/sources of capital and methods of minimising the impact of revenue and capital taxes over the years.

Dependent on the nature of property investments actually made, some investors may also require the services of other advisers from time to time. They might include architects, quantity surveyors, farm and/or forestry management consultants.

10

RESIDENTIAL PROPERTY

GEOFFREY J ABBOTT
Dip FBA (Lon) FRICS
Head of Sales and Purchases Department
and Investment Partner of Smiths Gore (Chartered Surveyors)

10.1 HIGHLIGHTS OF THE PAST FEW YEARS

The housing recession, which set in in August 1988 in the south east and rippled around the whole country, has now relaxed its iron grip in most areas.

Whilst the recovery is still very uneven, turnover of realistically priced houses has picked up in most parts of the country, and values are recovering in selected parts of London and the south east.

10.2 THE ALTERNATIVES

10.2.1 Personal homes

The purchase of a home is probably the largest investment which the great majority of us make without ever considering it an investment. It is the only form of property investment where capital gains are normally tax free. The owner, if he has more than one home, may elect which is his 'principal residence' and may vary this from time to time subject to notifying the Inland Revenue. A person required to reside in employer-provided accommodation may acquire a house and enjoy capital gains tax exemption on it, provided he intends in due course to live in it.

The capital gains tax exemption usually applies to a house and up to one acre of grounds, but exceptions exist above and below this amount and professional valuation advice should be sought.

In spite of the recent past, the purchase of a home has long been considered the safest and soundest form of property investment. The purchaser enjoys absolute control over his investment and may obtain tax relief at 15 per cent for interest on loans up to £30,000 for house purchase. Funds for purchase are traditionally obtained on mortgage from building societies and insurance companies, or the major clearing banks who entered this field in 1981.

Houses are normally sold by private treaty, but investment or let houses, and mortgage repossessions, are sometimes sold by auction. Factors to consider on house purchase include:

(1) style, location and potential planning factors;
(2) structural condition;
(3) availability of main services (gas, water, electricity, telephone, drainage);
(4) the local rate of council tax.

The length and cost of journeying to work is an increasingly important factor. Unmodernised houses may be eligible for local council improvement grants.

However, the most important question is whether you and your family actually wish to live in the house. First and foremost it is to be your home.

Insurance of property should usually be on the estimated cost of replacement (equivalent reinstatement cost) which may exceed the market value of the property. It should normally be index-linked to increase the sum insured in line with inflation of building costs.

10.2.2 Let houses and flats

Let houses and flats are occupied by tenants and produce a rental income. They are often referred to as 'investment' houses or flats and most postwar legislation has been viewed as favouring tenants. As a result the market shrank dramatically though the 1980s legislation to restore the market has had some effect.

Rent Acts

Many let houses and flats are covered by the old Rent Acts under which the tenant has security and the rent is fixed from time to time by the Rent Officer (an official of the local authority) at a 'fair rent' level which is generally well below market levels. Increases set by the Rent Officer may only be phased in over a period of years.

Protected shorthold tenancies (one to five years)

Under the Housing Act 1980, protected shorthold tenancies were introduced for new lettings of more than one year but less than five years, under which the landlord can regain possession upon expiry, provided certain conditions are fulfilled. Whilst the initial rent may be agreed between the parties, the tenant may apply to have the rent fixed by the Rent Officer at any time.

Assured and assured shorthold tenancies

These were introduced under the Housing Act 1988 for new lettings after 15 January 1989 at market rents, subject to a right of appeal to the Rent Assessment Committee who will look to comparable market lettings in the area. Both give the landlord greater rights to possession at the end of the term, but in the case of assured shorthold tenancies the landlord or his successors have the right to a court order for possession.

Corporate tenants

Corporate tenants are excluded from the security of tenure provisions of all the Acts, though tenancies predating 15 January 1989 are subject to the rent officer's assessment of a fair rent. Care must be taken to ensure that all sublettings to company employees are genuine, as 'sham' arrangements may result in a secure sub-tenancy.

Long leasehold houses (over 21 years)

Houses or flats let on long leases were common, particularly in the major cities. Under the Leasehold Reform Act 1967 the lessees of the majority were granted the right to enfranchise or purchase their freeholds.

Under the Leasehold Reform, Housing and Urban Development Act 1993 these rights of enfranchisement, subject to a number of conditions and exceptions, were extended to higher value leaseholders previously excluded from the 1967 Act.

General

In the case of old regulated tenancies, a 100 per cent or more increase in capital value can be released if vacant possession is gained.

Let houses and flats are considered a safe and secure form of investment if the location is selected carefully, management standards are high, and the investor understands the nature of the tenancy. Subject to the inevitable political risk of a change in legislation reversing the more favourable 1980s legislation, let houses and flats are now worthy of consideration.

10.2.3 Blocks of flats

The investment considerations for blocks of flats are similar to those for let houses and flats. However, the market in blocks of flats has tended to be determined by their 'break-up' value rather than by the income produced. This break-up value arises through an investor being able to acquire a complete block of flats at a figure which will enable him subsequently to dispose of the flats either to the occupying tenants or with vacant possession, if obtained, and so realise an overall capital gain.

In the late 1980s the competition for blocks of flats having a break-up value was dramatic. However, it is a high risk form of investment, as there is no guarantee of obtaining vacant possession, having regard to the high degree of security of tenure enjoyed by most tenants. Recently tenants have formed their own associations to try to control their landlords' operations, and the political risks and social problems for an investor operating in this market are considerable.

The situation is confused by the fact that tenants of flats were granted, amongst other things, under the Landlord and Tenant Act 1987, a right of first refusal if the landlord decided to sell his interest.

Further, the Leasehold Reform, Housing and Urban Development Act 1993 gave tenants, subject to complex rules and criteria, the right to initiate either the purchase of the freehold of their block of flats or an extension of their leases.

However, there have been a number of highly publicised abuses of the rules by certain landlords, and further legislation seems inevitable.

10.2.4 Holiday homes and time sharing

With increasing leisure time, the demand for holiday homes in the UK (which vary from a site on which to park a caravan to a substantial secondary house) has increased very considerably. The value of these properties is very much related to the personal choice of the purchaser, who is greatly affected by the ease of access to and from the major conurbations and the environment when he gets there. Lettings of these properties for holiday purposes are exempt from Rent Act protection. They can be good investments, with the added advantage that they can provide holiday accommodation for the family as well.

Holiday homes may also be purchased abroad. Specialist advice needs to be taken on such matters as local exchange control, the mechanics of purchase and availability of services. Good agents and lawyers are even more essential abroad than in the UK.

Partly as a result of this, a new concept of property ownership known as 'time sharing' became popular in the late 1980s. In essence, this provides for the investor to acquire an interest for a stated period (a week or a month) in each year in perpetuity or for a period of years. It effectively widens the spectrum of investment to encompass the smaller investor who can secure holiday accommodation with the added potential of capital growth.

It is sometimes associated with questionable sales techniques and even fraud, but it is an interesting concept for those who have limited funds which would otherwise be insufficient to purchase a holiday home. If the owner does not wish to use the accommodation each year, the property can often be exchanged if the location is in a major resort.

The method of sale varies according to the country, some properties being sold freehold and others on long leaseholds. An annual service payment is payable by the owner, together with the cost of electricity, water and other services used during a vacation. There are a number of companies specialising in this market who advertise nationally.

Holiday homes can be a sound investment but location is critical. If abroad, there are many possible pitfalls, not the least of which can be guaranteeing sound title.

10.3 PREVIEW OF THE YEAR AHEAD

Whilst the forthcoming General Election clouds the scene at the time of writing, turnover is recovering at healthy levels for realistically priced residential properties and most 'negative equity' positions are unwinding themselves.

The next year should therefore be characterised by increasing levels of turnover into those areas not yet benefiting, and values starting to rise in other areas as demand and supply move into balance.

Shortage is already a problem in the top end of the market which is likely to see the greatest growth in values.

11

AGRICULTURAL LAND, WOODLANDS AND MISCELLANEOUS

GEOFFREY J ABBOTT

Dip FBA (Lon) FRICS

Head of Sales and Purchases Department
and Investment Partner of Smiths Gore (Chartered Surveyors)

11.1 INTRODUCTION

The last two decades have been a period of dramatic change for the land using industries, in perceptions of desirable land uses generally and in the pressures on rural land of our predominantly urban population. Since 1939, pressure to increase self-sufficiency in both agricultural and forest products had led to significant changes in crop and livestock selection/husbandry and the rapid incorporation of modern technology into the rural industries.

During the 1980s, the domestic Green lobby and 'conservation interests' became increasingly significant, overlaid by international concerns such as damage to the ozone layer and global warming. The issues underlying these pressures for change are complex yet, because the great mass of our urban population has little direct contact with the countryside, the problems in the countryside are often seen in oversimplistic terms and the positions taken up can be illogical and/or inconsistent.

Further, few have yet acknowledged that the achievement of these objectives will ultimately have a dramatic effect on the life-styles and work practices of our urban populations. The majority of gasses which attack the ozone layer and cause acid rain emanate from urban chimneys, heating systems and exhaust pipes. Similarly much of the pollution in our rivers is the result of discharges from urban factories and sewage works.

The countryside is about diversity. An investment primarily in one form of land use will often directly or indirectly involve other land uses as well. Houses and woods are an integral part of farmland and all often overlay mineral deposits and are the natural habitat of the sportsman's quarry.

Throughout this chapter we seek to indicate typical cash yields on the various forms of land use but obviously many of the benefits of owning country property, which influence its value, do not come in the form of annual income.

Many purchasers of a vacant farm also get a nice house to live in and perhaps an interesting shoot as well; development possibilities (whether in the form of houses, leisure uses or mineral workings) or favourable capital or inheritance tax treatment in the future earn no income today; the surrender of the tenancy of a house or farm in due course can release significant latent capital value; and the mere ownership of a certain stretch of countryside can give the owner great personal satisfaction.

It is these factors and the post-war investment track record of country property which explain the historically relatively low initial yield typically earned on most forms of investment in land.

The much maligned Common Agricultural Policy in Europe is increasingly becoming involved in conservation objectives as opposed to product price support.

11.2 AGRICULTURAL LAND

11.2.1 Background

Usable agricultural land in Great Britain totals approximately 45,000,000 acres of which about 66 per cent is owner/occupied or vacant, and 33 per cent is subject to tenancy. They form two very separate markets with significant valuation and yield differences for otherwise physically similar properties. Within these overall totals there is an enormous diversity of soil types, topography, climate and physical location to which individual farmers apply their financial resources and technical/managerial skills. The result is the diverse range of land uses and end products still found in the countryside today.

Investors are strongly recommended initially to reflect quietly on Table 11.1 overleaf. Whatever the financial resources and skills he has to bring to bear on the property he buys, its many physical and climatic characteristics will rule the uses to which it is suited. Field scale bulb growing is only economic on the better soils and hardwood trees simply will not survive on solid rock at high altitudes. Finally, a good livestock farmer is seldom a good arable farmer and *vice versa*.

Within both the vacant and let (often referred to as 'investment') land markets there are therefore many sub-markets within which properties suited to different principal agricultural uses are grouped.

Table 11.1 Approximate distribution of soil grades and land uses

Soil Grade	England		Wales		Scotland		Great Britain		Principal Farming/ Forestry Uses	Principal Alternative Uses
	Percentage	Acres 000s	Percentage	Acres 000s	Percentage	Acres 000s	Percentage	Acres 000s		
I	3.3	806	0.2	8	0.3	49	1.9	863	Intensive arable cropping eg bulbs, vegetables, roots & cereals. No forestry.	Coarse fishing in drainage channels and lowly valued pheasant shooting. Principally 'dull' flatland but greater potential on poorer Grade II land out of Fens and similar areas
II	16.7	4,083	2.3	96	2.3	383	10.2	4,562	Arable cropping/intensive grassland eg cereals with roots and/or dairy cows. Limited forestry.	
III	54.0	13,203	17.5	729	13.6	2,175	36.1	16,107	Extensive arable cropping, rotational grassland eg cereals, oilseed rape & beans or grass leys for dairy cows, beef, sheep. Hardwood forestry mainly.	Pheasant/partridge shooting/roe deer stalking. Game fishing if suitable rivers/streams. Limited B&B, pony trekking etc.
IV	15.7	3,838	44.2	1,842	10.2	1,631	16.4	7,311	Permanent grassland/rough grazing eg beef and sheep rearing with limited dairying & cereals. Commercial softwood forestry.	Grouse shooting, Red deer stalking on open hill. Roe deer stalking in softwood plantations. Game fishing where suitable water. Extensive B&B, pony trekking, hill walking, rock climbing etc.
V	10.3	2,518	35.8	1,491	73.5	11,775	35.4	15,784	Rough grazings often with rock outcrops, eg principally summer grazing with hardy sheep breeds & hill cattle. Limited softwood forestry.	
TOTAL	100	24,448	100	4,166	100	16,013	100	44,627		

Note: MAFF Grades for England and Wales with Scottish equivalent.

Investors should also appreciate that a farmer runs a business. Like any other business, the actual financial results on any individual farm, however well the farming system is suited to the property, will reflect his managerial/technical skills and commercial judgements. As reflected in the rental market, the profit potential of a good farm is significantly greater than a poor farm. However, managerial skills on the individual farm remain critical to that unit's actual profitability. There are plenty of examples of poor farmers on the best land going out of business and good farmers on the poorest land making good money.

All investors should make a firm policy of sitting down with their advisers regularly to review whether this property or that one should still be owned or sold or perhaps passed down to the next generation. As part of these regular reviews, the potential of all land for higher value alternative uses should also be considered together with actions which might help to ensure its eventual release.

Could that droughty field cover potentially valuable gravel deposits, or might the field by the village be developed in 20 years' time? If the answer is yes, consideration should then be given of whether you will need that money in due course or whether it would make more sense to pass the land down to the next generation at purely agricultural value. Finally, a well-screened site is more likely to receive planning consent in due course than a prominent one out in the open. Should a belt of trees be planted now?

11.2.2 Highlights of the previous year

The farmland markets have continued to experience a strong recovery in values at a time of very limited supply. Vacant cereal growing land benefited most but even beef and dairy holdings held up well against a background of the BSE crisis.

Gross yields on let land have fallen by a further 0.75 per cent over the year and typically now lie around 3.8 per cent on the rents passing.

Demand for residential estates has also shown similar strength, though the importance of a balanced property has been well demonstrated.

The two most notable deals of the year were in the Midlands. In May 1996 the 1,600 acre Grade II/III soil commercial cereal growing Hatton Rock Farms north of Stratford-upon-Avon were offered in a competitive climate and quickly sold for over £4,000 per acre. The 6,890 acre multi-let Croome Estate soon followed and was sold to a traditional institution to show 3.7 per cent gross on the rent passing.

11.2.3 Vacant possession land

As vacant farmland represents over two-thirds of all farmland in Great Britain it is obviously the principal land market. By definition it is freehold land offered for sale with vacant possession or available for the purchaser to physically occupy. Over the years between 1 and 2 per cent is offered for sale on average each year in packages from five acres of bareland to 5,000 acres fully equipped with houses and buildings. However, offerings in recent years have been well below both historic levels and demand.

The principal buyers of most commercial farmland are normally farmers who buy the land to farm, though many others buy from time to time for various reasons. The market for particularly attractive stretches of countryside with high quality houses or for Scottish sporting estates is dominated by the wealthy, and in some cases the international wealthy, for reasons unlinked to the income which they may be able to earn from ownership of the property. In the case of land overlying potentially valuable minerals or which may be developed over in the future, the more imaginative investors or mineral operators and developers will normally compete to purchase.

Vacant possession land has been a very satisfactory investment since the Second World War, but values have fluctuated over the years and timing, as in all investment, has been a major factor for the most successful.

Given the diversity of the markets and understandable regional variations over time, reliable statistics about past land value trends are very difficult – and potentially dangerous if used for short-term comparisons. The only series which stretches back over the whole of the post-war period is the Oxford Institute/Savills series but it is based on averaging vacant land sales *at auction*. It can therefore make no allowance for properties withdrawn 'in the room' and subsequently sold privately. Further, it probably disproportionately reflects grassland value trends as auction is a more common method of sale in the livestock areas. It remains, however, the best guide to value trends over time and is set out in Table 11.2 opposite.

When selecting in which part of the country to buy, the private investor is understandably usually influenced by his background. As a general rule, investors in straight farmland should seek to acquire the best land in the chosen area, because history shows that given a competent level of farm management, the best land generates the greatest profits over the years.

Further, outside of the wholly commercial areas of farming such as the Fens, farmland with an attractive appearance has always tended to sell for a premium value. As conservation considerations become increasingly influential, the land markets are reflecting the conservation value of

Table 11.2 Average vacant land values at auction

With Possession £/acre		With Possession £/acre	
1951	88	74	636
52	76	75	539
53	73	76	734
54	75	77	991
55	80	78	1,327
56	78	79	1,769
57	73	**1980**	1,726
58	85	81	1,729
59	101	82	1,844
1960	123	83	2,082
61	124	84	1,978
62	134	85	1,935
63	168	86	1,697
64	214	87	2,001
65	235	88	2,178
66	242	89	2,654
67	258	**1990**	2,568
68	280	91	2,431
69	299	92	2,202
1970	245	93	2,208
71	262	94	2,333
72	596	95	2,484
73	757	96	3,560

otherwise well-farmed land. Enhancing the wildlife value of a property, by well-planned hardwood tree planting, pond maintenance and sensitive management of ancient pastures, should be an on-going management consideration of all investors.

In recent years an increasing level of grants and subsidies has been available for conservation policies, which are often based on the poorer quality soils. Increasing levels of such reliable 'high quality' income from government sources may well seriously distort the value of such inherently poor soils.

CAP reform has also established the form of agricultural support for the future — away from encouraging ever increasing output per acre and towards fixed payments per acre cropped or breeding livestock maintained, with currently 5 per cent of arable land being Set Aside.

Remembering what was said earlier about the importance of management to the actual financial results (see **11.2.1**), and that some of the benefits of owning vacant farmland do not come in the form of cash income, the monetary benefits for a well run unit may be expected typically to work out as shown in Table 11.3 overleaf.

Table 11.3 Monetary benefits of farm ownership per acre

	Intensive Arable	Extensive Arable	Dairy (inc. Quota)	Livestock Rearing	Hill Farming (inc. Sheep Quota)
Land Value, say	£4,250	£3,000	£5,500	£2,250	£1,000
Working Capital, say	550	450	1,300	550	450
TOTAL CAPITAL	£4,800	£3,450	£6,800	£2,800	£1,450
Net Profit, say (inc. rental value)	£400	£250	£415	£100	£100
Annual Return, say	8.33%	7.25%	6.10%	3.57%	6.90%

Source: *Smiths Gore Farm Management*

These overall yields, being an amalgam of the secure return to the investor as landowner (in the form of rental value of around 50 per cent of the net profit) and the higher risk return to him as a trading farmer, reflect the fact that farming is passing through a profitable phase. Also the vacant value of the farm is typically 200 per cent or more of its let land value.

There are many options open to the investor for the management of his vacant farm or land and he should take professional advice. He may manage his farm personally, or farm in partnership with another farmer, or he may have a contractual or profit-sharing arrangement with another farmer. Following the passing of the Agricultural Tenancies Act 1995, land previously 'let' on these complex arrangements is increasingly being let on new Farm Business Tenancies structured to suit the circumstances of the individuals.

The method chosen will depend on the investor's income requirement, managerial ability and capital situation. The choice will affect the amount of farming capital required, the level of return obtained, and the extent of involvement in the day-to-day running of the investment.

'Intensive livestock' is a specialist form of farming and is restricted mainly to pigs, poultry (chickens and turkeys), veal, barley beef and salmon or trout. These enterprises are usually capital-intensive in buildings and equipment and are restricted to small acreages (two to 20 acres). The investment can be speculative and the return is very dependent on expert management in a volatile market.

11.2.4 **Let or investment land**

'Let' or 'investment' land comprises about 33 per cent of the total usable agricultural acreage of Great Britain, having declined from around 90 per cent at the turn of the century. Most land is let under the old Agricultural Holdings Acts (AHA lettings) to a tenant who pays a rent and the investor may therefore not be able to live on the property or to farm it himself.

Traditionally, let land was worth two-thirds or more of its value with vacant possession. However, in the post-war period, legislation affecting the landlord/tenant relationship was seen as favouring the latter, and taxation policy has tended to favour the owner-occupier. As a result, AHA lettings are now generally worth only half of the land's vacant value.

From September 1995 all new lettings of farms (not being succession tenancies under the old Agricultural Holdings Act) are in the form of Farm Business Tenancies (FBTs) covered by the new Act. Subject to the length of the tenancy granted, the value differential between vacant and let land should be less.

Investment opportunities vary from single let farms to large residential estates; from 10 acres up to 5,000 acres or more.

AHA lettings are technically annual tenancies but which actually give security for life, indeed often with rights of succession, subject to certain rules, for up to three generations. However, one interesting court case (*Saunders v Ralph*) suggests that the succession rights under the 1976 Act may be retrospective in certain circumstances. Let farms which have passed down through the family for a number of generations may therefore have no further succession rights attaching to them.

The tenancy agreement must be examined by a professional adviser, since it forms the basis for all matters affecting the investment in the future.

Rent levels vary. Rents fixed under the old Agricultural Holdings Acts may be 50 per cent below the rents obtainable from FBT lettings. Examples of sitting tenant AHA rents per acre compared to FBT rents might be:

(1) for well-equipped Grade I or II soil arable farms in the Fens: £90 as opposed to £180 or more;
(2) for well-equipped Grade II or III soil arable farms (not Fens) and well-equipped dairy farms; £60 as opposed to up to £120; and
(3) for poorer land or poorly equipped farms: £40 as opposed to £80.

Currently three yearly rent reviews on AHA lettings are showing between 7 and 10 per cent compound annual growth.

Under most AHA tenancy agreements the landlord is responsible for insuring and for a major part of the cost of repairs to the houses and buildings though full repairing and insuring tenancies became common from the early 1970s.

Most AHA let land is owned by private families as part of substantial estates passed down through the generations, or is held by traditional institutions such as the Crown, the Church and numerous colleges and charities, most of whom buy for the long term.

Tenanted land may be one-third of the total stock of farmland in Great Britain but, because of this ownership pattern, only represents a very small part of the total farmland market each year. Supply to the market obviously varies but last year only 36,000 acres passed through the open market. This is only about a third of what was typical in the 1970s.

Currently, buyers of let farms are a broadly based group comprising tenants buying in their farms, private investors, family trusts, certain charities, both traditional and financial institutions and some foreign investors.

Management is customarily undertaken by professional firms of chartered surveyors, with land agency departments, or by resident agents on larger estates.

Investors should be aware that there is no fixed relationship between gross and net yields. A typical gross yield today of 3.8 per cent might net back on a full repairing and insuring let farm to 3.25 per cent, whereas on a traditional landlord repairing and insuring let estate it might be under 2.5 per cent in the short term. However, that let estate may well have latent potential to be released by active management which may compensate for the lower initial net yield. Each investment opportunity must be viewed on its own merits.

11.2.5 Finance

The basic rule for the investor in farmland is that he should have the majority of the funds available in cash. Except in special circumstances farmland investments should not be made on the back of borrowed money. The gross initial return to a typical investment in a let farm is currently only 4 to 5 per cent. Investment in a similar vacant farm is typically twice as high so the return to his investment in land (being the rental value of that land) is currently 2 to 2.5 per cent. A significant proportion of the purchase price therefore borrowed at say 7.5 per cent cannot be funded by the farm.

Within the agricultural industry, facilities for short-term borrowings of working capital are commonly provided by the clearing banks. Merchants' credit can also be taken but, when allowance is made for the discounts which may be lost, it can prove very expensive. Medium-term finance for machinery purchases, etc may also be provided by the clearing banks and various finance/leasing houses.

Long-term finance to the industry has traditionally been provided by the Agricultural Mortgage Corporation and the Scottish Agricultural Securities Corporation, with the main clearing banks participating more recently. Subject to the borrower's ability to service the loan, up to two-thirds of the agricultural value of a farm can usually be borrowed at competitive rates which may be variable or fixed and be for up to 40 years. Interest is normally tax allowable and repayment of principal is commonly by way of linked life policies.

11.2.6 Preview of the year ahead

With lower food reserves around the world, very volatile product prices and a stronger Sterling, the agricultural industry faces a less certain future than twelve months ago.

The excessive levels of demand of a year ago for commercial farmland have already thinned, and values look set to plateau for the current year. However, demand for residential amenity farms is increasing with the wider economic recovery, and values may well rise in these sectors.

11.3 WOODLANDS

11.3.1 Background

Woodlands cover just over 5 million acres or about 10 per cent of the surface area of Great Britain. This compares with between 20 to 30 per cent in most EU countries. Ninety per cent of UK timber consumption is imported, at a cost of £7.2bn in 1990. Annual timber production in Great Britain grew from about 3.5 million cubic metres in 1980 to 5.35 million cubic metres at the end of the decade. It is forecast to grow to 10 million cubic metres by around 2000. Consumption is also expected to rise over the period.

Of the national forest, some 25 per cent is made up of hardwoods (often referred to as deciduous woodlands) and 75 per cent is made up of softwoods (often referred to as coniferous or evergreen – but note the deciduous larch). Woodlands and forests take three principal forms.

Amenity and sporting woods and copses

These are normally found in lowland Great Britain in the form of hardwoods or mixtures. They are usually relatively small and can be politically sensitive locally, often being covered by Tree Preservation Orders. Whilst individual trees may be substantial and of significant value, these woods have little to do with commercial timber production. However, they can provide great enjoyment and satisfaction to the buyer.

Larger blocks of hardwoods

Typically found in lowland Britain, they can have a significant value but day-to-day management is often influenced by sporting and conservation considerations. Originally they formed parts of larger estates and can prove a very worthwile investment.

Commercial softwood plantations and forests

These are commonly found in the higher rainfall areas of the country, principally in the hills of Wales, the north of England and Scotland, with other pockets such as the Breckland Sands around Thetford on the Norfolk/Suffolk borders and the New Forest in Hampshire. Being based on fast-growing trees well suited to both the pulp industry and the saw-wood market, they are the backbone of commercial forestry. Conifers grow in western Britain almost twice as fast as in Scandinavia, Russia and most of North America, thus providing shorter rotations and a long-term competitive advantage.

Of the national forest approximately 40 per cent is owned by the Forestry Commission and 60 per cent by private investors/estates. The Forestry Commission was established in 1919 to encourage private owners to restore the productivity of their 3 million acres of woodland ravaged by fellings during the First World War and to create a State Forest of 1.75 million acres. The Commission's current estate is just over 2 million acres and principally made up of softwoods. As part of the wider privatisation programme, the Forestry Commission has had a target of selling 250,000 acres, or just over 10 per cent of its forestry portfolio, by the end of the decade.

Whilst the privately owned forest is more balanced overall between hardwoods and softwoods, the former tends to be owned by farmers and estate owners in lowland Britain. Much of the latter is in the hills having often been established by investors during the 1960s, 1970s and 1980s, with substantial incomes from other sources motivated by tax planning considerations available at the time.

Forestry planting still attracts substantial grants though forestry costs can no longer be offset against other income. The ownership of woods also has other valuable advantages:

(1) income from productive woodlands is tax free;
(2) assets comprising forestry business qualify for 100 per cent relief from inheritance tax after two years' ownership;
(3) the land element can attract capital gains tax rollover relief.

Investment in woodlands is essentially about investing in relatively low value land with a growing crop on it the rotation life of which may typically range from 40 years for some fast-growing conifers to 100 or 200 years for slower growing hardwoods. Normally, the first 20 years or more are about outgoings to establish the crop and manage it through to production age. From the commencement of thinnings, income may be expected to pick up from humble beginnings every five years for softwoods and ten years for hardwoods through to the bulk of the income from the felling of the final crop. A softwood crop planted today may be expected to show an internal rate of return of around 5 per cent per annum over the life of the crop.

Alternatively an investor may acquire an established plantation already in production and obtain a tax-free income. Such a wood is typically valued on the basis of a discounting of the expected net income stream in the 5 to 7 per cent range.

The underlying economic argument for investing in forestry is that the world has been consuming its forests at well in excess of sustainable growth rates for many decades. A significant shortfall of timber is therefore likely in the future. However, as much of the world's timber reserves are in the Third World, which is primarily concerned with short-term survival, the supply of timber on to the world markets may continue at in excess of growth rates. However conservationists were able to halt felling over a large area of the US in 1992 to protect the habitat of the Spotted Owl. This directly affected the supply and price of timber in 1992–93.

11.3.2 Market trends

Demand for attractive amenity woods and established commercial woodlands with a positive cash flow remains strong. With the value of the former underwritten by various conservation bodies, similarly well-roaded areas of good softwoods in production areas close to markets are highly sought after, with plantations in the 'golden triangle' in south Scotland achieving premium prices.

However poorer areas of softwoods in isolated areas, with poor access or younger plantations many years away from production, are heavily discounted.

11.4 MISCELLANEOUS LAND USES

11.4.1 Accommodation land

Accommodation land refers to small areas within a farm or estate which do not naturally fit in with the main land uses. They are often held for alternative use at a later date or as grazing land for conservation purposes (for instance a small area of permanent grassland). The expression can also be taken to mean those small areas of farmland which come up for sale from time to time, typically on the edge of a village or town.

Because of the limited acreage, accommodation land often appeals to the smaller investor with limited funds available, although it is usually more expensive to buy per acre than normal farmland. For the investor prepared to take on the problems of management and supervision they can sometimes generate a significant income from pony grazing. A portfolio of such units can give outstanding performance over the years if planning consent for an alternative high value use (eg residential development) is granted on one or more areas of accommodation land.

Accommodation land with vacant possession is sometimes held unused, but more often let on short-term arrangements.

Grazing for ponies and horses is normally done on a per head per week payment basis and often generates a premium income. Horses are however choosy grazers and pasture deterioration usually results from horse grazing over the years.

On specialist dairy/beef farms, other people's sheep are often bought in 'on tack' during the winter months to tidy up the pastures. Payment is usually on a per head per week basis.

11.4.2 Sporting rights

Sporting rights normally form an integral part of any land sale. Over most properties they form a minor element of capital value within the overall transaction. However, on Scottish sporting estates they are often the main constituent of value, assessed by past records of the bag or catch. In such cases ease of access will be a significant factor.

Sporting rights may be divided into three main categories:

(1) fishing – game and coarse;
(2) shooting – driven and rough;
(3) stalking – red and roe deer.

Sporting rights in England and Wales can be a legal estate and are on occasions reserved out of the sale of agricultural land and woods. In

Scotland, only salmon fishing rights can form a separate legal estate. They may therefore be acquired separately from the land for personal use or letting, and timesharing of stretches of well-known fishing rivers has become common. Since 1 April 1989 VAT has been payable on that element of the value of a land sale which relates to the value of the sporting facility. However a transaction will normally only become taxable where a sporting income or value is separately identifiable. There is a further concession that farm tenants will only be expected to pay VAT on the sporting element of their tenancy agreements if it is greater than 5 per cent of total rent.

The recent recession hit demand for sporting rights and values but both are now recovering.

Fishing

Salmon fishing

Capital values of salmon fishing vary enormously according to location and river reputation but can range up to £6,000 a fish or more. Sea trout are considerably less valuable. Rents can range from £50 to £500 per rod per day. Pollution and salmon disease can have a devastating effect on both rental and capital values. Salmon fisheries cannot be created artificially, and are principally associated with rivers in Scotland and parts of Wales and the West Country.

Trout fishing

This can be on freshwater chalk streams in the south (which command the highest rates and prices), on other rivers generally or on artificial or natural lakes or reservoirs. Demand has been high with rents almost matching salmon river rates on the very best chalk streams. There is evidence of some over-supply of man-made trout lakes in certain areas.

Coarse fishing

Coarse fishing normally occurs in standing or slower-flowing waters in middle England and East Anglia which are usually rented by angling associations or smaller syndicates. Prices and rents vary greatly but old ponds may provide a surprisingly large income close to large centres of population.

Shooting

Shooting rights are, subject to economic conditions, readily lettable to a growing number of field sports enthusiasts. Shoots vary from a well-organised grouse moor in Scotland or the north with accommodation, through to substantial pheasant or partridge shoots in the south or east, perhaps let by the day with beaters and a cordon bleu lunch, down to a rough shoot over a small farm enjoyed informally by friends. Sporting rents vary from significant sums on the very best shoots to a minor additional income to the farm of £1 or £2 per acre. Charges for the best pheasant shoots, mainly in the south, lie in the £17.50 to £25 per bird range, with the best grouse moors in the north and Scotland ranging up to £75 per brace after some disastrous breeding seasons.

Deer stalking

Red, Fallow, Roe, Sika and Muntjac deer are the quarry, though Red and Roe deer are the principal species. In the UK, Red deer stalking on the open heather hills of the Highlands of Scotland is the most well-known and the most highly valued at a cost of up to £250 per stag. Roe deer stalking is traditionally more highly valued on mainland Europe, but commercial lettings in suitable locations are becoming increasingly popular in the UK at between £125 and £400 per buck.

The build up of Roe deer numbers throughout the woods of Great Britain has resulted in professional stalkers shooting from high seats for vermin control purposes and the value of the carcasses. Red deer are also controlled in this way in the Thetford Forest in East Anglia. However, in the south west Red deer, and in the New Forest Fallow deer, are more commonly controlled by hunting with hounds.

Sporting generally

Sound game, vermin and habitat management practices can enhance the holding capacity and sporting qualities of a property but they cannot change the nature of it. For instance, grouse will only survive, let alone thrive, on a well-managed heather moor in the hills of the north or Scotland which benefits from peace, quiet and vermin control.

Corporate entertaining has increasingly influenced rental levels on the best sporting estates over the last 20 years but the quality of service they demand is also high. Commercial lettings of sporting rights are seldom therefore profitable in their own right but more a means of subsidising the owner's hobby.

Quality sporting rights as a separate investment is normally only for the very wealthy investor who can afford an often substantial capital payment, perhaps millions of pounds, with the prospect of significant annual outgoings. The less wealthy must therefore limit their ambitions to more humble rough shooting, a gun on a syndicate shoot or the purchase of a time share on a suitable river. For most investors, sporting rights will be an indirect benefit of the purchase of a farm, wood or estate.

Market trends

With increasing wealth, leisure time and transport facilities, demand for sporting rights has been increasing steadily. Capital performance has generally been very satisfactory with the market for the very best becoming international. However, they are about enjoying expensive hobbies and the recent recession had affected demand both to buy and rent sporting facilities though most sporting lettings found tenants again last year.

11.4.3 Stud farms and training establishments

Stud farms

Agricultural land may be developed for the breeding of thoroughbred bloodstock, riding horses or ponies. The demand has been increasing with over two million people now members of the various horse societies. For stud farms in the most favoured locations, such as Newmarket, Lambourn and Malton, demand remains relatively strong, although values have fallen and demand has slumped in locations further from the recognised breeding centres where the main stallions stand. The centre of the national bloodstock industry is Newmarket where the National Stud and Tattersalls Sale Paddocks, which have a worldwide reputation, are both based. Stud farms in the favoured areas command a substantial premium over VP farmland.

The environment of a good stud farm is of great importance if the young stock are to grow and develop properly. The type of soil, particularly to facilitate the building of bone, is critical and the best are to be found on free draining chalk soils. A stud farm typically varies in size from 50 to 250 acres and may be a private stud (where the owner maintains his own animals only) or a public stud (where one or more stallions are kept and the mares visit during the covering season and often the foaling season as well). Stables must be of high standard with special boxes and facilities for covering and foaling purposes. The cost of putting up post and rail fencing is high because of the need for small paddocks and double fences.

To establish a stud farm can take up to 20 years for the hedges and shelter belts to mature. Good quality residential accommodation at the stud will be required for the stud groom and other employees: for a medium-sized stud a minimum of five to six houses might be required.

Stud farms usually change hands by private treaty in a limited and highly specialised market. Purchasers will usually be closely connected with the bloodstock industry. It is exceptional for stud farms to be bought as an investment on a tenanted basis.

Training establishments or yards

At various centres in the country, but particularly at Newmarket, Lambourn and Malton, there are established training facilities with extensive gallops and all weather tracks. Training yards usually comprise a trainer's house together with a number of cottages and hostels for stable lads; a minimum of 15 boxes with tack, feed and hay stores; and often special open and covered exercising areas. Business rates are payable on both stud farms and training yards.

Market trends

The specialised markets for both stud farms and training yards had been expanding throughout most of the 1980s with the best being in a truly international market. However, the recent recession hit the racing industry hard. Most owners of studs are men of substantial wealth who weathered the troubles.

Many owners of training yards were not similarly endowed and many had increased their facilities during the late 1980s. The fall in values and the number of losses in training hurt them badly. However, with the economy strengthening, demand should now pick up fast.

11.4.4 Mineral bearing land

All minerals other than oil, gold, silver and coal usually belong to the freehold owner of land but may have been reserved to a predecessor in title. On acquisition, purchasers should always check that the mineral rights are included. The principal minerals are coal, sand, gravel, silica sand (glass), iron-stone, clay (brickmaking or china), limestone and in certain areas other special deposits (tin, copper, etc). With limited exceptions all coal belongs to The Coal Authority and oil/gas deposits to the government.

Strict planning regulation affects mineral excavation and specified areas are designated in most County Plans. Virtually no excavation is permitted on land classified as Grade I or II. Geological maps indicate the approximate location of minerals and resistivity surveys and test borings can establish mineral deposit patterns, depths and volumes. Development is usually carried out through a sale or lease to one of the principal operating companies.

The sale of mineral-bearing land incurs capital gains tax on chargeable gains. Profits from the commercial operation of mineral workings are liable to income tax (or corporation tax), with capital allowances (including a depletion allowance of, in general, 50 per cent of the royalty rate of the minerals) available for certain expenditure. Mineral royalties are taxed, broadly, as one-half as income and the other half as capital.

Tipping, fishing, boating and water skiing rights may be reserved and provide high levels of income and reversionary asset value on completion of excavation. The 'hole in the ground' was often worth more than the original land. However, with the evolving principle that 'the polluter shall pay', and the new tipping tax on landfill sites of £2 per ton of inert materials and £7 per ton of degradable materials, this situation is changing.

The end value of restored land is currently uncertain, and any hint of noxious materials on site could result in a negative value.

Minerals are a speculative investment if the land is purchased by an investor other than a mineral operator with mineral exploitation specifically in view. However, some farmland can produce high yields from unexpected mineral excavation. High prices should not be paid merely to hold a speculative 'mineral bank'.

11.4.5 Public leisure/entertainment, retail land uses and commercial uses for redundant farm buildings

Like most subsidiary forms of land use, these categories are all relatively marginal to the whole but potentially significant profit centres on individual properties in the right locations. The managerial skills required are, however, very different from those of a farmer or forester and, if management of the main activity is not to suffer, they are best treated as a separate activity. Their common characteristic is that they are intended to appeal to the general public. They come in three main categories, though they often overlap with each other.

The passive leisure land uses

The obvious examples are leased golf courses, caravan and camping sites and mobile home parks – though the higher the standard of the site and more extensive the facilities (a shop for instance) the less managerially passive they become.

These properties are usually located at or near seaside areas or in areas of scenic beauty. Mobile home parks may be for permanent (all year round) occupation in certain areas specified by local councils. Planning controls are stringent on all large-scale parks or sites. Special facilities are required under the Caravan Sites and Control of Development Act 1960 including washing and toilet facilities, electricity and roads. The Mobile Homes Act 1975 confers on caravan home owners a limited security of

ALLIED DUNBAR INVESTMENT & SAVINGS HANDBOOK

tenure. Planning permission is almost always required and not easy to get in areas viewed as being of high landscape value.

An investment of this type can be lucrative but is high risk, demanding considerable pre-acquisition investigation. The Caravan Club provides information on sites and the pitfalls associated with them. Fashions change and the weather greatly affects the income from holiday parks, particularly in coastal areas, where serious storms can result in large losses. Whilst the recent recession has affected the market, it has been an expanding, if often visually undesirable, area for investment.

The active leisure entertainment land uses

These are typically wildlife parks, pleasure gardens, theme parks, riding schools/pony trekking centres and grand houses open to the public. Planning permission is required for wildlife parks, pleasure gardens, golf courses and riding schools. Location is of paramount importance since it is essential to be close to urban populations with good road access. Initial development costs are high. It is probable that future legislation and higher design and maintenance standards will further aggravate the position. For country houses it is specially important to check the building status for planning purposes, since 'listed' buildings are graded under the Town and Country Planning Act 1971 and the Town and Country Planning (Scotland) Act 1972, which impose varying degrees of responsibility on the owner, including the need to obtain listed building consent for demolition, improvements or even minor alterations.

Houses having historic and amenity value are frequently opened to the public as a trading venture, enabling the owner to continue to live in the family home. The trading venture is intended to support the upkeep of the property and its general environment, in addition to the tax advantages of a 'one estate election'. Other large houses have been acquired for institutional purposes, such as research centres, out of town offices, training centres and health farms.

The problems with marketing wildlife parks, and more recently golf courses, demonstrate that an investment of this kind is highly speculative in all but the prime locations. It is more often seen as a means to an end by existing owners rather than as the reason for a purchase.

Retail land uses

Farm shops and garden centres are the obvious examples. Farm shops are usually ancillary to farm businesses; they enable the farmer to obtain better prices than he would on the wholesale market by cutting out the middleman.

184

Garden centres are normally run by individuals or small companies, but in a few cases they are larger enterprises with multiple sites. Planning consent is required.

The location of both farm shops and garden centres is important, the best sites being on main roads and close to large centres of population. The increase in leisure has stimulated the popularity of these enterprises, supplying requisites to the keen gardener and also to consumers increasingly interested in fresh farm produce, especially for the deep freeze. The 'pick your own' method of sale at certain seasons can be successful and at farms where it is in operation good car parking facilities are essential.

Enterprises of this kind can be a valuable source of additional income and capital if correctly developed out of a farm unit (which is usually owner/occupied) but they are seldom sold as investments.

Commercial uses for redundant farm buildings

The Government White Paper 'Rural England – A Nation Committed to a Living Countryside' pointed out that only 1.3 per cent of those living in the countryside now actually earn a living off the land. Now, 31 per cent of manufacturing and 25 per cent of service sector employment (and an even higher proportion of business start-ups) are based in the countryside.

Consequently, more and more planning authorities are viewing sympathetically well thought out schemes with good access for the re-use of redundant farm buildings.

SOURCES OF FURTHER INFORMATION

Useful addresses

Country Landowners Association
16 Belgrave Square
London
SW1X 8PQ

Tel: (0171) 235 0511

Department of the Environment
2 Marsham Street
London
SW1P 3EB

Tel: (0171) 276 3000

Agricultural Mortgage
  Corporation PLC
AMC House
Chanty Street
Andover, Hampshire
SP10 1DD

Tel: (01264) 334344

Ministry of Agriculture, Fisheries
and Food
Whitehall Place
London
SW1A 2HH

Tel: (0171) 270 3000

Agricultural Development and
Advisory Service (ADAS)
Oxford Spires Business Park
The Boulevard
Kidlington
Oxon OX5 1NZ

Tel: (01865) 842742

Royal Institution of Chartered
Surveyors (RICS)
12 Great George Street
London
SW1P 3AD

Tel: (0171) 222 7000

Incorporated Society of Valuers
and Auctioneers
3 Cadogan Gate
London
SW1X 0AS

Tel: (0171) 235 2282

Environment Agency
Kingfisher House
Goldhay Way
Orton Goldhay
Peterborough
PE2 0ZR

Tel: (01733) 371811

National Association of Estate
Agents
21 Jury Street
Warwick
CV34 4EH

Tel: (01926) 496800

Forestry Commission
231 Corstorphine Road
Edinburgh
EH12 7AT

Tel: (0131) 334 0303

Royal Institution of Chartered
Surveyors (Scottish Branch)
7–9 Manor Place
Edinburgh
EH3 7DN

Tel: (0131) 225 7078

Scottish Office of Agriculture and
Fisheries Department
Pentland House
47 Robb's Loan
Edinburgh EH14 1TY

Tel: (0131) 556 8400

Caravan Club
East Grinstead House
East Grinstead
West Sussex
RH19 1UA

Tel: (01342) 326944

Food From Britain
301–344 Market Towers
New Covent Garden Market
London
SW8 5NQ

Tel: (0171) 720 2144

Rural Development Commission
141 Castle Street
Salisbury
Wiltshire
SP1 3TP

Tel: (01722) 336255

12

COMMERCIAL PROPERTY

ANDREW BULL
ARICS, Partner in Jones Lang Wootton

12.1 INTRODUCTION

Review of 1996

Overview

The continuing low growth environment in those Continental European economies who are positioning themselves for Economic Monetary Union in 1999 is at least providing a stable backcloth for property, and as oversupplies decline and markets finally move out of recessionary mode, the prospects for a modest upturn are good, but there are no fireworks in sight. Free from the likelihood of first tranche EMU entry, the UK has bucked this trend, is already experiencing growth, and its markets are noticeably more buoyant than elsewhere in Europe.

In the office markets, activity continues to be driven by replacement demand and rationalisation. Genuine business expansion feeding through into new real estate requirements remains a rare event. However, the long flat trough at the bottom of the rental cycle has now been consigned to the past in most cases and rental growth at the prime end of the market should now be a real possibility for a number of cities in 1997.

Retail turnover remains flat in most countries, and in consequence high-street rents are weak. The luxury end of the markets seems nonetheless in some cities immune to these problems, nowhere more evident than in Paris and London. The best shopping centres are continuing to attract good business and the growth of cross-border retail activity remains a strong feature.

In the investment sector, the interest rate decline has given property a boost which now looks good value in many cases set against other asset classes. Prime office yields have been hardening in consequence in a number of cities, driven down in particular in the UK and the Netherlands by the continuing appetite from the German open-ended funds. Retail investment and the desire to reweight investment portfolios in its favour is strong, with Dutch, UK and now German cross-border demand noticeably increasing.

Speculative development remains very largely off the agenda, with major pre-commitments necessary in most cases to ignite enthusiasm and elicit finance. Against this trend, a new speculative development cycle is under way in central London.

United Kingdom

Office market conditions in London continued to improve during 1996. Demand for office space picked up significantly during the year, boosted by several major transactions Whilst take-up has improved, corporate rationalisation is resulting in the continued release of second-hand accommodation onto the market. However, the removal of obsolete office stock for conversion to alternative uses (eg hotel, residential) together with the recent low level of development activity has ensured that overall vacancy rates fell below 10 per cent during 1996. As a result, prime headline rents are under upward pressure, and tenant incentives are falling. Growing confidence in the real estate sector is resulting in increasing investment in office property by UK institutions and overseas investors.

Plans to build Europe's tallest skyscraper – the 385 metre Millennium Tower – in the City of London is also reflective of the level of confidence in the market. Elsewhere in the UK, strong demand from growth sectors is being offset by widespread rationalisation and cost cutting measures by major office occupiers, and as a result, net absorption remains low, and in general rents are stable.

The latest Central Statistical Office institutional property investment figures say the statistics reflect the surge in investor activity over the past six months.

Overall, UK institutions invested a net £170m in property during the third quarter of 1996; insurance companies were net investors to the sum of £480m and investment trusts to the tune of £60m. Pension funds were actually net disinvestors by £370m. This sum is not, however, lost to the property sector as the larger funds are now reinvesting these receipts to upgrade the quality of their portfolios. Meanwhile, the smaller funds are seeking an exposure to property through indirect media.

Jones Lang Wootton Investment Partner, John Stephen comments:

> 'The general recovery in the economy has boosted confidence in the property sector; the prospect of improving property returns has led to investment activity taking off over the last 6 months. Fund Managers want to get into a rising market which is attractive when compared with the current volatility in the equity and gilt markets.
>
> The retail sector, buoyed by the upturn in consumer spending, is the focus of buying attention. Shopping centres, retail warehouse parks and large shop units are keenly sought after. Investors are nevertheless selective in their

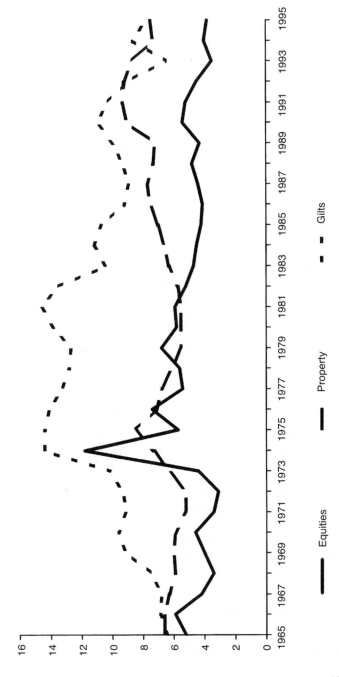

Figure 12.1 Property, equity and gilt yields 1965/95

Source: *Datastream, EIU, JLW, Hillier Parker*

Equities

Property

Gilts

requirements and have strict criteria determined by occupier trends. Retail warehouse parks will ideally have open retail planning consents without any restrictions on use, and prime unit shops should provide a minimum of 2,000 sq ft of well configured ground floor sales area.

It is interesting to note from the JLW Property Index that of the three traditional sectors, only retail showed positive rental growth every quarter for the 12 months to September 1996. The institutions clearly believe this trend will continue and are increasing their exposure accordingly.

As property has returned to favour, institutional investors are exploring opportunities in new areas including leisure, which is now an established sector in its own right. Institutions are considering investments in nursing homes, student accommodation and the private residential sector.

As UK and overseas institutions, particularly the German open ended funds, compete for a limited supply of suitable opportunities, there is now a ready market for lot sizes of £50m–£100m in London and the Regions.'

12.1.1 Types of investors

Property investments appeal to different types of investors dependent upon an investor's requirement for income or capital growth, and the level of risk the investor will accept. Properties can be subdivided according to location, type and size. Small industrial units and multi-million pound office investments are unlikely to be of interest to the same investor. Risk-averse investors such as insurance companies and pension funds will prefer to invest in 'prime' properties in established locations let to blue chip tenants on long full repairing and insuring leases. A factor of considerable importance to these investors is the security of rental income and capital gain. Other investors will, however, be prepared to accept a higher level of risk by purchasing 'secondary' properties if the return is considered to be sufficiently attractive.

The purchase of a commercial property involves the giving up of a capital sum now in exchange for future returns which can be either the benefits of owner-occupation, income flow and/or capital gain. Underlying any property investment decision will be the option of alternative investments, namely stocks, shares, cash, unit trusts and even works of art. In selecting an investment, the investor will seek the highest real rate of return on capital invested but, depending upon the object of the investment, may 'trade off' a reduced rate of return in consideration for increased liquidity or security of income. An investor's tax status will also be an important factor.

12.1.2 Property valuation

In its simplest form, the basis of property valuation is the capitalisation of rental income of a property over a term of years or in perpetuity (depending on whether the property is leasehold or freehold) at an investment rate of return which reflects all the elements of risk associated with that property (security of income, obsolescence of the building, economic factors and the cost/inconvenience of management). The capitalisation rate chosen to value the property will also reflect the expectation of future rental growth and consequently tends to be significantly lower than the yields available from fixed-interest securities. This phenomenon (also illustrated by the dividend yield of equities) is known as the 'reverse yield gap' and since the 1970s has varied between about 1 and 8 per cent.

12.2 TYPES OF COMMERCIAL PROPERTY

Direct investment in commercial property falls mainly into the following categories:

(1) retail including supermarkets and retail warehouses;
(2) offices including town centre, out of town and campus;
(3) industrial including factories, warehouses and hi-tech;

and, to a much lesser degree:

(4) farmland and forestry;
(5) leisure.

Most investors with a significant long-term investment portfolio aim to hold the majority of the investments balanced between the retail, office and industrial categories, where there is a well-defined investment market.

12.2.1 Purchase of commercial property

Due to the large amounts of capital required for the purchase of even the smallest commercial property, the commercial property investment market is, like the equity market, generally confined to UK and foreign insurance companies, pension fund and property companies, together with a number of wealthy private individuals or family trusts. UK insurance companies and pension funds began investing in commercial property in the mid-1950s, broadening their asset bases beyond the equities and government securities which had hitherto formed their principal media for investment. UK pension fund investment reached a peak as a percentage of their assets in 1979 and significant net new investment was not then seen until the late 1980s. At the end of 1996 the percentage of insurance companies and pension fund assets held in property was approximately 5.5 per cent. However, in excess of £4bn has been identified at the same date as an allocation to invest in the real estate market. This is due to the now widely held belief that those returning to property for the next few years will be at least equal to those leaving the UK stock market, and with little perceived risk.

In February 1996 rental growth became positive for the first time (see Figure 12.2). In most areas and all sectors the available vacant space continued to fall. As reported in the CBI survey in January, 32 per cent of companies expect to take more space or trade up their accommodation in the first half of 1997.

Figure 12.2 Rental growth turns positive

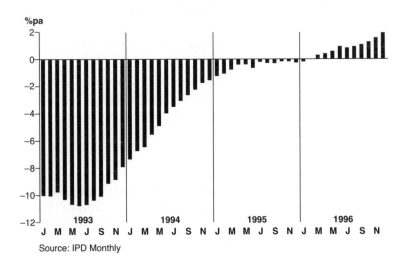

Source: IPD Monthly

12.2.2 Lease of commercial property

During the 1980s commercial buildings were generally leased for a term of 25 years with five-yearly rent reviews to the property's current open market rental value. During the early 1990s the supply/demand balance has been so radically altered that the market is one in which tenants' desires are paramount. There has been marked owner reluctance to grant shorter leases but the trend to shorter leases and the granting of tenants' options to determine leases continues. At the same time increased incentives by way of cash payments and rent-free periods have resulted in reduced returns to landlords. Under the terms of what is known as a 'full repairing and insuring' lease, the occupational tenant is responsible for (or for at least the cost of) carrying out all repairs to and insurance of the property. Whilst the day-to-day management of a commercial property investment is of vital importance in terms of maintaining the performance of the investment, and in particular in achieving the best possible rent on review, in the case of a letting of an entire building (as opposed to one which is in multiple occupation) the process is essentially one of collecting the rent and checking that the repairs and insurance are in place. In multi-occupied buildings the repairs and insurance are carried out by the landlord, or his managing agents, with the costs being recovered from the tenants. An investment in commercial property has historically been regarded as a passive investment, with the day-to-day and portfolio management responsibilities being undertaken by a firm of managing agents.

12.2.3 Rent reviews

Investments in commercial property provide regular opportunities for increasing the income obtained from the property through rent reviews. Since the Second World War the time period between rent reviews has altered. Formerly leases were granted with a period of 21 years between rent reviews, but latterly this decreased to 14 years, then to seven years and is currently five years. Generally, rent reviews result in the rent increasing to the then open market rental value of the property and most institutional leases provide for the rent review to be on an upwards only basis. As mentioned earlier, oversupply and reduced tenant demand resulted in rents falling, increased incentives and shorter lease terms. However, leases granted with terms long enough to have five-yearly rent review provisions have on the whole continued to include upward only rent reviews.

12.2.4 Rental growth

As can be seen from the Figures 12.3 and 12.4 on pp 194 and 195 showing rental growth in the three major investment sectors throughout the decade of the 1980s, and also the mean asking yield for the three sectors through the same time period, the rate of rental growth has varied enormously from a peak of about 30 per cent per annum to an actual decline in rental terms. At the same time, yields have altered by as much as 25 per cent.

12.3 SHOPS

12.3.1 General

Historically, three factors have affected the rental and capital value of shops: location, location and location. Due to the fact that the quality of the location can readily be ascertained, shops have been regarded as one

Figure 12.3 Rental growth by sector 1973/95

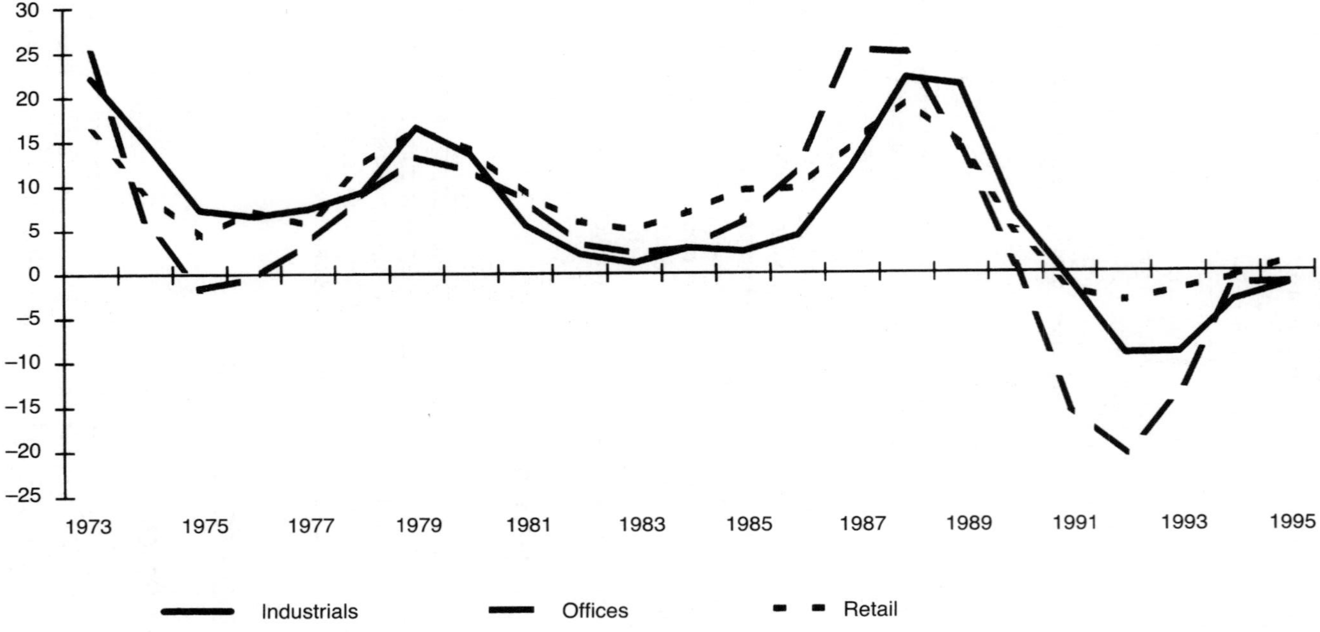

Source: *IPD, JLW FM Strategy*

Figure 12.4 Property yields by sector

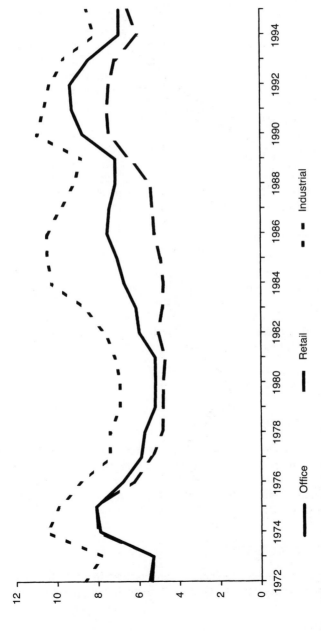

Source: *Hillier Parker.* Note: *average yields as at November.*

Office — Retail — Industrial

of the most secure forms of commercial property investment. In the past, principal high street locations were rarely subject to major change, except when a town centre redevelopment scheme or a new shopping centre was planned, when it was usually possible to predict the effect that these new centres would have on the existing shopping patterns within the high street. However, the future impact of out of town retail schemes and retail warehouse parks on high street shopping patterns is uncertain. With the announcement of the intentions of major retailers such as Marks & Spencer to set up a number of large-scale operations in out of town locations, the provision of sufficient and accessible car parking and an attractive environment will ensure that retail parks and out of town centres continue to prosper on the same levels as before. Otherwise, traditional town centres will be left to become fashion-dominated, durable-good centres, with food shopping moving out of town. The retailing sector is undergoing significant change, with many retailers repositioning in the market, restyling their outlets and merchandise, and taking over competitors. In addition there was dramatic growth in 'speciality' retailing in the past two years where a number of retailers have been successful in targeting specific markets and responding quickly to changes in consumer demand. Hence the more established chains experienced greater competition for prime pitches in the high street.

A large number of the best shop units in the UK are now owned by the institutions, although a proportion are still owned and occupied by the major retailing organisations. In recent years rental growth has been considerable throughout the retail sector. There has been keen competition to make further investment in this category, whilst the availability of suitable investments is extremely limited in relation to the amount of investment money available.

In the property investment market, shops are categorised as prime, secondary and tertiary.

12.3.2 Prime

Prime shops are those situated in the best trading locations along the principal high streets in the larger towns where major multiple retailers, such as Boots, W H Smith and Marks & Spencer, are to be found. The rental income obtainable from shop units within these locations varies enormously depending on the importance of the particular town.

12.3.3 Secondary

Secondary shops are shops either on the fringes of the best trading positions within the larger towns or in the best shopping positions in the smaller towns. Due to the shortage of prime shop units now available for commercial investment, the institutional demand for this type of property has grown in recent years. Since the prospects for rental growth in these locations have proved more erratic than those in prime locations, investors expect a higher yield.

12.3.4 Tertiary

Tertiary shops are shops on the fringes of the secondary trading positions and shops in neighbourhood shopping parades, including 'the corner shop'. There is a negligible demand from multiple tenants for representation in these locations. Therefore, covenant strength is poorer and the management load heavier. Consequently, demand for these properties derives principally from private investors. This market is usually very active with sales of all sizes taking place by private treaty or auction.

12.3.5 Out of town shopping

Out of town shopping has evolved through the recognition of the car-borne shopper and may generally be divided into food and non-food retailing. The main DIY specialists (Sainsbury's Homebase, W H Smith Do-It-All and B & Q) are often found grouped together and require units of 35,000–50,000 square ft. Out of town food retailers now include most of the major food chains. Good surface car parking and main road prominence are essential criteria.

12.4 OFFICES

12.4.1 General

In the early 1970s many provincial towns, as well as central London, became seriously over-supplied with office accommodation and rents either remained level or fell. This has started to happen again to a lesser extent in the 1990s. A factor in the demand/supply imbalance is the lengthy period from planning to completion of a development.

The quality of an office building is of greater importance than that of a shop unit. Occupational tenants are setting ever higher standards, requiring good quality finishes, modern lifts, central heating, adequate car parking facilities, the abilty to accommodate a growing range of sophisticated office equipment (notably computers, word processors and communications equipment) and, particularly in central London, double-glazing and air conditioning. The costs of maintaining offices, especially the mechanical services, the unified business rates, and the cost of refurbishing the accommodation, mean that the tenant and investor are subjected to high outgoings. These have increased as a direct result of technological changes having shortened the lifetime of buildings and services.

The most expensive office locations in the UK have historically been the West End and City of London. Since the tenant will be responsible for all outgoings under the terms of his lease, the actual cost of occupation will probably be double the cost of the rent alone. Due to the security and perceived prospects for long-term rental growth offered by buildings within the West End and City of London, there has been a strong institutional demand for investments. Increasingly, foreign investors as well as UK investors have been active in this market although recent over supply and falling rents in both the City and West End have resulted in more fluctuation and uncertainty in value, leading to reduced investment activity and caution amongst investors.

The other principal office areas in London follow a similar but less expensive pattern to that of the City and West End, although in the late 1980s an upswing in demand coupled with relatively restricted supply resulted in these locations experiencing dramatic growth in rents. Outside London, rents vary from centre to centre, with the towns immediately to the west of London along the M4 corridor being the highest outside London.

12.4.2 Conclusion

Offices form the backbone of most commercial property investment portfolios because of the amount of money involved and the past performance of rental growth on rent review. They are likely to remain a dominant feature of institutional portfolios and the preferred areas are those in central London and certain selected provincial centres. However, it is becoming necessary to spend large capital sums more frequently to maintain the quality of the investment. Over many years the cost of central London office occupancy and the inconvenience of commuting have encouraged companies to move their operations to suburban and provincial locations.

12.5 INDUSTRIAL

12.5.1 General investment: factories and warehouses

The declining importance in Great Britain of the industrial and manufacturing sectors, the volatility of the economy and the relatively short economic life of industrial buildings have resulted in investors requiring higher yields for factories and warehouse premises than for shops and offices. In this context, institutional investors tend to prefer warehouse buildings, as opposed to factories, due to the fact that these tend to be less specialised and therefore require fewer remedial works when a tenant vacates the premises. Industrial processes also tend to have a more destructive effect on the actual fabric of the property.

12.5.2 Location criteria

Although the uses of factories and warehouses are different, both in practical and in legislative terms, it is convenient to categorise them together, since the locational and investment criteria are similar. The most desirable investments in this category are situated on well-located industrial estates, close to major conurbations and motorway access points or the national airports. It is interesting to note that proximity to rail services is not an important criterion in the UK, being less important than a good supply of labour and good estate services for the factory owner.

12.5.3 Institutional criteria

The insurance companies and pension funds have developed certain criteria which they look for in modern industrial and warehouse buildings. These criteria relate to clear working height, floor loading capacity, the presence of sprinklers, the proportion of office space to warehouse space within the unit, the number of loading doors, the presence of a concreted hard standing in front of the unit and adequate car parking. Whilst these institutional criteria are often in excess of the criteria required by occupiers, investors would be wise to purchase units meeting institutional criteria, since they will find a wider market in which to sell the property in the future.

12.5.4 Yields

Yields available on prime industrial and warehouse investments are higher than those on prime shops and offices. Rental growth experienced over the late 1970s was, generally, very satisfactory but became static in the early and mid-1980s during the economic recession, and improved again in the late 1980s. Investment in modern industrial and warehouse buildings is a more recent trend than investment in offices and shops but now forms around 25 per cent of a typical portfolio. Opportunities do exist for non-institutional investment where very high yields can be obtained from obsolescent or poorly located properties, but these carry commensurate risk.

12.6 HI-TECH

Whilst many areas of traditional manufacturing industry were affected by the economic recession, the hi-technology field experienced considerable growth. This resulted in a new direction in the design and use of industrial buildings with tenants becoming increasingly discerning as to their preferences in building design and working environment. The most radical change has been the introduction of the building which comprises a two- or three-storey structure designed to permit the interchangeability of functions such as offices, research and development, laboratories or industrial. An out of town location, extensive car parking and landscaping with imaginative and functional finishes both internally and externally create a high quality corporate image. The first and still largest business park in the UK is Stockley Park off the M4 very close to Heathrow airport. Both back office and headquarters type functions are now moving to such business parks.

12.7 AGRICULTURE

Having experienced growth in popularity with institutional investors, at one point forming in excess of 5 per cent of some investment portfolios, farmland and forestry have been increasingly less popular as a result of falling values and the perception of a continued fall in values. In addition, investors have begun to appreciate that in many instances the economic support or tax benefits of these investments have been and are likely to be subject to political tinkering, thus dramatically altering the value of many investments at a stroke.

Smaller, more picturesque farms, especially those with attractive houses have, however, become increasingly attractive and prices have continued to rise for the successful businessman desirous of changing his place of domicile and lifestyle (see also Chapter 11).

12.8 LEISURE

Investments in the 'leisure industry' include hotels, marinas, golf courses, sports centres and entertainment facilities. The growing demand for leisure facilities, both home-based and from tourists, is resulting in increasing investment in this field. It is, however, regarded as an investment in management expertise rather than in the property which the particular leisure activity occupies, and great caution is therefore necessary. Quite often an investor's return will be geared to the operator's turnover or profitability rather than to the premises' rental value, which can sometimes be very difficult to determine.

Whilst the returns from leisure industry investments, in terms of capital gains, can be substantial for the astute investor, the risks are considerable and such investments are not recommended to small investors.

13

BUSINESS VENTURES (WITHOUT PARTICIPATION IN MANAGEMENT)

MIKE WILKES

Pannell Kerr Forster, Chartered Accountants

13.1 INTRODUCTION

There are always people with experience and no money looking for people with money and no experience. The former sometimes have the money and the latter have had the experience. That is not to say that, in general terms, such arrangements should always be avoided. There are plenty of good ideas which need financing and the rewards to the investor can be substantial, but such investments call for faith in someone else's judgement, nerves of steel and an instinct for gambling. Many ventures have turned out well after being (sometimes more than once) on the verge of disaster. Those who do not like walking along the edge of a precipice should keep to gentler paths.

The individual seeking after finance will often paint the picture of his prospects in rosy colours, not through dishonesty but because of enthusiasm, and such enthusiasm should always be discounted. Unfortunately it is often highly contagious, so that impersonal, dispassionate, professional advice is essential. The pitfalls should be considered every bit as carefully as the opportunities. It is easier to lose money than to make it; but money is seldom to be made without accepting an element of chance.

In some cases money, once put into a venture, is effectively locked in, come what may. At best it may be possible to withdraw it only at considerable cost. On the other hand, by good judgement and good luck (and any successful venture requires both), there are fortunes to be made. The essential feature of the investments considered in this chapter is that the investor relies wholly on the expertise of someone else – company director, active partner, racehorse trainer and so on – and will probably be involved in matters of which he is ignorant or, at least, inexperienced.

It must never be forgotten that taxation will make inroads into both income and capital gains, and, in this respect, professional advice should always be taken. There may be alternative ways of making investments so that, with this in mind, every scheme requires careful expert consideration. Equally, if losses are incurred, steps should be taken to see that the maximum tax advantage is obtained. The advice of an accountant or a solicitor or probably both can be invaluable, not only in dealing with legal and financial problems that are puzzling the prospective investor but often also in pointing out problems of which the layman may be totally unaware. The effects of taxation are touched on in the following sections, but complex problems can arise which it is impossible to deal with briefly. In every case the solution will depend upon the individual facts.

1981 saw the introduction of the 'Business Start-up Scheme' intended for the encouragement of investment in companies starting new businesses. Provided that the investment complied with the numerous, rigorous and complex provisions set out in no less than 16 sections of and two Schedules to the Finance Act 1981, the amount invested could be deducted from the income of the investor in computing his income tax liability.

The scheme was superseded by the 'Business Expansion Scheme' which, while similar in concept, was more generous in amount, wider in its application and subject to even more complicated legal rules. The scheme was, in many cases, viewed as a tax-saving vehicle rather than a way to take a stake in new ventures and came to an end on 31 December 1993. The 1994 Finance Act introduced a new investment incentive scheme, the Enterprise Investment Scheme, which replaced the Business Expansion Scheme and the 1995 Finance Act provided for the approval of Venture Capital Trusts (VCTs), yet another investment incentive vehicle. Although the avoidance of tax is the inducement to make such investments, the legislation includes a number of anti-avoidance provisions.

The view is sometimes held that professional advice is an expensive luxury which can be dispensed with. Nothing could be further from the truth. If it seems expensive it is because the mass of all-pervading legislation of recent years has made it dangerous to take any steps in commerce (or indeed in much else) without considering the application of statute law, statutory instruments and regulations. Professional advice taken at the outset often avoids difficulties and disputes at a later stage which may well prove far more expensive in legal costs.

13.2 THE CURRENT BUSINESS CLIMATE

Although smaller private companies were most affected by the recession, it must be hoped that the apparent upturn in the economy, and the various tax incentive schemes which have been introduced, will help to encourage the creation and expansion of new small businesses. If recent reports can be relied upon, property values are at last beginning to move upwards again, although experience has shown that we should be wary of 'false dawns'. Despite recent problems, Lloyd's finally appears to have started to address and resolve some of its major difficulties and some may consider that it is a more viable proposition now that corporate underwriting is a reality. As always however the potential profits are likely to diminish, in line with the reduction in personal risk, and certainly for the foreseeable future it seems likely that Lloyd's will still have to rely on individuals who are prepared to put their personal assets at stake.

13.3 MINORITY HOLDINGS IN PRIVATE COMPANIES

13.3.1 Introduction

It was for many years a feature of company law that a private company was one which restricted the transfer of its shares and any company which did not do so was a public company. Under the Companies Act 1980 (a statute enacted largely as a move towards European uniformity) this distinction was swept away and although the words 'public' and 'private' are retained, their meanings are now quite different. A public company is defined in the Companies Act 1985 (a consolidating Act bringing together the provisions of the Companies Acts of 1948, 1967, 1976, 1980 and 1981), and any company not within that definition will be a private company. The principal distinction is that a public company (denoted at the end of its name by the letters 'plc' or by the words 'public limited company') must have an authorised and allotted minimum share capital which is at present £50,000 but which may be altered by Statutory Instrument by the Secretary of State. At least one-quarter of that allotted share capital of a public company must be paid up before it can commence business. No such minimum capital requirements exist in relation to private companies. A company need no longer restrict the transfer of its shares to be a private company under the new Act. References in this part of the chapter to 'private companies' are intended, generally, to refer to the smaller family company where control rests in the hands of a few shareholders who are probably the directors or related to the directors. As regards the transfer of shares see **13.3.4**.

A minority holding in a private company may be acquired in a number of ways: it may be inherited; it may be bought from an existing shareholder; it may arise when a company is newly formed to undertake the starting of a business venture; or it may arise on the allotment of shares by a company taking over an existing company or undertaking.

A minority holding is, for the purpose of this chapter, any holding of shares or other securities which does not give the holder control of the company, and thus includes a holding of non-voting shares or debentures. Assuming that a company has shares of one class only, of which each has one vote, a holding of less than 50 per cent is a minority holding. However, in some companies there are different classes of shares and shares of one class only, for example, might carry a vote, the others carrying no vote or giving the right to vote on certain specified matters only. In other companies there may be one class of shares carrying one vote each and another class of which the shares carry a hundred votes each, so that a holding, in nominal value, of more than half the company's issued capital does not necessarily carry control. Careful scrutiny of the company's capital structure is vital before making an investment in a private company.

13.3.2 Powers of the minority

At general meetings of a company, a vote is first taken by a show of hands (subject to anything in the articles of association), giving each member personally present one vote regardless of the size of his holding. Under common law any one member may demand a poll, the votes then being counted, normally on the basis of one for each share held. The articles may include a requirement that a poll must be demanded by more than one member, but such a requirement is limited by s 373 of the Companies Act 1985 so that, except for certain purposes, an article is void if it requires the demand for a poll to be made by more than five members, or the holders of more than one-tenth of the voting rights, or the holders of more than one-tenth of the paid-up capital entitled to vote.

When a poll is held, each member has (in the absence of any contrary provision in the articles) one vote for each share held. Thus on a poll, one member holding 60 per cent of the issued shares will be able to outvote a dozen members holding the other 40 per cent between them.

An ordinary resolution requires a simple majority of members voting, so that a minority shareholder cannot, in the face of determined opposition, prevent its being passed. However, a special or extraordinary resolution, which is necessary for certain fundamental decisions, requires a majority of three-quarters of members voting, so that on a poll, where each share carries a vote, the holder of 40 per cent of the issued shares, although a minority shareholder, could block such a resolution. An extraordinary resolution is required for, among other things, winding up a company that cannot, by reason of its liabilities, continue in business, and the articles of the company may require such a resolution for various other purposes. A special resolution is necessary for, *inter alia*:

(1) the alteration of a company's objects (although, in that case, the holders of not less than 15 per cent of the issued share capital may apply to the court to have the alteration cancelled);
(2) the alteration of a company's articles;
(3) the change of a company's name (subject to the approval of the Department of Trade and Industry);
(4) a reduction of capital (subject to the approval of the court);
(5) the re-registration of a public company as private or a private company as public under the 1985 Act;
(6) the re-registration of an unlimited company as limited; and
(7) the winding-up of a company voluntarily.

In addition to considering the effective powers of the majority, it must be remembered that the day-to-day running of the company's business is in the hands of the directors. As a last resort, majority shareholders can remove and appoint directors; minority shareholders cannot. In this connection it is important to note that most companies' articles of association preclude the payment of a dividend in excess of that recommended by the directors. If, therefore, the directors feel it is desirable for any reason to retain the profits, or the bulk of the profits, within the company rather than distribute them by way of dividend, the minority shareholder may find that he is not receiving a satisfactory return on his investment and, even with the assistance of the majority shareholders, there may be little he can effectively do about it.

Arising out of the matters discussed in the previous paragraph, it will be appreciated that the majority could deal with the affairs of a company in a way which might be to the detriment of the interests of the minority, particularly where the minority controls 25 per cent or less of the voting power. The law, however, provides protection for an oppressed minority in two ways. First, the minority may petition the court to wind up the company on the ground that it is just and equitable to do so. This is, in many cases, an unsatisfactory course to pursue since the assets will be sold at their break-up value, the goodwill will disappear and the minority will not have achieved its object, namely that the company should continue to operate but that its interests should be safeguarded. Secondly, the minority may petition the court for relief under s 459 of the Companies Act 1985.

Protection under the 1948 Act was provided where the court was of the opinion that the company's affairs were being conducted in a manner oppressive to some part of the members (including the petitioner) and that to wind up the company would unfairly prejudice that part of the members although the facts would justify winding-up on the grounds that to wind up would be just and equitable. The court, on being so persuaded, could make any order which it thought fit. There is a considerable body of authority about what constitutes oppression for this purpose.

Under s 459 of the Companies Act 1985, protection is afforded by the court if it is satisfied that the conduct of the company's affairs is 'unfairly prejudicial to the interests' of some part of the members. A petition may also be brought under this provision based on 'any actual or proposed act or omission' of the company. The meaning of 'unfairly prejudicial' is not defined and awaits judicial interpretation.

13.3.3 Liability for uncalled capital

The essential feature of a limited company is that the liability of its shareholders is limited to the capital they put in or agree to put in, and no further demands can be made on them by the company or its creditors except where shares are issued which are not fully paid. The holder of such shares may be called upon by the company to pay up the unpaid balance, and failure to pay on a call may result in forfeiture of the shares. Any holder of partly paid shares must therefore always bear in mind that a contingent liability attaches to them. If the additional capital is required for development of the business, it will probably be all to the good. It sometimes happens though, that it is needed because the company is in difficulties and may amount to throwing good money after bad.

13.3.4 Transfer of shares

Difficulties may arise in connection with the disposal of a minority holding of shares in a private company. One of the hallmarks of a private company under the Companies Act 1948 was that it restricted transfers of its shares, and if the articles did not so provide, it was not a private company. The usual form, following reg 3 of Table A in Pt II of Sched 1 to the Companies Act 1948, provided that 'the directors may, in their absolute discretion and without assigning any reason therefore, decline to register any transfer of any share, whether or not it is a fully paid share.' It follows that, in such cases, the board must approve the proposed new shareholder and, where the articles are in the form set out above, the court will not inquire into the directors' reasons for refusing to register a transfer if none are given. Thus, whatever the value of the shares might be in terms of the assets and liabilities disclosed in the company's balance sheet, it may well be difficult to find a purchaser at anything approaching that value. The Companies Act 1948, s 28, which made restrictions on transfers essential for a private company, was repealed by the Companies Act 1985. There is nothing to prevent a private company from imposing such a restriction in its articles and in the case of any company whose articles already include it, it will remain in force unless the articles are amended. The articles of any company in which it is proposed to invest should therefore be examined with this point in view. The new Table A (under the Companies Act 1985), which sets out a suggested form 8 for the articles of association of a company, does not include any provisions relating to the refusal of directors to register a transfer of fully paid shares, but it is not unusual to see an express provision to that effect included in the articles of association of private companies.

Dealing with shares in a private company is often also restricted by a provision in the articles that a member wishing to dispose of his shares must first offer them to the other members at their fair value which is frequently determined in the absence of agreement between the intending seller and the directors, by the auditors, or an independent chartered accountant. The articles should therefore be examined with this in mind and also with a view to discovering whether, on death, a member's shares may pass to his personal representatives to be dealt with according to his will. In addition a minority shareholder who is an employee might be required under the articles of association to transfer his shares on ceasing to be employed by the company in question.

13.3.5 Loans

An investor may prefer to put money into a company by way of loan rather than by purchasing shares. A loan may be charged on all or any of the company's assets or its uncalled capital, or may be on a debenture, secured or unsecured. The nature of a debenture is difficult to define and Lindley J said in *British India Steam Navigation Co v IRC* (1881) 7 QBD 165, at p 172, '. . . what the correct meaning of "debenture" is I do not know. I do not find anywhere any precise definition of it'.

It is always necessary to proceed with caution when lending to a company. Its memorandum and articles should be inspected to ensure that the borrowing is *intra vires*, and the terms of any loan or debenture must be clearly set out and agreed. Independent professional advice is essential. In particular, where the lender is the settlor in relation to a settlement of which the trustees or a beneficiary are participators of the company, quite unexpected income tax liabilities may arise under s 677 of the Income and Corporation Taxes Act 1988 when the loan is repaid.

Money invested in a company by way of loan will normally entitle the lender to interest at a fixed rate. If the company fails he should not, if adequately secured, be out of pocket: if the company prospers he will receive his interest regularly, and in due course his loan will be repaid, but he will not share in the prosperity of the undertaking.

13.3.6 **Taxation**

Two applications of taxation must be borne in mind. First, when a dividend is received, a 'tax credit' is given equal in amount to the income tax at the rate of 20 per cent which would be payable on the aggregate of the dividend and the tax credit. The company thereupon becomes liable to pay advance corporation tax (ACT) on the dividend at a rate of 20 per cent on the aggregate, such ACT ranking as a credit against the company's corporation tax liability. Higher rate taxpayers will be given credit for the deduction; basic rate taxpayers will have no further tax liability.

Secondly, if and when shares are disposed of and a chargeable gain results, capital gains tax becomes payable. The Finance Act 1988 changed the base date from 1965 to 1982 which favoured many long-term investors, but that Finance Act also unified the rates of tax on income and capital gains so that the maximum rate of capital gains tax increased from 30 to 40 per cent.

Incidentally, a notional capital gain may arise where assets are given away or disposed of for consideration which is less than their full open market value. A person who makes such a gift or sale at an undervalue is treated as if he had received full market value. However, it may be possible for gains arising on such transactions to be deferred or 'held over'. The Finance Act 1989 abolished the general right to hold over gains on gifts, but the hold over provisions continue to apply to gifts of business property (and shares in unquoted trading companies generally fall within this category).

The tax payable on a capital gain arising from the sale of shares will normally be computed as follows:

Sale proceeds	x
Less incidental costs of disposal	x
	x
Less cost/31 March 1982 value	x
Less Indexation up to the amount of the gain (adjustment for inflation based on the increase in the RPI)	x
Less capital losses on other transactions in the year	x
Less £6,300 annual exemption – £6,500 from 6 April 1997 (unless utilised against other gains)	
Less capital losses brought forward (if any)	?
Net gains taxed at either 20%, 24% (23% for 1997/98) or 40%	x

13.3.7 Losses

Looking on the gloomy side, it is possible that a loss may arise on the sale of shares in a private company, or on its liquidation. Such a loss may arise because the investor cannot recoup his original investment, but even where he does get his money back, an allowable loss could still have arisen for disposals made prior to 6 April 1995 because of indexation (ie the adjustment made to reflect inflation and calculated as a percentage of the allowable cost reflecting the increase in the RPI during the period in which the investment has been held).

A major change was included in the 1994 Finance Act, which limited the amount of indexation relief which could be claimed for disposals made after 29 November 1993. The initial text of the Bill provided that, for such disposals, indexation relief could only be used to reduce chargeable gains to nil and would not be available to create, or increase, an allowable capital loss.

However, following representations, the Chancellor tabled an amendment to the Finance Bill (now incorporated in the Finance Act 1994) which provided for transitional relief for individuals, and trustees of settlements made before 30 November 1993. For losses realised on disposals made during the period from 30 November 1993 to 5 April 1995, indexation relief was available up to a maximum of £10,000. This indexation relief had first be used to reduce the net chargeable gains for 1993–94 to the level of the taxpayer's annual exempt amount of £5,800. Any unused indexation losses could be carried forward and used, with any indexation losses on disposals during 1994–95, to reduce chargeable gains for 1994–95. Any such indexation losses which could not be used during 1994–95 were not available to carry forward to 1995–96 and later years.

Example 1 – disposals prior to 30 November 1993

An individual invests £10,000 in December 1989. On 14 June 1993 he sells for £11,000. However, the RPI has increased by 18 per cent between 1989 and 1993. Before indexation he has a gain of £1,000 but after taking this into account he has an allowable capital loss of £800.

Example 2 – disposals between 30 November 1993 and 5 April 1995

The circumstances are similar to those in Example 1, but the sale takes place on 31 March 1994. Assuming the RPI has increased by 20 per cent between 1989 and 1994, there is an indexation loss of £1,000. This indexation loss can be set off against other gains arising for 1993–94, which are in excess of the annual exemption of £5,800. Any balance can be carried forward for use in

1994–95. If this cannot be utilised in 1994–95, no relief can be carried forward to 1995–96 and subsequent years. This example also assumes that other indexation losses arising during the period 30 November 1993 to 5 April 1995, when added to this indexation loss, do not exceed £10,000.

Example 3 – disposals after 5 April 1995

The circumstances are similar to those of Example 1, but the sale takes place on 6 December 1996. In this case the indexation relief is limited to the amount of the unindexed gain, ie £1,000, and no capital loss is created.

Reinvestment relief

Reinvestment relief was first introduced in the March 1993 budget as a relief for entrepreneurs on the selling of their own business. It was only given real substance in the 1994 Finance Act when the relief was extended for disposals made after 29 November 1993, and became available for *any* capital gain where the gain was reinvested in shares in a qualifying unquoted company. The 1995 Finance Act contained further extensions to the relief so that it is now available for gains reinvested in Enterprise Investment Schemes and Venture Capital Trusts.

Example

Wendy sells her shares in SAL Ltd in December 1996, for £20,000. She originally purchased the shares in January 1985 for £5,000. In May 1996 Wendy invested £10,000 in ordinary shares in a Venture Capital Trust. Wendy's capital gains tax position would be as follows:

	£	£
Proceeds		20,000
Less:		
Cost	5,000	
Indexation relief (say)	3,000	
		8,000
Net gain		12,000
Less reinvestment relief		(10,000)
Net chargeable gain		£2,000

If Wendy was a higher rate taxpayer, her combined income tax and capital gains tax relief could amount to 60 per cent (20 per cent income tax relief for the investment in the venture capital trust, and 40 per cent deferral of capital gains tax).

Capital losses are not normally available to be set against an individual's income, although they do attract capital gains tax relief. However, where an individual has subscribed for ordinary shares in a qualifying trading company and he incurs an allowable loss on disposing of the shares, he may claim relief from income tax instead of capital gains tax. This provision is to be found in s 574 of the Income and Corporation Taxes Act 1988. Note that this relief applies only where the taxpayer has subscribed for the shares and not where he had bought them from another shareholder, unless that other is his or her spouse, and acquired the shares by subscription. It applies only to ordinary share capital and stock and the company must be a 'qualifying trading company' in the terms of the definition provided by the section, that is to say:

(1) it must exist wholly or mainly for the purpose of carrying on a trade (other than dealing in shares, securities, land or commodity futures);
(2) it must be resident in the UK from its incorporation until the date on which the shares or stock are disposed of; and
(3) none of its shares or stock must have been quoted on a recognised stock exchange at any time since 12 months before the date on which the shares or stock were issued.

The relief will be given if the loss results from a sale at arm's length for full consideration, a distribution on a winding-up, or a claim that the value has become negligible giving rise to a deemed disposal. Partial claims are not allowed and if the loss exceeds income for the year of claim the excess may either be carried forward or set off against capital gains. Information may be obtained from the Small Firms Service of the Department of Trade and Industry.

13.3.8 Loans

Until relatively recently, professional advisers normally recommended that a person making a loan to a private company should do so on terms which made the loan a debt on a security. This is because such loans constitute an asset for capital gains tax purposes whereas normal loans are outside the scope of capital gains tax (which is fine until the investor seeks relief for a capital loss). As a general principle, losses are available to offset capital gains only if they arise from assets which are chargeable assets for capital gains purposes.

As already stated, as a general principle, a debt on a security does constitute an asset for capital gains tax purposes. This definition is itself obscure.

There is a further problem that even where a loan constitutes a debt on a security, relief may be withheld on the basis that the security is a 'qualifying corporate bond' (in this particular context, a qualifying corporate bond is one where the investor does not qualify for an allowable loss for capital gains tax purposes). It is possible to ensure that a debt on a security does not fall within the definition of a QCB, but it is necessary for the loan to have certain qualities and in particular the loan should normally contain provisions under which it may be converted into ordinary shares or preference shares. Professional advice is essential here.

Loans which are not debts on a security or QCBs

Even where a debt does not fall within the category considered above, it may in certain circumstances entitle the lender to relief as a capital loss if it becomes irrecoverable. The conditions which render the loan a qualifying loan for this purpose are in s 253 of the Taxation of Chargeable Gains Act 1992. These are as follows:

(1) The money lent must be used by the borrower wholly for the purposes of a trade carried on by him or for the setting-up of a trade subsequently carried on by him.
(2) The borrower must be resident in the UK. The Act does not say at what point the borrower must be so resident and neither does it require the business to be carried on here.
(3) The debt must not be a debt on a security. If it is it will fall within the provisions referred to previously.

13.3.9 Relief for financing costs

Interest paid on a loan to an individual is eligible for tax relief only if the money borrowed is used for certain purposes. These include the acquisition of an interest in a close company or in a partnership. In the case of a close company it must be used for the purchase of ordinary shares in a trading or estate company, or for the making of a loan to such a company to be used wholly and exclusively for the company's business. The individual will be entitled to the relief if: (1) he holds not less than 5 per cent of the company's ordinary share capital; or (2) he holds some part thereof, however small, and has in the period between the application of the loan and the payment of the interest been personally engaged in the conduct of the business in the case of a partnership, and 'worked for the greater part of his time in the actual management or conduct of the company', in the case of a company. During the same period he must not have recovered any capital from the company or partnership. For details of the complex provisions regarding this tax relief reference must be made to ss 360 and 362 of the Income and Corporation Taxes Act 1988.

13.3.10 **Conclusion**

It will be appreciated that many problems may arise in connection with company law and tax law. The latter in particular has become a matter of great complexity and specialist advice should always be taken. When all the legal hurdles are overcome, the sky's the limit and, if all goes well, the end result may be that the company 'goes public' or is taken over by a public company, leaving the shareholder with readily realisable shares in a company which may be or become a household name.

13.4 PRIVATE INVESTMENT COMPANIES

The first part of this chapter is concerned primarily with trading companies, but much of what has been said applies equally to private investment companies. These are companies which do not carry on a trade but invest, usually either in real property or in stock, shares and similar securities, and receive rents, dividends and interest. The line between property investment and property dealing companies is a difficult one to draw and presents a problem which the courts have often been called upon to solve. The question is essentially one of intention, but it is not always easy to decide how the available evidence (which may be scanty) should be interpreted. Some of the differences between dealing or trading companies on the one hand and investment companies on the other are dealt with below.

First, when a property is disposed of at a gain, the gain in the hands of a dealing company is part of its trading profit and is taxed at the appropriate rate of corporation tax. Where the disposal is made by an investment company, the gain may be a chargeable gain as defined for capital gains tax purposes and taxed as such. Secondly, an investment company is charged to corporation tax *prima facie* on the full amount of its income and must make a management expenses claim by virtue of which a deduction is allowed for the cost of management. Management expenses (nowhere defined in the legislation) are usually less than the expenses allowable against trading profits. Thirdly, an investment company, if it is a 'close investment-holding company', is less favourably treated than a trading company as regards distributions.

Because of provisions contained in the 1989 Finance Act, the company is generally ineligible for the small companies corporation tax rate. This means that it has to pay tax on its profits at the full 33 per cent rate rather than at 23 per cent. Furthermore, restrictions may apply to repayment claims for tax deemed to be withheld from dividends declared by the company.

In general the capital gains tax treatment of gains and losses arising on shares and loans to private trading companies applies equally to shares and loans involving private investment companies. However, there is one important difference: it is not possible to claim income tax relief under the Income and Corporation Taxes Act 1988, s 574 as described in **13.3.7**.

A further disadvantage which attaches to an investment company (or indeed to any company which makes chargeable gains) is that a double tax liability may arise on capital gains. On the sale of an asset by the company, tax becomes payable (as explained above) on the chargeable gain. That net gain increases the company's assets and hence the value of the member's shares in it. On a disposal of those shares by him a further chargeable gain may arise.

A private investment company has larger funds at its disposal than each individual shareholder and may thereby take advantage of opportunities not presented to the smaller investor. Furthermore, the minimum commission charged by a stockbroker may add disproportionately to the cost of investments of the smaller investor. Both these advantages, however, attach to any method by which small investors join together. So long as the basic agreement governing the project is carefully drawn up and fully understood by all those co-operating, a joint co-operative investment scheme may avoid the drawbacks of a private investment company while at the same time possessing many of the advantages. The taxation of unapproved investment companies (whether private or public) and their shareholders is discussed at **7.7**.

13.5 ENTERPRISE INVESTMENT SCHEME

13.5.1 Introduction

In his budget in November 1993, the Chancellor announced a new investment incentive scheme, intended to provide a 'targeted incentive' for new equity investment in unquoted trading companies, and to encourage outside investors to introduce new finance and expertise. The Business Expansion Scheme (BES), introduced by the Finance Act 1983, came to an end on 31 December 1993, and was replaced with the Enterprise Investment Scheme (EIS), with effect from 1 January 1994. There are numerous and complex conditions which must be satisfied in relation to the investor, the trade, and the investment. Although many of the rules included in the provisions were common to both the EIS and its predecessor, the BES, there are some important differences.

For shares issued by a qualified unquoted trading company relief is given to investors at the lower rate of 20 per cent on the amount subscribed for the shares in the year of assessment in which the shares are issued or the income tax payable by him, if lower. Tax reliefs, which are expressed in terms of tax, double taxation credits and tax deducted at source from annual payments, are ignored for this purpose.

In addition to income tax relief, an individual may claim capital gains tax deferral relief in respect of any other capital gain which is reinvested in an EIS during the period beginning one year prior and ending three years after the disposal which creates the capital gain. The maximum investment which may attract relief for 1994–95 and future years is £100,000 per annum. These limits apply to husband and wife separately. It is also possible to carry back up to half of an amount invested by an individual between 6 April and 5 October in any year to the previous tax year, subject to a maximum of £15,000. However, the relief carried back must not take the individual over the limit for the previous year.

Provided that the shares have been held for at least five years, the shares are exempt from capital gains tax on disposal. Unlike investments in the BES however, a loss on the shares' disposal after the five-year period has elapsed may still attract income tax or capital gains tax relief.

There is a maximum amount of money which a company can raise in a particular tax year under the EIS. The normal limit is £1m, but a higher limit of £5m is available for companies which are engaged in certain shipping activities.

It must be borne in mind that one of the conditions for the granting of this relief is that the company must, throughout the relevant period (see **13.5.4**), be unquoted. If, at the end of the five-year period, the company is still unquoted, the investor may find himself effectively locked in. If there is no quotation and the investor cannot find a purchaser for his shares he can realise his investment only if the company either disposes of its assets and winds up or sells its undertaking to a quoted company, so that its shareholders finish up with either quoted shares or cash. The directors may, however, be reluctant to accept the loss of directorships which would follow a winding-up and might well follow a take-over.

It must also be remembered that the EIS was introduced to encourage the investment of risk capital and that that is exactly what such an investment is. Tax benefits may follow an investment under the scheme but there is no certainty that the investment will be successful. Companies in commercial enterprises often have difficulty in producing a prospectus which is of much use to the prospective investor. Projections, by directors, of future profits should be read with caution. The cost of such professional reports as are required for a public flotation will often be prohibitive for new, small and possibly speculative enterprises.

13.5.2 Tax relief available

If all the conditions set out in **13.5.3** are complied with, a claim for relief may be made. It must be accompanied by a certificate from the company (authorised by the Inspector of Taxes) to the effect that it has, at all necessary times, complied with the conditions set out in **13.5.4**. The claim may be made at any time after the company has carried on the qualifying trade or activity for four months and must be made not later than two years after the end of the year of assessment in which the shares were issued. If the four-month period expires after the end of that year, it must be made within two years after the end of that period.

If a claim is allowed before the end of the qualifying period (see **13.5.4**) and any subsequent event results in a contravention of any of the conditions, the relief will be withdrawn. If the company fails to carry on the trade for four months by reason of a winding-up or dissolution for *bona fide* commercial reasons and not as part of a tax-saving scheme, the claim will not fail for that reason. Provision is made in the legislation requiring that information leading to a loss of relief must be sent to the Revenue.

13.5.3 Individuals eligible for relief

For an individual to be entitled to the relief under the BES he had to be resident and ordinarily resident in the UK at the time of issue. This requirement does not apply to investors in the EIS, and relief is available for non-residents if they are liable to UK income tax. There is a further relaxation in that an investor can become a paid director, without forfeiting entitlement to relief under the EIS. This is, however, subject to the proviso that the individual was not connected with the company or its trade prior to the issue of the EIS shares.

The words 'connected with' are given a very wide meaning. An individual is connected with a company if:

(1) he or an associate (defined below) is an employee of the company or of its partner, or is himself its partner or is a paid director of the company or of a company which is in partnership with it;
(2) he possesses (directly or indirectly) or is entitled to acquire more than 30 per cent of the company's issued ordinary share capital, loan capital and issued share capital, voting rights or such rights as would entitle him to more than 30 per cent of the assets available to equity holders on a winding-up;
(3) he has power to secure that the company's affairs are conducted in accordance with his wishes by means of the holding of shares or the possession of voting power of that or another company or by virtue

217

of any power in the articles or other document regulating that or any other company; or

(4) he is a party to a reciprocal arrangement under which some other person subscribes for shares in a company with which the individual (or any other individual who is a party to the arrangement) is connected.

For the purposes of (1) above, 'associate' means:

(1) the individual's husband or wife, parent or remoter forebear, child or remoter issue or any partner;
(2) a trustee of any settlement in relation to which the settlor is or was the individual or any of the persons mentioned in (1) (other than a partner), whether living or dead; or
(3) where the individual is interested in any shares or obligations of the company which are (with certain exceptions) subject to a trust or form part of a deceased's estate, any other person interested therein. It may, in this connection, be difficult to ascertain who is an associate and who is not.

The shares must be held in a qualifying company for at least five years and any relief claimed will be clawed back if shares are disposed of within the five-year period.

13.5.4 Qualifying companies

Two expressions used in connection with the qualification of a company require explanation.

(1) *The 'relevant period'*. In relation to 'qualifying companies' and 'qualifying trades' this means the period of three years beginning with the issue of the shares or, if the company was not at the time of such issue carrying on a qualifying trade, the period of three years from the commencement of such a trade.
(2) *A 'qualifying subsidiary'*. This means a subsidiary company which is not less than 90 per cent owned and controlled by the parent company, no arrangements being in existence by virtue of which it could cease to be so owned and controlled. That condition must be satisfied until the end of the 'relevant period' unless there is an earlier winding-up or dissolution for *bona fide* commercial reasons which is not part of a tax-avoidance arrangement and on which the subsidiary's net assets are distributed not more than three years after the commencement of the winding-up. The subsidiary must exist wholly or substantially to carry on qualifying activities or be a 'dormant' company, ie one which has no corporation tax profits and does not include the making of investments as part of its business.

The conditions to be complied with by the company are as follows:

(1) It must, throughout the 'relevant period', be an unquoted company which must exist wholly or 'substantially wholly' for the purpose of carrying on wholly or mainly in the UK one or more 'qualifying trades' (see **13.5.5**) or must carry on a business which consists wholly of either:
   (a) holding shares or securities of, or making loans to, one or more 'qualifying subsidiaries'; or
   (b) both (a) *and* the carrying on wholly or mainly in the UK of one or more 'qualifying trades'.

(2) The company's share capital must not, at any time in the 'relevant period', include any issued shares that are not fully paid up.

(3) The company must not, at any time in the relevant period, control (whether alone or with any connected person) another company or have a 51 per cent subsidiary or be controlled by another company (whether alone or with a connected person) or be a 51 per cent subsidiary nor must any arrangements be in existence at any time during the relevant period which could bring the company within any of the prohibited situations. An exception is made, however, for companies having subsidiaries which are themselves qualifying companies under (1) above.

(4) The original rules provided that a company's interest in land could not exceed one-half of its total assets. This condition was however removed with effect from 29 November 1994, under the provisions of the Finance Act 1995.

Another significant change from the BES rules is that qualifying companies can now include foreign companies. Provided that they trade in the United Kingdom, they will not be required to be incorporated or resident in the United Kingdom.

13.5.5 Qualifying trades

Some guidance was given by the Revenue, in a Statement of Practice dated 12 September 1986, of what, in their view, is meant by carrying on a trade 'wholly or mainly in the United Kingdom' referred to in **13.5.4**. Each case is determined on its facts including the 'totality of the activities of the trade'. Thus, regard is had to such factors as the location of capital assets, and the places where purchasing, manufacturing, selling and other things are done. The carrying on of some activities outside the UK does not disqualify the company if, in the Revenue's words, 'over one-half of the aggregate of these activities takes place within the country'. The phrase 'over one-half' suggests that some precise measurement must be possible. The Statement of Practice goes on to say that a company would not be excluded from relief solely because its output is exported, or its raw materials imported, or storage or marketing facilities exist overseas.

A 'qualifying trade' is one which does not to any substantial extent comprise:

(1) dealing in commodities, shares, securities, land or futures;
(2) dealing in goods otherwise than in an ordinary trade of wholesale or retail distribution;
(3) banking, insurance, moneylending, debt-factoring, hire-purchase financing or other financial activities;
(4) leasing (except for short term), chartering or ships;
(5) receiving royalties or licence fees;
(6) providing legal or accountancy services;
(7) oil extraction activities; or
(8) providing services of the nature of those set out in (1) to (7) for a trade carried on by any person who controls the trade carried on by the company.

A trade under (5) above is not disqualified if the company carrying on the trade is engaged, throughout the relevant period, in the production of films or in research and development and if all royalties and licence fees received by it in that period are for films produced by it, or of sound recordings or other products arising from such films or from research and development.

The trade must be carried on on a commercial basis and with a view to realising profits. It must have been carried on by the company for four months before the relief will be allowed and, if not carried on at the time of the issue, must be begun within two years thereafter.

13.5.6 Qualifying investments

For the investment to qualify for relief it must itself comply with a number of conditions:

(1) it must be made by the individual on his own behalf;
(2) the shares must be taken by subscription and not by purchase from an existing shareholder;
(3) the shares must be new ordinary shares which, throughout the five years from the date of issue, carry no present or future preferential rights to dividends, assets on a winding-up, or to redemption; and
(4) the shares must be issued for the purpose of raising money for a qualifying trade or activity carried on, or to be carried on, by the company.

The 1995 Finance Act contained provisions which relaxed the rules for shares issued after 28 November 1994 to allow relief to individuals, even where they are involved in the control of another company carrying on a similar trade.

Although the investment must be made by an individual, to qualify for relief, it may be made through an approved investment fund. Particulars regarding some of such funds are obtainable from the British Venture Capital Association.

13.5.7 Withdrawal of relief

Relief for investment in an EIS will be clawed back if an investor disposes of the shares within a period of five years, unless the disposal arises because the company has gone into liquidation. In these circumstances further income tax or capital gains tax relief may be due to the investor. Where the investor receives no payment as a result of the liquidation, the net amount of his investment may qualify as a capital loss.

The comments set out above should be taken as a guide only. They do not cover every detail of the proposed legislation but should help in identifying most of the difficulties to be faced in crossing this morass of regulations.

13.5.8 Venture capital trusts (VCTs)

In his 1993 budget the Chancellor announced proposals to create a new relief for investment in venture capital trusts. This announcement was followed by a consultative document, and the 1995 Finance Act contained provisions introducing the relief with effect from 6 April 1995.

VCTs are companies which are similar to investment trusts and to obtain approval they must meet a number of conditions, in particular:

(1) the ordinary share capital of a VCT must have been quoted on The Stock Exchange;
(2) the VCT must not retain more than 15 per cent of the income that it has derived from shares or securities;
(3) the income received by the VCT must have been derived wholly or mainly from shares or securities;
(4) the value of investments held by the VCT must consist of at least 70 per cent of qualifying shares or securities;
(5) at least 30 per cent of the value of a VCT's qualifying holdings must be made up of ordinary shares;
(6) the value of a VCT's holding in any one company must not exceed 15 per cent of its total investments.

It may be possible for a VCT to be granted provisional approval provided that the 70 per cent, and 30 per cent conditions mentioned in (4) and (5) above will be met within three years, and the other conditions in the current or next accounting period. This provisional approval will be withdrawn if the VCT fails to meet the conditions within these time periods.

13.5.9 Qualifying holdings

These must consist of holdings in unquoted companies which exist wholly or mainly for the purpose of carrying on a qualifying trade in the United Kingdom. For these purposes a qualifying trade is as defined for the EIS, and the gross assets of the unquoted company must not exceed £10m, immediately prior to the VCT's investment.

Income tax relief

Relief can be claimed by resident individuals aged 18 or over, and is available in two different ways.

First income tax relief at the rate of 20 per cent is given for amounts subscribed for new ordinary shares in the VCT, although the amount subscribed in any one year must not exceed £100,000. The relief is withdrawn unless the shares are held for at least five years.

In addition, dividends from ordinary shares held in VCTs are exempt from income tax, to the extent that the value of the shares acquired each year does not exceed £100,000.

Capital gains tax

Where investments in VCTs have qualified for income tax relief, disposals after five years are exempt from capital gains tax.

Reinvestment relief is also available for investments in VCTs, provided that the VCT shares for which the individual subscribes are issued during a period beginning 12 months before, and ending 12 months after, the date of disposal of the asset creating the capital gain which is to be deferred.

In common with investments in the EIS the deferred gain may be reinstated if the investor disposes of the shares, other than to his or her spouse, or ceases to be resident in the United Kingdom within five years of the issue of the VCT shares.

The relief is also withdrawn if the company ceases to be a qualifying VCT within three years of the issue of the shares, or within three years of the commencement of trading, if later, or the investor ceases to qualify for the 20 per cent income tax relief.

13.6 DORMANT PARTNERSHIPS

13.6.1 Introduction

It is not unusual for a person commencing a trade to find himself short of capital. In such circumstances an investor who is persuaded of the trade's potential viability may be prepared to put up the capital but not want to play any active part in the carrying on of the business. He is then a 'dormant' or 'sleeping' partner. Since partners are generally entitled to take part in the running of the business, this arrangement must be the subject of a special agreement.

Unless the business name consists of the names of all the partners, it must comply with the provisions of the Business Names Act 1985. This Act governs names which may and may not be used for business purposes and how and where they must be disclosed. A register of such names was formerly maintained but was closed in February 1982.

13.6.2 Loan creditors

It is important to distinguish a dormant partner from a loan creditor. If the investor receives a fixed rate of interest on his investment he is probably not a partner at all. Under s 2 of the Partnership Act 1890 the receipt of a share of the profits is *prima facie* evidence of partnership, although the receipt of such a share or of interest at a rate varying with the profits does not of itself make the lender a partner. This apparent contradiction was explained by North J, in *Davis v Davis* [1894] 1 Ch 393, and it appears from his judgment that the Act means that all the relevant facts must be taken together, no special weight being attached to the sharing of profits. It is difficult to see how the Act could be intended to mean that, although, in fairness to North J, it is equally difficult to see that it could be intended to mean anything else either. In the majority of cases there is (and there certainly should be) a written agreement making the position clear. If the agreement so declares, and the name of the dormant partner is included in the firm's name, there is little doubt of the existence of a partnership.

13.6.3 Rights and liabilities

Once it is established that the 'investor' (to use a neutral term) is a dormant partner and not merely a loan creditor, certain rights arise. For example, he is entitled to inspect and take a copy of the firm's accounts and, in the absence of any agreement to the contrary, to investigate their contents.

A dormant partner is, generally, personally liable for the firm's debts even if the creditors were unaware of his partnership at the time when the debts arose. This liability extends to the whole of the partner's personal fortune. Such an arrangement can therefore carry considerable personal risk, although this can be curtailed by the formation of a 'limited partnership'.

Under the Limited Partnerships Act 1907 it is possible for a partner to limit his liability to the amount contributed by him to the partnership at its inception, although there must always be at least one partner whose liability is unlimited. The limited partner may not receive back any of his capital so long as the partnership continues, and if any of it is returned to him, his liability up to the amount of his original contribution will remain. He is, of course, entitled to draw out his share of the firm's profits.

A limited partner must always be a dormant partner. Should he take any active part in the running of the business, the limitation of his liability is lost, and it will then extend to the whole of the partnership's debts and to the full extent of his personal assets.

The law relating to dormant partnerships is liberally sprinkled with traps for the unwary, and the law relating to limited partnerships is particularly unsatisfactory. No partnership of any sort should be entered into without taking legal advice, and although the law does not require a partnership agreement to be reduced to writing, it is always desirable that it should be. Whatever the relations may have been at the outset, it is only too easy for the partner entering too readily into informal arrangements to find the whole of his personal estate at risk in respect of liabilities which he played no part in incurring. It is when things start to go wrong that dissensions occur, and by then it may be too late to correct matters which should have been dealt with at the outset.

13.6.4 Taxation

A trading partnership, like any other trader, is normally assessed to tax on the basis of the profits of the trading year ending during the tax year prior to the year of assessment. For example, if the accounts are taken to 31 December, the profits for the year ended 31 December 1994 form the basis of the assessment for the tax year 1995–96. This general rule is subject to various complications relating to the opening years, the closing years, changes in partnership treated as a cessation, and losses. The 1994 Finance Act contained legislation to abolish the 'preceding year' basis of assessment for the self-employed, with effect from 6 April 1996. This change will however have immediate effect for businesses starting after 5 April 1994, although existing businesses will not fully change to the current year basis until the tax year 1997–98. There are complicated transitional provisions to ensure that profits are not taxed twice, and special rules will apply where a business changes its accounting date.

The assessable profit for the transitional year 1996–97 will be based on a 12-month average of the profits for the two-year period ending in the year ending 5 April 1997. There are however a number of anti-avoidance provisions which are intended to prevent manipulation of trading profits in order to gain a tax advantage. All these amendments have been made to simplify the introduction of self-assessment on 6 April 1996.

Having determined the amount of the assessment for, say 1995–96, that amount was apportioned among the partners in accordance with their profit-sharing arrangements for that fiscal year regardless of the way in which they actually shared the profit on which the assessment was based. It will be appreciated that this may have led to inequitable results. The change to the current year basis from 1997/98 will of course have the effect that assessable profits will relate far more closely to actual profits.

Earned income is defined in s 833(4)(c) of the Income and Corporation Taxes Act 1988 as income which is 'derived by the individual from the carrying on or exercise by him of his trade . . ., in the case of a partnership, as a partner personally acting therein'. Any partnership income not falling within that definition is investment income. Since a dormant partner (whether with limited liability or not) does not, by definition, act personally in the business, it must follow that any income derived from the partnership will be investment income. This will be of significance in relation to retirement pension schemes.

13.7 MEMBERSHIP OF LLOYD'S

13.7.1 Introduction

Some 300 years ago Edward Lloyd opened a coffee-house in the City which proved to be a popular meeting place for men with an interest in shipping. In 1692 he moved to larger premises on the corner of Lombard Street and Abchurch Lane, where the financial quarter had become well-established, which soon became known as a centre where ship-owners could take insurance cover. With the increasing size of ships and value of cargoes, the size of the risks grew and individual underwriters were obliged to join in syndicates, so creating the system which still functions today. Lloyd's itself, as in its coffee-house days, does no more than provide accommodation and facilities for the underwriters; it is not, and never has been, an insurer. Lloyd's was incorporated by Act of Parliament in 1871, and that and later Acts regulate the fundamental rules and authorise the making of byelaws by the members. An Act of 1911 authorised the underwriting of non-marine risks, regularising what had already become well-established practice.

Lloyd's of London published a business plan on 29 April 1993, which set out proposals intended to improve the profitability of Lloyd's by increasing capacity, cutting costs and capping losses arising prior to the 1986 account. However, the most fundamental proposal was to allow corporate membership of Lloyd's from the 1994 account. This introduced the concept of limited liability for the first time in the history of Lloyd's.

Members of Lloyd's (called 'Names') are grouped into syndicates and share in the syndicates' profits or losses. As regards losses, each member of a syndicate is liable only for his agreed share (unlike a partnership loss where each partner is jointly and separately liable for all losses) but at present that liability extends to the whole of his assets. Generally, a Name takes no part in managing the affairs of his syndicate. He is thus entirely in the hands of his Underwriting Agent (see **13.7.2**).

Income and gains received by Names comprise:

(1) investment income and capital gains on deposits and reserve funds (see **13.7.2**);
(2) investment income and capital gains on premiums received and invested by the syndicate; and
(3) underwriting profits (excess of premiums over claims) if any.

It must not be overlooked that both capital and underwriting losses may also arise. Figures are produced three years in arrears.

Following a series of unprecedented disasters, further problems surfaced in 1991 with claims of fraud and mismanagement, and some syndicates remained open until the Reconstruction and Renewal plan, since they were unable to reinsure to close. Names have suffered unprecedented losses.

Despite the drop in membership from the late 1980s, many Names increased their premium limits for 1996 and including corporate members the capacity of the market was over £11bn. Many non-corporate members, however, no longer have the readily realisable wealth formerly relied on (see **13.7.2**) and rely instead on bank guarantees secured against property.

It is suggested that much of the malaise stemmed from the Lloyd's Act 1982 which ruled that brokers could no longer own agencies managing syndicates. The intention of this was to prevent conflicts of interest but it probably resulted in brokers moving business elsewhere.

Certainly the problems of Lloyd's were considered. As well as many resignations there was much litigation and constant bad news which tended to scare off potential members. During 1996 Lloyd's announced details of a Reconstruction and Renewal plan, which involved the creation of a reinsurance company, Equitas, to reinsure 1992 and prior year liabilities. This gave Names an opportunity to end the uncertainty about past liabilities, and allow those who wish to leave Lloyd's to do so.

Whilst it may be possible to reduce the element of risk by taking out high level stop loss insurance policies and entering into members' agency pooling arrangements (MAPAs), one cannot avoid the fact that under the present regime an individual Name accepts unlimited personal liability.

13.7.2 Application for individual membership

The aspiring member must satisfy Lloyd's that he is a proper person to join their number. He must be sponsored by the existing Names, one of whom must be a director, employee or partner of the prospective Name's intended Members' Agent. The application form is posted in the Underwriting Room and the applicant is then interviewed by a sub-committee. The sub-committee, whatever other questions it may ask, always asks whether the applicant clearly understands that he will be trading with unlimited liability. The liability is not limited to the wealth shown (see below) nor to the amount of the deposit (see below). In the event of a substantial claim arising, the whole of the applicant's personal estate is at risk.

It is generally recommended that members should spread their risk among a number of syndicates. Membership of one syndicate only may mean a heavy financial loss in the event of a major disaster. MAPAs, which were first introduced on 1 January 1994, allows its members to take a smaller share in a wider range of syndicates, and thus help to reduce the exposure of each Name.

At an early stage, and certainly before election, the applicant must investigate the syndicate or syndicates which he hopes to join. Assistance in the choice of syndicate may be obtained from a Members' Underwriting Agent (not the same as a Managing Agent, although he may be so in practice). The policy for investing syndicate funds and the likely premium income will be explained by the syndicate's Underwriting Agent (see below) and the result of the last seven 'closed years' will be made available. A 'closed year' is one in respect of which the underwriting account has been closed by reinsuring any outstanding liabilities, usually at the end of the third year. The applicant should also enquire about the establishment of personal reserves, transfer to the Special Reserve Fund, and the form of accounts.

Applications for membership must be approved by the Committee, who apply a means test to the applicant's readily realisable assets which include Stock Exchange securities, life policies at their surrender values, reversionary interests and real property but not the applicant's principal residence. Gold (up to 30 per cent of the total), which must be held by an approved bank in the form of bullion or coins, is valued at 70 per cent of market value. Such things as shares in private companies, jewellery and antiques are not included. An applicant needs to show that he has readily realisable assets worth £250,000.

Where the applicant's wealth comprises items not readily realisable but is in other respects satisfactory, the Committee will accept, in whole or in part, a guarantee or letter of credit from an approved bank, as collateral for which the principal residence may be included. The object of the means test is to ensure that as far as possible, funds will be available at short notice to meet a claim, however large it may be. A booklet entitled 'Membership: the Issues' is obtainable from Lloyd's and sets out all the information which an applicant should know.

13.7.3 Conditions of individual membership

The Members' Underwriting Agent controls the underwriting affairs of the underwriting members of his agency. He maintains the accounts and records and deals with taxation, reserves, investments and other day-to-day matters as well as watching the statistics which give him a guide to current trends. It is also his duty to ensure that the rules laid down by the Committee of Lloyd's are complied with. Every underwriting member enters into an agreement with the agent which sets out the terms and conditions on which the agent acts, including his salary or fee and his rate of commission.

Every individual underwriting member is required to deposit with the Corporation of Lloyd's approved investments or cash which the Corporation holds as trustee. The Lloyd's deposit must be maintained at a minimum of £25,000. For further details enquiries should be made to the deposits department at Lloyd's. The investing of the deposit may be delegated to the Underwriting Agent or may, within the Committee's rules, be dealt with by the member. The income arising on investments deposited remains the income of the member.

A member's premium limit is the maximum premium income which may be underwritten by him in any one year. It is allocated to the syndicate and is then divided among the members in proportions agreed in consultation with the agent. The limit may be increased or decreased according to the deposit's market value and may be raised if additional amounts are deposited and evidence of sufficient means is produced. If the limit is exceeded the member is normally be required increase his deposit.

An entrance fee is payable in cash on election and varies according to the category of membership. Entrance fees are not deductible from profits for tax purposes. An annual contribution to Lloyd's Central Fund is also required. The Fund was set up in 1926 for the protection of policyholders in the event of the inability of a member to meet his liabilities out of his syndicate's trust funds, his deposit, his reserves and his personal assets. The reserve is the amount which, under the Rules, has to be set aside each year to meet the estimated cost of winding up the Name's underwriting accounts.

13.7.4 Taxation

The special provisions covering the taxation of the income of underwriters are in ss 450–457 of the Income and Corporation Taxes Act 1988, although the Finance Acts 1993 and 1994 contain further provisions which change the way in which Lloyd's Names are taxed from the 1994 underwriting account. The 1994 account profits will not be assessed for 1994–95, but in 1997–98, the year of distribution. In normal circumstances this charge would create a three-year period for which no syndicate profits would be assessable (1994–95 to 1996–97). However, as a result of the Reconstruction and Renewal arrangements many Names will be entitled to debt credits which will be assessable for 1996/97. These should be carefully considered by the applicant with expert advice. Briefly, the effect of the current legislation for underwriting years up to the 1993 underwriting account is as follows.

Underwriting profits will be assessed on the basis of the profits of the underwriting year ending in the year of assessment and not on the normal basis of the previous year. Thus the profits of the underwriting year ending 31 December 1993 will be assessed for the fiscal year 1993–94 although they were not finally ascertained for three years thereafter. Underwriting profits are profits or gains arising from underwriting business or from assets forming part of a premium trust fund. A premium paid for reinsurance is deductible as an expense. Losses of an underwriting business are allowed against other income of the year of assessment in which they are incurred, and any excess against that of the previous year if the underwriter was carrying on an underwriting business in that year. They cannot, however, be carried forward against general income of a later year but can be set against future underwriting profits, which includes personal Lloyd's income from the Lloyd's Deposit and Personal Reserves.

For many years it has been possible for Names to transfer part of their underwriting profits into a Special Reserve Fund. The object of this fund was to provide a source of money which could be called on in years in which a loss arose. However the old style Special Reserve Fund was quite limited, in that only a maximum of £7,000 could be transferred each year and tax relief was only available at a rate equal to the difference between the basic rate and the higher rate of tax.

A new type of Special Reserve Fund was introduced with effect from the 1992 account, although any existing old style special reserves could be transferred to the new reserve fund. Transfers to the fund will qualify for both basic rate and higher rate relief, and it will be possible to transfer 50 per cent of Lloyd's profits into the reserve each year, providing that the value of the funds held in the reserve does not exceed 50 per cent of the Name's overall premium limit. Any income or gains arising from assets held in the reserve are exempt from income tax and capital gains tax.

Withdrawals from the reserve will be made to fund losses, cash calls, or on resignation or death. This will be treated as underwriting income of the Name at the time of withdrawal. The tax calculation will be based on the actual value of the withdrawal rather than the 'book values' of the assets comprising the withdrawal. In effect the increase in the value of the fund attributable to income and gains will not be taxed as it arises, but on withdrawal.

13.8 INVESTMENT IN ANOTHER'S EXPERTISE

The first difficulty in making an investment of this kind lies in discovering the innovator whose expertise is to be given financial backing. The innovator seeking capital has many avenues open to him. He may consult the National Research Development Corporation, the Council for Small Industries in Rural Areas, Investors in Industry Group plc (formerly known as the Industrial and Commercial Finance Corporation) or the Small Business Capital Fund. Alternatively he may look for capital through his bank or a merchant bank, through local accountants, solicitors or insurance brokers, through the Rotary Club or the Round Table, through the local branch of the British Institute of Management or through the Small Firms Council of the Confederation of British Industry. The prospective investor can approach any of these agencies to inquire whether they know of any worthwhile ideas for which backing is sought.

Once the innovator has been located, the venture's prospects must be carefully examined, not only by the investor's accountant but also by an expert in the technical field where appropriate. Inquiry should be made as to how much of his own capital the innovator is putting into the venture. If he has little he cannot be expected to put much in, but his intentions in this respect indicate his real confidence in the venture. Plans should be carefully prepared and the amount required should be meticulously calculated, all contingencies being taken into account. The information required includes particulars of the product or process, with technical explanations and specifications of patents, if any. Its advantages over existing products or processes must be explained and the costs of development detailed, together with reasoned estimates of future sales. Mere hopes based on speculation will not do.

In general terms, an investor may back another's expertise by means of a private company, a partnership or a loan. A loan will probably be the least attractive method for two reasons. First, adequate security is unlikely to be available. Secondly, the income is limited to interest at a fixed rate, thus denying the lender any participation in profits should the venture prove an outstanding success – the greatest attraction of this type of investment. For private companies and partnerships, it is necessary to determine the appropriate proportionate interests of the investor who is putting in capital and the expert who is putting in expertise. Both may be of equal importance: indeed both are essential, but 50:50 holdings can mean deadlock and are better avoided if possible. This immediately gives rise to a problem which needs professional advice and probably tough negotiating.

Some of the legal aspects of the arrangement (including any liability for taxation on profits or gains arising) are dealt with in general terms earlier in this chapter. As has already been stressed, every case will present individual problems, and both commercial and professional advice should always be sought. Adequate financial and administrative control is essential for the investor, and he will usually be wise to insist on his own accountant auditing the books and his representative keeping a close eye on the running of the business.

13.9 RACEHORSES

13.9.1 Introduction

Investing in racehorses is not for the faint-hearted. The rules regulating racing in this country are made by the Jockey Club from whom detailed information may be obtained. Anyone proposing to invest in a racehorse is presumably already well-acquainted with the turf and will know something about horses. Investment may be either in horses in training or in stallions. (Investment in stud farms and training establishments is discussed at **11.4.3**.)

The increase in the cost of buying and running a horse led to an expansion of syndicated ownership regulated (for horses in training) by the Jockey Club 'rules of racing'. New syndicates are, however, no longer accepted by the Jockey Club and where a horse is owned jointly it must now be by way of a legally enforceable partnership of which each member is registered as an owner. The number of partners is restricted (as it was for syndicate members) to 12. The partnership agreement (which should be drawn up with legal advice) must be registered with the Jockey Club. All partners are jointly and severally liable for entrance fees, stakes, forfeits and jockey's fees. That is to say that any one of them may be held individually liable for the full amount and will then have to recover the due amounts from the other partners.

It is recommended by the Jockey Club that anyone proposing to become a part-owner by way of a partnership should contact them before taking any steps in the matter. The rules governing joint-ownership are complex and the Jockey Club would prefer to advise at the outset rather than unscramble an arrangement that contravenes the rules.

An interest in a racehorse may be bought through the medium of a limited company but it must be realised that the investor is then buying a share in the company and not a share in a horse. There are a number of public limited companies engaged in these activities.

13.9.2 Stallions

As well as investments in horses in training, investments may be made in syndicated stallions. In this case there are no rules of the sort set out for horses in training – *ad hoc* arrangements are made in each case. A stallion may stand at stud until it is 20 years old, but the value of a nomination falls as it approaches that age. A stallion will give about 150 services each season, covering each mare three or four times. Stud fees at present range generally up to about 1,500 guineas, although that figure may be greatly exceeded in special cases.

In a typical syndicate there will be 40 shares, most of which will be held by shareholders with one share each. The agreement usually provides for a committee, including the major shareholder or shareholders, to be set up. The committee will be empowered to decide all matters relating to the management of the stallion and the affairs of the syndicate as agent for the shareholders, although its powers regarding the stallion's disposal are usually limited. Generally each shareholder is entitled to one nomination per share for the season. The maximum number of nominations for the season is fixed, and in so far as it exceeds the number available to shareholders, the excess may be sold and the proceeds set against expenses which are borne *pro rata* by the shareholders. The agreement usually provides that the committee must approve mares to be served by the stallion and that a barren mare must also be approved by a veterinary surgeon. A veterinary surgeon will examine any maiden mare before service. Restrictions are usually placed on the disposal of shares and nominations, but it may happen that during the season in question the shareholder has no mare suitable for nomination and in such a case the nomination will be sold.

13.9.3 Taxation

Income tax

It was held in *Benson v Counsell* (1942) 24 TC 178 that receipts from the sale of nominations were receipts of annual income chargeable to income tax under Schedule D Case VI, although they were not trading receipts within Case I. This decision was based on the fact that the taxpayer had not bought the rights to nomination that he sold: what he had bought was an interest in the horse. The sale of the rights merely realised the horse's reproductive faculties and it thus became an income-producing asset. In 1915 the Earl of Derby unsuccessfully contended that a stallion at stud was 'plant' for the purposes of capital allowances (see *Derby (Earl) v Aylmer* [1915] 3 KB 374).

Capital gains tax

The sale of a share in the horse, whether it is a horse in training or a stallion, does *not* give rise to a taxable gain, since s 45(1) of the Taxation of Chargeable Gains Act 1992 takes out of the charge to capital gains tax any gain accruing on the disposal of, or of an interest in, an asset which is tangible, movable property and a wasting asset. There is no doubt that a horse is tangible and movable, nor that it is a wasting asset (ie one with a predictable life not exceeding 50 years).

13.10 BACKING PLAYS

It is possible that, somewhere, a playwright has just written a play that will take London by storm and play for years to packed houses. It is, on present showing, most unlikely. It is estimated that only one show in seven put on in the West End will be successful which suggests that somewhere along the line there is a failure to foresee what the public will and will not like. In past years flops have included *Stop the World I Want to Get Off, Exclusive, Metropolis, Sherlock Holmes, Someone Like You, Look Look, Dean, Barnardo, Can-Can, Fire Angel, King, Top People, Y, Ziegfeld, Troubadour, Bus Stop, Bernadette, My Lovely . . . Shayna Madel, Rick's Bar Casablanca* and *Children of Eden*. Together they have lost millions. The last one, alone, is said to have lost £2.5m.

This is not the place to consider the reasons for this failure rate but those tempted to put money into a play should realise that their chance of making anything out of it is slim. It is statistically more probable that money put in will be lost without tax relief. This is the ideal investment for those who enjoy losing money.

Those who put up the money for a theatrical production – the 'angels' – normally split the profits with the management: the angels usually take 60 per cent and the management 40 per cent, although the proportions are a matter for agreement. The agreement usually also provides for an 'overcall', ie a liability on the part of the angels to put up additional capital should it prove necessary. Before the profits are divided between angels and management there has to be deducted such of the fees and expenses of management as may be specified in the agreement. The agreement should be carefully scrutinised by an adviser familiar with these matters to ensure that the angel is getting his fair share.

Anyone determined to risk this gamble against heavy odds should first become familiar with the track records of various producers. The eager investor should then attempt to force his money on one who seems successful. If a producer makes the approach, consider why his usual sources of finance are not available. There is no central exchange through which investments can be made although assistance may be obtained from the Society of West End Theatre. Whilst not arranging investments itself, the Society will give advice and maintains a list of prospective backers. Since the backer will normally have no opportunity even to read the play he is simply betting on the producer's wisdom.

The cost of mounting a play varies enormously. A large-scale musical can cost millions to stage, and with production and running costs at their present levels a show has to run for a considerable time before the production costs are covered and anything is paid out. If the production is successful the investor will receive an agreed share of the net profits which will, first, recoup the costs and, thereafter, constitute income for tax purposes.

As a variant of the traditional method of financing, advantage may be taken of the provisions of s 574 of the Income and Corporation Taxes Act 1988 which enables losses on unquoted shares in certain trading companies to be set off against a taxpayer's income. The resulting loss is thus, to some extent, cushioned by income tax relief.

13.11 OPTIONS ON BOOKS

An investor with sufficient faith in a little-known author may back that faith by purchasing an option, exercisable usually for one year, to develop the book into a film or play. A little-known author is suggested as, in the case of a best-seller writer, the option is likely (if it is available at all) to be extremely expensive. It is, of course, much less expensive to buy such an option than it would be to buy the copyright outright.

Once the option is purchased it will become necessary to write or procure a script from the book and then to persuade a film company or theatrical producer to take it up. The time involved in these activities may necessitate the purchase of another year's option.

Would-be purchasers should consult a firm of literary agents for further advice. A list of agents is published in the *Writers and Artists Yearbook*.

13.12 PREVIEW OF THE YEAR AHEAD

The new Labour administration may well have a significant effect on future stock market and property values, interest rates, and investment opportunities. This uncertainty makes it difficult to predict the extent of further encouragement of the creation of new businesses, but generally, when one door closes, another opens.

Lloyd's produced a profit for the 1993 Underwriting Account, and profits are also predicted for the 1994 and 1995 accounts. Whilst corporate membership of Lloyd's may now appear to be a more attractive option than individual membership, as liability can be limited, this will inevitably mean that the opportunity to share in profits will also be limited.

SOURCES OF FURTHER INFORMATION
Useful addresses

Registrar of Companies/Registrar
  of Limited Partnerships
Companies Registration Office
Companies House
Crown Way
Cardiff
CF4 3UZ

Tel: (01222) 388588

Lloyd's of London
Lime Street
London
EC3M 7AH

Tel: (0171) 623 7100

National Research Development
  Corporation
101 Newington Causeway
London
SE1 6BU

Tel: (0171) 403 6666

Rural Development Commission
141 Castle Street
Salisbury
Wiltshire
SP1 3TP

Tel: (01722) 336255

Investors in Industry Group plc
91 Waterloo Road
London
SE1 8XP

Tel: (0171) 928 3131

British Venture Capital Association
Essex House
12–13 Essex Street
London
WC2R 3AA

Tel: (0171) 240 3846

Development Capital Group
    Limited
21 Moorfield
London
EC2P 2HT

Tel: (0171) 588 2721

Department of Trade and Industry
    Small Firms Service
To obtain address of nearest
    centre, dial 100 and ask the
    operator for Freefone
    Enterprise

British Institute of Management
3rd Floor
2 Savoy Court
Strand
London
WC2R 0EZ

Tel: (0171) 497 0580

Confederation of British Industry
Centrepoint
103 New Oxford Street
London
WC1A 1DU

Tel: (0171) 379 7400

Jockey Club
42 Portman Square
London
W1H 0EN

Tel: (0171) 486 4921

Society of West End Theatre &
    West End Theatre
    Managers Ltd
Bedford Chambers
The Piazza
Covent Garden
London
WC2E 8HQ

Tel: (0171) 836 0971

14

LIFE ASSURANCE

VINCE JERRARD LLB, ACII

Legal Director, Allied Dunbar Assurance plc

14.1 INTRODUCTION

Assurance contracts may be divided into three broad types, according to the nature of the primary benefits provided:

(1) life assurance policies (including single premium bonds) pay out a lump sum on death or on the expiration of a specified period;

(2) purchased life annuities pay periodic sums as long as the annuitant is alive;

(3) pension contracts provide pensions and other benefits and are available through one's work or occupation.

Within each of these categories there are further subdivisions. Pension contracts are dealt with in Chapter 15.

14.2 HIGHLIGHTS OF THE PREVIOUS YEAR

14.2.1 Life assurance business

After a couple of difficult years, the UK life assurance industry returned to growth in 1996. All three major product areas improved over 1995's performance.

The buoyant stock market, low building society interest rates and a constant stream of guaranteed products gave the investment market a record year, 50 per cent higher than 1995. The individual pensions market growth was an encouraging 23 per cent, signalling a return of confidence in an area in which it was particularly dented by the problems of personal pensions mis-selling in the late 1980s.

The 'restructuring' of the industry continued with more mergers, acquisitions and de-mutualisations. A further reduction in the number of active life companies is expected in future years.

14.2.2 Taxation changes

November 1996 saw the unveiling of the Revenue's proposed new regime for life policy taxation, originally announced in 1994.

The proposal involves a Consultation Document and 93 draft clauses of legislation. Consultation was due to continue until the end of April 1997 but it seems unlikely that any new regime will be enacted before spring of 1998 or brought into effect until a year after that.

The new regime, as proposed in the Consultation Document, would be quite radical in approach but somewhat less radical in effect in many areas.

There would still be a category of tax-favoured policies able to provide proceeds tax-free at maturity, death or encashment, even to a higher-rate taxpayer. The requirements for tax-favoured status would still include a minimum policy duration, payment of regular and level premiums (within a more flexible framework), and the provision of a sum assured of reasonable amount, in relation to premiums paid.

However, there would be no pre-certification of 'qualifying' policies as under the current regime (see **14.3.6**), and the testing to see if proceeds attracted tax would be carried out at policy termination.

On balance, if pre-certification has to be removed, the new 'qualifying' rules are reasonably attractive. However, other proposals, such as changes to the treatment of policies held in trust, removal of the '5 per cent per annum tax-free withdrawals' from policies, and the creation of some new chargeable events (including making gifts – even between spouses – chargeable), are certainly unwelcome as attacks on the reasonable expectations of existing policyholders.

A particular concern for the industry is the cost of the reforms which could be as high as £1bn, industry-wide.

Clearly the consultation process will be extremely important, with cost and protection of the interests of existing policyholders being of prime concern.

14.3 LIFE ASSURANCE POLICIES

14.3.1 Legal nature

Life assurance policies are contracts between the individual policyholders and the life insurance company. The general principle underlying life assurance policies is that the insurance company is the collecting house of pooled risks and investments of policyholders and offers benefits directly to them based on personal contracts.

The life company maintains the underlying investment funds in its own right but, depending on the policy's nature, undertakes to pay the policyholder either a specified sum, a sum which is increased periodically out of the company's profits, or one which varies with the value of part of the underlying fund.

An important characteristic of the life assurance policy as an investment is that it does not produce an income, as such, but is essentially a medium- to long-term accumulator. The income and capital gains of the underlying funds accrue to and are taxed in the hands of the insurance company, but the benefit is passed on, to a greater or lesser extent, in the growth in value of the policy. Many types of policy, however, allow regular or irregular encashment of part of the policy (withdrawal plans or encashment of bonuses) to serve as 'income', if required (but see 'Withdrawal plans and policy loans' at **14.3.4** and also **14.3.6** concerning part surrender of single premium policies).

14.3.2 Pre-conditions

To take out a life assurance policy an *insurable interest* in the life to be assured must exist, ie a pecuniary interest that would be adversely affected by the death of the life assured. At the time the policy is taken out, the policyholder must have an insurable interest in the life assured commensurate with the sum assured. Individuals have an unlimited insurable interest in their own and their spouses' lives.

Usually, where life assurance is taken out as an investment, the contract is applied for and held by a person on his own or his spouse's life, or on their joint lives, for his or her own personal benefit or for their joint benefit. Policies can, however, be the subject of gifts, in which case they are generally written in trust for the benefit of the beneficiaries (see **14.3.7**). They can also be assigned, by way of gift, or for value, or as security for a debt (eg as collateral security for a house mortgage or an overdraft).

14.3.3 Divisions and types

Endowment, whole of life and term assurances

All life policies provide life cover – a sum or sums assured payable on death. Most policies, other than temporary assurances, also provide investment benefits – sums payable on surrender or maturity. Life policies may be divided into endowment, whole of life and term policies, depending on the emphasis that is placed on savings or on protection (life cover):

(1) An endowment policy, which has a high savings element, is one under which the benefits are payable at the end of a predetermined period (the endowment period) or on death, if earlier.
(2) A whole of life policy is one under which the benefits are in general payable on death, whenever it occurs.
(3) A term policy is a temporary assurance, the sum assured being payable on death within a specified period only.

Both endowment and whole of life policies may be surrendered (ie cashed in) prematurely for a cash lump sum, the size of which depends on the contract's nature. Term assurances generally do not have an investment element as far as the individual is concerned, and so rarely have any surrender or cash-in value.

With profit, without profit and unit-linked policies

Within the endowment and whole of life categories, life policies can be of different types, depending on the way in which the sums payable by the company are determined:

(1) *With profit* contracts are policies under which a minimum sum is guaranteed to be paid by the life company, augmented from time to time by bonuses declared by the company according to its profits. These bonuses may be reversionary (bonuses added to the sum assured, either yearly or triennially) or terminal (bonuses declared at the end of the policy as an increment to the final payment). Reversionary bonuses may be simple or compound: simple bonuses are based only on the sum assured, while compound bonuses are based on the sum assured plus previous bonuses. Reversionary bonuses are usually expressed as a percentage of the sum assured or of the sum assured as increased by previous bonuses. Under a with profit endowment policy the individual receives at maturity the minimum sum assured plus the bonuses, reversionary and terminal.

A development in recent years has been the creation of what are called 'unitised with profits' policies. These are with profits business but are structured to give the appearance of unit linking, particularly in terms of the policy charging structure. Frequently, unitised with profits business offers a 'smoothed' growth, often with a guaranteed minimum rate, but the guarantee may only apply to maturity and death values and not to earlier surrenders.

(2) *Without profit* contracts are policies under which the life company guarantees to pay an absolute sum and invests the premiums in such a way as to produce that sum, bearing any shortfall in the return or retaining any profit in excess of the guaranteed return.

(3) Under *unit-linked* policies the life company maintains a number of underlying funds, which are divided, for accounting purposes only, into 'units'. The company undertakes to pay to the policyholder an amount equal to the greater of the guaranteed sum and the value of the units allocated to the policy. The underlying fund might consist of specific types of investment media often with a choice of geographical spread (such as property, equities, unit trusts, investment trusts, government securities, local authority and bank loans or deposits, or building society deposits) or the fund may consist of a combination of some or all of these ('managed' or 'mixed' funds). Out of every premium a proportion is allocated to the purchase of units which are credited to the policy. The movement in value of the underlying fund is directly reflected in the price of the units allocated to the policy and hence in the value of the policy benefits. Many types of policies give the policyholder himself the right to transfer his policy link from fund to fund at his option, by way of a simple procedure at low cost (eg a policy that is linked to an equity fund may be switched to become linked to fixed interest securities or bank deposits).

A life company generally has full investment freedom of the type of investments it chooses, subject only to the investments being a suitable 'match' for its liabilities. In the case of unit-linked policies the Insurance Company Regulations only permit linkage to certain types of assets, such as those listed in (3) above.

If the contract is one under which a guaranteed minimum or guaranteed absolute amount is provided, the investor knows that he will get at least that sum. At the same time, in the case of with profit policies, he has the advantage of having the guaranteed minimum augmented from time to time by reversionary and terminal bonuses, or, in unit-linked contracts, augmented by the movement of the value of the underlying fund (capital growth plus reinvested income).

Regular premium and single premium policies

A further broad division of life policies (of all types) depends on how premiums are payable:

(1) regular premium policies (also known as annual premium policies) are those under which premiums are payable annually, half-yearly, quarterly or monthly, either throughout the policy's duration or for a limited premium-paying period of time; and

(2) single premium policies are purchased by way of one single premium or lump sum (although such policies can usually accept further investment at any time).

Qualifying and non-qualifying policies

A brief introduction to qualifying and non-qualifying policies is given at **14.3.6**. The distinction between the two types of policy is important because their proceeds are treated differently for tax purposes in the hands of the policyholder.

14.3.4 Characteristics of regular premium policies

Investment and protection

All endowment and whole of life policies have an investment or savings element as well as a life insurance protection element. The extent to which the policy is slanted towards investment depends on the policy's nature and duration and the relationship between the premiums payable, the age of the life assured and the extent of the life cover provided.

In general, policies that have a low sum assured relative to the premiums payable over the policy life have a high savings or investment element, and conversely, high sums assured relative to the premiums payable mean that the policy is tilted more towards life assurance cover than towards investment. In considering life policies as investments, temporary or term assurances will be excluded, as these generally do not have a surrender value and benefits are payable only on death. They are usually taken out purely for life cover protection, to provide for one's family or to cover a prospective liability such as inheritance tax.

The type of policy that an individual should take out generally depends on his circumstances and objectives, weighing up not only the required degree of investment relative to protection but also the required degree of certainty of result relative to the potential for increased gain.

In general, the incidence of inflation and the conservatism of companies in guaranteeing a long-term return has meant that without profit policies have tended to provide a relatively poor rate of return compared with with profit and unit-linked policies.

A with profit policy gives the prospect of sharing in the company's investment performance where this exceeds that needed to meet the guarantee – but the need to satisfy the guarantee may still lead the company to a more conservative investment strategy.

With no guaranteed investment return a unit linked policy could be viewed as a little more risky but may also offer the prospect of better fund performance.

Withdrawal plans and policy loans

In the past, a feature of many regular premium policies with a high investment content was the facility, after a period of years, to operate withdrawal plans, under which the premium was reduced to a nominal amount, eg £1 per annum and regular or irregular sums could be taken from the policy by way of partial surrender to serve as an income, leaving the balance to accumulate. This withdrawal facility was challenged by the Revenue and withdrawn from qualifying policies issued on or after 25 February 1988. Policies issued before that date may continue as qualifying policies despite the presence of such an option. Substantially the same result may be achieved by taking out a series of smaller policies and cashing in individual policies from time to time while continuing the remainder and it may be possible to take withdrawals from a policy provided it has not suffered such a large premium reduction as was previously allowed. Many policies also give the policyholder the right to borrow from the insurance company at a beneficial rate of interest on the security of the policy.

14.3.5 Characteristics of single premium policies

In the main, the relevant single premium policies for investment purposes consist of single premium 'bonds' which are whole of life assurance policies. For many years these have been, in the main, unit-linked policies often marketed as property bonds, managed bonds, equity bonds, etc by reference to the initial underlying fund to which the policy was linked. There are also single premium endowment policies, but these are less significant.

In recent years, there has been considerable business written as with profit bonds. Although these did not generally incorporate the usual guarantees on future values, they did prove to be attractive in a time of recession and stock market uncertainty.

The main investment characteristic of single premium unit-linked bonds is the high allocation of the premium to investment in the underlying fund, with relatively low life cover. Virtually the entire premium is allocated to 'units', save only for the initial management charges, resulting, in effect, in the investment of most of the premium in the chosen fund. Most companies offer a wide choice of unit funds for the bond linkage.

Subsequently, at no cost or for a small administrative charge, the policyholder may switch his investment to one or more of the other funds and is thereby entitled to select a fund which reflects his own view of market conditions. Switching does not amount to a realisation for tax purposes, which is an important investment advantage.

The income produced by the underlying fund is reinvested, net of tax and annual charges, in the fund. A bond, therefore, serves as an automatic income accumulator as well as giving the investor the benefit of the capital growth from the fund, less a deduction for the insurance company's tax on capital gains.

At various times in recent years, market conditions have also made guaranteed income bonds very attractive for both life companies and investors. They may be structured as single policies paying annual amounts as a spendable 'income' by way of part surrender; or may be a combination of policies, some providing the annual 'income' and one providing the investment return at the end of the investment period, usually five years. The Revenue has challenged the efficiency of some of these arrangements, contending that the annual payments are actually Schedule D Case III income and not part surrenders of capital but legislation to be part of FA 1997 will confirm the position to be that which it was thought to be by the industry.

A case decided (on the hearing of a preliminary matter) in the middle of 1994 raised the question of how much life assurance protection a single premium bond had to provide for it to qualify as a life assurance policy. At first instance the judge decided that a policy providing a death benefit equal only to the surrender value at the time of death was not a life assurance contract.

An appeal against this decision in 1996 reversed it, but a further appeal is likely to be heard in 1998.

Withdrawals

Most unit-linked single premium bonds allow the investor the right to make regular or irregular withdrawals by way of partial surrender to serve as an income. The same result can be achieved by splitting the investment into a number of smaller policies and encashing individual policies in full from time to time. As these policies are not qualifying contracts they are not affected by the Revenue's attack on withdrawal plans referred to in **14.3.4** but see the section 'Withdrawals' in **14.3.6** below.

Ease of encashment

One of the most important characteristics of single premium bonds is the ease of encashment: there are few formalities other than production of the policy, a surrender form and proof of title. In the case of property bonds, some companies reserve the right, in exceptional circumstances, to defer encashment for a period so as to protect the general body of policyholders by avoiding forced sales of property.

14.3.6 Taxation

Taxation of the life company

The Revenue's review of life company taxation, announced in the 1989 budget, resulted in a statement by the Treasury in December 1989 and other changes announced in the 1990 budget. Legislation was included in the Finance Acts 1989 and 1990 to give effect to these changes. In the main, they took effect from January 1990.

The proposals were less radical than some of those originally canvassed and built on the existing 'I-E' (income-expenses) framework. The following is a very brief outline of an extremely complex tax regime.

The life company's management expenses are deducted from the investment income and capital gains of the life fund and the net amount is subjected to tax in the life company's hands at a rate of 25 per cent (24 per cent with effect from 1996–97) in respect of the policyholders' share of profits (20 per cent in respect of the policyholder's share of investment return corresponding to savings income, to reflect personal taxation, with effect from 1996–97) and 33 per cent in respect of profits attributable to shareholders in the case of a proprietary company. However, the expenses associated with the acquisition of new business are spread over a period of seven years.

As life companies are generally able to defer realisations of assets for a long period, they usually pass on this benefit in the form of a lower rate of deduction for tax on capital gains from the funds. This is especially true of unit-linked policies.

Previously, deferring capital gains had been achieved by investing life funds in units trusts. Much of the investment management could be achieved through the unit trust company selling its underlying assets, these being free of tax from capital gains. However, current rules (with transitional reliefs) charging tax on unrealised gains in life company holdings of unit trusts are promoting more direct investment by life company funds. See generally **14.2.2** for the current review of life assurance taxation.

Taxation of the policyholder

Qualifying and non-qualifying policies

The income tax treatment of a life policy in the hands of the policyholder depends on whether the policy is a qualifying or a non-qualifying policy. Policy provisions in standard form are usually sent to the Revenue by the life company for confirmation of compliance with the qualifying rules ('pre-certification'). Generally (although the rules do vary for different types of policy) a qualifying policy is one where the premium-paying period is ten years or more and where the premiums payable in any period of 12 months do not exceed more than twice the premiums payable in any other period of 12 months or $\frac{1}{8}$ of the premiums payable over ten years. In the case of a whole of life policy, the sum assured payable on death must not be less than 75 per cent of the premiums payable until age 75; and in the case of an endowment policy, the sum assured payable on death must not be less than 75 per cent of the premiums payable during the term of the policy, but for endowments this percentage is reduced by 2 per cent for each year by which the age of the life assured, at commencement, exceeds 55. Taxation of company-owned policies is considered later.

Qualifying policies

Tax relief on the premiums   In the case of a qualifying policy issued before 14 March 1984, the policyholder is eligible for tax relief on the premiums if the policy is written on his or his spouse's life, if either of them pays the premiums, and if the person paying is resident in the UK for tax purposes. The current rate of tax relief on premiums paid is $12\frac{1}{2}$ per cent. If eligible, the premiums may generally be paid to the life company net of the tax relief and the company will obtain the difference from the Inland Revenue. Tax relief is allowed to the policyholder to the extent to which the total gross premiums paid by him in the year do not exceed £1,500 or, if greater, $\frac{1}{6}$ of his taxable income after deducting charges on income but before deducting personal reliefs. Tax relief will not be available if a person other than the life assured or his spouse (such as an assignee) pays the premiums.

No life assurance premium relief is available for policies issued for contracts made after 13 March 1984. For these purposes a policy issued on or before 13 March 1984 is treated as being issued after that date if the benefits it secures are increased or its term extended (either by variation or by the exercise of an option built into the contract) after that date.

Policies intact   While the policies are held intact there is no tax charge to the policyholder.

Tax-free proceeds if kept up for minimum period   If a qualifying endowment policy has been maintained for at least three-quarters of its term or ten years, whichever is shorter, and has not been made paid-up within that period, the entire proceeds will be free of income tax in the hands of the policyholder. For a whole of life policy the appropriate period is ten years. If, however, a qualifying policy is surrendered or made paid-up within these periods, the profit ultimately made on realising the policy (whether by cashing in, death, maturity or assignment for value) is potentially subject to the higher rate of tax – but not the basic rate – as with non-qualifying policies (see below).

Capital gains tax   No chargeable gain arises on the disposal of either qualifying or non-qualifying policies (note that surrender and payment of the sum assured under the policy are treated as 'disposals' for these purposes) where the disposal is by the original beneficial owner or by an assignee who gave no consideration for the policy (eg received the policy by way of gift).

On the other hand, if an assignee realises a profit on a policy (or an interest under it) that he, not being the original beneficial owner, acquired for value, it is liable to capital gains tax in the same way as other chargeable assets.

To deal with the trade in second-hand policies (which were taxed under the then more favourable capital gains tax regime), anti-avoidance legislation was introduced in 1983 so that, broadly speaking, post-26 June 1982 policies remain in the same income tax regime despite being assigned for money or money's worth. Such policies may give a potential liability to both income and capital gains tax although the Taxation of Chargeable Gains Act 1992, s 37 prevents a double tax charge arising.

Person liable for the tax charge   See below.

Non-qualifying policies

Tax relief on the premiums   No life assurance premium relief is allowed on premiums paid under non-qualifying policies whether issued before or after 14 March 1984.

Policies intact   As with qualifying policies, while the policies are intact there is no tax charge on the policyholder.

Termination   On final termination of a non-qualifying policy, on death, cashing in, maturity, or sale, the only income tax charge, if any, is to higher rate income tax but not basic rate. To determine whether a charge arises, the gain – basically, the excess of the cash surrender value over the premium paid – is divided by the number of years the policy has been held ('top slicing'). Any previous withdrawals are also taken into account. This slice is then added to the taxpayer's other income for the year (after reliefs and mortgage interest). If the slice, then treated as the upper part of the individual's income, puts him in the higher rate bracket, the average rate of tax on the slice at the higher rate less the basic rate is applied to the whole gain. If the slice does not attract the higher rate of tax, the gain is, similarly, free of tax.

Note that it is only the income in the year of encashment that is relevant. If no chargeable events occur during other years, the individual's income, no matter how high in those years, is irrelevant. Thus, bonds or other non-qualifying policies can be realised tax-effectively in a year when the policyholder's other income is relatively low (eg after retirement).

Example 1 – no income tax charge

A basic rate taxpayer whose income after personal reliefs is £1,000 below the higher rate threshold cashes in a single premium bond that he has held for eight years, for a total gain of £5,000. This gain is divided by eight to produce a 'slice' of £625. The slice, when added to his other income, still does not take him into the higher rate of tax. No tax is payable on the gain of £5,000.

Example 2 – income tax on the gain

If the slice (£625 in the above example), treated as the upper part of the taxpayer's income, falls wholly in the higher rate band of 40 per cent, then the gain of £5,000 will be subject to income tax at the rate of 17 per cent (ie £850) being the difference between the relevant higher rate (40 per cent) and the basic rate of 23 per cent (tax year 1997/98).

Note that, on death, the gain which may be liable to tax is calculated, broadly speaking, as the cash surrender value immediately before death plus previous relevant capital payments under the policy, less the premiums paid. In this way the 'mortality profit' made under the policy at that time is not taxed as part of the chargeable gain.

Withdrawals Annual tax-free withdrawals or partial surrenders of up to 5 per cent of the premiums paid are permitted up to a total amount equal to the premium or premiums paid. Unused allowances are carried forward. If more than the 5 per cent annual allowance is taken a chargeable excess occurs. The excess becomes liable to the higher rate of tax (but is not liable to the basic rate) if, when added to the taxpayer's other income, it falls into the higher rate.

The 'top-slicing' procedure referred to above applies with some modifications: the first chargeable excess is divided by the number of years since commencement; subsequent excesses are divided by the number of years since the previous excess. The amounts withdrawn are taken into account in computing the gain or loss on final cashing in: the final gain or loss is equal to the cash surrender value, plus previous withdrawals, less the premium or premiums paid, less excesses previously brought into charge.

Example

Original investment in a bond of £5,000. The bondholder takes withdrawals of 6 per cent per annum for nine years and cashes in the bond after ten years for £8,000. The final gain on cashing in is £8,000 + £2,700 (ie 9 × 6% × £5,000) – £5,000 – £450 (ie 9 × 1% × £5,000) = £5,250. The 'slice' is therefore £5,250 ÷ 10 = £525. This slice is added to his other income in the year of cashing in to determine if any tax liability exists on the slice and, if so, the rate of charge, after deducting the basic rate. The net rate of charge, if any, on the slice is then applied to the gain of £5,250.

The Revenue's proposals for policy taxation mentioned in **14.2.2**, would result in a change to rules for taxing withdrawals (partial surrenders) from single premium bonds but the proposals are still at the consultation stage.

Person liable   The person liable for the tax charge is the policyholder if the policy is held by him beneficially, or the individual for whose debt the policy is held as security. Thus, if a policy is assigned by a parent to his or her child by way of a gift and the latter encashes it after attaining majority, the liability, if any, is the child's regardless of the donor's income and is determined by the child's income at the time of encashment.

Where a policy that is held in trust is cashed in, any chargeable gain is treated as income of the settlor and the tax is his liability, although the settlor can recover from the trustees any tax for which he is liable in this way. If a policy, previously held in trust, has been assigned to the beneficiary in execution of that trust and is subsequently encashed, any gain forms part of the beneficiary's income and is taxed accordingly.

Timing   Where the taxable event is the death of the life assured or the maturity, total encashment or sale of the policy, the gain is treated as arising at the date of that event. In contrast, however, withdrawals from policies are treated as happening at the end of the policy year in which they take place. For example, if a policy was effected on 1 June, a withdrawal in February 1996 will be treated as taking place on 31 May 1996 and so will be part of the 1996–97 tax computation for the policyholder and not the computation for 1995–96, the year in which it actually occurred.

14.3.7 Suitability

Life assurance policies are different from the normal run of investments in that they are capital assets that do not produce income as such. All income and capital gains produced by the underlying fund of investments accrue to the life company, while the policyholder receives the benefit in the form of an increase in value of his policy: the net income and gains after tax are taken into account in the value of the units or bonus additions, as the case may be. For this reason, life assurance policies are a very useful means of obtaining capital growth and accumulating income for medium- to long-term investment if immediate income is not required. This can be particularly important for higher rate taxpayers and various types of trust.

Both regular premium and single premium policies (qualifying or non-qualifying) also have the advantage that while they are held intact, the policyholder has no administrative burdens or tax returns to render, as the income and gains are the company's responsibility.

The medium- and long-term investor

Both single and regular premium policies are ideally suited to the medium- or longer-term investor seeking an institutionally managed investment. Life companies have considerable investment freedom and with profits policies reflect the results of investment across a wide spread of assets. Unit-linked policies offer a choice of property, equity, fixed interest, managed and many other types of unit funds, as well as the ability to switch investments between funds as market conditions change. Indeed, the keynote of most unit-linked policies these days is choice and flexibility to meet changing circumstances, so as to maximise the potential growth and protect the real value of the investment against inflation, particularly over the longer term; while with profit policies offer the relative stability of participation in the company's profits. For the individual who wants a direct link to a managed fund of commercial properties there are few investments comparable with a property bond, or a policy linked to a property fund, or a managed fund with a property content.

Qualifying policies issued pre-14 March 1984 may have the added attraction of tax relief on the premiums – something not available to other comparable forms of investment – as well as freedom from tax on the proceeds if maintained for the required period. The ability of companies to defer realisations and thus make deductions for capital gains liabilities at a rate lower than the life company rate on chargeable gains has been a continuing advantage (but see **14.3.6** for more recent changes to unit trusts held by life companies).

Beneficiaries

Life policies are suitable investments for individuals seeking personal investment benefits for themselves or their spouses, or for making gifts to beneficiaries. Since policies are automatic income accumulators, they represent useful investments as gifts for children or for children's own capital. As gifts of policies do not cause chargeable events, a higher rate taxpaying spouse can give a policy to a basic rate (or non-taxpaying) partner before encashment. In this way, any gain otherwise taxable may avoid being taxed by virtue of the new independent taxation regime introduced in April 1990 which no longer aggregates the investment income of married couples. Policies can also be taken out by trustees as investments of the trust, provided the power is given in the trust instrument to invest in non-income-producing property and provided an insurable interest exists, eg a policy on the life of a beneficiary for the ultimate benefit of that beneficiary.

A donor wishing to take out a policy for the benefit of children or other beneficiaries can do so at the outset by completing a standard trust form produced by the life company at the time of application. Trusts can range from very simple forms for the benefit of named beneficiaries absolutely (under the Married Women's Property Acts or corresponding legislation in Scotland and Northern Ireland, for spouse or children) to more elaborate forms, such as children's accumulation trusts and trusts where the settlor reserves a right to apply the benefits amongst a class of beneficiaries which may include the settlor himself (although to be efficient for inheritance tax purposes the settlor should be excluded from any personal benefit). Similarly, it is relatively simple to make a gift of an existing policy by assigning it to a beneficiary or to trustees for a beneficiary.

The tax considerations described in **14.3.6** should, of course, be taken into account, as well as the taxpayer's potential income and his tax position at the time of prospective encashment (as it is that time that is primarily relevant, not any time during the currency of the policy). Equally, note that the Revenue proposals for a new policy tax regime would create certain changes to the taxation of trust policies.

Companies

Companies have frequently found it useful to invest surplus funds in life policies, particularly where providing for a future liability or the replacement of an asset in the future. An insurable interest in the life of the assured must exist. In the past, the only tax consequence of such an investment has been that applicable to a close company in the case of a single premium bond or the premature encashment of a qualifying policy, but the Finance Act 1989 contained new provisions so that, broadly speaking, all policies owned by companies (and those assigned to secure a company debt or held on trusts created by a company) are treated, in effect, as non-qualifying policies and taxable to Schedule D Case VI income. In this case no credit is given for tax deducted in the life company's funds and no top-slicing is granted.

The new rules apply to policies effected on or after 14 March 1989 and those altered after that date so as to increase the benefits secured or extend the term.

A measure of relief is given in cases where a qualifying endowment policy is used to secure a debt incurred by the company in purchasing land to be occupied by it for the purposes of its trade (or in constructing, extending or improving buildings occupied for that purpose). In such cases, and subject to certain conditions, only the excess policy proceeds over the amount of the debt is taxable as a policy gain.

14.3.8 Charges

In the case of with profit and without profit policies, the company's charges are implicit in the premium rate for the sum assured. In the case of unit-linked policies, the company's charges consist of a proportion of each premium and charges inside the unit funds. For example, in the case of single premium bonds, typically an initial charge of 5 per cent of the premium is made. This is followed by annual charges in the order of 1.25 per cent of the value of the fund (although this does vary from company to company) deducted from the fund, either monthly or with the same frequency as the fund valuations. These charges cover items such as the company's expenses and profit margins. Such annual charges can become quite significant where the policy has achieved a high value. For this reason some companies have adopted the approach of using a policy charge which is designed to ensure that each policy contributes a fair amount to the company's expenses, irrespective of the policy's size. In such cases any annual management charge deducted from the funds is reallocated to the policy.

Switching a unit-linked policy between funds can usually be done for a small administrative charge that is far lower than the equivalent cost of switching other investments.

14.3.9 Mechanics

Life assurance policies are generally taken out through the intervention of an intermediary such as an insurance broker or salesman of the life assurance company, or a solicitor, accountant or estate agent acting as agent, or directly with the life company itself. The intermediary, although often the policyholder's agent, is generally paid a commission by the life company itself, although some insurance brokers charge the client fees (which are offset against their commission) for the work involved in preparing reports and undertaking financial planning for the client entailing the use of life assurance policies. The Financial Services Act 1986 introduced the concept of polarisation to the industry. This seeks to make clear to the consumer whether he is dealing with a representative of one company or a broker who will survey the market on his client's behalf.

14.3.10 Maintenance

Policies can be held in the individual's own name (usually in the case of policies held for the individual's personal benefit) or by trustees. As long as the policy is not cashed in there are no tax returns and no paper-work. It is only where excessive tax relief is taken on qualifying premiums or gains arise on the happening of a chargeable event (eg a single premium policy that is encashed or a qualifying policy encashed prematurely) that tax considerations arise. It is perhaps largely because of the ease of administration that many individuals with personal share portfolios take advantage of share exchange schemes introduced by life companies enabling them to exchange their shares for single premium bonds at reduced dealing costs.

Holders of unit-linked policies may receive annual fund reports, though the level of useful information provided varies between companies. Because the investment performances of unit-linked single premium bonds are directly related to the underlying funds, it is advisable to review the performance of the respective funds regularly with a view to switching between funds. This can be done with relative ease and at a low cost but for the majority of investors a carefully selected managed fund satisfies the requirements for a large proportion of their investment.

14.4 PURCHASED LIFE ANNUITIES

14.4.1 Legal nature

There are two broad types of purchased life annuities:

(1) Immediate annuities are contracts under which, in consideration of a lump sum paid to the life company, the company undertakes to pay an annuity to the annuitant for life, or for some other term, the rate of the annual annuity depending on the age and sex of the annuitant and on the yields prevailing for fixed interest investments at the time.
(2) Deferred annuities are similar to immediate annuities except that the annuity commences at a future date.

Both annuity contracts are direct contracts with the life company. Some annuity contracts provide for a guaranteed minimum number of payments; some allow the contract to be surrendered for a cash sum that takes into account the growth in the purchase consideration and any annuity payments that have already been made. Other types of annuity contract allow for a cash sum, representing the balance of the original purchase consideration, to be paid on death.

14.4.2 Pre-conditions

There are generally no pre-conditions to investment in purchased life annuities. The purchaser of the annuity is generally the annuitant himself or someone else who wishes to provide for annual payments to the annuitant.

14.4.3 Characteristics

An annuity contract represents a fixed interest investment providing either regular annual payments for the life of the annuitant (lifetime annuities) or for a fixed period (temporary annuities). These payments represent a partial return of capital plus a rate of interest on the investment. In the case of deferred annuity contracts the initial purchase consideration is accumulated at a fixed rate of interest before the annuity commences. Frequently, deferred annuity contracts are purchased with the object of taking advantage of income accumulation before the annuity commencement date and of cashing in the contract before that time (these are commonly known as 'growth bonds'). In general the life company fixes the rate of the annuity in advance, although cash surrender values may be related to yields on government securities at the time of cashing in. The actual investment yield earned by the life company is irrelevant to the annuitant, as he enjoys a guaranteed benefit.

In the past, two separate purchased annuity contracts were sometimes combined. For example, a temporary immediate annuity for a limited period was combined with a deferred lifetime annuity. This combination, known as a 'guaranteed income bond' (more frequently now written as a cluster of endowment policies), had as its object the provision of a short-term 'income' in the form of the temporary annuity, with the cashing in of the deferred annuity before the annuity commencement date to provide the return of 'capital'. The contracts were so structured that the cash-in value of the deferred annuity generally equals the total purchase price of the two contracts. The tax consequences of this combination have to be closely watched, especially for higher rate taxpayers (see **14.4.4**). Another combination is that of an immediate lifetime annuity, to provide an income for life, and a deferred annuity that can be commenced at a later stage to augment the income or, if the additional income is not taken, to pay a lump sum on death.

14.4.4 Taxation

The life company

In the past, annuities paid represented charges on the income from investments held by the life company for its general annuity business. To the extent, therefore, that the annuities paid equalled or exceeded the interest earned by the company, the interest did not bear tax, and could be passed on to the annuitants gross (although then subject to taxation in the hands of the annuitant).

The Finance Act 1991, however, made the taxation of general annuity business much the same as ordinary life assurance for accounting periods beginning after 31 December 1991 with a generally detrimental effect on purchased life annuities.

The annuitant

Annuities paid are divided into capital content and income content, according to actuarial tables prescribed by the Inland Revenue. For example, if a man aged 70 purchased an annuity of £1,800 per annum payable half-yearly in arrear for a consideration of £10,000, £900 of the annuity might be regarded as capital with the balance of £900 being treated as income for tax purposes. In other words, every annuity is deemed to be partly a return of the original capital invested plus a yield or interest element. The interest element of each annuity payment received by the annuitant is treated as unearned income, although since the abolition of the investment income surcharge for individuals by the Finance Act 1984 this is not currently a significant disadvantage.

Despite this treatment of payments as part capital and part income, the Revenue appear to regard annuities as substantially a right to income so that they cannot be transferred between spouses to take advantage of independent taxation.

In the past, if an annuity contract was encashed or assigned for value, or any capital sum paid on death, any profit made by the annuitant over and above the purchase price of the annuity, unlike single premium bonds, was subject to basic rate tax (as the company would not have paid tax on the income of its general annuity business) and higher rates if applicable. However, as part of the change to the company's tax position, the 1991 Finance Act also brought the chargeable event regime for annuities into line with that for life policies, eg by not charging gains to basic rate income tax.

Higher rate tax is charged in much the same manner as on single premium policies. In other words, the gain element is 'top-sliced' by the number of years the annuity contract has been in existence, and the resulting slice is added to the taxpayer's other income in the year of encashment to determine whether the higher rate of tax is applicable. The rate on the slice (less the basic rate) then applies to the entire gain. In calculating the amount of the gain the capital element of any annuities paid prior to encashment (but not the interest element) is included as part of the gain.

14.4.5 Suitability

Immediate life annuities are suitable for investors who wish to purchase a continuing income for the rest of their lives by way of a lump sum. Deferred annuities are a means of providing an income to start at a future date, or of accumulating a lump sum with a view to encashment at a future time when other income may be sufficiently low to offset the tax disadvantages of encashment.

14.4.6 Mechanics

Like other life contracts annuities may be purchased through an intermediary or from a life company direct.

14.4.7 Maintenance

As far as immediate annuities are concerned, annual tax returns and tax payments are necessary in respect of the interest element of the annuities. In the case of deferred contracts, no maintenance is required while the annuity contract is intact and not paying an annuity, since the income is income of the life company and not the annuitant. On cashing-in, tax returns are necessary and tax may be payable.

14.5 PREVIEW OF THE YEAR AHEAD

With confidence returning to investors and consumers in 1996 the prospects for the industry look better than has been the case for some years.

The rate of change in the industry shows no signs of abating and the anticipated proposals for a new policy tax regime are a cause for some concern.

Although all would subscribe to the need for client protection, there is a view that the current regime has gone too far by elongating the sales process while failing to deliver to consumers relevant, useful and succinct information on which to base their decisions.

14.6 CONCLUSION

Life policies remain a very simple way of making lump sum or regular investment, although they are best used for medium- to long-term savings.

They act as 'income accumulators' and the life company deals with all tax liabilities while the plan is maintained in force. Withdrawals can often be taken to provide the policyholder with a spendable 'income' and these too can often be taken very simply and with little paperwork. This makes policies easy to administer from the policyholder's viewpoint and they are attractive to many people as a result.

As a pooled investment, they offer a spread of risk normally unobtainable by individual investors, including exposure to the commercial property market. Inexpensive switching between the company's funds, the built-in life cover and the prospect of tax-free proceeds are also attractive benefits of investment through life policies.

The recent tax changes, which have increased liabilities on the industry, have already led to many contracts being repriced, but reduced tax rates applying to policyholder income and gains should provide some level of compensation for this.

SOURCES OF FURTHER INFORMATION

Useful addresses

Association of British Insurers
51 Gresham Street
London
EC2V 7HQ

Tel: (0171) 600 3333

National Association of Pension
   Funds
12–18 Grosvenor Gardens
London
SW1W 0DH

Tel: (0171) 730 0585

Inland Revenue Public Enquiry
   Room
West Wing
Somerset House
Strand
London
WC2R 1LB

Tel: (0171) 438 6420

Society of Pension Consultants
Ludgate House
Ludgate Circus
London
EC4A 2AB

Tel: (0171) 353 1688/9

LAUTRO (Life Assurance and
   Unit Trusts Regulatory
   Organisation)
Centre Point
103 New Oxford Street
London
WC1A 1QH

Tel: (0171) 379 0444

Pension Schemes Office
York House
PO Box 62
Castle Meadow Road
Nottingham
NG2 1BG

Tel: (0115) 974 0000

PIA (Personal Investment
  Authority)
Hertsmere House
Hertsmere Road
London
E14 4AB

Tel: (0171) 538 8860

IFA Association
12–13 Henrietta Street
Covent Garden
London
WC2E 8LH

Tel: (0171) 240 7878

Life Insurance Association
Citadel House
Station Approach
Chorleywood
Rickmansworth
Herts
WD3 5PF

Tel: (01923) 285333

Pensions Management Institute
PMI House
4–10 Artillery Lane
London
E1 7LS

Tel: (0171) 247 1452

15

PENSION CONTRACTS

STUART REYNOLDS LLB,

Divisional Director, Legal Department, Allied Dunbar Assurance plc

15.1 INTRODUCTION

Pension schemes in the UK can be divided, broadly, into three classifications: the State scheme; personal pension arrangements; and occupational schemes.

Approved pensions schemes have many of the constituents of the perfect investment: tax relief on contributions, tax-free growth, the prospect of a tax-free lump sum and a wide choice of underlying investments in large pooled funds to spread the risk. The major disadvantage is the need to purchase an annuity (taxed) at retirement. Recent changes have removed some of the problems which this can cause.

Not surprisingly, these benefits are carefully guarded by the appropriate authorities through a considerable number of rules and restrictions. This chapter summarises the main benefits and the conditions for their enjoyment.

15.2 HIGHLIGHTS OF THE PREVIOUS YEAR

Bad publicity as a result of the long-running pensions transfers and opt outs saga continued to dominate the headlines during 1996. Late in the year, almost two years after it issued its first set of guidance, the Securities and Investments Board issued further guidance designed to speed up the completion of the review. The review process had increasingly become bogged down by the sheer complexity of reviewing the facts of individual cases and the difficulties of gathering information about many different occupational schemes.

The revised guidance, which was subsequently adopted by the Personal Investment Authority, recognised that a major cause of the delays lay in the difficulties associated with obtaining information from the occupational pension schemes involved. The new process attempts to address this issue by placing more of the burden on scheme members to supply information, with some basic information either being assumed or obtained from scheme booklets. In practice, contact with the occupational schemes will remain unavoidable, to arrange the reinstatement of benefits for those investors who are ultimately found to have suffered loss as a result of bad advice. Moreover, it remains to be seen how many scheme members will be able to supply the required data without contacting the schemes directly.

Completion of the review remains the highest priority for both the regulators and the industry. Not surprisingly, given the complexity and scale of the review, a lot has still to be done.

The impact of the Pensions Act 1995 has become clearer over the course of the year. A vast amount of new legislation, in the form of statutory instruments, has been passed over the course of 1996 and early 1997. There have been changes to virtually every aspect of the regulation of occupational pension schemes, as well as major changes to the contracting out system.

Much of the key legislation takes effect from April 1997 and, in the run up to the deadline, schemes have had to devote considerable resources to the implementation of the new rules. Lawyers and actuaries, both of whom are given a more formal role under the new regime, have also been busy during the course of the year advising schemes on the new requirements. Even already well-run schemes will have found the change to the new regime an expensive process and the ongoing costs of compliance will also be significant. For those small schemes which do not benefit from specific exceptions (such as those for small self-administered schemes and certain insured schemes) the costs are significant and may lead some employers to move towards group personal pension plans.

Group personal pension plans are a series of individual personal pension plans with an employer contribution. The employer's involvement is essentially limited to paying its contributions (which benefit from tax relief) and, in some cases, arranging to collect the employees' contributions. As the employer does not act as a trustee of the individual personal pensions, and the pension provider takes care of the administration of the personal pension scheme, these arrangements will be an increasingly attractive alternative to occupational schemes for many small employers.

A further disincentive to those considering setting up an occupational scheme is the wide range of civil penalties and fines which can be imposed under the Pensions Act. The new pensions regulator, OPRA, has stated that it will be expecting compliance with the new rules from the start. Trustees and administrators of occupational schemes will nevertheless still be hoping that any early failings in complying with purely technical requirements will be treated with a degree of understanding.

Finally, before the election the Conservative Government announced that it intended to loosen some of the restrictions surrounding Free-Standing AVC (FSAVC) schemes. For example, FSAVC schemes can now accept transfers from other types of approved schemes and it is possible that in the future FSAVC benefits will no longer have had to be taken at the time that benefits are taken from the employee's main occupational scheme. The last requirement is a particular problem for those employees with early retirement ages, such as members of the armed forces.

A relaxation in these rules will be welcomed but these changes will simply add to the ever increasing complexity of pension arrangements in the UK which has continued unabated during the last year. Both the delays in the SIB Pensions Review and the welter of regulations under the Pensions Act are symptoms of this over-complication. Pensions are simple in concept – the accumulation of a fund to provide an income in old age. Making them simple in practice appears to be beyond the ability of both the pension industry and Government alike.

15.3 THE STATE PENSION SCHEME

The benefit the State provides to those in retirement falls into two main parts: the basic retirement pension and a supplementary earnings related pension (SERPS). Everyone is entitled to the basic retirement pension payable at State Retirement Age, subject to payment of the necessary National Insurance contributions. For an individual whose earnings have been at the national average level throughout their working life, the State will provide a basic pension of approximately one-third of the final earnings level.

The State Retirement Age is currently 65 for males and 60 for females. The State Retirement Age will be equalised in the future at 65 for both males and females. This will apply to women retiring after 6 April 2010 with a sliding scale for women retiring over the previous ten years. For women whose dates of birth are on or after 6 April 1955 the common State Retirement Age of 65 will apply. Women born before 6 April 1950 will benefit from the current age of 60. For those women with dates of birth between those dates the sliding scale applies. For each month (or part of a month) that a woman's date of birth is after 6 April 1950, her retirement date will be deferred by one month.

SERPS was introduced in April 1978 to provide an additional State pension based on earnings (within certain limits) rather than the flat benefit provided by the retirement pension. SERPS also provides a widow's benefit if a husband dies after retirement and also, in certain

Table 15.1 New State Retirement Ages for women

Date of Birth		Pension age (years/months)	New pension date
Before 6 April 1950		60/0	–
6 April –	5 May 1950	60/1	6 May 2010
6 May 1950 –	5 June 1950	60/2	6 July 2010
6 June 1950 –	5 July 1950	60/3	6 September 2010
6 July 1950 –	5 August 1950	60/4	6 November 2010
6 August 1950 –	5 September 1950	60/5	6 January 2011
6 September 1950 –	5 October 1950	60/6	6 March 2011
6 March 1951 –	5 April 1951	61/0	6 March 2012
6 March 1952 –	5 April 1952	62/0	6 March 2014
6 March 1953 –	5 April 1953	63/0	6 March 2016
6 March 1954 –	5 April 1954	64/0	6 March 2018
6 March 1955 –	5 April 1955	65/0	6 March 2020
6 April 1955 and after		65/0	–

circumstances, if he dies before retirement. SERPS is funded by the higher rate National Insurance contributions payable by both employers and employees. The self-employed do not contribute towards, or benefit from, SERPS.

In recent years the State pension scheme has come under pressure by increases in life expectancy and larger numbers of retired people in the population. These concerns led the Government to reduce the benefits under SERPS so that only those reaching State pension age in the years 1998 and 1999 will receive the original maximum benefits. Those reaching State Retirement Age in or after the year 2010 will receive a pension of only 20 per cent of their earnings (within certain limits) instead of the 25 per cent originally intended, and the relevant earnings to be taken into account will be the average of lifetime earnings and not the best 20 years' of earnings, as was the original rule for SERPS. A sliding scale will operate for those retiring in the years 2000 to 2009.

15.4 CONTRACTING-IN AND CONTRACTING-OUT

Those who are participating in SERPS (ie employees earning more than the lower threshold for standard rate National Insurance contributions) are said to be 'contracted-in' to SERPS. Since SERPS was introduced it has been possible to opt-out of the scheme (referred to as 'contracting-out').

Until 6 April 1988, this 'contracting-out' was only possible through an employer-sponsored occupational pension scheme which guaranteed to provide a broadly equivalent level of benefits to the SERPS benefits being lost. Since 6 April 1988, employers have been able to offer contracting-out on a 'money purchase' basis without having to provide the guarantee previously required. In both cases National Insurance contributions are reduced for both the employer and employee but with the loss of SERPS benefits.

However, this change still left the decision whether to offer contracted-out status firmly in the employer's hands. Further changes which took effect on 1 July 1988 gave the individual employee the right to contract out of SERPS on an individual basis, without his employer's consent. The personal pension plans which enable this are also money-purchase arrangements.

Contracting-out through personal pension plans involves the payment of 'protected rights contributions' to the relevant pension contract. The contributions are identified separately from any other contributions paid and create a 'protected rights fund'; it is the 'protected rights benefits' paid out of this fund at retirement which replace the SERPS benefits lost through the decision to contract out. The Pensions Act 1995 introduces a system of age-related contracting-out rebates which applies for the tax year 1997–98 and onwards.

Contracting-out via a personal pension plan is an annual decision and the individual can contract back into SERPS for the purposes of future benefits.

In general, contracting-out will be of benefit to younger employees but may not match the likely SERPS entitlement for some older people and for those on lower earnings.

15.5 TYPES OF PENSION CONTRACTS

There are two main types of pension contract in the context of life assurance investment:

(1) Personal pension plans for the self-employed and individuals who are not in pensionable employment take the form of deferred annuity contracts between the individual and the life company directly and are purchased by single or regular premiums.
(2) Occupational pension schemes take the form of contracts between the trustees of the scheme (set up by the employer) and the insurance company (in the case of an insured scheme) and provide benefits for employees as a group or on an individual earmarked basis. Controlling directors of director-controlled companies other than investment companies are also eligible for occupational pension schemes.

Since April 1988 individuals have been able to opt out of their occupational pension scheme and provide for their own benefit via a personal pension plan. It is often not advisable to do this if the occupational pension scheme is a good one. Alternatively they will be able to top-up the pension provided by their occupational scheme by making Additional Voluntary Contributions to that scheme or by effecting a free-standing AVC (FSAVC) plan with a pension provider of their choice.

15.6 CHARACTERISTICS OF PENSION CONTRACTS

As with life assurance policies there is a wide variety of types of investment. Companies offer with profit contracts with a level of guaranteed benefits but the right to participate in profits and unit-linked contracts with a wide choice of unit funds and the ability to switch between funds to provide growth on top of any guaranteed benefits. A recent development has been a series of guaranteed equity funds, where investors can benefit from the performance of an index, usually the FT-SE 100 Index, but are protected from stock market falls.

It has become common in recent years for employers to split their pension investment between an insurance company and other investment media by what is known as a 'self-administered scheme'. One of the attractions of such an arrangement is the facility of investing part of the pension fund in the employing company itself either by loans or equity investment (see **15.7.6**).

An attraction of all pension contracts is that the income and capital growth produced by the investment of the premiums accumulate on a gross basis, because pension funds are not generally subject to UK income tax or capital gains tax.

As the contracts provide essentially for retirement annuities and pensions, they cannot generally be surrendered for a cash consideration: benefits must take the form of pensions (part of which can be commuted on retirement) and life cover (including a return of the premiums with reasonable interest, which in the case of unit-linked contracts means the growth in value of the units). An important feature of many of these contracts is the 'open market option' at retirement, enabling the annuitant to use the accumulated fund built up for his pension to purchase an annuity or pension from any other company offering a higher rate. Although funds invested in these contracts generally remain 'locked in' until retirement, a facility offered by many insurers is the availability of loans, on commercial terms, to companies taking out pension schemes or to individual members of these schemes (see **15.7.6**).

15.7 ELIGIBILITY, TAXATION, CONTRIBUTION LIMITS AND BENEFITS

15.7.1 The life company

The income and gains attributable to the life company's pension liabilities are effectively free of UK tax, and it is thus able to pass on to its policyholders the entire gross increase in value of the assets and income, after deduction of its charges, without any deduction for UK tax.

15.7.2 Personal pension plans

Eligibility

You will be eligible to make contributions to a personal pension plan (PPP) if you are in receipt of 'relevant earnings'. This means either earnings from non-pensionable employments, or from businesses, professions, partnerships, etc. Generally, you are not eligible if you belong to a pension scheme operated by your employer, but you are eligible if it provides only a sum assured payable on your death while in the employer's service. Controlling directors of investment companies are not eligible for any form of PPP in respect of earnings from such a company nor are certain other controlling directors who are in receipt of benefits from their employer's occupational scheme.

Tax relief on premiums and limits

If you have relevant earnings, and pay either single or annual premiums to a PPP within the limits mentioned below, you enjoy full tax relief on those premiums in the relevant years. However, an 'earnings cap' applies so that contributions to a PPP will only be possible in respect of earnings up to £84,000 for the 1997/98 tax year (previously £82,200 for the 1996/97 tax year). The legislation provides that this figure will be increased in future years in line with the RPI (although this did not apply for the tax year 1993–94).

Employees can pay premiums net of basic rate and any higher rate relief is claimed through the PAYE coding. The 20 per cent lower rate band does not affect the rate at which employees can deduct basic rate tax. The self-employed must make contributions gross, and claim relief through their annual tax return, a separate claim or, in some cases, by a reduction in subsequent payments on account under the self-assessment system. The annual limit for contributions to PPPs is 17.5 per cent of your 'net relevant earnings'. This means relevant earnings from your non-pensionable employment or business, etc, less certain deductions such as expenses, trading losses and capital allowances. The limits for older tax-payers are currently as shown below.

An amount not exceeding 5 per cent of your net relevant earnings can be used to provide a lump sum payable from the PPP in the event of your death before age 75. Premiums used to provide this life cover must be included as part of the contributions you are permitted to pay to your PPP.

Age at beginning of year of assessment	%
36–45	20.0
46–50	25.0
51–55	30.0
56–60	35.0
61 and over	40.0

Contributions may be paid to a PPP and a s 226 contract (see **15.7.4**) at the same time but the contribution limits apply to the 'aggregate' of contributions to the two plans (although the 'aggregation' is not always straightforward and paying contributions to both a PPP and a s 226 contract can restrict the overall contribution possible in some cases, particularly where contributions are above the earnings cap).

If your employer pays contributions to your PPP, these too must be taken as part of the maximum contribution which can be made to your plan. Employer's contributions are not treated as the employee's income. Protected rights contributions paid to your PPP to enable you to contract out of SERPS can be paid in addition to the maximum permissible contribution calculated as the appropriate percentage of your net relevant earnings.

Years for which relief is granted

Generally, relief is given against net relevant earnings of the tax year in which the contributions are paid. However, you can elect to have any premium you pay treated for tax purposes as if it has been paid during the preceding tax year, or, if you had no relevant earnings in that year, for the premium to be relieved against earnings in the tax year before that; ie there is a 'carry-back' period of one or two years.

To the extent that premiums paid in any year fall short of the permitted maximum of net relevant earnings, it is possible to 'carry forward' the shortfall on unused relief for up to six years and use the shortfall (on a first-in first-out basis) to obtain relief against a premium paid in a subsequent year, to the extent that that premium exceeds the maximum percentage limit of net relevant earnings for the year in which it is paid. The amount of relief which is available in any year as a result of the carry back and carry forward provisions is restricted to the amount of net relevant earnings for that year.

Benefits payable and age at which they may be taken

The PPP scheme established by the pension provider can allow the individual to make more than one contract (or arrangement) under it. The advantages of this are that, as benefits from an arrangement can, generally, be taken only once if they are to include a cash lump sum, multiple arrangements can give the opportunity to take benefits in stages.

Your pension may start being paid at any age between 50 and 75. It is not necessary for you actually to retire before the annuity can commence. In certain occupations the Revenue allow an annuity to start earlier than the age of 50 (eg jockeys, motor racing drivers, cricketers, etc).

It is no longer necessary to purchase an annuity when benefits from a personal pension are taken. The annuity purchase can be deferred until age 75. Until then, or the date when the annuity is purchased if earlier, income withdrawals are taken up to a limit broadly equal to the amount of the single life annuity which could have been taken. The amount of income withdrawals has to be reviewed every three years and the withdrawals are taxable in the same way as annuity payments.

Should your PPP incorporate a sum assured, on your premature death the lump sum would be paid and this can be arranged to be free of inheritance tax by writing it in trust where the PPP scheme itself is not set up under trust. The whole of any annuity payable either to you, your spouse or your dependants will be treated and taxed as income (and not, as is the case with purchased life annuities, partly as income and partly as a return of capital – see **14.3.4**). The annuity is taxed under Schedule E and subject to the PAYE system.

A lump sum may be taken from the PPP, between the ages of 50 and 75, up to a maximum of 25 per cent of the fund then being used to provide you with retirement benefits.

You are permitted, instead of taking the annuity from the life company with whom you hold the contract, to utilise the fund built up for your annuity to purchase an annuity from any other company, thus obtaining the best terms then available ('open market option'). If your PPP is provided by an organisation which is not a life assurance company, your pension (and life assurance) must be provided by a life company.

15.7.3 Contracting-out via a PPP

Scheme certificates

If a PPP has an 'appropriate scheme certificate' from the Occupational Pensions Board it will be able to receive protected rights contributions (and may be funded by them entirely) and so enable the individual employee to contract out of SERPS. A PPP which receives only protected rights contributions (a 'PPP(PRO)') can be effected by an employee who is a member of a contracted-in occupational scheme but wishes to contract out on an individual basis.

Contributions

Protected rights contributions consist of a National Insurance rebate. For the tax year 1997/98 and onwards the rebates are age-related and vary between 3.4 per cent and 9 per cent of the individual employee's band earnings (the earnings between the upper and lower earnings limits). Both employer and employee continue to pay full National Insurance but the rebate is paid by the DSS to the individual's plan after the end of the relevant tax year.

(From April 1993 to April 1997 a system of flat-rate rebates operated with an incentive of 1 per cent of band earnings payable for those over 30.)

The protected rights pension must commence between State pension age and the age of 75. From 6 April 1996 males will be able to take their protected rights pensions at age 60 in the same way as females. It must increase at 3 per cent per annum or the rate of the RPI, whichever is lower, and must not discriminate between males and females, married or single people in terms of the annuity rates offered. No lump sum benefit can be taken from the protected rights fund.

A protected rights pension must continue for the benefit of a widow/ widower or dependant on the individual's death, at a rate not less than one-half of the individual's pension. On death before retirement age the protected rights fund can be paid to the deceased's estate or nominees but no life assurance sum assured can be included in the protected rights benefits.

15.7.4 Retirement annuity contracts (s 226 contracts)

In many ways s 226 contracts were similar to the new PPPs but there are some key differences, eg no employer's contributions; contributions paid gross and the tax reclaimed; no facility for an employee to contract out through a s 226 contract and no general entitlement to take benefits before the age of 60. One important way in which a s 226 contract could be more favourable than a PPP was in providing a cash commutation equal to three times the annual annuity payable after the cash had been taken. This figure is often more than the 25 per cent of the fund available as a lump sum under a PPP. (Contracts entered into on or after 21 March 1987 are subject to a maximum cash lump sum of £150,000 per contract.)

The earnings cap does not apply to s 226 contracts and the contribution limits are also different from those which apply to PPPs.

No new s 226 contracts could be entered into after 30 June 1988 but contracts in existence by that date can continue much as before. Contributions can continue to be paid to such contracts and regular contributions can be increased in the future.

Note that, although many s 226 contracts contain an open market option to allow the annuity to be purchased from a life company other than the one with whom the pension plan has been effected, exercising such an option after 30 June 1988 has the effect of transferring the policy proceeds to a new PPP (unless the policyholder has a second s 226 contract already in existence with that other life company). Thus, in the absence of another s 226 contract, the benefits will be paid out of a PPP with the resulting less favourable calculation of the maximum cash lump sum compared to the s 226 contract.

15.7.5 Occupational schemes

These are schemes provided by an employer for the benefit of some or all of his employees but they are not available to directors of investment companies. To be effective, the scheme should be approved by the Pension Scheme Office (PSO) which is a branch of the Inland Revenue.

'Approval' will prevent contributions paid by the employer being taxed in the employees' hands as a benefit in kind. 'Exempt approval' gives the additional benefits of the gross roll-up in the fund and tax relief for the employee in respect of regular contributions he makes to the scheme. Exempt approval also means that the employer's contributions are deductible business expenses without relying on the normal rules for deductibility applying to Schedule D income. In most cases approval is given under the PSO's discretionary powers which are extremely wide-ranging.

It is not possible for an employer to make membership of an occupational scheme (other than one providing death in service benefits only) compulsory. Employees are able to opt out of their employer's scheme and so become eligible to effect their own PPP, independent of the employer. In general, leaving an occupational scheme is unlikely to be wise except where its benefits are extremely poor; expert advice should be sought if this is contemplated.

Contributions

The employer must make some contribution to the scheme although the employee may indirectly provide the necessary funds by agreeing to a reduction in salary — 'a salary sacrifice'. Contributions by the employer to an exempt approved scheme are deductible business expenses, although relief on non-regular contributions may be deferred by being spread over a maximum of five years. The employee may make personal contributions of up to 15 per cent of his remuneration. Personal contributions attract tax relief at the highest rate paid by the individual.

Unlike PPPs there are no specific limits on the amount of contributions which may be made to an occupational scheme; instead (subject to the various 'income capping' rules referred to below) the controls operate on the level of benefits which is allowed. If a scheme becomes 'overfunded' (ie where the scheme has more capital than is necessary to meet its prospective liabilities), payment of further contributions may be restricted or capital may have to be returned to the employer. If a refund is made to the employer it is taxable at a special rate of 40 per cent.

Benefits and limits

The benefits that can be provided by an approved occupational scheme are regulated by a series of Inland Revenue limits. These limits have been restricted over the years including important changes announced in the 1987 and 1989 budgets. Each generation of limits has in general been preserved or 'grandfathered' for those who were members of existing schemes at the time of the budget when the changes were announced. Other changes, the majority of them relatively minor, have also been made at other times. Details of the earlier limits can be found in previous editions of this work and in the *Allied Dunbar Pensions Handbook*. The limits which apply to members joining new schemes are summarised below.

The Inland Revenue limits are based on a percentage of the individual's 'final remuneration'. This must be calculated in one of the two ways permitted by the PSO, namely:

(1) the remuneration in any of the five years preceding retirement, leaving service or death (as applicable) together with the average of any bonuses, commissions, etc averaged over at least three consecutive years ending with the year in question; or

(2) the highest average of the total earnings over any period of three consecutive years during the last ten years of service.

Certain items are excluded from the calculation, such as share option and share incentive gains and golden handshakes, and some controlling directors have to use the second definition of final remuneration. There is also a maximum amount of earnings that can be taken into account and this is £84,000 for the 1997/98 tax year (previously £82,200 for the 1996/97 tax year). This figure should increase in future years in line with the RPI (although indexation did not apply for the 1993/94 tax year).

Within this framework, an individual can accrue a pension at the rate of one-thirtieth of final remuneration for each year of service with his employer up to a maximum of two-thirds final remuneration. To achieve this it is necessary to achieve 20 years of service.

The benefits can be taken on retirement between age 50 and 75. The benefits must be in the form of a pension but part of the pension can be commuted for a tax-free lump sum. The maximum lump sum is three-eighths of final remuneration for each year of service or 2.25 times the pension available before commutation, if greater. The maximum lump sum, again available after 20 years of service, is one and a half times final salary.

It is also possible to incorporate widows' and dependants' benefits, including a lump sum of up to four times salary, together with a refund of personal contributions, which can be paid free of tax.

Company directors

In general, the same rules apply to 'controlling' directors as to any individual in an occupational pension scheme. However, because a director of a family company is in a rather different position from an ordinary employee, the Revenue have imposed some limitations on directors with at least 20 per cent control, eg the measurement of final salary is more stringent than for non-controlling directors. Directors with 20 per cent control and members of families controlling more than 50 per cent of the company are not eligible to join a company's approved pension scheme if it is an investment company.

15.7.6 Loans and self-investment

A very important development in recent years has been the use of pensions in connection with loans made to the pension planholder or occupational scheme member. This helps to reduce one of the disadvantages of pension schemes, ie capital invested in the fund is 'locked-in' until retirement.

Typically, a lender who makes an interest-only loan to the individual might expect him to repay the capital out of any lump sum to which he is entitled from his pension. Such lump sums will not be assigned to the lender as security for the loan but, for example where the loan is for house purchase, the mortgage over the property, assigned life assurance protection and the existence of the pension cash entitlement will usually satisfy the lender's requirements.

It is important that the pension contracts remain independent of the loan arrangements and that effecting the pension does not guarantee the availability of the loan. The pension must not be taken out to obtain the loan as the pensions legislation requires the pension scheme to be solely for the purpose of obtaining retirement benefits.

Another approach to 'unlocking' some of the pension fund is for the fund to be invested, in part, in shares of the employer company, in making the loans to the company or in purchasing premises from which the company trades.

There are restrictions on the availability and amount of loans that can be made to the employer company under the Social Security Act 1990. In addition, Inland Revenue rules have also restricted this type of 'self-investment'. Loans are limited, for the first two years of a scheme's existence, to 25 per cent of the fund's value excluding transfer values, followed by a limit of 50 per cent of the fund.

The other approaches, which are also subject to restrictions, are usually only available to self-administered schemes in which the trustees have wide powers of investment compared to 'insured schemes' where the investment is usually confined to a policy issued by the insurance company concerned.

15.7.7 Contracting-out via an occupational scheme

As already mentioned, it is possible to use money-purchase schemes to contract out of SERPS.

A contracted-out money purchase (COMP) scheme will receive protected rights contributions as is the case with a PPP. However, from April 1997 a COMP will receive the payments partly in the form of monthly direct flat-rate payments from the employer and partly in the form of age-related payments from the DSS as with a PPP. The total rebates from all sources range between 3.1 per cent and 9 per cent for the 1997/98 tax year.

With a COMP, the Inland Revenue's limits on maximum benefits apply to the aggregate of the protected rights and non-protected rights benefits; a contracted-in occupational scheme member may obtain the maximum benefits from the occupational scheme, in addition to the protected rights benefits, from a PPP(PRO) effected to contract out of SERPS. The age-related incentive payable from April 1993 did not apply to a COMP.

Protected rights benefits from a COMP can be taken at age 60 by both males and females.

15.7.8 Unapproved occupational schemes

These may be established by employers to provide benefits greater than those otherwise allowable. In this way, for example, benefits in excess of two-thirds of final salary can be provided and top-up pensions can be given to employees with short service or those who are subject to 'income capping'.

There are none of the special tax benefits normally received by approved pension schemes and employer contributions will only obtain relief under the normal business expenditure rules, but lump sums can be paid free of tax from funded schemes. However, such schemes do retain certain tax benefits including, in some cases, the ability to roll up income at the basic rate of tax rather than at the special rate of tax applicable to some trusts. In appropriate cases this can result in a saving of tax where the employee is a higher rate taxpayer, as is likely to be the case. In addition, until 30 November 1994 it was also possible to set up offshore schemes with enhanced taxation benefits. Although the employee is subject to tax on payments into the scheme (whether set up offshore or not), it was also possible to arrange for a degree of tax-free growth and freedom from tax on lump sum benefits. This is no longer possible as the Finance Act 1994 imposed a new tax charge on schemes set up to avoid tax in this way. The new rules apply to all schemes set up after the 1994 November budget and existing schemes which are varied after that date.

15.7.9 Free-standing AVC schemes

Since October 1987, all occupational scheme members are entitled to top-up their pensions by making contributions to a separate pension scheme of their own. Such a 'Free-Standing' Additional Voluntary Contribution (FSAVC) scheme may not be commuted for a cash lump sum and must be aggregated with the occupational scheme to determine the maximum permitted benefits. The overriding limit on personal contributions, 15 per cent of salary (capped where appropriate), remains.

Although regulated by the occupational pension scheme tax legislation, FSAVC schemes also have similarities to PPPs in that they are individual arrangements independent of the individual's employer. The maximum limits on benefits and contributions are, however, those applicable to occupational schemes (see above). An employee's contributions to such schemes must be paid net of tax relief at the basic rate.

As long as contributions to the FSAVC do not exceed £2,400 per annum, the employer need have no involvement in an employee joining an FSAVC scheme. Even where the contributions exceed £2,400, the employer's involvement at the outset is restricted to providing sufficient information to allow the maximum contribution which can be paid to be calculated by the FSAVC provider. In some cases the funds built up in the FSAVC together with the benefits from the employer's scheme may exceed the Inland Revenue limits. Where a scheme is overfunded in this way any over-provision is returned to the scheme member subject to a tax charge. This charge also applies to AVC schemes established in-house by employers.

15.8 SUITABILITY

Personal pension plans and occupational pension schemes provide highly tax-efficient benefits. In consequence they are suitable for and extremely attractive as investments for those with earned income who wish to provide for personal cash and income during retirement and protection for their wives and families during their working lives. Because the premiums are deductible for tax purposes from earned income, the effective cost is relatively low, while the tax-free growth inside the pension fund enables substantial accumulation of funds for pension benefits. The emerging benefits, in the form of tax-free cash commutation and pensions, receive beneficial tax treatment. However, the fact that pension benefits can only be taken after certain ages tends to make such schemes suitable only for those prepared to take a long-term view.

15.9 PREVIEW OF THE YEAR AHEAD

This year will see the first test of the reforms introduced by the Pensions Act and the new pensions regulator OPRA. Attention will quickly focus on the way in which OPRA exercises its considerable new powers. The regulator has a difficult balance to achieve: overly strict implementation of the new rules could deter some employers from operating schemes and defeat the primary objective of securing better pensions provision. On the other hand undue leniency could lead to the new rules, and ultimately the regulator, being discredited.

The Maxwell affair can be seen, in part, as representing a failure of the self-regulatory system under the Financial Services Act. Whether OPRA can prevent a scandal on a similar scale depends as much on the effectiveness of the new whistle-blowing obligations of scheme actuaries and auditors, as on OPRA's own efforts. The actuarial profession has always played a key role in the management of occupational schemes. With their new obligations to report Pensions Act breaches to OPRA, actuaries have been effectively cast in the role of policemen. The sound of the policeman's whistle could become a familiar sound – only the best run schemes will have managed to have complied with every detail of the Act's requirements.

Some will argue that the policeman should have come equipped with a radio or at least regulatory powers similar to those under the Financial Services Act. OPRA, and the actuarial and audit professions' 'Special Constabulary', will be looking for a solid start, with no major scandals, if confidence in the system is to be built up.

The new Labour Government will face the challenge of defusing the 'demographic time-bomb'. As the population ages there will be fewer contributors in employment to pay the pensions of those in retirement. Current private pension provision is inadequate – most people simply do not pay enough, early enough to secure an adequate level of pension provision. The basic State Pension and SERPS is likely to provide only the barest level of subsistence for many of those due to retire in the next century.

Immediate changes are unlikely to be at the top of the new Government's agenda. Although personal pensions and occupational schemes will continue to have a key role to play the Labour Government intends to set up a review of pensions and the financial insecurity of the elderly. Any proposal which seeks to provide some form of compulsory private pension provision (such as proposed by the Conservative party in March of this year) may be seen as a further means of reducing the need to rely on State provision. The mechanics of such a system, and the way in which it interrelates with existing schemes, are likely to prove more complex than they appear at first glance.

The system of contracting out using personal pensions is a good example of past experience. Intended as simple money purchase arrangements, funded by once a year payments from the Department of Social Security, contracted out personal pensions have seen three major changes to the contribution structure and various changes to the tax rules, as well as changes to the regulatory system. All this has taken place within ten years. During that time pensions scheme legislation and Inland Revenue guidance has expanded to fill three considerable volumes. Making changes to the existing system may only add a further layer of complexity.

This complexity comes at a price. New pensions providers with little experience of the pensions market have pinned their faith in simple products at a competitive price, but provide little or no advice to help consumers fight their way through the maze. The established providers are fighting back by re-emphasising the importance of getting advice to select the right product rather than simply the cheapest. With a further period of change ahead, there will also be an emphasis on selecting products which have the flexibility to adapt to changing circumstances.

Finally, the fear of adverse tax changes is likely to surface during the year. Removal of tax-free lump sums, a reduction in higher rate tax relief or an increase in the rate of tax which can be recovered on dividend income are all no doubt all be the subject of speculation. If the rumours prompt more investors to start making contributions that will be no bad thing; in the final analysis the purpose of a pension is to secure a realistic level of retirement income regardless of the tax advantages.

15.10 CONCLUSION

The tax-deductibility of premiums, tax-free growth and prospects of a tax-free lump sum make pensions an extremely attractive investment.

There are, of course, some restrictions (lack of access to the fund until a minimum age, ability to take only a proportion as a lump sum, limits on the investment permitted, etc) but these do not detract from the investment benefit of pensions where the pension is effected for the right reasons, ie as long-term planning for retirement.

SOURCES OF FURTHER INFORMATION

See end of Chapter 14.

16

COMMODITIES

WILLIAM ADAMS
Head of Metals Research, Rudolf Wolff & Co Ltd

This chapter is aimed as an introduction to the commodity markets and a brief review and forecast of markets themselves. The areas covered are:

(1) Introduction to commodities.
(2) Types of commodities: softs, metals and financials, physical and futures.
(3) Characteristics of commodities.
(4) Methods to participate in the markets: cash, futures, options and managed funds.
(5) Recent market performance.
(6) The outlook for the year ahead.

16.1 INTRODUCTION TO COMMODITIES: WHAT THEY ARE

The commodity markets had their origins in the Industrial expansion of the 19th Century. Industrialisation led to a rapid growth in demand for basic commodities which caused increased volatility in prices as supply became more dependent on the arrival of shipments from abroad. This price volatility meant more efficient means were needed to price and allocate commodities. The early commodity markets therefore enabled traders to buy and sell contracts for physical commodities, on the basis of today's prices for delivery in the future.

Today's commodity exchanges still provide this service, although they have generally evolved to provide more of a pricing mechanism, where traders buy and sell the right to a commodity (a future), than trading the physical commodity. That said, the commodity exchanges are still backed by physical commodities and if a future contract becomes prompt, then it is the physical commodity that has to be delivered or taken-up.

The primary reason for the markets is still to provide a means whereby trade users can fix the price at which they sell or buy their raw material commodities in the future. For fabricators using commodities, this means that the price of their finished goods can be determined before being produced, by locking-in (hedging) the cost of the commodities needed to produce the finished goods. Likewise a producer can plan in advance whether it is profitable to continue producing the commodity in the period ahead. If the future price is above the full cost of production, the producer can sell futures against forward production and guarantee a profit for the period ahead.

Today's commodity markets are very sophisticated and form an integral part of the world financial markets where banks, producers, consumers, merchants and investors are all participants.

This chapter largely deals with the concepts of the commodity markets with insight into those commodities that can be bought and sold through, or are regulated by, the London Clearing House, The London Metal Exchange, The London Commodity Exchange, and London International Financial Futures Exchange.

16.2 TYPES OF COMMODITIES

16.2.1 Softs and metals

The raw material commodities can be sub-divided into two categories: soft commodities and metals.

The term soft commodities loosely describes all non-metallic commodities: cocoa, coffee, sugar, rubber, grain, potatoes, wool, edible oil, nuts, etc. The London Commodity Exchange is Europe's primary soft commodity exchange, operating markets in coffee, cocoa, sugar, the BIFFEX Freight Index and UK domestic agriculture markets.

The London Metal Exchange (LME) is the centre for trade in the main non-ferrous base metal futures such as aluminium, copper, zinc, lead, nickel, tin and aluminium alloy. The London Bullion Market Association (LBMA) looks after the interests of London's bullion markets. The bullion markets are physical markets and not futures markets.

The London Clearing House (LCH) deals with the clearing and settlement of the futures markets. Membership of LCH guarantees the fulfilment of the contract to both buyer and seller, thus avoiding the need for both buyer and seller to be concerned with each other's financial health. In effect, the LCH becomes the counterparty to each trade that its members carry out with other members.

16.2.2 **Physical and futures**

The commodity markets can be broken down into 'physical' and 'futures'. The physical markets deal with trading of the actual commodity and would normally result in a physical exchange of the commodity. A futures contract deals with commodities that are traded for delivery at a pre-defined future date and in the majority of cases the commodity is not expected to be delivered. As a futures contract is a tradable contract, it is generally liquidated before the contract becomes prompt. This means that the contract is cancelled by a corresponding and opposite contract, which means the trader's net position is square and that any difference in buying and selling prices is settled in cash.

By buying and selling in the futures markets against a physical position, the hedger is able to safeguard himself against the risk that the value of his unsold goods will depreciate through a fall in price or, alternatively, against the risk that pre-booked forward sales will show a loss if the commodity price rises.

Example

A merchant who has taken delivery of 25 tonnes of copper, but has not yet found a buyer for the metal, can sell one futures contract, the basis being the price at which he bought the physical metal. When he finds a buyer for the physical metal, he then buys back his futures contract on the basis of the price at which he sells his physical metal. This means that while he holds the 25 tonnes of copper in stock, he is not vulnerable to a fall in the copper price, as any fall in the copper price is offset by a profit on his futures contract.

This mechanism for hedging risk works when the futures markets are liquid, that is when there are sufficient buyers and sellers to make a two-way market.

Market liquidity is increased by the existence of speculators. The speculator buys or sells a commodity on the expectation of making a profit. By taking the opposite view in the market to the hedger, the speculator takes on the unwanted risk that the hedger wants to avoid.

Investment in physical markets is complicated by having to pay the full cash cost of the commodity, the warehouse and insurance costs, etc. Metals have the advantage over soft commodities in that they are generally less bulky and are not perishable.

Investing in futures avoids many of the disadvantages of physical commodity investing. The speculator can avoid taking physical delivery of the commodity as long as the future contract is closed before the contract becomes prompt. By dealing in futures, the speculator is able to trade softs as easily as metals, without the worry of the commodity perishing, or the more expensive storage costs.

16.2.3 Financial futures

The third category of futures are the financial futures which regard money as another commodity. Financial futures grew rapidly in the 1980s and have enabled traders to use their money more flexibly by trading and hedging interest rates, bonds and stock market indices in the same way they would trade other raw material commodities.

These financial futures contracts are structured, regulated and cleared just like the raw material commodities and provide opportunities for invest-ment managers, financial treasurers and traders seeking profit opportunities.

The interest rate market contracts are the most important of the financial futures. These range from short-dated three-month papers to long-maturity government bonds and are denominated in most of the world's major trading currencies. The major contracts are traded in three time zones, providing around-the-clock access.

Stock index contracts are also well established and becoming increas-ingly popular, as are the option derivatives on the stocks. In addition to speculation, these products enable investors and fund managers to hedge their portfolio rapidly or to gain immediate access to the market (see **6.3–6.5** on futures).

16.3 CHARACTERISTICS OF COMMODITIES

Commodity markets are sophisticated, internationally traded and price movements are often volatile. It is these characteristics which provide many attractive trading opportunities.

16.3.1 International markets

The word commodity is defined in an economic sense as 'an exchange-able unit of economic wealth'. In most cases these units of economic wealth are internationally recognised and therefore have a real value which is recognised and traded internationally. This widespread need for the commodities also means the markets are liquid and have high turnover as each commodity often passes through many traders'/industrialists' hands before being consumed. The liquidity, high volume and interest in these commodities means that in most cases it is possible to trade large volumes fairly quickly without disrupting the balance in the market.

16.3.2 Frequent opportunities

The prices of commodities continuously fluctuate as buying and selling pressure shifts. The driving forces for prices in the long term are the supply and demand fundamentals. In the short term the markets may move in the opposite direction to that suggested by the fundamentals factors, but this divergence provides further opportunities for trading. In the futures markets because the prompt date is a date in the future, the contract can be sold short. This means that the trader can sell the contract before buying it back at a later date. Therefore even if traders expect prices to fall, they can still trade and profit from a falling market. This second dimension to the futures market is not available to most private investors in equities. However, the futures markets can at times be very volatile, and the investor directly involved in a commodity will need to follow the market closely and is best advised to seek the guidance of an established broker and investment advisor.

16.3.3 Real assets

Raw material commodities are real assets with intrinsic values. This means that they could always be sold for cash and in the long term they are a good potential hedge against inflation or currency depreciation.

16.4 METHODS OF PARTICIPATION IN THE COMMODITY MARKETS

There are many opportunities for investors to participate in the commodity markets and a host of investment vehicles that can be used to do so. The following deals with the more direct approaches of investing in commodities and commodity futures.

16.4.1 Physical (cash) metals

Possibly the least speculative means of getting involved in the metals is to buy physical metal. Once bought, the investor pays insurance and warehousing costs, but because payment has been made in full and there is no gearing involved on the initial capital investment, he does not have to pay additional margin payments.

The time to buy cash metals is when prices have fallen considerably below the costs of metal production, which in theory should eventually lead to production cutbacks at plants that are no longer economically viable. This brings about a change in the supply and demand balance of the metal.

It should be made clear that an oversupply situation in the metal markets can last for a number of years, so this type of investment should be seen as a long-term investment.

In addition, it should be realised that world production costs also fluctuate; in times of falling metal prices, producers attempt to cut production costs in an effort to remain economically profitable.

The long-term cyclical nature of commodity prices is inherent in the markets, as high prices encourage additional production and less consumption, which turn a market which has a balanced supply and demand into one where there is a supply surplus. This leads to lower prices. Conversely, in a period of low prices, consumption increases and production decreases, which eventually leads to a drawdown in stocks and higher prices as demand for metal outstrips supply. These cycles mean that the further prices diverge from the world production costs, the more likely there is a change in the direction of the price trend. These factors influence the market over the long term and may take a few years to change the direction of a commodities price.

16.4.2 Cash and carry

The cash and carry is a risk-free way of trading in commodities, for a known return on funds employed. In addition, a cash and carry sometimes provides opportunities for a capital gain.

This method of trading takes advantage of markets where forward prices are at a premium to cash (spot) prices. This premium is known as a 'contango'. In normal (contango) market conditions, the futures price is above the cash price (the exception to this occurs when there is a physical shortage of the commodity for nearby delivery; when this happens forward prices trade at a discount to the cash price. The discount is known as a backwardation). Normally the contango reflects the cost of storage, insurance, and the opportunity cost of tying up money while holding the physical commodity. In other words, the contango reflects the interest payments lost by not having the money in the bank, plus the cost of insurance, plus the cost of storage.

A cash and carry is traded by buying a commodity for immediate delivery and simultaneously selling an equal amount of the commodity for a future delivery date. In a contango market, this means you are buying at a lower price and selling at a higher price. The difference is the gross profit. Occasionally while the investor is holding a cash and carry, a shortage in the commodity occurs and the market's contango narrows or even turns into a backwardation. In this case the holder of the cash and carry can sell his cash commodity and simultaneously buy back his future position, thereby making a capital gain.

16.4.3 Futures

The basic commodity traded on the exchanges is the outright futures contract. This provides the investor with a high risk vehicle to trading commodities and requires the services of a futures broker. The buying or selling of a futures contract by an investor/speculator involves them taking a view on whether prices are set to rise or fall during the period of the futures contract. At any time during the life of the futures contract, the contract can be closed-out by making a corresponding and opposite trade.

For example if an investor buys one March 94 Cocoa then to close out his position he needs to sell one March 94 Cocoa before the March 94 Cocoa contract becomes due. If on 4 January he sells one LME three months copper, with a prompt date of 4 April, then when he closes the contract he needs to buy one lot of LME copper on the basis of the three months' price and then adjust the contract to the prompt date of his original short position, in this case 4 April.

Because dealing in futures is for forward delivery, only a proportion of the value of the contract is initially required as payment. This initial payment, known as initial margin, is normally around 10 per cent of the value of the full contract. Therefore an investment in £100,000 worth of copper will only require an initial outlay of £10,000. This means that the funds the investor initially commits are geared at 10 per cent.

Your risk, however, is on the full £100,000 value of the commodity; therefore a 10 per cent move in the price of the commodity against the investor would mean a 100 per cent loss on his initial funds. Should the value of the commodity move against him, then he would be required immediately to provide funds equal to the open position loss of his futures contract. This difference is called variation margin and is paid in addition to the initial margin. Both initial and variation margin are used by the broker as collateral against any difference in the current market value of the contract and the starting value of the contract when the investor initiated the trade.

It is this gearing and the need for variation margin payments which gives the commodity markets their high-risk reputation. Of course it is the ability to make 100 per cent on the investor's funds with only a 10 per cent movement in price which makes the market attractive to speculators.

16.4.4 Options

A less risky way to invest in the commodities is to buy options. An option is a traded contract which gives the buyer the right to buy a futures commodity at a specific price (strike price) at a predetermined date in the future; the buyer does not, however, have the obligation to buy the futures contract. The risk is limited to the initial payment that the buyer has to pay for the option, which is known as the premium. The advantage of trading options is that for a predetermined cost there is the potential for a significant gain.

Traded options are based on underlying futures contracts. If the option becomes profitable, the holder of an option can at any time prior to the declaration of the option lock in a profit by one of the following means:

(1) trading a futures contract against the option position;
(2) selling the option and making a profit out of the difference between the premium he paid to buy the option and the premium he collected when he sold the option;
(3) waiting until option declaration and notifying his broker that he intends to declare the option, in which case the option position is converted into a futures position at the strike price of the option. The investor then has to sell the futures contract to take the profit.

If the futures price moves in the opposite direction to the option, then the option holder allows the option to expire and his loss is limited to the initial premium he paid.

There are numerous types of options and by combining various types, the investor can produce option strategies which provide different opportunities.

The basic options are call and put options. A call option gives the buyer the right to buy a futures contract and a put option gives the buyer the right to sell a futures contract (see also **6.6**).

A grantor (uncovered seller) of an option takes on unlimited risk, as by selling the option he gives the buyer of the option the right, but not the obligation, to take up a futures contract at a predetermined price on a predetermined date in the future. Option grantors are traditionally the trade (consumers and producers) who use options as a means of raising cash. Investment fund managers and risk seekers also grant options, but option granting is a high risk activity, whereas option buying will provide an investor with a highly leveraged position with a limited liability.

16.4.5 Managed funds

Investing in commodities through managed funds provides the ideal vehicle for investors to get exposure to the risk/rewards that the futures markets offer, but do not have the time, inclination or expertise to follow and trade the markets.

Types of fund on offer vary the level of risk/reward; some offer a guarantee that at least the initial sum will be returned after a pre-set period, but this guarantee means that the fund is relatively lowly geared and therefore less risky than a highly geared fund where the initial investment is at risk.

Essentially there are two types of funds that invest in commodity futures, options and derivatives. The traditional type of funds are the Unauthorised Collective Investment Schemes, which pool investors' money so that the investment benefits from a diversified portfolio investing in futures and options. These funds are generally registered offshore and are open-ended funds which work on a unit allocation basis (see also **8.12**).

The second category of funds is the Futures and Options Funds (FOFs) and the Geared Futures and Options Funds (GFOFs). These funds have recently been authorised by UK regulators and work in a similar fashion to the Authorised Unit Trusts, which traditionally were not allowed to invest in futures. At the moment these new funds have not been widely developed.

Funds generally operate on the basis that the fund manages the money it raises by investing the money with a number of Commodity Trading Advisors (CTAs). This enables the fund managers to select the best performing CTAs and as market conditions change, the allocation of money with each CTA can be optimised. The fund manager monitors the returns from the CTAs and handles the fund's administration and risk management.

Normally, the only cost to the investor will be standard brokerage charges plus a small management fee of between 1 and 3 per cent and an incentive fee which is assessed on the performance of the fund. This fee generally averages around 15 to 20 per cent of the increase in value of the fund in an agreed accounting period.

Commodity funds generally have full discretion over the money invested with them, although some funds specialise in certain market segments and have pre-set risk management principles.

The performance of all funds relies heavily on the fund manager's judgement and how accurately he anticipates the markets.

In selecting a fund manager, the investor needs to see how the manager has performed in the past. Although this by no means guarantees future performance, it does give some insight into how skilled the manager and the operation is.

The traditional funds are registered overseas to provide tax incentives for investors.

Generally, the minimum investment into this traditional type of funds is around £10,000. The advantage of managed funds is that they provide individual investors and institutions with access to a market which is growing rapidly in volume and which provides numerous opportunities for investors to diversify their investment portfolio.

16.5 COMMODITIES' RECENT MARKET PERFORMANCE

16.5.1 Financial markets

Early 1996 saw the equity and bond markets pause, but from September onwards, the US markets have pushed ahead again. Strong corporate earnings and few pressures on inflation, apart from falling unemployment, have supported the rally. The inflow of money into mutual funds has been one of the driving forces in pushing the equity markets, and therefore indices, higher. The FTSE rose 10 per cent while the Dow Jones increased by 26 per cent.

16.5.2 Soft commodities

Coffee

At the beginning of last year the market was just recovering from hitting contract lows on its long fall post the 1994 frost. Prices remained range bound during the spring and summer, and slid towards the lows in September as the new crop was sold.

Expectations of lower production in Brazil and Central America in 1997 caused prices to rally from December onwards. News of problems in Colombian production lead to an explosion in January/February with prices rising 55 per cent to the $1.75 to $1.90 per lb range.

For the balance of the year a strong market is expected until there is evidence of a recovery in production. If the lower estimates for production become fact, the market could well rise another 20–50 per cent.

Cocoa

Fears over the delivery of Ivory Coast mid-crop saw prices rise as the trade bought large quantities for September delivery. Prices rose sharply from £900 to all but reach £1,200, as scares over the delivery of the cocoa caused the sellers to chase for cover. In the end the material was delivered – a total of 29,757 lots or 297,570 tonnes, which is an exchange record.

Since then prices have been weaker with values losing all their previous gains. It is believed values have fallen to a possible low point around £875, and it is expected that there could be some recovery in the order of 10–15 per cent over the coming months.

This will, however, depend on the Ivory Coast's production being below 1m tonnes this season compared to 1.3m last.

Sugar

At the beginning of 1996 prices were peaking on both fundamental and technical strength. With the Thai crop delayed the trade was forced to cover in other origins and this caused a short-term logistic problem.

Crop predictions were for another surplus year and prices dropped below 10c/lb, having peaked at 12c/lb.

In mid-year funds became aggressive buyers and caught the trade short; prices again moved higher but peaked at 11.76c/lb. This move was totally against the fundamental outlook.

This year the market is trading between 10 and 11c/lb, awaiting off-take from the two major buyers (Russia and China). The market still remains in surplus, and until there is a more balanced production/consumption outlook, the longer term 10–12c/lb range should remain intact.

16.5.3 Base metals

Throughout the first three quarters of 1996, most metals remained under pressure. Much of this was the result of continued de-stocking which carried on from 1995. The main event, however, was the sell-off in copper that was sparked by the Sumitomo crisis in May and June 1996. This saw copper prices fall by $1,000/tonne in two months. The fall was the result of a combination of producer, option short and fund selling, against concerns that vast quantities of copper would be released onto the market; in the event this fear proved ill-founded. The weakness and volatility in copper had an impact on all the base metals, with the result that trade business became noticeably quiet, and the markets remained under pressure, as shown in Table 16.1 overleaf.

Whereas copper has been the leading metal for the base metal complex, this seems set to change. The supply/demand balance for copper is about to shift from supply deficit to surplus. As a result, prices should move considerably lower. The other base metals are not in such a weak fundamental position; supply constraints and strong demand are expected to draw down stocks and further price gains are likely.

Table 16.1 Summary of 1996's performance: price and stocks

	LME 3 months prices					LME stocks movements				
LME	Start	Hi	Lo	Last	Pct	Start	Hi	Lo	Last	Pct
Cu	2650	2712	1733	2130	−20	315175	356800	90050	125350	−60
Al	1703	1703	1302	1547	−9	589925	970275	589925	951275	+62
Zn	1022	1121	992	1065	+4	662400	662400	516550	506825	−23
Pb	713	862	660	705	−1	130750	130750	88175	118600	−10
Ni	8000	8850	6360	6430	−20	44676	49350	31998	48900	+9
Sn	6310	6650	5675	5850	−7	11860	11860	8450	10610	−11
Aa	1495	1505	1175	1390	−7	62860	86640	62860	74440	+18

16.6 OUTLOOK FOR COMMODITIES IN 1997/98

16.6.1 Financials

Following a very strong performance in 1996, following on from 1995's, the US markets look overbought and a correction seems overdue. Any major correction in the US equities would be likely to impact other stock markets. In addition, with the Japanese banking industry facing difficult times, any major upheavals could cause a ripple effect through the US Treasury auctions, which may increase the cost of borrowing, hence raise interest rates. Overall the outlook for the financial sector is turning bearish as the upside potential seems limited compared to the potential for a significant downside correction. As is always the case in trying to predict a turning point, it is ultimately the timing which is all important.

16.6.2 Base metals

With most of the base metals falling in 1996, as shown in Table 16.1 above, some good buying opportunities have been seen. Some of the metals have already rallied, but a combination of improving fundamentals, low stock levels and fund buying are expected to lead to further gains. The exception to this is copper, where the shift to a supply/demand surplus is likely to lead to significantly lower prices. With the world economy pausing in 1995 and 1996, world growth is expected to expand again in 1997. A recovery in Japan and a general low inflationary environment should underpin steady growth.

Whereas in 1994 and early 1995 the market was driven by strong consumption, late 1995 and 1996 have been consolidation years, but supply factors are now expected to drive most of the metals higher.

Copper

Copper is in a confusing situation and much depends on the action of the Chinese. Fundamentally, a host of new copper production is set to create a supply surplus, which in turn should lead to a build up in stocks and lower prices. However, the Chinese have recently been looking to buy copper to rebuild their strategic stockpile. If they choose to do this now, then the forecast surplus could be wiped out in 1997 and the current low stocks levels would suggest significantly higher prices; but this seems unlikely. Being shrewd traders, it would seem rational for the Chinese to wait for lower prices before they re-stock. With bearish fundamentals dominating over the next three to four years, it is expected producer forward selling eventually to cap any rally above the $2,400–2,500 level.

Aluminium

Aluminium prices sank to a low of $1,305/tonnes in October 1996 on fund and disappointed liquidation selling. The excessive sell-off provided an ideal buying opportunity, which the funds took. Prices have since rallied to $1,660/tonne and the rate of rise seems to have caught consumers off-guard and, therefore, under-hedged. As such, any dips in prices should be well supported. A recovery in demand, plus a return of consumer buying after two years of de-stocking, should underpin the firmer prices. Although stocks are still relatively high and there is idle smelter capacity in the US, the producers who control the idle capacity are in no apparent hurry to re-start it. As stocks fall back towards more normal working levels, higher prices should be sustainable.

Zinc

Zinc prices look set to rise towards the $1,400/tonne level. After years of depressed prices, which has seen little investment in new production capacity, the outlook is for a few years of supply deficit. This should bring stocks back to more normal working levels by the end of 1997. Beyond that, a shortage is likely to develop, which could lead to considerably higher prices. Out of all the base metals, zinc is thought to have the best fundamentals.

Lead

After a very tight first half of 1996, lead prices have been trending lower, with prices hitting a low of $634/tonne in February 1997, 26 per cent below June 1996's high. The extent of the sell-off is surprising, especially as the market has ignored various supply disruptions that are likely to tighten up primary supply. However, the high prices in mid-1996 led to a significant pick-up in exports from China and an increase in scrap collection – over 50 per cent of refined lead is sourced from recycled scrap. At the moment, longer-term bearish fundamentals are depressing lead prices, but with stronger demand expected in 1997, plus the recent disruptions to primary production, in the short term, firmer lead prices are likely. Should the funds get involved as well, then a rapid recovery in lead's fortunes could be seen. At the moment, total commercial lead stocks are below critical levels, so the market is vulnerable on the upside.

Nickel

Nickel demand has suffered as a result of cutbacks in stainless steel production. The stainless steel industry has seen a rapid increase in production capacity, especially in South Africa and the Far East. The flood of stainless steel onto the market has now caused production cutbacks and hence less demand for primary nickel. This is only a temporary set-back, as stainless steel is a metal with huge potential demand. Once demand absorbs the new capacity, higher prices should follow and idle production capacity will then need to restart. Once this happens, nickel demand and prices should rise.

Tin

Tin is expected to continue its recovery; stocks are falling towards critical levels, which may now cause periods of supply tightness. The level of Chinese exports will remain an important swing factor in the tin market. New smelter capacity is coming on stream, but a lack of investment in tin mining is likely to result in a concentrate shortage. Economic growth should underpin demand, especially as industrialisation takes hold in South East Asia, India and China. In addition, the likelihood of significantly higher aluminium prices should have a positive impact on tin in the packaging industry. Should fund buying spread across all the base metals, then another period of strong tin prices are likely, similar to the 1993–95 bull run.

16.7 HOW TO PARTICIPATE

Commodity markets involve a high risk and it is essential for the investor to fully understand the whole workings of the market. That said once the concepts and risks have been grasped then commodities provide a wide range of investment opportunities.

The key to successful investing in commodities lies in a full understanding of the opportunities available, to have access to up-to-date information, and most importantly to know how to interpret this information. This information can be found through experienced brokers and professional advisors.

Further information should be initially sort from the market exchanges and the London Clearing House, details given below:

London Metal Exchange Ltd
56 Leadenhall Street
London
EC3A 2BJ

London Commodity Exchange
1 Commodity Quay
St Katherine's Dock
London
E1 9AX

London International Financial
    Futures Exchange
Cannon Bridge
London
EC4R 3XX

London Bullion Market
    Association
6 Frederick's Place
London
EC2R 8BT

London Clearing House
Roman Wall House
1–2 Crutch Friars
London
EC2R 8BT

GOLD AND OTHER VALUABLES

JOHN MYERS

Solon Consultants

17.1 INTRODUCTION

17.1.1 A long-term hedge in precious metals

Traditionally, investors have looked upon precious metals and other valuables as a long-term hedge against political or economic chaos. When inflation has soared, when currencies have weakened, when stock markets have plummeted, precious metals have gained in attraction; historically, the greater the fear, the higher the price rises. Gold is the archetypal precious metal, sought for its allure and its rarity, and its habit of reasserting its worth when ephemeral standards fail.

Many still regard gold as intrinsically valuable, internationally acceptable and negotiable. For these reasons, it maintains a historical image as the ultimate form of money, a store of wealth unaffected by wars and political turmoil. However, recent events have tarnished that image. Hedging, with the help of futures, options, gold mining shares, physical holdings and indices, has damped oscillations. Also, exchange controls have weakened. That has made it easier for wealthy people who dread war and local hyperinflation to shift into dollars, marks, Swiss francs or yen, instead of gold. Political crises across the world have therefore had little impact on the bullion market of late. The Gulf conflict, the breakup of the former Soviet Union, and successive Balkan wars, again involving Sarajevo, have only marginally affected the price.

Could a central bank still run wild and cause unbridled inflation? Perhaps; but what protects savings is a government that wants to protect them. Any government can allow inflation, as Russia has recently, to finance government by creating new money. It can do so, unless gold reserve requirements are so stiff that no human can determine economic policy – only gold can. Few democracies in the 1990s would accept this.

Those who nonetheless want a return to the gold standard do not trust governments. Most people are not as pessimistic about the motives, capabilities and skills of the money managers. In practice, nations no longer settle balance of payments' deficits with gold, and gold no longer backs currencies. Nor are countries and trading blocs willing to let the ebb and flow of their gold supply determine economic activity and the fate of their people. Admittedly, in times of calamity, gold is always likely to be a safe and valued haven. Otherwise, gold will remain something to use in jewellery and dental work, and as the main ingredient of coins in collectors' hands.

Yet the interplays of demand and supply in bullion markets remain complex. Unlike other commodities, dream and doubt, more than industrial utility, have often driven demand. The actions of the 'official sector' have governed supply and prices more than the efforts of producers. (Central banks are responsible for gold's role as a quasi-monetary standard and, for the moment, control almost one-third of the supply.) Yet, with enthusiasts, gold holds its reputation, perhaps sullied, as a long-term insurance against the collapse of economies, markets and currencies. Bullion 'bugs' state confidently that the metal will sustain, or even increase its value in times of great uncertainty.

Maynard Keynes dismissed the metal as 'a barbarous relic'. Others insist that 'something that has been a store of value for 5,000 years will not go out of fashion'. They also point to the physical characteristics of bullion bars, wafers or coins. The metal is largely immune to the effects of weather, moisture, oxidation or sea water, and to the corrosive effects of most acids and alkalis. Gold hoarders go on believing that their holdings will endure, and offset any severe downturn in portfolios of stocks and shares during a monetary or political crisis. Furthermore, prices of gold and platinum are usually expressed in US dollars. The 'bugs' therefore see these metals as a hedge against sharp falls in non-dollar currency markets.

For a few financial planners, the strength of the case persists. They still recommend wealthy investors to keep perhaps 5–10 per cent of their assets in precious metals. Some intrepid souls, with cash to spare, continue to hold 10–15 per cent of their wealth in gold. The truly enchanted are even bolder. In February 1997, the *New York Times* featured the fiscal conservatism of an American retired investment banker, Robert F Hague. He keeps 90 per cent of his portfolio in gold bullion, coins, unit funds, and individual equities. Hague told the journalist: 'I've felt for many, many years that we're going to have to use gold to straighten out our financial system. The reason the economy and the market look so good is the excess of credit and debt. It's all false. There will come a time when we recognize gold as the ultimate money.'

Others disagree. Experts point to the negligible annual return produced by gold bullion or coins – an average of just 0.46 per cent from 1991–1996. Investors have also been critical of the gold 'bugs', especially in America. Investing in commodities such as gold and silver 'is not for most average investors,' says Thomas O'Hara, chairman of the US National Association of Investors Corporation. 'Gold is very risky; it provides no regular income, such as occurs from investing in common stocks,' he says. Metal prices are 'volatile and subject to manipulation from speculators'. Investing in gold or silver is 'primarily for very wealthy individuals'. Others should perhaps be careful not to become gold's fool.

Most investors should 'stay away' from gold, agrees John Markese, executive director of the American Association of Individual Investors in Chicago. If a person 'just has to buy some gold', then owning shares in a broadly based natural-resources mutual fund is probably the safest route. Nevertheless, the gold component 'should not be more than 10 percent of the value of the investor's mutual-fund portfolio,' he says.

From a positive standpoint, gold has unique properties – superior electrical conductivity, ductility and malleability. Gold is also beautiful. These qualities are timeless, and the reason that gold provides a long-term store of value. The importance of gold as a 'safe haven' has diminished in recent years; however, the possibility of world political turmoil, even if small, makes some investment in gold or gold mining shares prudent.

Silver and platinum have also become respectable vehicles for investment. Admittedly, they are riskier than gold. The prime use of silver, for example, is as an industrial material, with at least a chance that its price will fall during a recession. Platinum is an alternative, but prices are highly volatile. Its popularity has depended largely on its use in automotive catalytic converters that, with technical developments, now require decreasing amounts of the metal. Nevertheless, worldwide demand has risen, boosted at the margin by low-cost platinum jewellery sales in Japan.

In principle, buying gold and platinum should help to even out the volatility of an investment portfolio. John Goodrich of Colonial Consulting made the point in *Money Management Letter*, 24 February 1997: 'The statistics available are irrefutable that if you broadly diversify your equity holdings with non-correlating assets you can increase the sums invested in equity while reducing volatility and risk.' The historical evidence is that prices of precious metals, like gold, have oscillated spectacularly on occasion. They are not investments for the nervous or the needy. Records show that, in times of low inflation – for example, the early 1990s – shares, bonds and unit trusts substantially out-perform gold and other precious metals.

On balance, the unpredictability of prices makes precious metals unsuitable investments for individuals with limited capital. Nor are these commodities wise purchases for investors who might require liquid funds in a personal emergency, or a reliable flow of income from their savings.

17.1.2 Recent developments

In this century, gold has recorded five major price rises in world markets. Its history, of course, is as a coinage metal and a measurement of national wealth. In 1934, as part of America's 'New Deal', the bullion price was upgraded and fixed in US dollar terms at $35 per ounce. This lasted for 40 years until President Nixon severed gold's links with the dollar. On the open market, bullion then reached $200 per ounce, mainly because of petrodollar inflation and weak central banking strategies.

A quarter of a century ago, in the inflationary 1970s, investors rushed to convert paper money into gold. The price of an ounce of gold rose to $825, the last big surge in the gold price. It then dropped to $300 an ounce in mid-1982, only to rally again, reaching $500 per ounce in June 1983. Since 1987, gold has fallen back. In 1991 the dollar price averaged $362.26, down 6 per cent on 1990, and declined further to a six-year low of $336 in April 1992. This was despite the Gulf War, continued turmoil in South Africa, and the collapse of the Soviet Union.

By March 1993, gold had tumbled yet again, and was fixed at a consecutive seven-year low of $326, with the most pessimistic predicting still lower prices. Against their expectations, gold recovered to show a strong price performance in 1993, which it sustained during the 1994 bull market in commodities. For gold 1994 and 1995 were years of consolidation with prices remaining within a steady $370–395 trading range. This left the average dollar price for 1995 at 7 per cent above its 1993 average, the first increase since 1990.

In this period, new buyers entered the market on a large scale. For the first time, China surpassed the US as the world's largest buyer, importing 350 tonnes or 10 per cent of world output in 1992, when China lifted exchange rate controls on semi-official currency swap markets. China's dollar depreciated by 30 per cent and, within days, Hong Kong's gold outlets reported an upsurge of 20 per cent in demand from Chinese customers.

Chinese consumption grew by 130 per cent in 1994 as wages increased and people sought a hedge against inflation rates, which rose to a post-1949 high. Demand remained high throughout 1995, due to the lifting of exchange rate controls, the rapid depreciation of China's currency, and a traditional cultural affinity for gold. The market is also growing in other South East Asian countries, where many people buy gold partly as a guard against economic, financial and geopolitical uncertainties.

Purchases in South East Asia rose to about one-third of the world's annual gold consumption. Steady sales of gold occurred in Thailand, Taiwan, Singapore, Malaysia and South Korea.

In 1996, the World Gold Council reported a fall of 4 per cent in gold sales on the world's principal markets. The main factor was a sharp drop in Japan, and to a lesser extent in China and Europe. According to the Council's annual study, sales in Japan in 1996 dropped 40 per cent from 1995 to a seven-year low, because of 'continued consumer caution'. In Taiwan, another important market, gold sales dropped 23 per cent because of an economic downturn and record joblessness. In Europe, buying of the precious metal was down by 6 per cent, because of 'weaker investment demand'.

India consumes more gold than any other country in the world. There, buying continued to climb, rising 6 per cent to a record level of 500 tonnes of gold, mainly because of a favourable economic and political climate. Supported by strong jewellery sales and investment demand, US demand rose by 6 per cent to a record 350 tonnes. Gold prices have fluctuated around $350, reaching their lowest point since 1993, weighed down by the withdrawal of speculative investment funds and fears that central banks would sell gold.

Thus, in the 1990s, the metal has acted out of character, like a commodity. The price has mainly reflected demand from fabricators of jewellery and electronics. Some commentators hope that, in the late 1990s, the Eastern Bloc nations might provide a stimulus to the market as they seek to back their currencies with bullion. These commentators also highlight gold's traditional popularity in Eastern Europe as a store of value, and they anticipate a rise in private hoardings there. When the Baltic states successfully persuaded the Bank of England to return their pre-war reserves, commentators viewed it as evidence of renewed interest in gold's monetary role.

Generally, central banks prefer not to upset markets, but methods other than outright sales may be used to 'mobilise' gold reserves. They can be physically disposed of through the minting of bullion coins. Other indirect means are call options on reserves, and low-interest gold loans to producers.

In Russia, gold is now in use as a form of money. The Russians have been minting gold roubles to steady their own currency and to stabilise the economy. A surge in demand has encouraged miners, and gold output has been rising in the Krasnoyarsk and Khabarovsk territories, the Irkutsk and Amur regions, and the Evanki republic. The Chairman of the Russian Federation's State Committee for Precious Stones and Metals hopes that Russia can sustain gold production at an annual rate of 160 tonnes.

17.1.3 **Other precious metals**

Platinum, palladium and rhodium have industrial uses in manufacturing and jewellery fabrication, which make them prone to the effects of world recession. About a third of platinum output goes into catalytic converters for the automobile industry, but this demand is highly susceptible to the development of better technologies. In early 1992 the market faltered when a US company announced a breakthrough, which eliminated the need for platinum. Prices recovered when later reports showed that the new device was merely an add-on to existing converters.

Palladium's prime role is also as a catalyst, in electronics as well as the automobile industry. Demand for this metal is similarly susceptibility to the effects of substitution but, overall, continued expansion in the electronics industry has masked cuts in the use of palladium. Rhodium plays a crucial role in the automobile industry, which consumes around 90 per cent of it. This role looks set to continue, as does demand for this more exotic member of the platinum family. However, precious metals dealers comment: 'Companies that use costly materials in electronics are looking for alternatives. They are always striving to use less precious metal on circuit boards, but they can't yet completely abandon it in all cases.'

The miniaturization of electronics also has detracted from physical demand. However, higher sales volumes of devices such as digital pagers and cellular telephones has partially offset the decline.

In the 1990s, the 'wild card' in the market for platinum has been the uncertainty of supplies from its main producers. Labour unrest in South Africa continues to affect this sensitive market, and political problems beset the second major producer, Russia. Seven years ago, South Africa produced 75 per cent of the total world output of platinum, and the former Soviet Union 20 per cent. Demand reached record levels in 1991, but so did supplies. Russia increased exports by a third, causing a fall in prices to a six-year low. The closure of the South African Boschfontein shaft by Rustenburg Platinum, the world's largest producer, in March 1993 also affected prices.

By 1996, dealers in London noted that prices for platinum-group metals were falling, and they saw little prospect of higher levels in the latter part of the year or 1997. Nevertheless, platinum jewellery has been popular for more than two decades in Japan, and represents more than a third of the total market for the metal.

17.1.4 **Gold coins, a popular choice**

Thus, investors, who wish to secure an interest in precious metals such as gold, silver, platinum or palladium, have a choice of media. Most are ill-suited to ordinary investors. For example, gold jewellery makes a memorable gift, but does the buyer really want to ask his or her spouse to sell the Patek Phillipe to pay a child's tuition bill? The alternatives include:

- Buying bullion, which comes in bars made by fabricators and is usually kept in a bank vault. This incurs expensive storage and insurance charges.
- Avoiding the cost and risk of keeping gold bars under the bed, by using the services of commercial banks that hold the metal for their customers in 'gold statement accounts'. When a customer wants to draw on his or her account, the bank advances the cash equivalent of the gold's value at the prevailing price, less commission.
- Speculating in gold futures contracts through a commodities broker. This approach is for gamblers who, undaunted by the wild swings in gold prices in the past, think they can predict future values, or gain a turn by hedging.
- Investing in mining stocks – through equities of companies that mine gold and other precious metals, or diversified funds that specialise in mining companies. Mining stocks have not been stellar performers of late; in 1996, few funds recorded significant growth. Gold funds generally pay modest dividends, locking in at least some returns. However, performance can vary widely, as can annual charges and management fees.
- Buying government-minted coins, such as sovereigns from the Royal Mint or American Eagle coins produced by the US Treasury. (Rare coins are another matter; they are usually considered speculative. See Chapter 19.)

Of these possibilities, gold coins are popular as bullion investments. Eighty per cent of individual investors, who physically own gold, only hold coins, according to the World Gold Council. Enthusiasts believe that, 'when the price of gold moves, collectable coins move faster and further.'

Governments of many countries other than the UK and the US mint bullion coins. Examples are the Russian Chervonetz, the Mexican Peso, the Austrian Corona and Philharmonic (it has a fiddle on the obverse), the Luxembourg Lion, the Australian Nugget, the South African Krugerrand and others enjoying culturally redolent names. So, Mauritius has its Dodo; France, its Napoleon; China, its Panda; Canada, its Maple Leaf; Japan, its Hirohito and its Akihito.

The Royal Mint's Britannia depends upon an aesthetic appeal (as a Coin of the Year) to justify a premium over its bullion value. The coin is struck in 22 carat gold, and on one side depicts Britannia standing amid the waves brandishing her trident; on the other, she holds a shield and olive branch. Although the Britannia competes with the American Eagle, it has a significant difference: the US mint produces tens of thousands of Eagles, while Great Britain limits production to five hundred each of the 1, $\frac{1}{2}$ and $\frac{1}{4}$ ounce sizes. The set sells for $1,650 and the individual $\frac{1}{10}$ ounce coins for $105. However, the retail price seems high, given that bullion today (March 1997) sells at $350 an ounce.

In 1995, prices of American Eagle bullion coins remained within a narrow trading range. Dealers gear rates to gold and silver prices, to which they add a small premium. However, as they are all legal tender (that is, genuine coins produced in limited quantities), they could eventually attract the interest of collectors. Demand might then exceed supply.

Another example is the Australian 'kangaroo', launched in March 1991 as 2 ounce and 10 ounce bullion coins and 1 kilogram 'nuggets', which are 99.99 per cent pure gold. The largest coin has a face value of A$10,000 (more than £4,000), but dealers link sales prices of the coins to the market value of bullion. The 1 kilogram nugget is the heaviest legal tender since South Sea islanders used large stones to pay for goods.

In earlier decades, the Krugerrand was largely responsible for gold coins' success. In 1978, South Africa sold the highest amount ever recorded by any country in a single year. Since trade sanctions disappeared, the South Africans have re-launched the Krugerrand internationally. However, a general deterrent for the UK private investor wishing to invest in gold coins, or for that matter wafers and bars, is a liability to pay VAT. Although investors can still avoid the tax, by buying and holding gold offshore, UK demand for this form of investment collapsed after the Chancellor imposed the tax in 1982. However, demand in Germany for gold coins and bars has risen dramatically since the authorities removed the 14 per cent VAT rate in 1993.

As with all purchases of precious metals, experts advise buyers to deal only with reputable sources. Two years ago, an advertiser in Florida promised to turn a $60 investment in gold coins into $9,200 within a short time. Trading watchdogs in the State described the plan as 'nothing more than a classic pyramid scheme'. Prudence also dictates that, when selling gold coins, the investor should check prices with several bullion merchants or coin dealers. Prices can vary 5 per cent or more from one dealer to another. With gold currently trading in the range of $330–380 an ounce, 5 per cent can be substantial.

17.1.5 Silver, platinum and palladium coins

In this decade, silver coins have become more popular with mints. Dealers and traders sold more than 5.3 million silver dollar American

Eagles between December 1990 and March 1991, a record volume for a silver bullion coin. One factor in the success of the Eagle was the anticipated rise in silver prices. Another was patriotism during the Gulf War. Also, investors favour silver coins and bars to hedge positions in silver futures and shares of companies that mine silver.

The latest entrant is the Canadian silver dollar, introduced in 1996. That coin and a gold Can$100 coin went on sale from 1 March. The mintage is limited. For example the gold coin commemorating the Klondike gold rush is in a limited 'edition' of 35,000, although the 1996 proof silver dollar is more widely available; it records the 1811 arrival of the McIntosh apple-growing family to Canada.

In April 1995 the British Royal Mint launched a £2 silver coin to commemorate the 50th anniversary of the United Nations. However, discerning collectors and traders are beginning openly to challenge the Mint and its promotion of commemorative coins to collectors and investors. Many experts claim that they would not usually form part of a serious collection, and that they represent a poor return on investment. Dealers generally estimate that the realisable value would be no more than 40–60 per cent of the original price. Glendinning, the specialist coins and medals auctioneer, also contends that the supply of commemorative coins considerably outstrips demand. Whereas their production was once a rare event, the mints have launched many new issues in the past two decades.

Investors can buy a silver version of the Royal Mint's UN coin for £26.50. Base metal and gold versions of this coin have been available since late 1995. Another Mint product is a silver 36-coin collection, priced at £1,200, with each coin representing a UN Member State. The coins are in limited production, and purchasable on a monthly subscription basis.

Both the silver Kookaburra (released April 1990) and the platinum Koala feature in Australia's bullion coin programme. The Koala is one of only a few platinum bullion coins currently on the market. One of the earliest was the platinum Noble from the Isle of Man, minted originally in 1983. Following that example, the Australian Gold Corporation selected platinum because of the metal's rarity. Only about four million ounces of platinum are produced worldwide annually, compared with forty million ounces of gold. Japanese buyers account for about 50 per cent of world demand for platinum, and the designers chose the Koala image on the coins partly to develop sales in Japan. According to the Gold Corporation, the day after the coins appeared there, dealers sold 4,093 ounces of the platinum Koalas at prices averaging $515 per ounce. The coin is available in 1 ounce, ½ ounce, ¼ ounce and ¹⁄₁₀ ounce sizes, with nominal values in Australian dollars of $100, $50, $25 and $15.

Russia also markets a set of four historical commemorative coins, two made of silver, one of platinum and one of palladium. The full set has been selling for about £500. As the Russians urgently need hard currency, they have been aggressively selling palladium coins to collectors and metal speculators. The content is 99 per cent palladium, and the price 20 per cent above the metal's daily spot market price. Carrying the image of a ballerina, the coins bear a face value of 25 roubles. The coin contributes to what the Russians hope will be a long-lasting series of 'palladium ballerina' coins. Of 30,000 minted, 3,000 were of proof quality.

Knowledgeable dealers believe that the palladium coin serves as an important long-term precedent, and that palladium, which industry employs in electronic components, could be the investment metal of the next century. Only three countries (Russia, South Africa and the United States) have enough palladium reserves to mine the mineral commercially, but other countries, (Bermuda, France, the Isle of Man and Tonga) have produced special-issue commemorative coins manufactured from imported metal. The Russian coins are just one case of the increasing competitiveness with which foreign mints are seeking customers. Mexico, for example, has been offering the Mexican Rainbow Proof Coin collection consisting of a set of gold, silver and platinum coins. When the Mexicans launched them, they priced the first year's coins bearing the date 1989 at £440.

17.1.6 Selected forms of investment in valuables

Various bodies offer alternatives to investment in physical gold and other precious metals. Some institutions have 'certificate programmes', through which a private investor can specify how much to invest (usually a minimum of £500 or $1,000). The institution then puts all the orders together and buys ingots at the going market rate. The institution then divides the purchase between all the investors, issuing certificates to each. Suppliers can subsequently arrange delivery and storage. Prudence dictates that investors should make certain that the organization that they are dealing with is trustworthy; that they make the purchase in their individual names; and that they receive proof of ownership.

Other forms of investment have recently affected the gold market, helping to change its structure. The growth of speculation in the futures and options market has been an area of some controversy. The price of gold has declined gradually in real terms over the past four years, and some commentators see a vicious circle in the effects of hedging by producers. To cover future price rises when they open new mines, owners sell gold forward; they raise gold loans that they will repay later at a fixed rate.

The more that prices are capped at $350 per ounce or less (a World Gold Council estimate), the greater the incentive for producers to hedge to protect their profitability. Other analysts disagree, pointing to a reduction in hedging by mining companies when the market plunged to a seven-year low. Whether or not hedging by producers has a counter-productive effect, the options and futures market provides flexible instruments for speculators to exploit any short-term volatility in the gold price.

In North America, for example, 50 publicly traded and closely watched firms mine gold as their exclusive or primary line of business. These firms have the same exposure; their output is a globally traded, volatile commodity. They can manage this exposure using a rich set of instruments, including forward and futures contracts, gold swaps, gold or bullion loans, rolling forward commitments called spot deferred contracts, and options. Perhaps most important, firms in the gold mining industry now reveal details of their risk management methods. Quarterly reporting gives investors extensive information on firms' use of forward sales, swaps, gold loans, options, and other explicit or embedded risk management activities. The data enable analysts to measure the risks.

A spot deferred contract is a long-term forward sale of gold in which mines can choose annually whether to deliver against the contract or wait to deliver the gold. Ultimately, they must deliver the gold committed under this contract, but the mine has the option of deciding whether to defer delivery, perhaps because spot prices exceed the contract price. The mine would agree a new delivery price that covers the market forward price plus the loss that the mine would have borne had it met its forward commitment. Thus, spot deferred contracts are similar to rolling one-year forward contracts, except that the former ensures that a creditworthy mine has long-term access to forward contracting (at market rates). A mine reduces the risk of being unable to roll over an existing forward position. If a mine were to rollover a forward contract in which it had a loss, it would have to record the accounting loss on the contract at the rollover. With a spot deferred contract, mine owners roll forward these losses until the ultimate delivery of the gold, and defer accounting losses.

Firms that apply insurance strategies use either exchange-traded, or over-the-counter, gold put options. Alternatively, they dynamically replicate 'puts' by trading forwards and futures. Thus, firms can choose from a rich menu of risk management instruments that allow them to customize their gold price exposure.

Mining equities and funds offer the investor an alternative route. Shares in technologically proficient mining companies with large reserves and low production costs may on occasion be more attractive than investing directly in their physical output.

17.2 HIGHLIGHTS OF THE PREVIOUS YEAR

17.2.1 Central bank and related factors

In 1996, bullish stock markets and strong currencies took attention away from precious metals, as did a spate of selling by central banks, especially those in Europe. Ostensibly, they bought dollars to meet cash requirements for a single European currency by 1999, dealing bullion markets a heavy blow. To counteract this trend, in February 1997, the European Union ruled that member states' central banks could not use proceeds of gold sales to meet the entry criteria for monetary union.

Nevertheless, central banks are still likely to sell gold. The main reason is that the banks are seeking to improve the investment performance of their reserve assets. In that context, many analysts expect gold to trade between $330 and $380 a troy ounce during 1997, and commentators have focused on central bank sales. For example, Raymond Chan Fatchu, president of the Chinese Gold & Silver Exchange Society, said: 'Gold prices have been a victim of dishoarding by central banks, particularly Belgium, Holland, Portugal and even Canada. If not for their selling, gold would now be at $500 an ounce.' Central banks both sold gold directly and leased bullion to cover forward sales.

Analysts also suggest that mine production in the past year fell behind jewellery demand, which would normally have caused a rise in prices. The gold reserves released by central banks made up for the shortfall. Last year, mining output rose to 2,300 tons from 2,000 tons in 1995, while jewellery consumption soared to 2,700 tons from 2,000 tons. The gold price initially rose from $388.10 (December 1995) to $417.70 (February 1996), the highest price in more than five years.

Explanations abound why gold finally broke through its $400-an-ounce ceiling of recent years, shrugging off crises in Bosnia and Herzegovina, wars in Kurdistan and the Chechen Republic, and the Mexican peso crash. Technically, the scene for a rally was set late in 1995, when the South Africans moved to lock in the then current price. They decided to sell about 300 tonnes (not yet mined) for future delivery. The South African forward sales coincided with a shortage of 'lendable' gold to cover the sale. The effects were to push the current price of gold higher, and cause a 'spike' in the cost of leasing the gold to cover a forward sale. Then, late in January 1996, the Barrick Gold Corporation of Toronto announced that it was cutting its forward gold-selling by one-third. This was a move that some analysts expected other mines to follow, and Ashanti Goldfields confirmed it was taking similar action. Any suggestion that miners will stop selling gold they have not yet dug lifts market prices. And as prices rise, miners have even less incentive to sell forward because they might get more for their gold by waiting.

Many other factors contributed to the temporary price rise. Although inflation remained low efforts to reverse portended a rise in inflation in the longer term. In addition, a gap existed between production and demand. Mine output has been falling since 1993, reaching 2,250 tonnes in 1995, with 600 more tonnes entering the market as scrap. Commenting on the trends, Deutsche Morgan Grenfell's chief economist attributed gold's surge to an easing of interest rates by the Japanese, German and US central banks. Analysts suggested that discount rates in the three countries had fallen to record lows in an attempt to stimulate their sluggish economies. He noted: 'People expect all this stimulation to spill over and blow up, they see growth in the money supply and in economic output increasing in the future. Meanwhile, when interest rates were low and investors saw the possibility of future inflation as growth picks up, they bought gold.'

Gold in Japan remained at 1,400 yen per gram, mainly because the yen had depreciated, or the dollar appreciated, in line with a lower dollar price of gold. Japanese analysts generally believe that gold mining costs, though they may vary from one mine to another, will be the 'last defence against declining gold prices. If the gold price drops below that level, mining companies must reduce production or close unprofitable mines.'

What could determine the future price of gold, these analysts feel, is how much metal the central banks will make available and whether mining companies continue to sell unmined gold for future delivery. The imbalance between mine and scrap supply, and the demand, should have forced the price up over the last three years, but it held remarkably steady because of the central bankers' involvement. In a thoughtful study of the gold-leasing market, Ian Cox, a British expert, reckoned that about 50 central banks will continue lending gold to earn a return on a sterile asset.

17.2.2 Other precious metals

The absence of investors in silver last year reduced price volatility, although silver remained the most volatile of the precious metals. The difference between the low and high COMEX settlement price in 1996 was $1.12, the lowest since 1992. Measured monthly, volatility for the year peaked at 8.1 per cent in June and hit a low of 3.9 per cent in December. Volatility is the spread between the monthly high and low prices, as a percentage of the low price for the month.

Futures trading activity in silver declined for the second consecutive years in 1996. Trading volume on the New York, Tokyo and Chicago exchanges fell to 25 billion ounces in 1996, down 8 per cent from 1995. Total open interest at year-end 1996 stood at 252 million ounces, down 5 per cent from 1995, the lowest annual trading volume and year-end open interest since 1993 and 1992 respectively.

COMEX remained by far the largest silver futures market by volume, accounting for 97 per cent of total trade. The COMEX market share increased in 1996, as the volume and open interest dropped more sharply than in New York. Total open interest in COMEX silver options slipped 13 per cent in 1996 to 300 million ounces. Nevertheless, open interest in calls went up 2.5 per cent to 250 million ounces, while put option open interest fell sharply to 50 million ounces. The put/call ratio at the end of 1996 was at an unusually low level – a level seen only once before in the COMEX silver option market, and that was at the cyclical bottom in silver prices in early 1993.

In 1996, India's imports of silver reached higher levels, according to the Gold Fields Mineral Services consultancy, based on official statistics and the firm's estimates of smuggling. Good harvests contributed to the rise in Indian silver consumption, particularly in the northern tribal belts, where the rural population often chooses to save heavy silver jewellery. A fall in the local price of the metal also helped to increase demand to 2,442 tonnes in 1996, marginally higher than the previous year, but below the record 3,422 tonnes in 1994. India is the third largest silver consumer, after the US and Japan, and a major consumer of silver jewellery.

17.3 COUNTERFEITS AND FRAUDS

17.3.1 Counterfeit coins

One problem of purchasing coins made from gold bullion or other precious metals is the risk of forgeries. In the 1970s, when inflation was soaring upwards, interest in UK sovereigns was so high that the Mint found itself unable to produce enough. As a result, dealers increased the premium (the difference between the face value and the metal value). The coins began to sell at almost one and a half times their face value. The opportunity attracted middle eastern forgers, although, in practice, the vendors and buyers could easily detect the counterfeit coins.

Controversy over the long-running Hirohito coin scandal still has residual effects on market sentiment in Japan. Originally issued in 1986 to commemorate the 60th anniversary of the late Emperor's accession to the throne, the Japanese police alleged in 1990 that 100,000 were middle eastern fakes. Coin dealers affected by confiscations denied there was any conspiracy or crime. The affair took a new turn when a UK dealer began civil action against the Japanese government for the return of seized coins. The dealer alleged that the Tokyo police, contrary to their statements, had effectively abandoned their investigations in 1990. As a result, confidence in the Hirohito coin collapsed and investors cashed in 3 million coins worth 300bn yen at their face value.

The Hirohito coin scandal caused a delay in the issue of the Akihito coins (called Heisei after the new emperor's era). In the event, the authorities decided to release only 2 million coins; the original plan was to issue 3.8 million Heiseis. To discourage forgers, the coins contain 30 not 20 grams of gold. This amount represented about 50,000 yen worth of gold in a coin that the Japanese sold for 100,000 yen. However, despite the Hirohito scandal and the delayed issue, the Japanese bought most of the 2 million coins.

17.3.2 Gold mine frauds

Fraud has also beset precious metal investing. Typically, promoters sell interests in gold mines that are nearly worthless or non-existent. Telephone salespeople may call offering gold not yet mined. They say they will sell it for $100 under the going price.

Such frauds are an international problem. One US commentator believes that there are 'probably 30 to 40 gold mining scams going on now in the United States'. He cautions investors to be distrustful of salesmen who offer interests in gold mines. Typically, they promise gold for perhaps half the market price; the explanation is usually that the mine owner has a special process or patented techniques for extracting the metal.

New fingerprinting techniques developed by scientists, led by Watling and Herben at the Western Australian Department of Minerals and Energy Centre, should make salting of gold mines, a technique used since the mining industry began, a problem of the past. 'Salting' is the addition of precious metals from one mine to another, to give the illusion of great discoveries of gold, as happened in Kalgoorlie, the centre of the new Western Australian gold rush. A new mine suddenly was found to contain ores with a gold content ten times higher than normal. Watling presented evidence at a conference in 1994 to prove that the gold came from two sources, and that one was added artificially.

This process, recently perfected, will give every mine a unique fingerprint. The fingerprinting technique will affect not only salters of mines and gold thieves, but also fraudsters who claim that gold ingots originate from a specific mine. Watling hopes that experts will fingerprint much of the world's gold so they can identify its origins with certainty, and gold will no longer be an untraceable international currency. Watling is applying the same technique to diamonds from De Beers.

However, even such advances do not always prevent fraud, as investors in the Busang mine on the island of Borneo, Indonesia, found to their cost. In February 1997, a small but reputable Canadian mining firm, Bre-X, hailed it as the biggest gold discovery of this century, with 71 million ounces worth £15.5bn. In May 1997, it turned out to be the biggest illusion since the days of Houdini.

Samples from the site had been tampered with to boost their gold content. Mining consultants, Strathcona Mineral Services Ltd, showed that the find was not economically worthwhile. Strathcona's president, Graham Farquharson, wrote in a letter to Bre-X's chairman: 'The magnitude of the tampering with core samples that we believe has occurred . . . is without precedent in the history of mining anywhere.' The effect has been to reduce investment interest in unit trusts that hold shares in gold mining companies, and in exploration companies. It was Mark Twain who, during the 1849 gold rush, remarked: 'A mine is a hole in the ground with a liar standing next to it!'

17.4 OPPORTUNITIES AND COSTS

17.4.1 Investment potential

Who should buy gold, in what form should investors purchase it and how much should they invest in the metal? 'It depends on the investor' says one dealer. 'Many large portfolios might have at least a small percentage in gold. A person who has little money to invest and is conservative should concentrate on gilts. If you are more aggressive, you could have a larger holding in gold.' These recommendations seem optimistic, given gold's resistance in recent years to the anxiety factor. For many investors who still wish to hold gold, coins make sense, because they are easier to sell than bullion. Alternatively, investors can buy precious metals in bars or wafers which may, for an extra price, have decorative stampings. A 100-ounce gold bar is about the size of a brick. Dealers sell wafers in various weights, down to a few ounces, although premiums are higher on smaller unit weights. Hoarders could store gold coins, bars or wafers in a safe-deposit box or home safe.

The safest way of buying gold, either in the shape of coins or bars, is at a high street bank, which will reduce the risk of theft, increase security and avoid VAT, if the owners hold the gold in offshore branches. Some banks offer gold purchase programmes, and (given adequate security) may be willing to finance these purchases. If an investor buys on credit, the bank will want to keep the gold in its vault and charge for storage. For example, some clearing banks in Jersey will deal in Kruggerands and Maple Leaf coins for mainland customers. Reportedly, they charge £1.50 per coin for the service, with a minimum charge of £10. Insurance during transit is 50p per coin. Storage is 25p per coin per quarter (minimum charge £5 per quarter). Insurance for storage is 0.175 per cent per annum of the gold's value, with the minimum premium set at £35.

17.4.2 Costs of ownership

Among other factors, the transaction costs put off some investors. Other deterrents are the imposition of VAT, storage expenses, and the lack of dividends or interest from precious metals investments. Investors should remember that, unlike bank deposits and securities, gold's value depends on changes in the general market for bullion. Storage, dealing and insurance costs can erode profits from investments in gold bars or coins.

17.4.3 Advisers

Even to investors who have good reasons for acquiring precious metals, financial advisers offer words of caution. Anyone who buys gold or another precious metal, or gemstones, should use a bank, a specialist trading house or a reputable dealer. In any event, making sure he or she can obtain possession of the asset when it, is important for the investor. In times of great financial crisis, banks may be closed.

In Britain, investors can buy gold coins through dealers, precious metal brokers, investment consultants, some banks and jewellers. They sell and buy gold sovereigns and half sovereigns in quantity, and the products of other countries' mints. Advantages can flow from choosing coins in popular demand. The premiums charged (ie the difference between the price of the coin and the value of the bullion it contains) are higher for coins that sell in low quantities.

Many financial advisers suggest that individual investors interested in gold would be wise to choose shares of gold mining companies or gold unit trusts. In contrast to coins, ingots, futures or options, gold stocks represent a productive asset, ie a company, and may even pay dividends. Typically, the shares of gold-mining companies rise two or three times the percentage increase in gold prices. Gerald Perritt, editor of the *Fund Letter*, explained that once these companies cover their high fixed costs, the additional revenues fall mostly to the bottom line.

17.5 TAXATION

17.5.1 Tax planning

The income, capital gains, capital transfer and inheritance tax considerations reviewed in Chapter 18 on arts and antiques are generally relevant to valuables. The same advice applies to careful tax planning.

17.5.2 VAT

Until 1982 purchase of bullion coins did not attract VAT if the coins were still legal in their country of issue. Following the Exchange Control (Gold Coins) Exemption Order 1979 and the Value Added Tax (Finance) Order 1982, there are now two main ways for UK private investors to buy gold bullion coins. One is to pay the VAT, which would make it more difficult to realise a gain from the transaction. The other is to buy the coins overseas and store them there at a cost.

Dealers may promote other approaches in advertisements or through direct mail circulars, but investors should treat them with caution. In the UK, when VAT-registered traders (who buy and sell gold coins by way of business) sell bullion coins back, the dealer who buys them should pay the VAT on the transaction directly to HM Customs & Excise.

On 1 April 1993, the Chancellor of the Exchequer introduced a special scheme for accounting and paying for VAT on gold transactions. The scheme applies to certain supplies of gold that are liable to VAT at the standard rate. Under this scheme the buyer and the seller treat a standard-rated supply of gold as a taxable supply for registration. Under the terms of this scheme, the buyer must account for the output tax that the seller charges when supplying the gold. The buyer retains the right to claim input tax credit in the same VAT accounting period in which the supply takes place. VAT leaflet 701/21193, 'Gold and gold coins', available from HM Customs & Excise, offers guidance.

The forfeiture provisions of the Customs & Excise Management Act apply, even if the smuggled gold is found in the possession of an innocent purchaser. It is, therefore, in the best interest of buyers to satisfy themselves that importers have complied with the regulations before agreeing to complete a purchase. The questions to ask are: Where has the gold come from? Who has imported it? Have they paid VAT on it? Why are they selling it? How is it delivered? Is a quick settlement demanded? Is the seller new to the gold market? Does he regularly supply large quantities? What references can he offer? Such basic checks on the history and reputation of the supplier, and the documents, are clearly advisable in view of the growing number of frauds.

VAT regulations also apply to silver and platinum. As in the gold and silver markets, zero-rating for VAT applies only to transactions between wholesale traders. In the past, zero-rating was not necessary as transfers of metal among traders in London were relatively unimportant. The rapid rise in demand for platinum has increased the need for speedy inter-trader movements of metal. Note, though, the future of zero-rating is in some doubt pending decisions on EU VAT regulations.

17.6 PREVIEW OF THE YEAR AHEAD

17.6.1 Demand and supply

Gold demand should outstrip supply (excluding central bank and forward sales) in 1997 and 1998. Economic forecasters expect no substantial increase in inflation during 1997, and no serious decline in the dollar. A surge in demand for gold jewellery seems likely in India, the Middle East and the Far East. That demand should be higher than supplies and imports of refined gold, thus reducing gold inventories over the next two years. India is a fast-growing and large market for gold, and could account for 20 per cent of refined gold consumption in 1997.

Political uncertainties could also affect demand. Suppose relations between the major powers became tense, or a large regional conflict breaks out? The demand for physical gold and shares of gold mining companies might then surge, and the gold price could rise.

Observers estimate total demand for gold from industrialized fabricators to increase from 2,950 tonnes (1996) to about 3,200 tonnes (1998), that is, an average annual increase of 4 per cent. As noted above, consumption may be at a high level in the Far East, where many countries have large populations and improving per capita incomes. Over the next three years, sales in North America and the Far East should go up by 3–4 per cent, and demand in Indian and Latin American gold consumption by 9–10 per cent.

In the Middle East, demand for gold has revived. Purchases of gold in OPEC states generally correlate with movements in the price of oil. As oil prices rise, so do local incomes and the demand for gold. Industry specialists are forecasting a 1–2 per cent per annum increase in the world oil price in 1997 and 1998. If this prediction is accurate, demand for gold jewellery is likely to be marginally higher in the Arabian peninsula. To the north, Turkish consumers and tourists already enjoy a wider choice of gold jewellery. The tourist trade has stimulated demand; about half the gold jewellery made in Turkey now leaves the country.

Different factors have influenced demand in Japan. On the one hand, the Japanese have suffered a series of calamities and worrisome incidents, including terrorist gas attacks, an earthquake, and fears for the future of financial institutions. On the other, low interest rates are likely to prompt renewed interest in a pure-gold deposit plan. Under this plan, subscribers buy bullion for a fixed term in monthly instalments. At the end of the contract, the subscriber can choose to have jewellery made from the gold, or claim its value.

In the electronics sector, gold has two main applications. Gold bonding wire forms the connections in semiconductor integrated circuits, and gold salts improve the reliability of electroplating. US and Japanese consumer electronics, telecom products and computers benefit from these qualities. Observers anticipate continued growth in the electronics industry's demand for gold. However, analysts also believe that strong growth in sales of computers, cellular telephones and related equipment will be offset by a more efficient use of gold in these products.

The use of gold in official coins has depended on a lower local bullion price to stimulate production. Marginal shifts in currency parities and the dollar value of gold could lead to modest falls in local bullion prices. In turn, that could produce slight increases in the volume of coin production in major markets.

Lured by better returns in stocks in international markets, funds have been shifting assets out of gold. The prospect of higher interest rates in 1997 has also taken the lustre out of investing in the metal. Market watchers anticipate further weakness for gold in coming months, continuing a downward trend caused by the strong dollar, a robust stock market and an absence of physical demand. 'Gold is not going to go up if the stock market is doing well,' said Tim Porter, an analyst with Refco, New York. 'We have a strong dollar and rumours of European central bank selling. Rumours move markets.'

In 1997, the London Bullion Market Association (LBMA) sought to improve market information and reduce the scope for rumours. The LBMA began to quantify how much bullion cleared in London, the international settlement centre. Every working day in January 1997 the marked cleared about 37 million troy ounces of gold, worth $13m. These figures underestimated the volume of transactions; they reflect net transfers between the Association's eight clearing members. Commentators suggest that analysts should multiply the LBMA statistics by at least three (and possibly by five) to show the full scale of the global gold market. The monthly figures from the Association are likely to become a key indicator in monitoring the market.

The true interactions of supply and demand lead optimists to stake their hopes on new markets in Asia. As one expert commented: 'There is tremendous demand potential in Asia linked to the new middle class.' Agreeing with this assessment, Bette Raptopoulos, a gold analyst at Prudential Securities, suggests: 'We could still see gold reach $450 to $460 in 1997.'

Bullish traders point to a healthy balance of demand, often exceeding production, and uncertainties that affect output from Russia, the world's second-biggest producer. They predict a correlation between gold and other metals, as the economic cycle swings worldwide from high interest rates and recession to low interest rates and recovery. A few, like gold guru Julian Baring, look for a price of $500 per ounce at some point in the next four years.

17.6.2 Central banks' sales

One factor to set against optimism is the activity of the official sector. Central banks, particularly in EU countries, have little incentive to maintain their reserves at current levels. A widely reported prediction suggests that the prospect of European Monetary Union may eventually lead central banks to become net sellers by the turn of the century. However, investors should weigh this possibility against central bank conservatism, and the likelihood of delays in monetary union.

In spite of these reservations, economic researchers anticipate a rise in gold sales by central banks. Rabobank's Economics Research Department recently commented: 'Gold no longer has a significant formal role in the international monetary system, and it hardly influences public confidence in the monetary authorities.' Merrill Lynch suggests that 'many observers are looking for sales of between 500 and 1,000 tonnes from central banks'.

Market supplies will therefore come partly from central bank sales, expected to average 175 tonnes per annum in 1997 and 1998, that is, 25 tonnes below the 1996 level. Motivations for gold sales vary by country. They include a need to meet call options, distress sales from countries short of foreign exchange, and opportunistic sales of surplus stocks when reallocating a central bank's reserve assets. Nonetheless, a prime concern of specialist advisers is the vast hoard of gold that central banks hold (about 35,000 tonnes, or roughly one-third of all that humankind has ever found and kept). They fear that the hoard when released will affect the market's dynamics. Analysts believe that changes will occur as supplies come under a new generation's control. Bankers trained in portfolio management are less sensitive to gold's mystique.

Other factors are also influencing expectations. Analysts question bullish predictions that former Eastern Bloc countries will seek to back their currencies with gold. Conversely, these countries need to sell gold reserves to earn hard currency. Evidence also emerged in January 1997 that Japanese investors were selling gold futures to cover losses in the Tokyo equity market.

Another report suggests that 'inflation indexed' Treasury notes could end gold's use as a hedge against inflation. The *Wall Street Journal* pointed to a high demand for 10-year notes, suggesting that investors were finding new ways to hedge against inflation. Industry analysts generally feel that the report was premature. John Lutley, president of the Gold Institute, points out that the inflation-indexed bond is only 'a piece of paper backed by the good faith of the government, just like social security. The great advantage that gold has had over the millennia is that there is not a government around that can control the price of gold.'

17.6.3 Growing jewellery demand

Demand for jewellery fabrication worldwide has surprised some with its ability to withstand the effects of recession. The use of gold in jewellery has increased for the past twenty-five years. In a recent paper, Gold Field Mineral Services outlined reasons for considering jewellery as 'gold's salvation'. Jewellery fabrication grew at a lower rate than per capita wealth in the period 1970–95. Yet, over the same period the real gold price almost doubled, and jewellery demand is sensitive to price changes. Growth in demand extends beyond the industrialised countries. Admittedly, jewellery holdings per person have grown faster in the OECD countries, reflecting their wealth. Nonetheless, developing countries, especially in the Middle East and Asia, are adding to demand.

In many parts of India, gold is a favoured means of saving. For cultural and social reasons, Indian families mainly buy gold jewellery, so that they can parade their prosperity. Also, Indians hoard bullion ingots, legally since 1990, when the government withdrew gold control.

Gold processing in India has also increased sharply since 1995, and further growth seems likely. Several fabricators intend to build factories to produce gold jewellery, with up-to-date designs, fine polish, and a guaranteed 18-carat gold content. They hope to sell this jewellery in domestic and export markets. In the past, production has mainly been in the hands of small retail goldsmiths, producing 22-carat jewellery.

The Indian industry will soon challenge Italy for market leadership. However, the market for Italian gold jewellery has recovered following a decline in 1992 and 1993. Sales have risen at home and abroad, partly because of the lire's weakness. The Italian fabricators foresee further export growth in other parts of Europe, Asia and Latin America.

If holdings of gold jewellery continue to grow at the present rate, the additional gold required will be considerable. Much of the potential for growth comes from increased prosperity in the Pacific Rim countries. When the Indian government lifted import restrictions on gold, the market for jewellery fabrication and hoarding increased. This trend looks set to continue. The Chinese, Korean and South East Asian markets remain strong, and demand in Kuwait picked up as the country re-established itself after the Gulf war.

A continuing growth of demand for precious metals does, however, rest on several assumptions; that an increasing world population will become more prosperous, and that jewellery will retain its appeal. It is also a prediction for the rest of the decade, not just for 1997, and does not take into account uncertainties in the market for retail jewellery. Given that gold does become increasingly popular as an industrial product for jewellery rather than a tradable commodity, gold prices should eventually stabilise. As one Chinese observer recently remarked: 'It's like a silkworm biting into a leaf: with slow bites, it consumes the whole tree. Jewellery demand is like that. Gold prices may fall to $350 or less but, at that stage, jewellery consumption will speed up, taking the bullion price to $360 or more.'

17.6.4 Future developments

Falling mine production

One factor likely to reduce gold supplies in the future is a decline in mine production. Western mine production has probably reached a peak, although analysts do not expect output to fall immediately, and they think it unlikely that producers will increase output in response. The main factors are rising production costs, reduced capital expenditure, and falling exploration, and the limiting effect on each of a low gold price. In the US, Canada, and Australia, surface ores have gradually become depleted. This means that extraction must increasingly focus on deep-lying deposits, and on sulphide ores, both of which involve more costly production.

In the developed world it is also less likely that many valuable ore reserves remain undiscovered. In the developing countries, terrain is often hostile and investment in production can be risky. In South Africa, still the world's largest producer, capital expenditure has fallen sharply since 1986. The industry has rationalised extensively, increasing productivity but focusing output on the highest grade ores and shortening the life of the mines. Continued low investment will reduce South African output. Some predictions suggest that production will fall by 30 per cent over the next five years. Conversely advances in technology promise to boost the South African gold mining industry. Executives in the industry hope the technological advances will transform the production process and its economies.

In recent years, two large gold mines have closed, other mines have reorganised and South African gold output has steadied at about 600 tonnes a year. However, to make profits the mines need technological advances that reduce costs, or consistently higher gold prices. Otherwise, production is likely to go into slow and steady decline.

Russia and the former Soviet Republics also have production problems. The mining areas are often remote and hostile, and equipment poorly developed and limited in supply. Nevertheless, the way is now clear for the development of Sukhoi Log in Siberia, the world's largest known gold deposit, according to Star Mining Corporation, the small Australian company that has 34.9 per cent of the venture. The agreement had taken six years to negotiate. If all goes well, the construction of a conventional hard rock, open pit mine will begin at the end of 1996. Production should rise from 300,000 troy ounces in 1998 to more than 2 million troy ounces by 2003. Cash costs would be among the lowest in the industry, no more than $180 an ounce, despite the difficulties of mining in Siberia.

The Lena gold fields, which contain Sukhoi Log, and several other substantial gold deposits, are in the Bodaibo region of Russia's Irkutsk province. While Sukhoi Log is being developed, the joint venture company, Lenzoloto (Lena Gold) will have cash flows from alluvial mining, which has produced at least 30 million troy ounces of gold since 1850, making Lena Gold one of the biggest gold producers in the world industry. Lena Gold expects to produce about 220,000 ounces from existing operations, rising to 300,000 by 1998. Kazakhstan, formerly part of the Soviet Union, predicts a substantial increase in gold output in the next three to four years.

During 1993 the Republic produced about 14 tonnes of gold and seeks foreign investment to increase this rapidly to between 42 and 56 tonnes. The aim is to build reserves to back the country's new currency. A Kazakhstan gold mine, the Bakyrchik, in an arid region of the north-eastern steppes, is one of the world's biggest gold deposits with about 8 million troy ounces, but the ore is very complex and difficult to process. Bakyrchik Gold, a London quoted company, is in a joint venture with Altynalmas, the organisation responsible for Kazakhstan's precious metals' and precious stones' production.

Technological change

Western industrial groups are eager to win potentially lucrative stakes in the former Soviet Union's gold mining industry. They have found that bacterial leaching technology offers an edge over traditional mining methods. The technology, new to the western gold industry, uses bacteria to break down refractory or difficult ores to release the gold locked inside. Another attraction of the technology is that it is environmentally friendly. For example, bacteria can process ores containing toxic material such as arsenic and leave no harmful waste.

Two Western companies have recently signed gold deals with CIS partners which specifically called for the introduction of bacterial leaching. Lonrho, the UK-based conglomerate, reportedly won the right to develop a gold mine in Uzbekistan, primarily because it had access to the Biox bacterial leaching process developed by Gencor of South Africa. Biox has been in use at the Fairview mine in South Africa, at São Bento in Brazil, at the Harbour Lights and Wiluna mines in Western Australia, and by Ashanti, Lonhro's associate in Ghana.

Although Gencor is so far the front-runner in gold bacterial leaching, rivals are beginning to emerge. The Moonstone Group, a small exploration company in the Channel Islands, is participating in a joint venture to explore for gold and diamonds in Kazakhstan. The company claimed the BacTech system made the deal possible. The chemistry department of King's College London developed the system with Australian backing.

17.6.5 Silver, platinum and palladium

According to experienced analysts, investment demand will continue to be a pivotal factor in the direction of silver prices. However, they also believe that the underlying fundamentals for silver are continuing to improve, as demand exceeds supply and above-ground inventories fall. CPM Group's 1997 silver survey concludes that:

> 'Investors are monitoring the silver market closely, with the view that the huge shortfalls in newly refined silver supply relative to fabrication demand will eventually lead to a period of significantly higher prices.
> That said, it is unlikely that investors will re-enter the silver market forcefully without a sharp correction in the US and other equities markets, or some other major economic or financial disturbance. Should EMU (European Monetary Union which is due in 1999) stumble, some investors would likely seek shelter in silver, gold and platinum against erratic movements in the currency markets and related European financial assets.'

Other analysts expect investors to be net disposers of silver this year, selling perhaps 200 million ounces of silver bullion. Then, in line with the CPM Group's forecast, 'silver prices reasonably could rise as high as $6 by late 1997. Already some fabricators are beginning to take steps to protect themselves as inventories could fall to only about 4.7 months' worth of demand.'

In January 1997, the LBMA released data on bullion market trading for the first time in January 1997. The data showed that the eight London silver clearing banks cleared about 248 million ounces, including spot transactions, forwards, options and other silver trades, per day in December 1996. In the following month the Association stated that the volume cleared in January 1997 averaged 294 million ounces of silver worth $1.4bn.

Platinum has bullish prospects because Japan, the largest consumer of platinum, is beginning to see a modest recovery in the yen. Optimists also expect platinum to remain around the $450 mark, while they predict that silver will trade between $5–6 an ounce.

Platinum and palladium have recently been leading the precious metals' sector. Yet analysts are now warning of sharp reversals as speculators take their profits. They expect prices to prove volatile. 'Platinum's rise has been vertical and that cannot be sustained,' according to a technical analysis from Investment Research, Cambridge. Trend Analysis chartists also warned against misjudging the moves in the precious metals markets. 'People may think this is the beginning of a major bull market but I am sure it is not. It is a correction and when it is over prices could fall sharply.'

Dealers said concerns over a decline in Russian exports of platinum and palladium were fuelling demand for these metals, especially in Japan. Russia is the leading producer of palladium and the second largest exporter of platinum after South Africa, and its internal problems stimulated stock-building of platinum group metals. Changes to Russia's exporting administration and delays in passing the 1997 budget postponed the start of negotiations with Japanese importers, and consequently exports.

In the first few months of 1997, Russia has exported virtually no palladium. However, commentators expect exports to resume by the middle of the year. Re-opening of trade talks between Russia and Japan caused a sharp fall in platinum and palladium prices in May.

A twist was added to the Russia-Japan problem, when workers at Russia's huge Norilsk mining and processing plant voted to strike in mid-March over unpaid wages. Workers at the cash-strapped plant in Arctic Siberia were last paid in full in October. However, dealers said they had already factored the strike issue into the price.

17.7 CONCLUSION

Few are willing to forecast large price rises for gold. Of course, pessimists might take into account Sir James Goldsmith's prediction of a 'meltdown' in the global financial system, and purchase bullion bars or gold coins. Others seeking an investment in precious metals may prefer unit trusts holding mining equities, or direct investment in major mining equities. Analysts generally believe such investments will outperform the physical commodity in the short to medium term.

Platinum, palladium and rhodium are likely to remain fascinating, if risky, investments. The platinum group metals will probably sustain their market in the automobile and electronics industry, with rhodium being resilient to the development of substitutes. Even with alternatives reducing the platinum content of catalytic converters, continuing environmental concern for greenhouse gas emissions is likely to increase the number fitted to new cars.

17.8 OTHER VALUABLES

17.8.1 Diamonds and De Beers

Apart from precious metals, investors can also consider gemstones like emeralds, sapphires, semi-precious stones and diamonds. In investment terms only diamonds are significant, and the Central Selling Organisation still dominates the market. This is the London-based marketing organisation of De Beers.

Only about one in six of the diamonds mined ends up in rings or other jewellery, but these account for most of the diamond output's value. Buyers put the remainder to industrial use. The market's performance therefore largely depends on the success of its promoters in stimulating demand. To this end, De Beers spends large sums on advertising and sales promotion, a concerted effort to persuade more women and men to buy and wear diamonds as jewellery. One result has been to stimulate demand through retail jewellers, but the markups make it more difficult for the investor to achieve gains. The addition of VAT accentuates the problem.

Yet, over the decades, De Beers has succeeded in mass-marketing what was once an aristocratic luxury without greatly diminishing its value. Diamonds remain 'the gem of gems' even though millions own them. De Beers' aim is long-term stability and prosperity for the industry. In its view, price fluctuations would undermine confidence in the value of diamonds. So far, the strategy has succeeded. However, it is potentially vulnerable to persistent recession and threats to the world-wide cartel, as more governments wonder about alternative approaches to marketing diamonds other than going through the Central Selling Organisation.

De Beers has kept firm control over the supply and price of the world's diamonds for nearly a century. However, diamond prices have not always kept pace with inflation, and for a time, Russia stood accused of breaking faith with the cartel by flooding the market with bootleg gems and synthetic diamonds. Furthermore, the cartel is struggling to gain control over the output of new mines, which could deflate values. Despite these challenges, De Beers remains bullish.

17.8.2 The market

Antwerp, the medieval Belgian city, is the world's diamond-trading capital, home to about one-third of De Beers' handpicked buyers and accounting for 60 per cent of all transactions. Traders experienced a slump in 1992, when falling demand and the Angolan civil war disrupted government control over freelance miners in the Lunda Norte region, the net result of which was a massive flow of Angolan diamonds. However, according to the trade publication *Diamond International*, the diamond market has improved recently with Antwerp disposing of £21bn worth of rough, polished and industrial diamonds in 1995.

Antwerp's industry association, the Diamond High Council, is confident that the US market will continue to grow and that the Japanese market will also recover. However, a question still hangs over Europe's resurgence. One major threat to Antwerp's monopoly is emerging competition from other diamond centres, mainly in the Far East.

Since 1992 Japan has surpassed the US as the world's largest market for diamond jewellery. In 1967 only 6 per cent of Japanese brides received diamond engagement rings; in 1995 the level was 77 per cent. According to Toshiyuki Momozawa, president of the Jewellery Trade Centre in Tokyo, 'De Beers gets the credit for this'. 'They took the same concepts they had used on the Americans and were able to convince the Japanese that the diamond lasts forever, it is a good investment and is the only kind of engagement ring.'

The problem is that recently this has not necessarily been the case. Although some larger diamonds hold their value and may even appreciate, smaller stones of a carat or less can be money losers, especially if bought at marked up retail prices. In 1989 wholesalers sold a top-quality one-carat stone for $18,000; in February 1996 similar stones were selling for about $15,700, a 14 per cent decline. By far the best diamond investment during those years would have been in paper form, that is, De Beers stock, which has improved in value over the years.

De Beers is hoping that Japan will serve as a wedge into a larger Asian market. Business is booming in the Asian 'tiger' economies, and dealers covet the potential of China with its young, growing and newly prosperous urban population of 280 million. Mark Cockle, executive editor of *Diamond International*, says; 'Its safe to say that every company is looking for a new Japan,' and 'China could be another Japan and America rolled into one.'

17.8.3 Diamond production

Russian mines produce top quality diamonds, and the country has some newly discovered diamond fields. However, an acute shortage of cash constrains opportunities to add to the supply. In turn that exacerbates the political uncertainties and the weakness of the rouble. Russia's progress is likely to have a radical impact on both the domestic and world markets by the turn of the century. Now, the Yakutia-Sakha Republic accounts for 99 per cent of the former Soviet Union's total diamond production. Analysts expect mining to deplete these fields by 2010. However, the newly discovered fields in Asiatic Russia, around St Petersburg and in the Karelian Republic could bring riches. De Beers conservatively estimates that just one field will yield 250 million carats.

The output of gem diamonds from the new fields is much higher than the Yakut fields' output, which is in turn better than the output of gem stones in South Africa. The diamond content of the Yakut ore ranges from 0.6 to 4 carats per tonne of ore, with 2–3 carats per tonne on average. Industry sources predict that an annual production of between 3 and 6 million carats is likely over the next 30–40 years. Prospecting and development of the fields are likely to be both expensive and time-consuming. Nevertheless, American, British and Australian investors have already placed and won tenders to develop five diamond-bearing areas.

Russia and South Africa also face competition from other countries. For example, Australia is now a large producer of diamonds. Most of the stones are industrial grade only, but a proportion are of gem quality. Australia's Argyle diamond mine also produces some of the rarest stones in the world, a few of which have sold for more than US$1m a carat.

17.8.4 De Beers and Russia

A new marketing agreement healed a threatened breach between South Africa's De Beers' cartel and Russia, sustaining trade worth £1bn a year. It leaves De Beers as 'the sole and exclusive buyer of all rough diamond exports from Russia', according to the authoritative *Diamantaire* newsletter. Alongside the agreement is a deal under which western banks, headed by NatWest Markets, advanced funds to Almazy Rossii-Sakha, Russia's biggest diamond producer.

Analysts believe that Russian stocks of rough or uncut gem diamonds might run out as early as 1998. To cover a possible shortfall, De Beers has medium-term plans to increase production. For example, it has already embarked on a four-year project to double the Orapa mine's annual output in north east Botswana to 12 million carats. The corporation reports that demand for rough diamonds remains robust, in spite of a recent weakness in Japanese demand and markets for world diamond jewellery. Sales at each of the CSO's sights in early 1997 averaged $500m.

17.8.5 Investment

The traditional image of diamonds as a good investment is not as appealing as many perhaps imagine. While other commodities fluctuate in price, influenced by the weather and economics, the price of rough diamonds has stabilised or risen. Given that price performance, and the financial strength of De Beers, investment in diamonds should be secure. However, De Beers deals only in rough diamonds, and sells only to about 150 diamond dealers, a select client list. Membership is by invitation. Outside this narrow market, prices for cut and polished diamonds rise and fall, sometimes dramatically.

With valuables like gemstones, which vary in quality, investors face problems. To follow the recommended practice in the alternative investment markets, investors should purchase the best. The difficulty is that the best is becoming scarce and very expensive in many classes of alternative investments. Diamonds are no exception. One of the consequences is interest in other gemstones, such as sapphires, which are almost as durable as diamonds. A Sri Lankan government agency and the Gemological Institute of America have jointly developed a grading system for sapphires. An established grading certificate is an important supporting document when buying or selling diamonds or sapphires. Other gemstones, for example emeralds, are less appealing, because miners are still extracting them in large quantities.

Diamonds are a compact way of holding wealth, with their long-term trend appreciation slightly above that of inflation. Experts can more easily examine large loose stones, free of jewellery settings, for flaws, colour, 'fire' and brilliance, and comparing stones is easier. An internationally recognised organisation, such as the Gemological Institute of America or the Diamond High Council of Antwerp, should certify and seal the gems.

SOURCES OF FURTHER INFORMATION

See end of Chapter 19.

18

ART AND ANTIQUES

JOHN MYERS

Solon Associates

18.1 INTRODUCTION

18.1.1 A form of alternative investment

Bring and buy works of art and antiques! Why? Ultimately, as any auctioneer, dealer and lover of art and antiques will say, it is not their investment or exchange worth but their civilising and aesthetic values that are important. Also, the promoters of these 'alternative investments' confidently advocate these tangible assets as sound purchases for 'financially secure and intelligent buyers'. The assets they have in mind are, ideally, works of artistic, cultural or historical significance, that is, items that are 'museum-worthy by any standards', which will appeal to collectors. Advocates of these purchases generally recommend clients with money to spare to allocate to 'traded artifacts' up to 10 per cent of their capital (excluding the equity value of their main home). These advisers declare that possessions such as works of art and antiques can protect their clients against inflation and currency fluctuations.

On occasion, larger institutional investors and corporate bodies also buy paintings, sculptures and antiques to diversify their holdings of securities and real estate. The apologists argue that these investors can afford to ride out slumps lasting up to a quarter of a century, if beneficiaries can wait and the eventual return is adequate. Pension funds and similar bodies are generally free from tax on their gains in art and antique markets. On the other hand, these assets cost money to insure, conserve and store. Capital appreciation has to be substantial to make up for these costs and the interest foregone.

Nonetheless, buyers often see art and antique objects as investments, the values of which can rise and fall as critics and curators appraise anew the aesthetic, historic or functional worth of a school, genre or work. Other factors that prompt the eager are TV and press features, active marketing by auction houses and dealers, and ingenious ways to improve the liquidity of alternative investments. Specialist sales, fairs and exhibitions, magazines for collectors, the track record of works sold in each field, and the findings of art historians, sway decisions to buy. However, to allow values to 'mature', prudent advisers counsel buyers to keep items for years, even for decades. Speculative trading in works of art and antiques is, they say, too risky, with too volatile rewards to justify gambling on perfectly timing a purchase and a sale. Even experts make mistakes in picking the undervalued piece that is sure to re-enter fashion next month or next year.

18.1.2 The dividends

The advocates of the alternative investment argue for including fine art and antiques in private or funds' portfolios as long-term investments on grounds which are, essentially, those of the economist: while the number of buyers in the markets is tending to go up, the supply stays static or declines. On the one hand, the flow of 'discoveries' or 'retrievals of lost works' is restricted. On the other, valued items do disappear through fires, thefts and other calamities; and, perhaps more significantly, museums and galleries steadily drain from the market the works they obtain and keep. Of course 'coffin chasers' (that is house clearers and others who deal with collections left after death) generate a regular supply and 'receiver chasers' have other sources, respectably illustrated by Phillips' sale of Asil Nadir's office furnishings for £4$\frac{1}{2}$m. In theory, the problems of Lloyd's Names should also have ensured a steady flow of art on to the market. Christie's offered a way through Coutts & Co for Names to use works of art as collateral, so that they could obtain bank guarantees for 'funds at Lloyd's' purposes.

Advocates of this alternative investment market believe it appeals to individuals and institutions looking for assets that are in growing demand, diminishing supply, and promise a long-term upward movement in prices. The cosmopolitan origins of buyers who attend major sales suggests that this argument has gained wide acceptance. They create an international demand for authentic items of quality. Apparently these buyers are confident that works of art and rare antiques are safe homes for spare capital, or revenue otherwise subject to tax, though the works bring their owners no income and involve some risks. Many deny an investment motivation. Such motives degrade the purity of endeavour among aesthetes, who seek a cultural dividend, the delights of living with satisfying works that give pleasure. Equally, boards of directors and partnerships buy works of art to improve their standing in society, or to enhance their employees' working environments. The prime movers in these firms will claim that investment is no more than a secondary motive.

Experts concur with the analysis. Nevertheless, they point out that works of art and antiques, unlike shares, have no clearly defined market, no bourse to provide verifiable price indices. One ordinary share in a company will be identical to another of the same category in the same company, but works of art and antiques will vary in many respects. These variations in detail, provenance, condition and quality, and the divergent circumstances and terms of sale, mean that like objects will differ in price. As John Andrew remarked in *The Independent* in February 1997: 'Add the effects of restoration, repairs, alterations, copies and fakes to the pricing formula and a minefield appears.' He goes on to suggest that: 'The biggest trap to snare the unwary in the field of antiques is a lack of knowledge. The prudent individual who carefully researches before buying a consumer durable, or seeks professional advice when investing money, generally throws caution to the wind when buying antiques.'

Andrew gives, as examples of costs and rewards, four Charles II silver lockets, genuine antiques, bought for £905 in about 1982, and sold at auction for a net sum of £1,764 in 1995, to give an equivalent annual return of $5\frac{1}{4}$ per cent compound interest, well below the 10 per cent per annum compound increase in the *Financial Times* Share Index over the same span. He also mentions a silver salver made in Sheffield in 1895, bought in January 1983 for £185, and sold in early 1997 for £350. This represents a $4\frac{1}{2}$ per cent compound annual return. However, between 1983 and 1997, the stock market rose at a compound annual rate of 12 per cent. Of course, these figures do not allow for the pleasure dividend that an owner of fine antiques gains from possessing them.

18.2 RECENT DEVELOPMENTS

18.2.1 The market's performance

In the 1980s and early 1990s, collectors paid spectacular prices for works of art; millions for a fine Impressionist or an Old Master. Many people outside the art world, and some inside, consider it absurd to pay £20m or more for a painting. Some experts dismiss this view, arguing that the doubters fail to take account of the 'edifice of values that provide a logical basis and grounds for such prices'. Others recall Euripides: 'Man's most valuable trait is a judicious sense of what not to believe.' The evidence is ambivalent.

The Art Sales Index shows that, over twenty years, the average price for works by Cézanne, Degas, Manet, Monet and Renoir sold at auction rose from £37,000 to £271,000, equal to a compound annual investment return of 10 per cent.

Comparable figures come from the Antique Collectors' Club, whose records date back to 1968. Their data suggest that old mahogany tables and oak cupboards are outdoing both house prices and the stock market. The club's index focuses on the selling prices of particular items in good condition. Data for 1995 showed a leap of 14 per cent after a downturn in the early 1990s. One highlighted performer was a mahogany night table, a convenient piece of equipment to have beside the bed, which can hold a chamber pot. In 1987, it would have cost £875. In 1996, observers say, 'it was going, going, gone for about £2,500', a compound growth in value of 11 per cent a year.

In 1995, the club's figures suggest that a serpentine-fronted mahogany chest of drawers would have cost about £5,500. The price in 1996 was £9,000, an amazing 80 per cent increase. Over the same span, a walnut cabriole-legged dressing table has reportedly risen in value from £5,000 to £7,500, up 50 per cent. A Regency mahogany writing table went up from £5,000 to £8,000 (60 per cent), and a small Victorian worktable from £400 to £500 (25 per cent). The club claims that virtually no antique furniture has fallen in price in 1995 or 1996, and predicts that none will drop in 1997 either. On average, it expects a price rise over twelve months of 8 per cent, with some items up three times that amount.

Generally, the art market seems to have performed less well than the club figures for antiques would indicate. The Daily Telegraph Art Index, prepared by Art Market Research in North London, and calculated on a base of 1975 = 1,000, recorded a decline over the past eight years, as Figure 18.1 reveals. In December 1989, the newspaper's Art 100 index stood at 8,609; by June 1996, it had fallen to 3,885. The chart plots the equivalent annual compound rate of interest for £1,000 invested in 1975 and realised in the year shown. The rate fell from $16\frac{1}{2}$ per cent for a work held from 1975 to 1989 to $6\frac{3}{4}$ per cent for a work held from 1975 to 1996.

Figure 18.1   Daily Telegraph Art Index: equivalent compound interest per annum

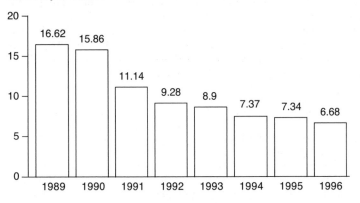

18.2.2 **The fundamentals and the opportunities**

Markets for art and antiques have developed considerably in recent years, especially over the last two decades. Negative and positive factors have affected growth. At times, investors chose to buy these tangible assets because of failures of stock markets and interest-bearing securities to protect their capital against inflation. Immediately after the October 1987 Stock Market crash, auction houses' sales attracted record volumes of works, for which bidders paid record prices. Sothebys, for example, sold van Gogh's *Irises* for £30m. The same artist's *Portrait of Dr Cachet* brought the highest price at auction for a work of art; the auctioneer took a bid of £50m in May 1990, at the peak of the art boom.

With a spread of higher disposable incomes and an increase in leisure expenditure, a demand has emerged for assets which have a worth and an interest beyond their monetary cost. Social changes have also made an impact: for example, dealers and auctioneers report that young, wealthy buyers have been entering the market for works of fine art, such as paintings, prints, ceramics, engravings and sculptures.

As noted above, popular television programmes, features in newspapers, magazines and books have stimulated wide interest in the hunt for works with hidden value. Admittedly, fewer antique shops can afford today's retail rents and overheads, but antique centres and antique fairs have burgeoned, placing many sellers in one location.

At times, antique markets attract large crowds, as anyone visiting London's Portobello Road on Saturday morning can testify. Dealers come from all parts of the country, and start trading between themselves almost at the crack of dawn. Other London street markets are Camden Passage (on Wednesdays) and Bermondsey (on Fridays). Paris has its flea markets and, in America, antique fairs in Atlanta and other centres of wealth are popular. The enthusiasts in Georgia start at about 5 am and stand in line for the early-risers' pick of antiques and collectables.

Choice pieces can pass through several hands on their route up-market via dealers outside the main centres and street markets to a major auction or a listed antique shop. The more reliable dealers belong to the London and Provincial Antiques Dealers' Association or the British Antiques Dealers' Association. Their members usually offer a receipt with a full description; if it proves incorrect, the buyer has a basis on which to claim a refund.

Analysts of alternative investments have studied the ways the markets work. One place to chase bargains is the car boot sale, where the discerning might find 1960s designer objects. Another start for the sifting process might be a house clearance. The trash can go to the local tip, and ordinary bric-à-brac to a second-hand fair. The inlaid metal match-box case that is left seems unusual, and might really be a jewelled gold piece from the Fabergé workshop, worth thousands to a connoisseur at the top of the pyramid, who can trace its history from the St Petersburg archive. Or, of course, it might be a mass-produced design, or sometimes a stolen piece.

Also gaining in popularity are international antique fairs. Some are well known and fashionable; for example, the eight-day March art and antiques fair at Maastricht celebrated its tenth year in 1997 and attracted 50,000 visitors. So many planes arrived for the fair, that they caused an aerial traffic jam. Newer is the two-year-old Asian Art Fair in New York, also run in March. Others include fairs at the Royal Academy in London, Chelsea Town Hall and Olympia, and the British Antique Dealers' Association fair at the Duke of York's headquarters in King's Road, Chelsea.

18.2.3 Market weaknesses and strengths

More people are entering the art and antiques market. To what extent can they rely on the assets they buy proving a worthwhile investment, given the repugnance of monetary motives to the aesthetes? In truth, auction-eers and dealers who profess horror at the idea of buying a painting as an investment were, on occasion, the same auctioneers and dealers who persuaded buyers to invest large sums of money in the late 1980s, some-times in second- and third-rate works, only to see them plunge in value. Values for first-class objects stayed reasonably solid, and bidders are paying high prices for exceptional works. Although handsome short-term profits are not much in evidence, recent sales have demonstrated that works of art can still perform well as long-term investments.

'A lot of record prices are being achieved now but there isn't any hype in the market,' said Melanie Clore, head of Impressionist and Modern art at Sothebys in London. 'That's because there is hardly any speculative buying. But people know that pictures of really great quality in really great condition are going to hold their value.' Of course, buyers hope works of art will do better than hold their value. After all, art works earn no return for their owner between one sale and the next. Instead, as observed above, they cost money, both to insure and to maintain.

This flight to calibre and bijou quality, and away from large-scale but second-rate works by famous names, means that investing in art is not lim-ited to the monied rich with conservative tastes. Impressionist and Modern paintings by leading artists can still command a premium, but auctioneers and dealers are also reporting strong sales to buyers with eclectic tastes; they have been fuelling reviving prices in the contemporary art market. Auctions of post-war and contemporary British art have a growing appeal to collectors, and many lots have fetched far more than their pre-sale estimates. Indian and Chinese buyers have been evident, and Far Eastern collectors have rekindled demand for jade objects.

Good provenance, quality and freshness to the market are crucial factors in the sale of art and antiques. It is worth noting that the areas which have withstood the slump over recent times have been those which appeal to the connoisseur rather than the speculative trader. An increase in private buyers was noticeable at auctions in London and New York, when falling prices attracted knowledgeable collectors. Of late, they have included few Japanese bidders. One reason for their absence is that hundreds of high-priced paintings are reportedly languishing in Tokyo, Osaka and Kyoto bank vaults as their owners wait for markets to reach new peaks. Trade sources suggest that some works have been secretly sold to dealers at a loss. Another reason is that the Japanese art market has been preoccupied in recent years with a series of scandals. Reports of debts, bribes, tax evasion, fraud and jail sentences do little to build confidence.

18.2.4 Protecting alternative investors

Perhaps a few hundred people might today pay more than £10m for a work of art. For them, the main attractions can include the market's performance and the opportunities to 'collateralise' art, a development that, until a few years ago, seemed to have a bright future. After several years of rapid escalation, demand for works sold at auction declined amid controversy over Sothebys leveraged sale of *Irises* to the Australian entrepreneur, Alan Bond. The arrangement led to accusations that auction houses were artificially inflating prices. The J Paul Getty Museum later bought the painting for an undisclosed sum, after Bond failed to pay off his £16m loan from Sothebys. The rate of interest on such loans can be as much as 4 per cent above prime.

The loan system can inflate prices, whether the borrower secures the painting or not: like a roulette player with chips on house credit, he finds it tempting to raise the stakes. Pre-financing by the auction house creates a synthetic floor, while a dealer who states a price sets a ceiling. If the borrower then defaults, the lender recovers the painting, writes off the unpaid part of the loan against tax, and can choose a time to offer the work for resale at its new inflated price.

Apart from lending money to foster buying, some auction houses gave guarantees to sellers. The practice added to critics' concerns about the ethics of the trade. If a collector has a work of art that an auctioneer wants to sell, the latter can issue a 'guarantee' that the collector will obtain, say, £3m from the sale. If the work does not make £3m, the collector still receives the payment, but the work remains with the auction house for later sale. Guarantees are a strong inducement to sellers, but clearly risky for the auction house.

Leading dealers dislike the system of guarantees and loans. They argue that it creates a conflict of interest. One dealer is on record with the comment: 'If the auction house has a financial involvement with both seller and buyer, its status as an agent is compromised. Lending to the buyer is like margin trading on the stock market. It creates inflation. It causes instability.' The advocates defend the policy as 'right, proper and indeed inevitable'. They claim that guarantees are given 'very sparingly'.

Persistent criticism can lead to government controls and levies, which test the industry's stability. These factors and growth in alternative investments have encouraged auction houses to examine their own practices and develop the range of services they offer, sometimes leading to controversy. Conflicts of interest and claims of sharp practice have focused the attention of regulators, as has the growth of outright fraud and theft. Unethical behaviour has come under the scrutiny of the media and authorities in several centres of the art trade. For example, reports have focused on 'puffing the bid' – fictitious bidders inflating the price by displaying false interest.

Scandals have also emerged from the trade in art and antiques, which has traditionally thrived in the 'informal economy'. In Spain and Italy, for instance, operators in a lively black economy have poured money into art. For these buyers, art and antiques represent a store of value, a haven for assets and a form of currency. Their interest supports the market internationally, especially in fields which appeal to Latin tastes. However, many in the market, as well as in government, have become increasingly concerned about the growing internationalisation of art theft and fraud, and not only in the European Union. The Japanese police have strengthened supervision of art dealers. They suspected that art works were being used in tax evasion and as 'stage properties' in large-scale economic crimes. Similarly, in May 1992, a Swiss government report expressed concern at the country's role as a transit centre for objects of doubtful origin – not a novel feature of the Swiss scene – and for 'money laundering operations'. New import controls are seen as likely, but perhaps not for a year or two.

In the US, there has been a contest between the auctioneers and consumer affairs bodies. Teams of officials have pored over leading auctioneers' records, identifying such exotic-sounding practices as 'bidding off the chandelier' (the puffing by fictitious bidders to drive up the price) and the more normal 'buying in' (leaving a work unsold because it does not reach the seller's undisclosed reserve price). Stiffer controls are being applied in the US, including those governing loans. The New York State legislature has also taken a close interest in the art market. It has shared with the city's Consumer Affairs Department concerns about chandelier bidding, the undisclosed reserve and auction houses' lending practices. The current consumer affairs code says that 'if an auctioneer makes loans or advances money to consignors or prospective purchasers, this fact must be conspicuously disclosed in the auctioneer's catalogue'. These developments are likely to have repercussions in Britain and other parts of Europe, as auction players often adopt the same tactics worldwide.

According to a US official, in the past these were 'gross irregularities' in some art auction houses. At the time, chandelier bidding amounted to 'an industry practice, both above and below the reserve'. The spokesman was also concerned about the practices of not announcing buy-ins and of keeping reserves secret. The auction houses contended that, if bidders knew the reserve, it would chill the market. Art dealers, lobbying the agency, maintained that the reserve should be disclosed and that bidding should start at it.

The English poet, Shelley, in his *Adonais* wrote of 'Month following month with woe, and year wake year to sorrow'. When he penned these lines in 1821, Shelley might almost have had in mind London auction houses a century and and three quarters later. From January 1997, they have suffered a surge of hostile media reports that accuse them of dealing in looted works of art, of 'chandelier bidding', and smuggling. Auctioneers have also been under fire for accepting items that are 'not quite genuine'.

In March 1997, the BBC's *Watchdog* programme criticised Bonhams for an alleged failure to enquire properly into the background of two lots in its 'Rock and Pop' sale. A month earlier, Channel 4's *Dispatches* programme had challenged Sotheby's alleged involvement in a smuggling case. Clearly, auctioneers are wise to have and follow rules which require them to handle only objects that have secure export papers and provable provenances (that is, reliable records that show the history and previous ownership of a piece).

The media *causes célébres* have reinforced press criticisms that auction houses sell art on less than fair conditions. Godfrey Barker put the point forcefully in the *Daily Telegraph*, 14 March 1997: auction houses, he claims, typically 'say to all 50,000 buyers who pass each year through their gilded doors, "All goods are sold with all faults and imperfections and errors of description. Buyers should satisfy themselves prior to the sale as to the condition of each lot and should exercise and rely on their own judgement as to whether the lot accords with its description".'

He argues that the conditions of sale are unfair, and compare poorly with measures to protect buyers of consumer goods. Barker suggests that auction houses try to keep their conditions of sale under wraps, and that, when a disaffected bidder has a complaint, they often settle out of court. His article claims that '100 to 150 cases a year in London are muffled in this way'. In contrast, art dealers comply with a code which generally leads to refund without question.

Recently, British antique dealers have demanded reform in the way auctioneers sell artifacts. A new code of conduct may include clauses on:

- legal responsibility for the authenticity of goods sold;
- a ban on 'chandelier bids';
- auctioneers declaring an interest when they have given guarantees;
- preventing auctioneers charging commissions to both buyers and sellers;
- withholding from auction staff details of bids received in advance ('commission bids').

For their part, the auction houses have sought to demystify the auction process to reassure the new breed of collectors and investors. They have employed capable people to explain the significance of the terminology and the practices, and the business of reserves. Representative bodies try to set standards and to control their members' practices with professional codes. Yet, dealing in art, from a gallery or an auction house, is perhaps not a profession; instead, it is a trade or a financial service. Its critics argue for regulation, for setting up an independent regulator, an art industry equivalent to the Securities and Investment Board. The auction houses and dealers have doubts about the ideas; some outsiders think they may have merit.

18.2.5 Continued internationalisation

Despite these uncertainties, buyers around the world have been persuaded by plausible arguments that alternative investments might protect them against calamity. As a result, many of the markets for art and antiques have become more international: since the 1970s, North American, Continental European and Middle and Far Eastern investors have begun to frequent sales rooms in great numbers.

A few years ago, rich art buyers revived Russia's market. Prime among them, in Moscow and St Petersburg, were banks, which had made immense profits in 1992 and 1993 from trading currencies. The most notable were Inkombank, Stolichay, Alpha-Bank, Voznozdenie, Menatep and Moscovia. Six years ago none of them owned significant paintings; today they hold Old Masters and contemporary art. Self-promotion is one reason why the banks bought. Another was their anxiety to store value in what appears, for now, to be a stable international currency – art. What mattered most were special tax provisions that favoured investors in 'outstanding art collections' (a heritage measure to keep great art in Russia).

International developments have had a further effect. In recent years, London's traditional dominance as the centre for art and antiques sales has been challenged, in particular by New York, Geneva, Frankfurt and Paris, which nowadays are attracting important specialised sales. London still accounts for two-thirds of art sales in the EU, but regulatory changes are putting at risk London's strength in the art world.

In some alternative investment markets, furniture being one example, the vigour of American demand has meant that market prices have been set mainly in New York. Generally, the mobility of alternative investments, combined with the wider geographical spread of dealers and auctions, should mean that prices are less vulnerable to the effects of inflation and volatile exchange rates.

18.3 NATIONAL HERITAGE ISSUES

18.3.1 Export controls

The establishment of the Single Market has caused concern over the possible repatriation of art works to their countries of origin. However, this concern is not a recent phenomenon, and governments have tried in various ways to prevent objects of long-standing cultural value and national heritage works, whatever their origin, from leaving the country permanently.

A Holbein painting was withdrawn from sale following a public outcry at the prospect of the picture leaving the UK. It was eventually bought by the National Gallery for £10m under private treaty. *The Old Horse Guards, London* by Canaletto, was bought by the composer Andrew Lloyd Webber for £10.2m, after similar fears that it would be sold abroad. In 1994, an export ban was placed on the £7.6m *The Three Graces* sculpture by Canova, which prevented it from going to the Getty Museum in California. The controversy over these sales illustrates the growing influence of the heritage lobby on the international market for art and antiques. With museum purchasing funds still under tight control, despite the odd lottery fund windfall, the government has come under increasing pressure to apply export controls to prevent the erosion of Britain's national heritage.

How does the export licence system work in practice? Owners of heritage works of art and antiques have to allow for the imbroglio of export review when planning a sale in world markets. Consider a typical case. Treasure hunters, using a metal detector, unearthed an early seventeenth-century gold signet ring near Foulsham, Norfolk. Research showed that they had found a *Memento Mori* (*Remember that thou shalt die*) ring made to solemnise the marriage of Edmond Anguishe and Alice Drake. Their impaled arms are on one side of the ring's bezel; on the reverse, a benign skull in a flower, foliage and scroll border.

Advisers felt that the ring would find its best market abroad, and interested parties applied for an export licence. The Reviewing Committee on the Export of Works of Art held that this object is a genuine part of the national heritage, and ought to stay in the UK. Their appraisal states that the ring is important 'to the local history of Norwich, which in the early seventeenth-century was the second or third city in the Kingdom . . . and for the study of jewellery and its social history. It is a rare object, the only surviving ring of its type linked to Norwich goldsmiths. The few in museums belonged to aristocrats or the landed gentry, and show their engraved arms, whereas this ring comes from a town-based family of merchants. This ring therefore gives a new social context for such luxury objects.'

In March 1997, the Department of National Heritage deferred a decision on export until 11 September 1997. They hope that a buyer in Britain will offer at least £21,172.50 for the ring, or show serious intent to raise funds for its purchase. Also, the Department agreed to take offers from public bodies for less than the stated price through a private treaty sale. The reason is that such purchases can bring tax benefits to both parties.

This export licensing system is designed to strike a balance between the various interests concerned in any application for an export licence – for instance, the protection of the national heritage; the rights of the owner selling the goods; the exporter or overseas purchaser; and the position and reputation of the UK as an international art market. However, the licensing system's main purpose is to keep in the UK cultural goods considered to be of outstanding national importance.

Under the present system, the Waverley rules, a specialist reviewing committee advising the National Heritage Secretary, can recommend a moratorium on the granting of an export licence for up to six months. The delay is to allow museums and public galleries the chance to purchase. The success of this system depends, however, on these bodies having or raising adequate funds to meet the high prices of works deemed of national interest. In 1991 the Secretary of State resorted to placing long-term export bans on several items, limiting their potential market value.

The criteria defined in the *Waverley Report on the Export of Works of Art* (1952) depend on the answers to three questions. Is the object so closely connected with British history and national life that its loss would be a misfortune? Is it of exceptional aesthetic importance? Is it of exceptional significance for the study of some particular branch of art, learning or history? The Waverley Committee recommended a minimum age limit of

100 years in 1952. Committee members did not want to discourage 'the vigorous two-way traffic that we should like to see, bringing important works into the country to fill the many notable gaps in our collections'.

Subsequently, the Government adopted a lower age limit of 50 years. Under the present export licensing controls, works produced more than 50 years ago and valued at or above defined monetary limits fall within the control. Exceptions are an artist or a producer's own works that he or she plans to export. The artist or producer's spouse, widow or widower has similar rights. Advocates of the 50-year rule believe that it properly allows the authorities to decide whether a work meets the Waverley criteria, whether or not its artist or producer still lives.

The export control can apply not only to paintings but to all works of cultural significance, including archives, manuscripts, sculpture, machinery and so on. In practice, the effect of the export control can differ according to the nature of the object. Many national treasures are valued out of the reach of all but the wealthiest investor, but government heritage policy is likely to affect the art and antiques market as a whole, and EU policies, reviewed below, even more so.

18.3.2 Art and the Single Market

The Single Market has affected the movement of works of art both out of the EU and between the member states. Since January 1993, imports and exports have been subject only to spot checks at member states' frontiers, making illegal trade much harder to detect. Some countries, notably Spain, Greece and Italy, fear the loss of many important works. The UK government's prime concern is that trade restrictions will harm the country's art trade, while auction houses anticipate endless bureaucratic wrangles.

An EU export licence is now required to export a cultural object out of the Union, if its value exceeds a stated threshold. These thresholds are defined by age and value, much as they have been under UK export rules. In some cases the thresholds are comparable with those set for a UK licence; in others the threshold is set at a higher level, as the chart below shows. For comprehensive details contact the Department of National Heritage, tel: (0171) 211 6164.

Auction houses also face what has been described a 'an unprecedented threat' from three new areas of legislation:

- *Droit de suite* – a levy on the resale of contemporary art. The EU wants to apply it to Britain, but dealers say it would devastate the international market in twentieth century painting in London, worth about £300m a year.
- *Unidroit* – a treaty which returns 'stolen' goods. The *unidroit*

agreement, which has been signed by a number of governments, covers stolen or illegally exported cultural objects. The British Government has been pressed to sign the treaty, which would allow original owners to reclaim artefacts on proof of origin.

- The imposition of Value Added Tax on art imports into the European Union after 1999 – a pressing issue. Until 1994, there was no import VAT in the United Kingdom and dealers in London could persuade sellers from across the world to send their works of art here.

Category by type and age	Threshold (£)
Elements forming an integral part of artistic, historical or religious monuments which have been dismembered and which are:	
more than 50 years old, but less than 100 years old	no licence required
more than 100 years old	zero
Manuscripts more than 50 years old, including maps and musical scores	zero
Architectural, scientific and engineering drawings produced by hand, more than 50 years old	11,900
Arms and armour, more than 50 years old	39,600
Drawings by hand on any medium and in any material, more than 50 years old	11,900
Portraits or likenesses, which are more than 50 years old, of British historic persons	119,000
Paintings in oil, tempera or other media, which are more than 50 years old (excluding portraits), of British historic persons	119,000
Books which are:	
more than 50 years old, but less than 100 years old	no EU licence required
more than 100 years old	39,600
Collections and specimens from zoological, botanical, mineralogical or anatomical collections	39,600

Droits de suite

Payment of artists' royalties, known as *droits de suite*, varies across Europe, from none in the UK, Ireland and the Netherlands, to between 3 and 5 per cent of the selling price in other member states. These sums are payable by the seller, direct to the artist or his/her estate, provided the sale is over a threshold figure and the work is still in copyright (that is, produced by a living artist, or one who has died within 50 years). The European Commission is seeking to extend this system. Supporters argue that the levy assists artists; opponents, including the UK Government, argue that it is a disincentive to trade. London dealers fear that its introduction would shift trade to the US and Switzerland, 'devastating a thriving international market in twentieth century painting, worth about £300 million a year'. A survey by the Department of Trade and Industry has estimated that *droit de suite* alone could rob the UK of an annual £68m in art sales and 5,000 jobs in the art trade.

In March 1996, the European Commission proposed harmonising national systems that cover 'resale rights' for artists. The purpose is to allow artists to share profits when dealers trade at high prices in a work by an artist who had originally sold it at a far lower price. The proposal applies to pictures, collages, paintings, drawings, engravings, prints, lithographs, sculptures, ceramics and photographic works. In 1997, the European Parliament and Council drafted a new directive on the resale rights that will benefit originators of works of art.

Unidroit

A recently introduced EC directive on the return of 'cultural objects' has been a focus of controversy in some member states. This directive entails the forming of central authorities or 'art tribunals' in each country. They would have the power to demand the return of an item illegally exported, with compensation if the buyer had exercised due care in the purchase.

This right of return expires after 75 years for public collections and 30 years for private collections. Because the legislation is not retroactive, the British Museum will not be compelled to relinquish the Elgin Marbles.

VAT

In December 1993, the member states reached agreement on the harmonisation of VAT payable on sale of works of art imported into the EU. The Seventh VAT Directive on works of art took effect on 1 January 1995. Its effect is to tax works of art imported into and sold within the UK, which has the largest art and antiques market within the EU. Britain's negotiators had sought to maintain the country's status as an international centre. The basis for taxing works of art, which had applied in the UK (that is VAT on the auctioneers' commission and premium, but not on the whole price) now applies throughout the EU.

For items imported from non-EU countries into the UK, the rate of VAT is $2^{1}/_{2}$ per cent from 1 January 1995. This special rate applies until 30 June 1999. Then Britain must come into line with the rest of the EU and charge a rate of not less than 5 per cent. However, it has been agreed with the EU that a review on the impact of the import tax will take place in 1998. The $2^{1}/_{2}$ per cent tax will make an imported work of art less than 1 per cent more expensive than it is at the moment, when bought by an EU purchaser. For a non-EU purchaser, however, it could be cheaper, since any VAT payable should be refundable on re-export. However, auctioneers and dealers feel that the effects will be harmful.

Confirmation of the adverse impact of VAT on the London market came in a recent sale of institutional assets. The British Rail Pension Fund decided not to sell in London a pair of Canalettos and 22 other paintings. Sotheby's auctioned them in New York in January 1997. The fund had begun investing in art in the 1970s, and spent £40m on about 2,400 pieces. It has now disposed of more than 2,200 for £150m, showing a positive annual return of $5^{1}/_{2}$ per cent above the retail price index. Selling the Old Masters in New York represented a departure; earlier sales by the fund had mainly been at Sotheby's, London. As a result of the decision, BR's pensioners are more than £6m richer, while London auction houses and dealers are worrying more about VAT.

They have formed the British Art Market Federation, which is lobbying hard against the new legislation. If the Government has to implement all the measures in full, auctioneers contend that Britain will lose a lucrative source of revenue and employment. A limited exodus from Bond Street in Central London has already begun. Pace Wildenstein, a large firm of art dealers, has sold its Bond Street premises. Phillips opened premises in both New York and Geneva in 1996 'so that we are covered whatever the outcome'. See also **18.7.5** and **18.10.1**.

Dealers estimate that 40 per cent or more of art works sold (by value) come from Switzerland, America, Japan and outside the EU. Thus, it will make sense for many to buy and sell through New York.

The art trade elsewhere in the EU, apart from Paris, is mainly domestic, so that London dealers see an envy of London's status as a world centre since the eighteenth century. Published estimates show that the London market turns over £2.1bn a year, compared to £3.5–4bn for the EU as a whole, Britain included. The British may not be large-scale buyers of art, but the London market is like the City is to international money markets: an entrepôt.

Take a Japanese collector who intends to sell a modern painting. If he chooses to make the sale in New York, and attracts a bid of $4m, the buyer will pay the auctioneer 15 per cent on the first $50,000 and 10 per cent on the rest ($402,000) on top of the hammer price. The seller pays 2 per cent, plus expenses – probably a figure in excess of $100,000. The same transaction in London would attract the same costs, but the buyer would have to pay an additional 5 per cent import tax on $4,502,000

($225,100). The seller meanwhile would have to pay an additional 2 per cent *droit de suite*.

Thus to carry out the transaction in London would cost more than 60 per cent more than it would in New York. This position will apply in 1999, when London's existing preferential treatment will cease. Already, the 2.5 per cent import tax has caused measurable damage to London trade. The UK's imports of art and antiques are already on the decline; the trade fell by 28 per cent in 1996 to £665m.

See also **18.7.5** and **18.10.1**.

18.3.3 New export controls in France

Paris is planning new art export controls to prevent masterpieces from trickling abroad, a measure that might lower art prices in France. The new law would, however, retain the existing principle of compensation for works declared 'national treasures'. The art establishment wishes to strengthen the 1992 laws, but French dealers fear that new restrictions could prompt collectors to remove valuable works from the country. Critics also feel that the new law would be difficult to enforce with open EU borders.

The current system has been widely condemned, especially since a payment for a Vincent van Gogh painting, still in a private collection, took most of France's budget for acquisitions. In this case, owners of van Gogh's *Jardin à Anvers*, one of the Dutch artist's last masterpieces painted in 1890, won 145m francs (£17m) from the French state, under a court order, when the authorities refused to allow its export.

Pierre Rosenberg, the director of the Louvre museum, said the 1992 law was 'disastrous' because it had barred exports without giving museums the cash to buy new works. 'The French heritage is threatened as never before.' He noted that Rubens' *Decapitation of St John the Baptist* and Poussin's *Agony in the Garden of Olives* both recently left France. The government has turned down only 39 out of 11,000 applications for export permits.

For their part, French dealers believe that restrictive laws do not work. One Paris auctioneer pointed out that 'Italy is probably the most prohibitive country in Europe but people just smuggle works out. The law is so strict that no one asks for permits' – a view that the English media might endorse!

18.4 HIGHLIGHTS OF THE PREVIOUS YEAR

18.4.1 Export controls revised

During 1996, the Department of National Heritage consulted the museums and art trade worlds on several important issues:

- Estimates of a fair market price for export-deferred works of art. In particular, the Department has sought opinions on a proposal to exclude a dealer's commission from the fair market price, where the commission is on a sale to a connected third party.
- Whether any extra conditions attach to a private offer from a UK buyer to purchase an object under export deferral.
- Whether, the National Heritage Secretary should encourage an owner to prefer a public offer to a simultaneous offer from a private source.
- The application of the Waverley rules to works by living artists.

Consultation on these issues followed the Reviewing Committee on the Export of Works of Art's reports and recommendations. The Committee advises on the principles that should govern the controlled export of works of art and antiques under the Import, Export and Customs Powers (Defence) Act 1939. The members examine cases where a work of art or an antique's 'national importance' leads to the refusal of an export licence. They also advise when a special exchequer grant will go towards the purchase of an object that otherwise would go abroad, and the Committee supervises the operation of the export control system.

Controversy over the fair market price arose when the Reviewing Committee considered Jean-François de Troy's painting *La lecture de Molière*. The members expressed reservations about the inclusion in the fair market price of the dealer's commission charged by the applicant to its related US company. The Committee also urged the Secretary of State for National Heritage only to take account of private offers, if the UK buyer has given satisfactory undertakings. These should include assurances on public access, proper maintenance, a minimum retention period and, for a collection or set of objects, the integrity of the collection. Consultation led to changes in the private offers' policy, which imposes strict conditions on a private offer to purchase an object under export deferral.

In another case, the Reviewing Committee considered an application to export *The Painter's Room* by Lucian Freud (1943). This was the first occasion on which a work by a living artist had come before the Committee. Sotheby's had applied for a licence to export the painting to a purchaser in the US. The value shown on the export licence application was £515,812.50.

The Department of National Heritage's Expert Adviser came from the Tate Gallery. He stated why he felt that the work should stay in Britain, asserting that *The Painter's Room* was a vital *oeuvre* from Freud's first phase, and the largest picture that he had painted to that date. The painting 'declared arrestingly the preoccupation with concentrated realisation of motifs from observation that would be a central feature of his art over the succeeding half century. Memorable in its clarity and strangeness, it was Freud's first key work.'

Against that, Sotheby's argued that the painting stood as an early work within the scope of Freud's output, and was stylistically atypical. 'The depiction of such an estranged world and the absence of human beings, were not characteristic. Later works do not bear any resemblance, and Freud's style quickly evolved into a more realistic and dramatic one.' The painting did not identify with the style upon which Freud built his reputation. It stood more as curiosity than as an established and characteristic work.

For tactical reasons, the Reviewing Committee submitted no recommendation. In due course, the Secretary of State for National Heritage decided to defer a decision for two months, hoping to see an offer at the recommended price of £515,812.50, or higher. The Tate Gallery announced a serious intention to raise funds for the purchase, extending the deferred period to four months. Later, the owner refused separate offers to purchase from the Tate and the Chatsworth House Trust at the stated price. The National Heritage Secretary therefore refused the export licence.

This case prompted the Reviewing Committee to express reservations about deferring a decision on a licence for any living artist's work, whatever its merit. The members felt that Freud's painting raised an important point of principle: whether the export of works by living artists should stay under control. However, they noted that removing such works from UK export control would not prevent action under European Union regulations that govern trade in cultural goods.

The Reviewing Committee felt that the system could act to a living artist's detriment. Suppose a painter or a sculptor is important enough for heritage conservationists to oppose its export. Probably the artist already enjoys an international reputation, and the value of the artist's work might rise if buyers learn that his or her work is 'of national importance'. A licence deferral could allow national galleries to fill gaps where public collections do not already cover the early part of an artist's *oeuvre*.

In practice, the market for the artist's work is unlikely to fall, merely because the Secretary of State might not issue an export licence. It also seems unlikely that many works will come before the Reviewing Committee. The Freud painting was the first by a living artist to come before it in 42 years. If more do come forward, it is doubtful if matching offers would be forthcoming for all living artists' works subject to licence deferral.

On the other hand, the Waverley Committee's original arguments in favour of the higher limit support the exclusion of works by living artists from the regime. Any restriction on the export of work by living artists could limit the spread of their international reputation. Nor would the export controls apply to artists who export their own work. Many of these artists are under contract to sell their output through dealers, who would be subject to export licence controls. Anomalies could then arise. A dealer, or an overseas buyer, could evade the controls by selling the work back to the artist. He or she could export it legally under his or her own name and then resell it to the new owner, bringing the control into disrepute.

Export controls apply not only to the work of artists but to the archives of authors, musicians and other public figures. They might prefer to sell their papers through an agent. The latter would be subject to controls and might reduce the price offered because the Department might withhold a licence for the early part of the archive. Agents might also see advantages in breaking up a collection of papers.

See also **18.10.1**.

18.4.2 Museum financing

The balance is shifting in top range art and antique markets towards museums and galleries. They are mounting massive exhibitions and launching 'museum stores' that profit from art and antique merchandise. Art museums have become big business around the world, and especially in America, where reduced revenue from the public purse and corporate parsimony have prompted cultural institutions to seek other sources of funds.

Many museums and galleries in America have large endowments and collections of almost immeasurable value. Yet they suffer from seesaw support; up and down attendances, membership and other sources of income. So these institutions are shifting to new forms of financing, for example, to large bond issues; to underpin these issues, they are seeking credit ratings. The first to try the approach was New York's Metropolitan Museum, which, in the 1980s, suffered substantial cuts in New York City funding. In 1987, with support from a State educational authority, the Museum floated a $40m issue. By 1993, the Museum was able to re-finance its debt, and secure another $22m at preferential rates. The issues were successful; by early 1996, the Museum had won a higher rating from credit agencies, as did the Art Institute of Chicago.

Reports are becoming more common of innovative financing by museums and galleries, and raised credit standing. As an example, Moody's Investors Service now rates New York's Museum of Modern Art as A1 for an issue of $34.7m (£21m) of debt. Cultural institutions across the Atlantic and in other parts of the world have learnt how to operate in debt markets, without the cushion of government backing or costly bond insurance programmes. New York's Natural History Museum and Boston's Museum of Fine Arts are among other cultural institutions that have used publicly-traded debt to finance capital projects. One benefit is a lower interest rate than banks charge for loans. The bonds are tax-exempt, offering investors and savings advantages; they do not have to pay Federal taxes on the income. American investment bankers have been struck with 'museums and galleries' strong balance sheets, low debt, and efficient financial management of large-scale events'.

These institutions apply their borrowing mainly to capital projects. However, they do not offer their collections as collateral. Nor do the agencies treat these assets as formally available for debt servicing; but the credit raters nevertheless feel that, in straitened circumstances, the institutions could sell some works of art from their inventories. The American experience might well be a precedent for the UK, although it would probably require changes in the charities' law.

Some other public museums are experiencing organic growth. Perhaps the most spectacular growth has been in Seattle. To house new donations of art, three major art museums there have added 200,000 square feet of floorspace over the past five years. The largest, the Seattle Art Museum, a showcase for contemporary art, has tripled in size, added 2,556 pieces of art and put an additional 8,000 new members on its rolls since 1991. The greater purchasing power of art museums could have a substantial impact on world markets.

18.5 PURCHASING ART AND ANTIQUES

18.5.1 Quality and provenance

The consensus of expert opinion is that the buyer should be concerned with the features which establish a work as one of quality. The condition of a painting, for example, is an important factor, as is its provenance, that is, its origins and history. An investor who acquires a work (which he plans to hold for some years before disposing of it, possibly in an overseas market) will want to make sure in advance that its ownership, authenticity and quality are established beyond reasonable dispute, and that it is marketable.

When negotiating to buy an asset, the investor therefore needs to go further in his investigations than would be necessary merely to check that the vendor has a good title to the piece. The research carried out into the history and previous ownership of the work should also indicate clearly the probability that it is a genuine item. A bill of sale which includes a full and authentic dossier of the purchase will be helpful both for the purposes of an inventory of assets and an eventual disposal. Preferably, the dossier will be endorsed by valuers of repute, who will be in a position at some time in the future to verify the statements made.

These precautions are advisable for several reasons. Basically, they provide the buyer with evidence that the vendor has a good title to the piece. Equally, the research is important because there are frauds and forgeries in the alternative investment market, as well as reproductions and 'restorations' which can be difficult to distinguish from the genuine article. Occasionally, the forgery may turn out to have a high value in its own right, but on the whole the investor needs to take due care that the work's authenticity has been verified. It is also important to bear in mind that certificates may be counterfeited.

18.5.2 Fakes and forgeries

Dealers and auction houses take steps to reduce the risk of forgery and mistaken identity. Some offer the buyer a five-year guarantee against forgery. Because the largest houses trade in volume and compete intensively for material, they can sometimes be an unwitting conduit for fakes, particularly in ill-documented but now increasingly expensive areas of art. In sectors of the market where fakes are relatively common, some will inevitably turn up at auction; and where the rewards can be measured in millions of dollars, fakes will breed.

Successful fakers may discredit sections of the market and even distort history, but it is sometimes the 'experts' more than the artists who are to blame. When anyone dares to pry into their secret world, they close ranks. Many did so when Tom Keating, Britain's most celebrated forger, faced criminal charges over a handful of his 2,000 or more fakes. The same pattern of events occurred when another trickster, Eric Hebbom, was accused of faking many drawings by Old Masters. Nothing is guaranteed; even the Mona Lisa may not be the original. Leonardo's masterpiece went missing from the Louvre for 11 months in 1911 after an audacious theft and some people still claim that a copy was substituted for the real work. In 1985 the J Paul Getty Museum in California reputedly paid $7m (£4m) for a 6th century BC Greek statue, known as a *Kouros*, only to find that its provenance could not be substantiated and it was very likely a fake, possibly made by one of Rodin's assistants in

Paris in about 1900. The handiwork of some well-known forgers has itself become sought after. A case in point is that of Tom Keating, whose works have fetched up to £27,500 at auction. One buyer, however, paid £1,500 for an 'original' Keating only to find that it, and its certificate, were themselves fakes.

Nobody can say for sure how much of the art on the market has dubious origins or how many 'wrong' artworks find their way into Britain's salesrooms. Some experts believe that half the items most sold on the market may not be 'right'. Dealers, auctioneers and gallery curators privately admit that faking is on the increase. In the case of most paintings by Cézanne and Seurat, provenance is impeccable and there is no reason to believe they are fakes. Then again, hundreds of fake post-Impressionist works have been turned out over the years and an unknown percentage of them are on the walls of leading galleries all over the world.

As Keating demonstrated, fakes are frequently first rate; several of his 'Samuel Palmers' are still regarded by some people as 'among Palmer's finest works'. In the Netherlands, the Rembrandt Research Project, set up 15 years ago to distinguish true Rembrandts from works produced by pupils and followers, had by 1994 reduced the Dutchman's oeuvre to less than half the previous total. Elmyr de Hory, an exuberant Hungarian, fooled the market for years with a profusion of faked Picassos, Matisses and Modiglianis and, at the time of his death, had no idea what had happened to a batch of skillfully forged Old Masters.

In recent years, money launderers have discovered that buying and selling fakes can double their profits. Colombian drug barons were the first, but now the Russian mafia has cornered the market in fake icons. This led to the murder of 30 icon dealers last year. Dealers have to cope with innumerable forgeries. Of course, the art world dislikes discussion of widespread fakery. A book on the subject (*Fakes, Forgery and the Art World*, published by Richard Cohen Books in 1995) met with the studied hostility of members of the art establishment. Publication was halted at the last moment by the publisher on the advice of lawyers, and a second firm agreed to publish only after some specific allegations about people still in the business were modified or omitted from the text.

Who are the fakers? They are usually talented artists who are consumed by the belief that their genius has gone unrecognised and are bent on revenge. Eric Hebborn was born in Romford, Essex, in 1934. While a student in the 1950s he undertook work as a part-time restorer and discovered a gift for filling in missing bits of pictures in the style of the original artists. Later, after he studied works by the Dutch painter Willem van de Velde, he attempted a van de Velde of his own and signed it with the artist's name. He redrew his preparatory drawing on to an old canvas and prevented paint seeping into the age cracks by filling these with a jelly-like substance that resisted his paintbrush and would later dissolve in water. He took care not to use colours such as zinc white and Prussian blue that were not available in van de Velde's day and the paints he did use were ground in a clearer oil than linseed and had a mixture of artificial resin added. He copied a signature from a photograph.

Hebborn was not exposed until 1978 when a curator visiting the Pierpont Morgan Library in New York noticed something odd about a drawing of a boy supposedly by Francesco del Cossa, the 15th century Italian artist. The ink lines had been scratched over with what appeared to have been a 20th century razor blade. A long investigation ensued and Hebborn's career as a forger was at an end, or so the establishment claimed. He had the satisfaction, however, of knowing that three sets of 'experts' had pronounced his Cossa an original.

The way a scam unfolds is revealed in the example of de Hory, who worked closely with an unscrupulous couple, Fernand Legros and Réal Lessard, in the 1960s, passing off bogus Dufys, Dérains, Modiglianis, Vlamincks and Matisses. Their tactics, de Hory once revealed, were to secure expert opinions, if possible, from the artists' surviving relatives, such as Jeanne Modigliani and Alice Dérain, or to forge them. The fraudsters also paid impoverished collectors to certify that they had previously owned the pictures. Alternatively, they would put a painting in an auction and, if nobody bought it, they had only to pay the handling fee to reclaim it – a small price for the picture's appearance in a reputable catalogue as genuine.

One of the century's greatest forgers was Hans van Meegeren, a Dutchman who throughout the 1930s and early 1940s specialised in superbly crafted fakes of the 17th century master Johannes Vermeer. He was generally successful (though less so than the dealers who profited from his activities) and stumbled only after it was suggested in 1945 that he had handed over a Vermeer, *The Woman Taken in Adultery*, to Hermann Goering, an act of criminal collaboration. Van Meegeren retorted that he had knocked off the Vermeer himself and then sold it to Goering, thus hoodwinking the Nazi, and to prove this he produced *Jesus Preaching in the Temple*, without models and in the presence of six witnesses, to a standard that astounded the experts.

Fakers provide the artefacts, but dealers and valuers provide the market. Keating, who died in 1984 after a spectacular career, insisted that he had always been quite open about his forgeries. 'It was other people that weren't,' he said. After he was exposed in 1976 and under investigation by Scotland Yard's art fraud division, dealers and auctioneers became singularly reluctant to talk. The art market is built upon confidence: when trade is going well, business prospers but a scandal can easily start a downward spiral. Keating's 'crude daubs', as he called them, made it more difficult for dealers to convince buyers of the value of a unique, original production of a famous mind. A few scribbles by a master are worth far more than a fine painting by an unknown artist or a forger. Faked art continues to be sold, alongside and often indistinguishable from the real thing. A Fabergé egg sold in good faith by Christies in 1977 for $250,000 as an imperial egg (one of only 57 in the world) was denounced eight years later by the same company in New York. Reportedly, about $5m was paid to the buyer's estate in compensation and costs.

Most cases against fakers or their associates hinge on the intention to deceive, which has to be proved. Auctioneers will normally offer recompense for fakes only if the buyer can provide proof, usually within five years, and even then only if it can be demonstrated that the saleroom was not reflecting general opinion at the time, or that they could only have uncovered the truth by unreasonably expensive scientific means.

18.5.3 Crime and punishing losses

Some of the Metropolitan Police art and antique unit's cases are unusual and instructive. In 1996, its officers detected forgeries in art gallery archives. Spurious documents formed part of an ingenious fraud by three parties. One seeded archives with an 'authentic' provenance for a bogus painting that the second created. The third sold the fake. Any buyer or dealer who checked the archive for the history of the work would find file entries that endorsed the claims. The fraud came to light when a dealer uncovered false claims for a water colour by Ben Nicholson, the English artist. In parallel, the art and antiques unit traced fakes claimed to be the work of Jacob Epstein and Giacometti. These paintings also had ersatz origins.

The case prompted detailed scrutiny of documents that buttress claims. For instance, appraisers focus on labels affixed to frames, which purport to chronicle a painting's itinerary from museum to gallery, to owner, to dealer, to saleroom. Letters, extracts from critics' reviews and curators' reports, invoices, receipts, insurances, bills of lading, customs declarations, all lend support to assertions that the work is genuine, and is worth a large sum. Doubts can arise when the sources are critics and curators who are no longer alive, or auction houses and galleries which have gone out of business. Prudent dealers now carry out the type of investigation that merchant bankers, accountants and research specialists conduct when a client buys a company; today, many art experts launch a 'due diligence' enquiry.

Clearly, it is unwise to accept without checking that any provenance is bona-fide. Of course, an error in the provenance does not prove that a painting is a forgery, but it is advisable to take care. The due diligence process usually means verifying original documents, contacting the experts and critics cited in the support materials, and studying catalogues of an artist's work. To reduce the risk, collectors can also take advice from an art foundation that specialises in a named artist. For a fee of £250 or more, depending on the costs incurred in checking the work, an expert will supply a 'photo certificate', which includes a signed opinion and a photograph.

Fears about paintings with false provenance have affected sales. In some sectors, evidence of large-scale fraud and forgery has brought a market to a virtual stop, as happened for example with some Russian avant-garde art. Art historians have disputed the origins of paintings sold at auction and, in December 1996, Sotheby's withdrew six Russian avant-garde paintings at short notice. A gulf between the opinions of Russian and Western experts is making it difficult to authenticate pictures that are in demand. The buyers affected are mainly rich Western collectors of works by such artists as Malevich, Rodchenko, Popova and Exter. Their works belong to experimental schools that sprang up during the turbulent years between 1905 and Lenin's death in the early 1920s. Fakes make for a factious and fractious market. Given a lack of consensus on the authenticity of works, few major auction houses will now sell these controversial avant-garde paintings.

The forgers and fraudsters of these Russian works rely on the muddled paper trails left by the artists, who lived through the dark days of the century's history. Stalin denounced experimentation in art as in music and literature, and artists died, or went to labour camps. Their works festered in musty storerooms, or vanished altogether.

Generally, the cognoscenti worry that fakes are widespread. In some categories, some claim forgeries are almost as numerous as the genuine article. Many doubtful paintings, these experts believe, remain undetected in private collections and great museums. A recent book tells of a Yugoslav forger, who allegedly 'sold a museumful of fakes to the Tito government'. Out of almost 4,000 items, the author believes, all but a few dozen are of disputable origins. Yet the collection is still open to the public in Zagreb. Even more spectacularly, according to this book, a Mexican fabricator has faked an entire phase of ancient Inca art, many of the artefacts being on show in American galleries.

18.5.4 Choosing an adviser

When making a purchase, it is usually helpful to have details in a dossier about the artist to whom the piece is ascribed. In the art market, for instance, it is common to use the names of artists to denote works 'in the style' of a particular painter, or paintings by unidentified members of a school associated with a famous artist. Therefore, not all paintings listed in an auction catalogue under the name 'Manet' will be by that painter; and it is important for buyers to appreciate the esoteric distinctions employed by the specialists in auction houses to indicate the provenance of a work.

Ideally, those chosen to advise should have a wide knowledge of the field. Thus, a specialist offering guidance on the purchase of works of art should also be able to direct its installation, placement and maintenance. Ideally, he or she should have a background in art history, curatorial experience, an intimate knowledge of the art market, and up-to-date familiarity with trends in prices and values. In addition, care should be taken to check that the adviser has a good understanding of handling, shipping, conservation, restoration, insurance and security. Curators of art galleries and museums will sometimes indicate formally which dealers specialise in particular areas.

18.5.5 Exporting art

An intending buyer of art or antiques should keep other precautions in mind. Suppose, for instance, that the plan is to send an item out of this country; authorisation may be needed. Some categories of antiques, collectors' items and other artifacts do not need a specific licence. They are covered by the Open General Export Licence (Antiques), which does not need to be applied for. Exporters need only inform customs officials by naming the licence in export documentation. A Specific Export Licence must be applied for (from the Department of Trade and Industry) by those wishing to send historic manuscripts, documents and archives of any value out of the country. Any object covered by the regulations which exceeds the thresholds of age and value will need a UK export licence.

Licence applications have to be accompanied by a black-and-white photographic copy of the item; and the decision whether or not to permit export will be influenced by independent advice. Where the item is regarded as part of the national heritage, the issue of a licence may be delayed or refused on the advice of experts in the field. The procedures may include reference to the Department of National Heritage's Arts and Libraries' Reviewing Committee on the Export of Works of Art, described above.

In the past many licence applications have been made; few have been rejected. For example, in one recent year, 6,550 applications were made for export licences with a total value of £963m: only 24 failed to receive approval, subject to an offer to purchase at a specified price being made by a public collection in the UK within a reasonable time.

It is prudent to bear the requirement in mind when deciding to acquire a work of art or an antique of exceptional interest. When these items come onto the open market some foreign buyers may be deterred by the inconvenience and delays of up to seven months in the review procedure, and by the inherent risk that their offer will merely represent the buying-in price for a domestic museum. The absence of such foreign buyers could mean lower bids and less attractive gains when the time comes to dispose of the item.

National heritage bodies

The National Gallery
The National Museums of Scotland
The Ulster Museum
The National Trust for Places of Historic Interest or Natural Beauty
The Historic Buildings and Monuments Commission for England
The Trustees of the National Heritage Memorial Fund
The Historic Churches Preservation Trust
Any local authority (including National Park authorities)
Any university or university college in the UK
Any museum or art gallery in the UK which exists wholly or mainly for the purpose of preserving for the public benefit a collection of scientific, historic or artistic interest and which is maintained by a local authority or university in the UK
The British Museum
The National Museum of Wales
The National Art Collections Fund
The National Trust for Scotland for Places of Historic Interest or Natural Beauty
The Friends of the National Libraries
The Nature Conservancy Council
Any government department (including the National Debt Commissioner's)
Any library the main function of which is to serve the needs of teaching and research at a university in the UK
Any other similar national institution which exists wholly or mainly for that purpose and which is approved for the purpose by the Commissioners of the Inland Revenue.

18.6 CHARACTERISTICS

18.6.1 Prospects of capital appreciation

Can alternative investments be justified by private investors or by trustees and fund managers with powers to buy fine art or antiques? Essentially the question is whether the capital appreciation over a period of say, ten years, 25 years or even longer, will warrant the diversion of funds and the expenditure incurred in holding the asset.

Frequent reports in the press of record-breaking prices paid for pieces at auction may seem to support the case for alternative investment. In 1989, as the market approached a peak, some ten-year and 20-year investments paid handsome dividends. The increasing number of investments which have provided significant capital appreciation short-term also represents an interesting trend that helps to endorse the advocates' case for buying arts and antiques.

Their counsel to both private and institutional investors is to buy the best examples that can be afforded and to take expert advice from a reputable dealer or appraiser. They suggest that an artist's early work will, in general, be less valuable than later, more mature, examples. Reasonably enough, they also point out that prices can fall, as happened with Georgian silver after a boom in the 1960s, with 19th century fine art in the mid-1970s, and with many categories of art and antiques in the early 1980s and the recent 1990s. However, even expert advice is fallible, particularly where attribution is concerned. A case in point is the work of Rembrandt, which has suffered the attentions of a Dutch government committee (see **18.5.2**). The majority of works once attributed to him have now been reattributed to his pupils. Works have lost up to 90 per cent of their value, and the controversy has spawned a 'Save Rembrandt Society'.

18.6.2 Art as investment

One sector of the alternative investment market comprises investors who are nervous about the future. Some works are low in weight, small in size, and high in value: they are portable, easily concealed and readily negotiable in markets around the world. Those who fear political, economic, social or tax repression in their own countries tend to regard alternative investments as a means of safeguarding their wealth.

Some market sectors, on occasion, seem to meet demanding investment criteria. Conversely, anecdotal evidence could make enthusiastic bidders at auctions pause. According to one press report, a battle tableau by Ernest Meissonier, a much-favoured painter of a century ago, sold in London in 1892 for £20,700; again in 1913 for £6,300; and again in 1964 for £4,340. Lazare reports that John Singer Sargent's oil sketch *San Virgilio* sold for £7,350 in 1925 and just £105 in 1952. A scholarly study of London art auction transactions between 1952 and 1961 found that the average work appreciated just half a per cent a year, a poor return in anyone's passbook. More recently, a painting by Henry Fuesli, an 18th century Swiss/British artist, bought by Rudolf Nureyev in 1988 for $1.16m, was sold in January 1995 for $761,500 (£488,141).

To set against these warning illustrations, there are some promising examples of the gains to be made. Paintings by the Scottish Colourists, S J Peploe, J D Fergusson, Frances Cadell and Leslie Hunter, have shown an average annual appreciation rate of 19 per cent from 1975. Similarly, Renoir's *Tête du Femme* was sold for £1.35m in 1987 and exchanged hands again in 1988 for £1.98m (an appreciation of 35 per cent in one year).

18.6.3 Costs of ownership

Typically, rates of return are only attractive if the owner is prepared to put a value on the pleasure of holding such works of art in his home or at his place of work. The investment may also be justified if the money used for the acquisitions would have been taxed at a high rate. Nevertheless, some items could have been a poor investment for the buyer, after taking into account outlays to meet insurance premiums, dealers' or auctioneers' commissions, any liability to capital taxation or VAT, the interest foregone, and security and maintenance costs. The lack of income flows means that the buyer of alternative investments is dependent on capital appreciation; yet he has to deduct the following costs from any gains he may achieve:

(1) costs of acquisition and disposal, including premiums and dealers' commissions;
(2) holding costs (insurance, storage, etc);
(3) valuation and provenance research fees incurred;
(4) revenue and possible tax benefits foregone by tying up capital in the asset;
(5) the value of time spent dreaming about the market and, increasingly, the advice of market experts or consultants;
(6) capital gains tax payable on realisation of the asset, or inheritance tax payable on its transfer.

Substantial gains are necessary to justify such an investment in financial terms; or, alternatively, the investor has to be convinced that the assets he acquires can be relied upon to sustain their worth in times when traditional investments fail. Figure 18.2 shows how much an investment of £1,000 must grow to produce the equivalent of 8 per cent compound between 1997 and 2007. The interest rate represents an inflation rate of 3 per cent, and a target annual return of 5 per cent. In other words, the painting bought at auction for £1,000 net in 1997 should fetch a net sum of £14,133 in 2007 to match these targets.

Figure 18.2   Increase in values required equivalent to 8 per cent compound per annum

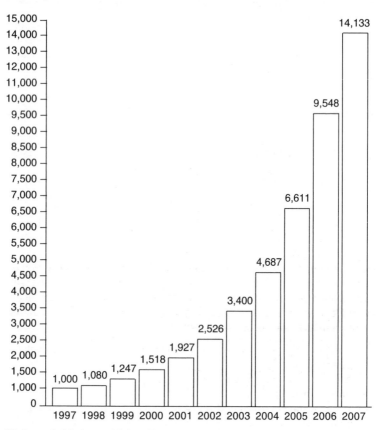

Note: 8 per cent includes 3 per cent inflation and 5 per cent compound interest per annum

18.6.4 The Chester Beatty collection: a precedent

In 1991, 13 paintings from the collection of the late Sir Alfred Chester Beatty were offered at auction. They included works by Toulouse-Lautrec, Dégas, Renoir and Chagall. The trustees had previously considered donating van Gogh's *Sunflowers* to the nation: instead they sold at auction for £24¾m. Had they donated it, the family would have received £5½m under the government's acceptance in lieu scheme. That returns a quarter of the tax deducted as an incentive to donate works of art to the nation.

The sale at auction was subject to combined inheritance and capital gains taxation. The capital gains tax of £3.07m was calculated as 30 per cent of the difference between the valuation and the sale price at auction. The inheritance tax was levied at a variable rate (between 65 and 80 per cent) because the painting had been exempted at the time of an earlier death in the family. Otherwise the rate would have been 60 per cent. At the 80 per cent rate, the balance left for the family would be £3–3½m, probably not enough to settle the full tax on the estate.

18.6.5 Buying at auction

Sales to meet tax bills provide auction houses with a flow of works to offer. Many people who like the idea of buying at a sale worry that they will find it hard to conform to usual practice, that a sudden twitch will leave them with an unexpected heirloom and an unwelcome bill. The pace can be fast, the enthusiasm contagious, and bidding strategy complex. The amount paid is also likely to include extras, such as a 10 per cent buyer's premium and VAT on the auction house's services.

In reality the buying process often begins a month or more before the sale date. Catalogues appear and can be bought on subscription, by order or at the auctioneer's offices. The descriptions of items have various nuances; for instance, only information printed in bold type may be guaranteed. There will be an estimated price range, but no disclosure of the secret minimum bid acceptable to the vendor, the 'reserve'. Critics ask, 'Is this secrecy necessary?' Should the buyer be told whether he is bidding against an actual rival or the consignor's reserve? Auctioneers argue that the confidential reserve is a defence against the collusion of 'auction rings'. It is only worth organising a ring when the participants know that the reserve is low enough to ensure a good profit.

Before the sale, lots are commonly exhibited. They are sold 'as seen', so it is important to study the condition of an item in advance. Before bidding at many major auctions, it is necessary to register, ie to give name, address and bank reference. A 'client card' for previous registrants can speed the process. At the auction, the registrant may take a pre-reserved seat and a bidding number. It is, in practice, virtually impossible to bid by accident. Just when to start bidding is a matter of strategy. Some buyers come in early and raise quickly to deter competitors; others wait to avoid inciting other bidders with their keenness. Care is advisable when the bidding pace seems unusually fast, or the auctioneer does not indicate the source of the bid. Often he or she will say 'on the left' or 'the bid is with me' or some similar words that convey the origin and authenticity of the bid. Payment may be cash, approved cheque or, in some instances, by credit card.

18.6.6 Independent sources of information

Research pays off before buying at auction or through a dealer. An independent source of information on the prices of paintings sold at auction is the Art Sales Index. This lists the results of auctions for about 60,000 items each year which were sold for £500 or more. Using this source, an analysis has been made of transactions for a representative selection of 20th century Modern masters. The analysis shows a compound rate of appreciation in excess of 14 per cent per annum between 1971 and 1991. Such rates of growth make it easier to argue the case for the allocation of funds to alternative investments.

The growth of interest which has already taken place has prompted the development of improved sources of information on available media, prices and the advantages and limitations of particular types of investment. There are already computerised databases providing information to help determine sound investments. 'Artquest', provided by the Art Sales Index, holds details on paintings, drawings and sculptures which have been sold at public auction around the world. Another recently developed database is the 'Thesaurus of Fine Art Information'. This allows dealers, collectors, and museums who subscribe to it to search through details of forthcoming auction sales, for any category of antique or collectable of interest. The gradual evolution of a more or less formal infrastructure of information sources in the alternative sector of the investment market will add to the understanding of the opportunities and prospects.

These sources and others tend to show that the average annual appreciation over the past 40 years has tended to outstrip the rate of inflation, although there has been considerable volatility from artist to artist and from sale to sale.

18.7 TAXATION

18.7.1 Tax planning

To attain positive returns, investors should plan to avoid unnecessary tax liabilities. For instance, if the investor eventually wishes to contend that isolated purchases are for the purpose of building up assets as long-term investments, then it is mandatory to record the acquisition of chargeable assets in his tax returns. This step would help to support a claim that capital gains, rather than income tax, should be the basis for calculating any future liabilities when, despite the parity of the rates of tax, there are advantages in doing so for the individual taxpayer.

The private investor also may be faced with claims by the Inland

Revenue that purchases and sales of alternative investments are adventures in the nature of a trade. This would lead to an income tax liability if the investor is held to be carrying on the trade on his own account, or to a corporation tax liability if he has set up a company for the purpose.

18.7.2 Capital gains

Alternative investments are subject to the general law on capital gains tax, although there are special exemptions. In broad terms the amount of the chargeable gain is the difference between the cost of the asset and the sale proceeds, less an adjustment for the inflationary element of the gain accruing since March 1982. For any asset held on 31 March 1982, there is the opportunity to base the cost of acquisition at its market value on that date. There is however no charge on unrealised gains from assets held by an individual at his death.

Special considerations apply in the case of works of art and other alternative investments. Thus, a gain accruing on the disposal of an asset which does not exceed £6,000 (from 6 April 1995) is generally exempt from capital gains tax with marginal relief (see Capital Gains Tax Act 1979, s 128). In this connection the exemption on articles which provide a gain of not more than £6,000 (for instance, individual pieces of antique silver) would become relevant.

Exemptions also arise for individual objects of artistic, historic or scientific interest (and collections of such objects) which are accepted by the tax authorities as forming 'an integral and major part of the cultural life of this country'. These are often referred to as 'national heritage property'. Under the *douceur* arrangements (see **18.7.4**), gifts of such alternative investments to national heritage bodies (and gifts of these alternative investments to charities) are not charged to capital gains tax. In the case of sales, the notional capital gains tax liability is one of the factors relevant in calculating the sale price that can be negotiated. There is a similar exemption applying to gifts of qualifying heritage property made for the public benefit.

Where national heritage property (accepted as such by the Commissioners of the Inland Revenue) is transferred by way of gift from one individual to another, or where such property is transferred into or out of settlement, the transfer will be treated for capital gains tax purposes as giving rise neither to a gain nor to a loss, provided that appropriate undertakings are given with regard to location, preservation and access. This means that any gain is carried forward, and will be chargeable when the donee disposes of the property in a manner which does not qualify for conditional exemption.

18.7.3 Inheritance tax and estate duty

Inheritance tax replaced capital transfer tax with effect from 18 March 1986. It was introduced in the 1986 Finance Act and applies to gratuitous transfers by individuals. The major difference between capital transfer tax and inheritance tax is the treatment of lifetime transfers. Outright transfers between individuals are exempt if the transferer lives on for seven years. Gifts made within seven years of death are charged at death rates, but the charge is tapered where the gift occurs more than three years before death.

The charge on death is retained within inheritance tax, as are most of the exemptions and relief available under capital transfer tax, including transfers between spouses domiciled in the UK. Trust-related transfers remain subject to the full range of charges at the time the transfers are made. The cumulation period for all chargeable transfers has been reduced to seven years and the threshold below which tax is not chargeable is £154,000 (from 6 April 1995). A flat rate of 40 per cent replaced the former four-rate system.

Estate duty applies to property inherited before 13 March 1975. This may still be relevant to the sale of objects which have been previously exempted from estate duty. Estate duty will not be charged if exempted objects are sold by private treaty to a national heritage body or have again been transferred on a death and have been conditionally exempt on that occasion. Special rules apply when property which has previously been exempted is sold after 6 April 1976. The way in which this property is taxed depends on what had happened since the original exemption was granted – either capital transfer tax or inheritance tax or estate duty only may be payable. This is a complex issue and is dealt with fully in Appendix III (p 46) of *Capital Taxation and the National Heritage* (see bibliography at the end of Chapter 19).

18.7.4 Tax liabilities in practice

The Treasury has become more flexible about the art it will accept in the form of heritage sales to museums as a means of saving tax. On the other hand, museum purchasing grants in the UK have been severely curtailed, which limits the opportunity for private treaty sales.

Suppose a beneficiary has inherited a painting that auction houses believe will fetch £100,000 under the hammer, after allowing for commission and expenses. When the painting was bequeathed it was worth, on valuation, £80,000. Capital gains tax would be payable on the difference between the valuation and the sale price (on £20,000). Inheritance tax would be payable on the sale price net of capital gains tax, leaving the vendor with just over £50,000.

If a museum will buy the painting the vendor receives a *douceur* (usually a quarter of the amounts payable in capital gains and inheritance taxes). In this instance a museum would gain the painting at a bargain price, and the beneficiary would receive more than £65,000. The problem is that museum purchasing grants have been frozen for six years, and the National Heritage Fund and the National Art Collections Fund have limited resources. The Treasury also sets aside a sum of about £12m a year for passing on works of art to the State in lieu of tax. The object can only be set against inheritance tax, not against capital gains tax.

The Commissioners of Inland Revenue exercise their powers under the National Heritage Act 1980, the Inheritance Tax Act 1984 and supplementary Finance Acts. As indicated above, they may accept certain property, in whole or part, in lieu of inheritance taxes (and its predecessors, estate duty and capital transfer tax), and of liability to pay interest on these taxes. However, the National Heritage Secretary has first to agree that the property is 'pre-eminently of national, artistic, historic or scientific interest, or has important historical associations, taking account of its valuation and condition and the benefits of adding it to a national, local authority, or university collection.'

When it receives a relevant offer, the Revenue's Capital Taxes Office refers it to the Museums and Galleries Commission. Once the Commission has taken opinions from independent experts, it advises the Secretary of State whether the property offered is suitable for 'acceptance in lieu'. Qualifying property under these procedures include pictures, books, prints, archives, manuscripts, works of art, furniture, craft objects, historic objects, scientific objects, and other items.

The National Heritage Secretary also has the power to direct the placing of this property, and can permit accepted items to remain *in situ*. In practice, the public has a right to see these items. The Secretary of State receives advice from the Museums and Galleries Commission on the location (both temporary and permanent) of the property. The Royal Commission on Historical Manuscripts advises on the location of records, archives and manuscripts. Chattels accepted in lieu therefore go on public display in museums or galleries, and *in situ* offers must provide for public access.

Under the National Heritage Act 1980, the Secretary of State for National Heritage reimburses the Commissioners of Inland Revenue for the tax forgone. In its accounting, the Revenue treats this payment as tax due. Currently, the annual provision under the in lieu 'vote' is £2m. However, as announced in July 1985 and noted above, the Department of National Heritage and the Revenue can draw sums from the reserves to cover the cost of large, important items.

18.7.5 **VAT**

HM Treasury has produced The Value Added Tax (Works of Art etc) Order 1983 (SI No 809) which exempts from VAT disposals of works of art and other objects (including manuscripts, prints and scientific objects) which are of national, scientific, historic or artistic interest, or which have an historical association with a particular building. To qualify for exemption, these heritage objects have to be disposed of by private individuals in the course of business either as private treaty sales or gifts to one of the approved lists of public galleries and similar institutions or in settlement of tax debts under the *douceur* arrangements. This change is also now incorporated in the Value Added Tax Act 1983, Sched 6.

On 1 January 1986 a new harmonised system of customs duty and temporary importation reliefs came into effect under the Value Added Tax (Temporarily Imported Goods) Relief Order 1986 (SI No 1989). The relevant HM Customs & Excise Notices are 361 and 712. The latter is an information 'package' about the VAT second-hand scheme for works of art, antiques and collectors' pieces (mainly for dealers in fine art and antiques who are VAT-registered). VAT leaflet 701/12/89 gives guidance on 'Sales of antiques, works of art etc from stately homes'. The new regulations apply to works of art brought in primarily for exhibition but later sold. VAT leaflet 701/36/86 also contains guidance on the insurance of second-hand goods such as works of art.

From the beginning of 1995 changes occurred arising from the first stage of implementing the EC Seventh VAT Directive. Further changes followed the Royal Assent to the Finance Act. The measures affect dealers in works of art and antiques. From 1 January 1995, VAT on all these goods has been accounted for on the margin between their buying and selling prices. Details of the new arrangements are explained in HM Customs & Excise VAT Information Sheet 1/95 which supersedes Information Sheet 3/93, dated 1 June 1993. The new arrangements require traders registered for VAT who make supplies of second-hand goods to traders registered for VAT in other member states to submit EC sales lists showing the full net value of any supplies made. Full details appear in HM Customs & Excise Notice 725: *VAT; the Single Market*.

The Finance Act 1995 introduced a 2.5 per cent effective reduced rate of VAT on imports of those works of art and antiques which are currently fully relieved from VAT at importation. Details can be found in HM Customs & Excise Notice 712. The relief previously afforded by Regulation 47 of the VAT (General) Regulations ceased to be available and such importations become subject to VAT at the standard rate. Supplies of goods through auctioneers and agents who act in their own names will be treated for VAT purposes as supplies both to and by them. A special accounting scheme will allow auctioneers who sell works of art and antiques to calculate their VAT on a margin basis. A new VAT Notice 718 gives more detailed guidance on these changes.

The works of art eligible for the margin scheme include:

- Pictures, collages and similar decorative plaques, paintings and drawings, executed entirely by the artist's hand, with some exceptions.
- Original engravings, prints and lithographs produced in limited numbers from plates executed entirely by the artist's hand.
- Original sculptures and statuary in any material, executed entirely by the artist (subject to certain provisos).
- Tapestries and wall textiles made by hand from original designs in limited numbers (not more than eight copies).
- Industrial pieces of ceramics executed entirely by the artist and signed by him.
- Enamels on copper, executed entirely by hand, limited to eight numbered copies, bearing the signature of the artist or studio, with certain exceptions.
- Photographs taken by the artist, printed by him, or under his supervision, signed and numbered, and limited to 30 copies.

Antiques are defined as objects, other than works of art or collectors' items, which are more than 100 years old. See also **19.6.2**.

In October 1995, HM Customs & Excise issued a revised edition of VAT Notice 702 (imports and warehoused goods). It replaced the January 1994 version, and reflected changes from the EC Seventh VAT Directive. These include new ways to value imported and re-imported works of art, antiques and collectors' pieces.

Subsequently, HM Customs and Excise sought views on the procedures that affect people who import their personal assets into the UK. These assets can include valuables, works of art, antiques and collectables. Details of the forms and procedures appear in *Customs Notice 3: Bringing your belongings and private motor vehicles to the UK from outside the EC*. The Department has canvassed views on the unnecessary problems that the procedures can cause, and ways to improve them. Documentation can be onerous when such moves occur. It is worth checking on any changes that emerge from the consultation.

See also **18.3.2** above.

18.7.6 Stamp duty

Stamp duty is normally payable only when the transfer is of an interest in an alternative investment, and not when it is the work itself which is being transferred, since chapels are transferable by delivery and no document is required to effect a transfer of the interest.

18.7.7 PAYE and NI

Regulations are in force to prevent employers avoiding PAYE and national insurance payments by remunerating their staff in kind. These regulations cover gifts of precious metals, fine wines, diamonds, and other assets for which 'trading arrangements' exist that enable employees to swap assets, often for cash.

18.8 MECHANICS

18.8.1 Suitability

Research on individuals' investment preferences indicates that works of fine art and antiques, perhaps not surprisingly, only begin to figure to a significant extent in the portfolios of the wealthy. Initially, investors concentrate on property, building society investments, insurances, unit trusts or investment bonds, and possibly equity investments or gilts or National Savings certificates.

Thus the more esoteric investments tend to be bought when extra capital is available. Neither individuals nor pension funds have so far engaged in the purchase of alternative investments as a routine policy, although the British Rail Pension Fund was, at one time, an exception; the Fund invested approximately £40m in about 2,000 works of art, but its trustees and managers subsequently decided not to make any more purchases in this market.

In November 1988 the BR Pension Fund disposed of 31 museum-worthy pieces of silver for £2m, having paid £400,000 for them ten years previously. In 1989, the Fund sold paintings and sculptures, including works by Manet, Renoir, Monet, Picasso, van Gogh and Cézanne. Altogether the items put on sale realised £38½m, leaving the pensioners with more than £30m after paying all expenses and commissions. In 1990, the Fund sold its collection of 19th century continental 'European art' and Victorian paintings for £6m compared with its mid-1970s purchase price of £1.2m. One of a batch of 16 Old Masters owned by the Fund, which were sold at Sothebys in December 1994, went for £3.4m, compared with a purchase price of around £150,000. The Fund has seen a 14⅓ per cent annual cash rate return and a 6⅔ per cent real rate of return, but later sales have generated lower annual rates of return. (See also **18.3.2**.)

In general, pension fund investment managers see a problem in the marketability of such assets. It is not easy to convert alternative investments into cash at short notice without sustaining losses. In addition, pension fund trustees and investment advisers are cautious about committing themselves to a line of action which might be criticised in the future. Trustees and investment advisers say that it is difficult to obtain accurate valuations on a regular basis and, even when valuers can supply a dependable service, there are few reliable and independent indices on which to compare their portfolio's performance, as they can with equities. There is also a lurking suspicion that funds should not be invested in areas which are regarded as unsuitable for investors who may need income or capital at short notice, and which cannot be readily converted into cash.

On the other hand, the infrastructure for making alternative investments is gradually being established, and in the course of the next few years there may be improvements in the information sources and the indices available to investors and trustees. A well-publicised example is the service provided by London-based art investment managers Poensgen Sokolow. They produce the quarterly Art Market Analysis, and offer portfolios of important works with starting prices of around £10m. The improvement of the information facilities and the build up of reputable sources of impartial market intelligence might eventually help to make such alternative investments attractive, both for individuals and for investment managers with responsibilities for closed funds such as small self-administered pension schemes.

18.8.2 Sources of information

For the moment, the sources of information and intelligence are diverse and scattered. There are, in each of the areas of alternative investment, several specialist journals. In addition, there are various societies or clubs, which give the collector access to specialist knowledge. Auctioneers produce useful catalogues which highlight pieces coming onto the market; and those interested can find out about the prices paid at these sales.

The specialist journals and some of the directories produced by associations of dealers and auctioneers identify the areas in which particular firms are knowledgeable. The dealers will usually charge high commissions to cover their costs of holding expensive assets for periods, which can sometimes be prolonged, before a buyer emerges. Auction sales are, on the whole, a source of more competitively priced items, although many of the leading London firms now charge a commission to both vendors and buyers.

It is, however, becoming more difficult for the private collector to keep pace with developments in his or her chosen fields of alternative investment. Although London remains an important centre of trading activity in art and antiques, many important sales are nowadays being held outside the UK, which has become a net exporter of such pieces. In earlier times, collectors could rely on a steady flow of fine works.

One development which will undoubtably help in the dissemination of information is the Internet, which gives access to art, artists and major museums worldwide. Art and the Internet might seem strange companions. While art is traditionally considered material culture – paintings, sculpture, etc – the Internet is the realm of the immaterial, the virtual, the unreal. But recently there have been exciting artistic developments on the Internet. New Websites featuring gallery tours, excellent computer art reproductions and links to artists are appearing daily. However, this new approach is unlikely to signal the end of art as everyone knows it. Museums will not permanently shut down, and real art will not go out of style. When photography was invented around 160 years ago, some visionaries insisted it was the end of painting. Events proved them wrong. Similarly, the World Wide Web is unlikely to bring 'real' art to its knees. Most of the Websites emphasise that they do not replace art, but rather enhance the enjoyment and understanding of it. Frequent 'surfers' of the Internet will be aware of art-related Websites. For the uninitiated, the Internet can be a threatening place, and it may seem easier to pick up a book than to fight a path through the Web. But many of the really interesting Websites have material not available in books.

For anyone linked to the Net simply wanting to find out what art resources are available, the easiest approach is a keyword search tailored to a specific medium, artist or museum. However, keyword searches often produce lists of possibilities too copious to follow at one sitting. Does one want to visit the Louvre or the Metropolitan Museum of Art or the Smithsonian? It is all possible in a virtual sense. At http://www.metmuseum.org/, the surfer can take a tour of the Metropolitan's collection, with spectacular computer reproductions of its famous artworks. The Web browser can also update himself or herself on the museum's plans, sign up for membership and shop in the museum store. Most museums with rich endowments have sites like this on the Internet.

Websites are advantageous to museums for a number of reasons. First, they are useful advertisements. Viewers can see almost any of the works in the museum's collection, even if the works are in storage. Also, more sensitive objects like drawings and textiles are often hidden away for years for preservation purposes. Through the Internet, visitors can see them without risking damage to the works. Not all Websites correspond to actual museums. There are a number of Internet services that maintain only virtual collections of art. Time Warner's *ArtsLink*, for example, contains an 'Artist in Residence Program', a site that provides selected artists with exhibition space on the Internet. There, the viewer can see artworks and read the artists' biographies and statements. A printmaker, Francis Crisafio, has a home at this site, contactable through Time Warner's home page at http://pathfinder.com/twep.

There is virtually no end to the online resources available on the arts. Only a fraction has been mentioned here. But so as to avoid the intimidation of the sheer abundance available one should start slowly, perhaps by taking a leisurely tour of a favourite museum or completing a key-word search of a popular artist. Then an enquirer can roam around art on the Internet. Another approach is to use CD-ROMs of art directories, featuring artworks and artist information. These services are updated regularly and are available on subscription.

18.8.3 Advisers

In recent years the established London firms have experienced competition in specialised fields from provincial dealers and auctioneers. To keep abreast of news and intelligence on alternative investments today requires a complex web of contacts and information sources. In this context, it is important to locate one or two of the specialists among the dealers and in the auction houses who can be relied upon to assist the dedicated and wealthy enthusiast.

To a degree, investors seeking advice on specific pieces can depend upon appropriate museums or art galleries, where curators are normally willing to give an opinion on the quality and authenticity of a work. Curators are also likely to be familiar with the market and with dealers who specialise in a sector, although they are usually reluctant to recommend a particular firm. Curators do not normally give opinions on market values.

Leading auctioneers are more willing to express a view on the price a piece might command if offered for sale, and specialist dealers also have opinions on the value of an item in their field of expertise. Such valuations are important if the investor plans to make a sale; they will help him or her to arrive at a sensible reserve figure.

Dealers and auctioneers are generally keen to offer help, in particular to itemise and appraise assets. At the outset, their valuers advise on insurance cover and the security of precious items, pending sale. They then prepare a full inventory of the chattels, identify those which are of value and make arrangements for the disposal of the residue. Any gifts or bequests will also be valued for inheritance tax purposes, and recommendations will be made on the handling of any works which have national or historic interest. The experienced auctioneer or dealer also advises on how best to sell items for disposal.

Given that the market for art and antiques has become international, it is important to choose with care a time and a place when specialist collectors are likely to be at a sale. The valuer will charge a fee, and the auctioneer or dealer will be thinking of a commission on sales.

Before confirming instructions for an inventory and appraisal, it is advisable to discuss the eventual consignment contract for an estate which may include important pieces. Some firms in the art and antiques market refund part of their valuation fee if any of the items they appraise are sold through their auction or dealing rooms within a year or so of the appraisal. There may also be opportunities to negotiate lower commission rates on sales. Within the trade, auctioneers and dealers are often prepared to cut their selling commission from 10 to 6 per cent, and there is certainly scope for reductions in standard rates when the estate is large and valuable.

A further point to bear in mind when negotiating commission rates is the possibility that an item at auction may not reach the reserve price suggested by the valuer. In some instances, the auctioneer may be willing to make no charge to the vendor, or levy a reduced commission, if a lot fails to sell at the reserve which the firm has recommended. Auctioneering and dealing in art and antiques are highly competitive businesses and many firms are willing to consider special terms when an estate contains worthwhile items.

For buyers who use the services of dealers there are often the attractions of 'buy-back' offers. These usually have many caveats attached to them. The dealer may undertake to buy back at a price geared to his valuation at the time of the repurchase; or he may only be willing to commit himself to buy back at the original price paid by the investor. Almost no dealer is willing to purchase at the original price plus inflation since the date of the transaction; and, if any do make such an offer, the buyer might well consider it prudent to make such checks as he can that the firm is likely to be still in business at a future date when a resale might be contemplated.

The professionals who advise on alternative investment can also help when it comes to reviewing a portfolio. To offer sound advice, they should be in close touch with the market trends, so that they can recommend optimum times for the disposal of pieces which have reached a current peak in value. Equally, they should be well placed to identify pieces coming onto the market which would make a collection more representative and therefore more valuable in terms of the chosen theme.

18.8.4 Commercial galleries

New collectors may not necessarily understand the more recondite points of aesthetics when collecting art, but they are often keenly aware of the financial implications. They are also conscious of the social benefits of being a part of the collecting 'realm', and the prestige of owning museum-calibre works. In this context, one American dealer offers a useful checklist for those entering the art market for the first time:

- 'Use the expertise of dealer-owned galleries which represent the artists they exhibit. Ask for biographical materials on the artists. Seek advice from individuals in the art industry.
- Let the dealer know which artists are of interest, so that he can send details of exhibits and new works. Probably, the collector will then have early and first-hand information, and a place on a special list for private previews.
- Galleries do not always display all their inventory. It is worth asking to see the 'back rooms', and putting questions to knowledgeable staff.
- Dealers seldom give a 'collector's discount' to occasional buyers. However, in major centres, it is not uncommon for dealers to offer perhaps 10 per cent discounts. Most works are marked up substantially to allow for price negotiations.
- Whenever possible, view a one-person exhibition to see several pieces of an artist's work. This should reveal the depth of an artist's vision and quality of his or her work.
- Take time and advice when making a purchase. Most dealers will hold an item for 24 hours or longer, or offer first refusal.

Commercial galleries normally put on three kinds of exhibition: one-person shows, theme shows, and exhibitions from stock. Galleries tend to show from stock at the quieter times of year. From the standpoint of the exhibitor, the one-person or theme show is the best way to achieve the preferred effect: they allow the gallery to suggest the cultural significance of an artist's work. A few galleries can put on first-class exhibitions from stock because their backroom holdings are strong. They are able to mount exhibitions of acknowledged masters, or works that can reasonably be described as 'museum-quality'.

Some of the galleries and dealers are promoting art and antiques as alternative investments because they believe there are worthwhile opportunities to create and manage portfolios. They contend that the investor can specialise in one or two categories of investment but still spread the risks by diversifying the selection within these categories. In addition, they suggest that it is possible to use market intelligence and research to time purchases and sales to maximum advantage and to build up interest among potential bidders.

18.9 MAINTENANCE

18.9.1 Safeguarding the investment

A prime consideration in the mind of the investor who buys works of fine art or antiques ought to be security. Robbery, accidental damage, fires, floods and other catastrophes remove many works from the market each year, usually forever. Computer systems are now being introduced to log details of missing works such as the Art Loss Register and the New York based International Foundation for Art Research. Their aim is to deter robbers by making details of stolen works quickly available to auction houses, dealers and collectors.

The immediate conclusion is that a purchase should be held safely. For economic reasons, a bank vault may be considered when items are not continuously on display. Even when the items are bulky, the cost of hiring vault space will be far lower than the valuation and subsequent insurance premiums for pieces held in less secure places. In other cases, the collector's pieces should be insured against all risks, and the items in a collection should be revalued at five-yearly intervals, or more frequently, to ensure that the insurance cover is adequate.

18.9.2 Insurance

Brokers and insurers who carry out these valuations with the aid of expert dealers or auctioneers will at the same time advise on cost-effective outlays on security measures, ie expenditures that will bring more than just compensating savings in premiums. The valuers will, in particular cases, photograph pieces in a collection to provide a record in case of damage or loss.

A point to note is that the London head offices of insurers charge travelling and subsistence expenses, so it is usually sensible to contact the nearest regional office. However, if the item is a particularly specialised work of art, a prudent course is to consult fine art brokers. They may advise that it is unnecessary to insure well-known items against theft, giving substantial savings in premiums, on the grounds that any subsequent disposal by the thief in the art market would lead to his capture. For example, in 1994, the gang that removed, in 50 seconds, one of Norway's greatest icons, Edvard Munch's painting *The Scream*, from Oslo's National Gallery, were captured when they tried to sell it to members of the Metropolitan Police's art and antiques unit, who masqueraded as unscrupulous dealers.

By and large, burglars usually avoid stealing such items unless they already have a buyer or can realise the value of precious metal or gemstones from which an antique is made. Most thefts of antiques are opportunistic and involve works of art valued at less than £1,000. Some are planned, either through handlers, or because the thieves mistakenly believe they can convert antiques into cash.

Steps are now being taken to create one global law on stolen goods, which will enable the owners to repatriate their property while the unwilling buyers can seek compensation from the auction houses or dealers that handled the sale. More than 50 nations gathered in Rome in June 1995 to initiate an agreement.

A collector may also wish to put his art or antiques on show. This can present problems. As values rise, it can be difficult to insure valuable exhibits. When the Metropolitan Museum of Art's show 'van Gogh at Arles' was being planned in the early 1980s, it was assigned a global value for insurance of about £1bn. Today it would be £5bn, and the show could never be considered. In the wake of the May 1990 sales, every van Gogh owner wants to believe his painting is worth £50m and will not let it off the wall if insured for less. Even then, the problem is compounded by enthusiastic dealers or auctioneers: when consulted on insurance values, they may be tempted to set the maximum imaginable price on a painting to maintain the image of its market value and tempt the owner to sell.

18.9.3 Security

One of the security measures which is often overlooked is to preserve confidentiality when buying an alternative investment. News of purchases attracts those inclined to steal, a problem also faced by owners who have to allow access to the public to gain the tax exemptions referred to earlier.

In addition to tighter security, it is important with some works of art and antiques to consider the 'ambient' conditions in which a piece is to be displayed. Adverse lighting can, for instance, cause a valuable watercolour to fade, and many items of antique furniture need a suitably humidified atmosphere to survive without deterioration.

Normally, specialists in the field will advise on the best methods of preserving the qualities of a piece. They are also a useful source of information on firms which carry out restoration and repair work to appropriate standards, and on removal firms which have a good record of handling delicate and valuable pieces with due care.

Recovery of stolen works is being helped by improved information sources. The Art Loss Register and the Thesaurus Group's *Tracer* magazine are reinforcing the authorities' efforts to track down lost and purloined items. The Thesaurus Group also offers computerised screening for items registered as stolen against pre-sale catalogues. The registry is also useful for dealers. Artscope International and police intelligence bureaux' hotlines improve the chances of tracing the products of theft and burglary.

18.10 PREVIEW OF THE YEAR AHEAD

18.10.1 Export licences

In March 1997, the Department of National Heritage issued a *Guidance Notice* on export licences for cultural goods such as antiques, works of art and collectors' pieces. This *Notice* makes clear when an export licence is required; it sets out how to apply for a licence, and gives details of how decisions are reached on licence applications. It follows consultation with museums and the art trade in 1996 (referred to above) about what can be included in a fair market price, and attaching conditions to private offers, the treatment of works by living artists. The results of the consultation exercise are as follows.

Fair market price

In addition to the base price, the Reviewing Committee on the Export of Works of Art may allow several additional elements to be included in the recommended fair market price. These elements are:

- the buyer's premium;
- reasonable conservation costs;
- the dealer's commission on a sale to a third party, which will not normally include a commission on a sale to a connected party.

Conditions attached to private offers

The *Notice* set out the revised policy that, if an owner receives an offer to purchase from a private source, he or she is free to accept or reject it. Owners are under no compulsion to sell. However, where an owner does not accept an offer from a private source, Ministers will determine whether to grant the licence. In so doing, they will take an offer into account only where it includes a signed undertaking with a public institution that the owner will:

- guarantee reasonable public access;
- provide satisfactory conservation conditions;
- not sell the object for a specified period.

Treatment of works by living artists

The present export control on works by living artists will remain unchanged. In other words, the National Heritage Department has rejected the advice of the Secretary of State's Reviewing Committee.

18.10.2 Far Eastern interest

Dealers and collectors from the nations of South East Asia have made their presence felt in the auction houses in the last few seasons. There has been a corresponding interest in artwork from the region, a reflection of their booming economies. Korean, Taiwanese and Hong Kong buyers have been particularly active, and mainland Chinese collectors are becoming a force in the market. Their main interest, for the present at least, is in reclaiming their cultural legacy that has been in the possession of Western collectors.

The strong interest shown in works of the South East Asian nations is coupled with the anxieties of wealthy Hong Kong collectors about the change of sovereignty. These factors and the possibility of renewed Japanese interest are likely to ensure the region's continued presence in the market.

18.10.3 Prudence

'Times have changed,' said Franck Giraud, who runs Christie's Impressionist and Modern painting department in New York. 'The players have become more educated, they know what they are looking at and if they don't, they come to these sales armed with professional advice.'

Recently, it has been the private buyer, with a sound knowledge of the determinants of quality and provenance in a specialised niche, who has sustained the market in art and antiques. Collectors can take both pleasure and gain from a work of art, the two forms of appreciation. It also seems possible that ownership of art will seep out of America towards Europe and the Far East. Art management specialists who take on responsibility for high value portfolios are likely to increase in number. In the UK and Europe, governments will continue to regulate the market, inhibiting it in some cases, but ensuring wider access in others, not least through better protection for the consumer.

The last few years have illustrated that if art is a market it is a highly knowledge-intensive one. To make informed judgements, the prospective investor needs expertise or access to it. A connoisseur's intuition, and familiarity with the *patois* of the auction house and dealer, are as vital as knowing what is on sale, where, and when. As the French art expert Jacques Attali recently pointed out, 'nobody is in a position to establish laws for a market as unstable and as irrational as this. Each work of art is singular; each motivation is unique; each transaction has its own requirements'. In the coming years, he says, buyers will become more and more discriminating. The supply of recognised works of art will diminish, but new types will appear on the market. The art market will become 'a kind of avant-garde of museums, a selection process of what may subsequently become part of our collective memory'. It is in keeping with his remarks to add the footnote 'investments can damage one's financial health'.

SOURCES OF FURTHER INFORMATION

See end of Chapter 19.

19

COLLECTABLES

JOHN MYERS AND IAN SOMERVILLE

Solon Associates

19.1 INTRODUCTION

19.1.1 Collectables as alternative investments

Investors in alternatives look for safe havens for their hard-earned funds, but with an eye to pecuniary and gratifying rewards. Collectables, many now believe, can satisfy these objectives. The number of desirable items is small, and values increase whenever the demand for them exceeds the supply. Prices can be low enough for individuals of modest means to choose a field in which they can build collections and become experts. Generally, the marketplace is driven by these individuals, not by investors. Collectables also offer scope for applying ingenuity and imagination; an existing set can be thematic, but then divided and combined with new examples to form a fresh topic.

As David Hirsch pointed out in *Stamps* (4 June 1994) the key to success in investment in collectables is insight. He believes that, if a collector develops the confidence to spot a good buy and act on his or her judgment, he or she should fare well. Hirsch advises against following the flock and merely buying what is popular today. A good collectable should hold its value regardless of fleeting opinions. Collectors should heed advice from experts, but buy only if the case is convincing. For investors *qua* investors the trap is to view the accumulation of holdings as a hobby. A collector 'needs' items to complete a collection. In contrast, an investor 'needs' nothing, and acquires items solely on their merits as investments. Of course, if the purchases can perform double duty as enjoyable collection items, that is a bonus, and a reward in kind if the financial element fails.

In the high reaches of the market for collectables are items that qualify as 'conditionally exempt' pieces. The Inland Revenue publishes a register of these items on the Internet at http:/www.cto.eds.co.uk. A free leaflet, IR 156, *Our heritage – your right to see tax exempt works of art* is also available. The Revenue hopes that the World Wide Web site and the leaflet will improve public awareness of the register and rights to see the objects it lists. On the register are 18,000 entries that cover many items of national, scientific, historic or artistic interest. Among them are works by Leonardo da Vinci, Dürer, Titian, Rubens, Van Dyck, Manet, Monet, and Picasso. British artists represented include Hogarth, Reynolds, Gainsborough, Stubbs, Constable, Turner, Moore and Hepworth. Other entries refer to Chippendale and Adam furniture, silver by de Lamerie, and clocks by Tompion.

Figure 19.1   Items on public view

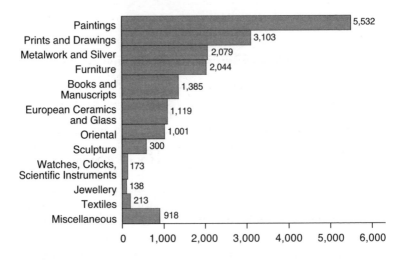

Source: Inland Revenue: items accepted giving exemption from inheritance tax

Objects like books, manuscripts and scientific collections, of national, scientific, historic or artistic interest, can qualify for conditional exemption from inheritance tax. To gain tax exemption, the owner has to agree to keep the object in the UK, preserve it and allow reasonable public access to it. The Revenue will charge inheritance tax when the owner persistently fails to keep the agreement.

To comply with the public access provisions, an owner can allow viewing of the object by appointment and make it available on request to public collections on short-term loans. The object then features on the Revenue's computerised register, updated monthly. It describes each entry, and gives the name and address of a contact point. It also shows the broad location, usually the county, in which each object is normally available for viewing.

Payments for exempt collectables are the high part of a framework for prices in alternative investment markets. Another strut in this framework is the movement in the costs of living extremely well. *Forbes* magazine has measured shifts in these costs, illustrated in Figure 19.2. Wealthy individuals with spare cash are accustomed to rises of up to 14 per cent a year in the desirables they purchase.

Figure 19.2 Cost of living extremely well

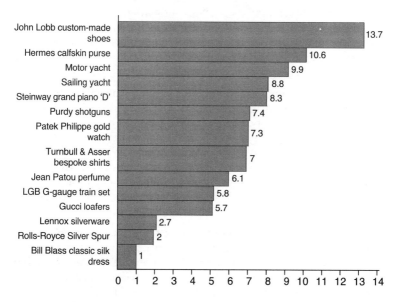

Source: Forbes magazine. Prices estimated from similar products

An investor who buys a desirable piece can be a collector, but a collector is wise not to think of him- or herself as an investor. It may happen that way, but the outcome is fortuitous. Nevertheless, some advisers feel that a significant portion of almost any client's savings for the future should be put into collectables. The argument is that these investments can complement other forms of investment, but not replace them.

The urge to collect has become a smart fashion, and seems to extend to an ever-widening range of items with memorable, nostalgic, or merely eccentric qualities: classic postage stamps, old cars, numismatic coins, Oriental carpets, banknotes, scrips, medals, vintage wines and spirits, musical instruments, playing cards, *objets de vertu*, bric-à-brac, scientific instruments, and printed ephemera, to name but a few. The enthusiasm for collecting such items has stimulated the formation of many bodies, including the Ephemera Society, which was set up in 1975; its membership, of more than 1,800 worldwide, benefits from a lively range of activities and publications.

Despite this evidence of enthusiasm, many investors remain wary of collectables. Caution is, of course, sensible when considering esoteric investment media, but several factors have made them more appealing. Players on the stock markets are constantly aware that equities can be volatile. Every threat of a crash can send shareholders scurrying to spread their risks. In times of uncertainty, collectables can offer a hedge against escalating prices; for many people with catholic tastes, they warrant a small proportion of an investment portfolio.

Collectables in common with art, antiques and valuables can attract wealthy buyers from all quarters of the world. They use their cash or borrowing power to diversify their assets, in the manner of new Renaissance merchant princes. Quality of life is one aim. Another is diversification. The buyer of an alternative investment compares an opportunity to buy a collectable with the risks involved with stocks and shares. When equity markets teeter on the edge of decline, an art deco ornament or a rare musical instrument might hold its value, or perhaps record spectacular gains.

A case in point was one example of a Venini glass vase which, in the 1960s, sold through a department store at £20. Five years ago, at a Geneva sale, a bidder paid 176,000 Swiss francs (£70,000) for it. The glass had original qualities. Valuers had not expected such a high bid; their successive estimates for other Veninis offered for sale proved to be too low. The appraisers recalled that a bidder who had paid £500 for a Venini glass vase in 1978 could not find a buyer to take it off his hands at a higher price. He chose not to sell at the time, and was wise to wait: at an auction in 1984, the same vase fetched £25,000, twelve times the auctioneer's estimate, equal to an annual compound rate of return of 92 per cent. In 1987, another Venini vase attracted a successful bid of £52,000. The pre-sale estimate was less than half that amount. The more recent transaction at £70,000 was also well above the auction house's estimate.

Another case also arose at a Geneva sale of 20th century collectables. French and Japanese dealers bid strongly for a delicately carved glass table lamp. Originally produced commercially by Daum and Louis Majorelle less than a hundred years ago, the lamp went to a Japanese dealer for 1.58m Swiss francs (£675,000). The seller had bought it about 20 years ago for less than £5,000, a compound annual rate of appreciation of 30 per cent.

These glass collectables are perhaps exceptional examples. Illustrations from markets in a wide range of media may give a fairer picture.

19.2 DEVELOPMENTS IN COLLECTABLES' MARKETS

19.2.1 Vintage stock certificates

Collectables with obvious appeal for the alternative investor are vintage stock and bond certificates. Enthusiasts and scripophilists will pay five- or six-figure prices for a rare item, as happened in 1991 when a collector laid out £70,000 for a Bank of England promise-to-pay bill, issued to back loans to the Russian Imperial government. The certificates' value lies in their historic and aesthetic appeal, and in the signatures which appear on them, not their face value. Thus, an 1856 share certificate of the American Express Company, signed by Mr Wells and Mr Fargo and with a nominal value of $500, recently sold for £500.

Certificates from the early industrial revolution are in high demand, particularly those that shipping and railways enterprises issued. Some collectors hold on to pre-Communist bonds from former Eastern bloc countries in the faint hope that the certificates will eventually be redeemable. They recall 1991 when the then Soviet government paid 54 per cent of the face value of devalued bonds. However, the compensation settlement had a time limit. Dealers later received a mass of certificates from owners who missed out, causing a slump in the market for Russian bonds. The trade in vintage bonds from other pre-revolutionary regimes should be an area for speculation.

19.2.2 Rare books

Collectors have amassed books since the times of monasteries and chain libraries. From the Renaissance to the French Revolution, books were popular among readers for what was in them, not for their packaging. By the time Jane Austen's novels were entertaining England, the *nouveau riche* had begun to see books as artefacts that conferred a desired status on their owners. Some buyers began to value the printing and binding more than the content.

The market for collectable books is segmented. One sector is the 'first edition market' – a specialised field. With some works, a book's value may depend as much on the presence and quality of its dust jacket, as on its other qualities. Scott Fitzgerald's *The Great Gatsby*, for example, had a typographical error on the jacket of its first edition, but only on a few copies. With this error, a copy might fetch £3,000; without, a mere £150.

Inscriptions in books by the author or a famous owner, or a relative, or an influential friend of the author, can also enhance values. In 1991, Sotheby's sold a copy of the late Graham Greene's rare first novel, inscribed with a message to his wife, for £13,200. The price was double the previous record for this volume, set a year earlier. In other cases, inscriptions have increased values by even more.

In collectable books, as in other areas of the market, it has been works of the finest quality that have withstood downturns. As noted in Chapter 18, the art market declined in the 1990s. Standard reference works or *catalogues raisonnés*, on the other hand, have experienced little change in demand. These volumes have more than aesthetic appeal, they are in constant demand from art dealers, and can fetch four figure sums at auction. Rare works have also weathered the recession. A successful book sale at Phillips raised more than £500,000, with the main attraction being manuscripts by David Garrick, the eighteenth century theatre luminary. Another generally successful area has been antiquarian textbooks. Christies' sale of the Loughlin collection, of mainly sixteenth to eighteenth century works on mathematics and other sciences, did well for the vendors. The highest price, £280,000, was for a finely bound copy of du Bellay's 1549 *Instructions sur le Fait de la Guerre*.

The advice to collectors of rare books could easily be restated in many other fields of alternative investment: 'Buy the best of what you like. Rely on your own instinct, but work closely with knowledgeable dealers. Develop a collector's eye by looking at a large number of books. Browse in specialist shops. Search out auctions, fairs and even car boot sales.'

One of the latest trends in collectables is the 'hypermoderns', ie books which have been published within the last two decades, or even the last two months. For example, an original copy of John Grisham's *A Time to Kill*, his first mystery, will fetch £500 today: of the 5,000 printed, the publisher destroyed 3,000. Meanwhile, in American hypermodern-speak, the author 'garped', a term used to describe a breakthrough book derived from *The World According to Garp*, the book that made John Irving's mark with critics, readers and collectors.

19.2.3 Numismatic coins

Rare coins have recently been treated almost on a par with the holding of shares and bonds, and some brokers, particularly in the US, have recommended them to their clients as a substitute for stock market investments. The market for coins has been greatly enhanced by a wider acceptance of a grading system. Agreed methods of categorising coins according to their quality help to structure the market for collectors and investors. With this help, enthusiasm for coin collecting is reviving. 'The interest in coin collecting has never been as great since the late 1960s and early 1970s,' according to Mark Rasmussen of Spink, the coin dealers.

The heyday for coin collecting began pre-decimalisation. In the early 1970s, collectors examined coins they received in change to fill date-runs of denominations, which were soon to vanish. The practice became almost a national obsession and, in a decade of high inflation, it became fashionable to put money into collectables, as savings in financial instruments did not pay a real return. The sharpest rise in prices for British historical coins occurred in 1973–1974 when the stock market was collapsing. Although the coin market paused for breath in the first few months of 1974, it then started on a steady upward climb. Five years later prices for English coins had increased on average by 150 per cent. 'Casual' date collectors became numismatists, and began to build sets of historical coins, only to drop out of the market in the late 1970s and early 1980s. Rare coins of quality became too costly to collect.

Before the end of the 1970s, two interrelated factors had caused prices to rise further. Investment buying in the US gained impetus when buyers could invest in collectables, via retirement plans, and receive tax relief on their purchases. The Reagan administration cut out this concession in 1980. Booming bullion prices also helped. In January 1980, silver peaked at $52.50 and gold at $835 an ounce. Many coin dealers trade in bullion as an adjunct to their main businesses. The profits they were generating from this activity were substantial. As coin markets were buoyant, they channelled money into their coin dealing operations. The price for US historical coins rose sharply until, inevitably, the bubble burst; in the first half of 1983 prices fell. Those who had purchased coins as an investment were disillusioned, while many genuine numismatists had long since stopped adding to their collections. The specimens they sought were financially out of reach.

The most important determinant of value is a coin's condition, within a range from mint state to poor. An uncirculated 1887 silver crown bearing the Jubilee portrait of Queen Victoria would sell for around £60. However, a coin with signs of wear on its raised surfaces would be worth only £10 and, in a poor state, £2–3. Coins are not an investment. When money gain hopes outweigh the interest in coins for their own sake, problems are likely.

Coins can tell enchanting stories and reveal a nation's history. One enthusiast reminds audiences that coin collecting is the oldest collecting hobby, traceable to the invention of coinage in the seventh century BC. He comments: 'Most people are drawn into the hobby for a variety of reasons. Pride of ownership and desire to expand or complete a collection once it is started are sufficient for many collectors. The profit motive is another prime incentive for collecting coins. Others enjoy their coin collections because they have an interest in art, history, geography or science.'

Keen players would like coins to become respectable as the basis for investment funds they are setting up. A typical institutional scheme requires an initial tranche of capital, say £50m, to fund dealing in collectable coins. The strategy is to acquire enough coins which will appreciate over a short enough period to generate worthwhile returns for the investor. A key question is how to calculate 'worthwhile'. Some coins will gain in value, others will lose. Whatever happens, the fund has to meet its overheads, which include regular valuation of its portfolio. One analyst estimates that sets of coins need to appreciate, on average, by more than 40 per cent to give investors a 20 per cent return. In the case of one such fund, the promoter's filings with the US Securities and Exchange Commission claim that similar types of investment have previously achieved returns of this figure or more.

The promise of success is echoed in fresh price records at coin auctions. Not long ago, a Wall Street investment fund paid £600,000 for an 1804 US silver dollar, a record at the time for a coin sold at an auction. The coin was one of only 15 known examples. The earlier record price paid for a coin was for an American doubloon, dating from 1793, sold in 1979 for £250,000. Rare coins have a long-established market among collectables, but with rarity goes a high premium. A 1982 gold coin issued when British Forces relieved the Falkland Islands sold for £2,200. It was in mint condition and one of only 25 struck. At a Christie's sale, an 1890 halfpenny sold for £1,380. This ordinary halfpenny is stamped with the word 'Oakley' on its obverse and is deformed by a bullet shot. Apparently, Annie Oakley, the great American sharpshooter, used to shoot coins thrown up in the air. These were then stamped with 'Oakley' and given to the audience.

Over the last two years the rare coin market has also attracted a share of the controversy caused by aggressive selling practices. Some dealers in the US have sought to encourage investment in coins by establishing certifiable grades of quality. Associated with this is the practice of 'slabbing'. Coins graded by one of two grading houses, the Numismatic Guarantee Corporation or the Professional Coin Grading Service, are sealed in plastic 'slabs'. However, the market in slabbed coins is not strong and, in at least one case, the Federal Trade Commission has challenged the objectivity and consistency of the grading.

Certification of quality, if performed consistently, could show pointers to how the market in collectables might develop. Through the American Numismatic Exchange some coin dealers have sought to create their own version of the modern stock market. The Exchange enables dealers to trade over a computer network. Investors can buy and sell as they wish through the network, without having to wait for auctions and sales.

Critics argue that coins are not equities, they are 'limited edition objects', so values tend to be set on a subjective basis. Nor, they argue, are coins liquid assets. Investors should allow for delays in finding a buyer who will pay the 'right price' for a rare coin.

Advocates of the coin bourse claim that it has helped to stabilise a volatile market. In theory, if such a bourse develops, it might trade in coin futures and coin options. Equally, it could conceivably extend its remit into other alternative investments. Syndicates and funds could be set up to trade in certificates backed by physical assets, hedged on the Exchange. An information infrastructure could follow, as the traders and investors seek better intelligence on the fundamentals and technical performance of particular assets. These ideas may seem far-fetched but informal coffee-house trading years ago in the City led to the spectacular and speculative commodity, insurance and shipping markets of today. At the time, it seemed an equally unlikely proposition.

Interest is already rising in the new *Euro* coin. Europe's Mint Directors issued a report in November 1996; they covered issues such as the face value, the images, diameter, thickness, weight, colour, composition, edge and shape of the coins. Work is still in progress on edge lettering and latent image, storage and distribution, collector coins and precious metal bullion coins, including a new heptagonal coin. The European Commission has set up a design competition and appointed a jury. In May 1997, the EU Council plans to choose a design in the light of the jury's views, public consultation and the experts' proposals.

19.2.4 Phonecards and trading cards

Printing cards at times seems like printing money. They are 'instant collectables', fancy goods mass-produced for a few pence and retailed to collectors at premium prices. Nowadays, the main market is cards: plastic telephone cards; glossy trading cards; and even cards that reproduce works by international artists. They satisfy the basic requirements of popular collectables: they are small, easily stored, easily displayed, issued in sets, and durable. Instead of limiting editions by setting a closing date for orders (really just a feeble justification for using the term 'limited edition'), card-makers strictly control editions by stated numbers, deliberately creating scarcity and boosting resale value among collectors.

Private publishers of telephone cards have developed an instinct for alluring commemoratives, and are becoming as responsive as the brasher trading cards to the latest comic book, film and television crazes. Even BT itself has promoted similar issues, featuring Pink Floyd for example. Worldwide, telephone cards are today's fastest-growing collectable, with more than four million collectors worldwide. Japan's 1.3 million telephone-card collectors now outnumber its stamp collectors. The Germans, with one million collectors, are Europe's keenest. France has 800,000 and Britain 75,000, of whom two-thirds are reckoned to be children.

In Britain, prices for limited-edition telephone cards are rising steadily. A set of two privately printed BT cards of Garfield, the strip cartoon cat, is worth £150 if unused. When the 20-unit cards were issued only three years ago, mainly to collectors, each of the 482 sets (a few of the 500 made were scrunched in manufacture) carried the premium price of £11. They would buy £2 worth of telephone time. Most of the balance is profit for the publisher. So the pioneering anorak-toting collector-publishers have found themselves alongside promoters of commercial products, charities, sports teams, schools and regiments, all keen to coin their own currency.

Promoters have accounted for about 20 new cards a month through BT and its manufacturer. BT charges £2.16 each for a minimum permitted order of 1,000 five-unit promotional cards. For a time, Britain's most valuable privately published telephone card was a money-spinner for members of the Messerschmitt Owners' Club. The club published 500 five-unit BT cards (50p worth of telephone time) at £11 each. Club members bought 300, collectors the rest. Three years later, they are worth £150 each unused. One of Britain's biggest telephone card dealers, Kevin Baker of Spalding, Lincolnshire, published 1,000 sets of three five-unit cards for a Romanian relief charity. They cost him £7 a set to produce and sold for £15, of which a proportion went to the charity. These cards are now worth £35–40 a set. Kevin Baker believes: 'Because of the rapid development of the hobby, there isn't a single card in existence that is not going to go up in value. As more card phones are installed, production runs are bound to increase, but there will always be a finite number of early editions as small as 500.'

Major companies have less interest in limited editions than in mass advertising. Kellogg's issued three million 20-unit advertising cards two years ago. So far, they are not worth much more than their £2 face value. However, 5,000 Coca-Cola advertising cards in a 1993 Icelandic edition, micro-chipped for exclusive use on trawlers, are worth £30 a card to collectors. A card with a captive clientele is BT's own 20-unit 'For use in HM prisons only'. Outside the prisons, they sell for a mere 25p in used condition. Unused ones could be worth £8–10. BT's current 20-unit *Beano SOS* cards, to enable children to call home, cost £2 each new. America now has its first set of erotic telephone cards, with antique Oriental paintings of copulation. Non-erotic BT took an airbrush to its 1993 artwork for Sloggi bras: the £10 card is worth £15 today.

World-record prices for cards, both ancient and modern, have little to do with the smartness of publishers and everything to do with the age-old combination of rarity pursued by wealth. One of BT's trio of first-ever commemoratives, a 900-strong edition of 100-units for the 1987 Muirfield golf championship, is now worth £2,500 unused. A unique used and battered Taiwanese definitive (standard-issue) telephone card of 1983 was recently bought by a Japanese collector for £28,000. The most expensive card, bought for $451,000 (£250,000) at Sotheby's New York five years ago, is an American card for Piedmont cigarettes of 1910, showing the baseball ace Honus Wagner. A non-smoker, Wagner forced Piedmont to withdraw the card, but this one survives.

19.2.5 Collectable cars

Classic cars have a more limited appeal, but remain cosmopolitan. A Porsche 959, a Ferrari F40 super car, or the Bugatti Royale may attract bidders from almost any part of the developed world. Their chances of gain have been considerable, as are the prospects of losing money. Within a single year, 1988–89, the price of some Aston Martin DB6s rose tenfold, from £10,000 to £100,000. Prices then fell, however, and eventually moderated to a lower 'realistic' level, at least 50 per cent below the peak figure.

The frenetic activity in the market sprang, to some extent, from wealthy, middle-aged enthusiasts, nostalgic for their youth. Foreign buyers also stoked the price furnace. These buyers have not disappeared, although ageing Rolls-Royces and Bentleys still glut the market. Fondness for the highly charged sports car is undiminished, and the old Ferraris, Jaguars, Maseratis and MGs continue to command high, but not hyped, prices. Old cars with character, the Volkswagen Beetle, the Morris Minor, the Mini-Cooper, are attracting a new generation of enthusiasts willing to pay around £5,000 for a model in good condition.

Buyers of classic cars are encouraged to drive them. Unless it is a museum-quality machine, an ageing vehicle could benefit by being fired up to full running temperature on a regular basis. If it costs too much to insure the car for the road, the buyer is advised to change the oil periodically, to jack up the car to protect the suspension, and take other steps, such as dehumidifying the garage, to prevent deterioration. According to claimed, if not acclaimed, experts, the trick is to pick the few vehicles, or to find a whole new class of collectables, that will increase in value. Some specialists believe that old vehicles can offer investment possibilities. Collector cars can be worth five- and six-figure sums. However, experts say that few vehicles are legitimate investments that will serve as a hedge against inflation. A noted collector of Rolls-Royce *Silver Ghosts* cautions against overweening faith in rarity. He insists that it is no more than an enthusiast's market.

The cost and relative scarcity of even the finest US models may put them out of reach for many car collectors. Generally, values have stayed high but almost flat for several years North American magazines such as *Cars and Parts* and *Old Cars Price Guide* can help collectors follow the changes in US collectable vehicle prices. *Cars and Parts* publishes graphs every month that show the change in collector car prices, while *Old Cars Price Guide* gives prices for thousands of vehicles, based on condition. Advisers recommend that prospective buyers check the *Guide* before making a purchase, and call in an appraiser. Such moves can help a buyer to avoid over-paying.

19.2.6 Collectable wines and spirits

Some French wines, for example fine vintages of Latour, have recorded an average annual appreciation of around 20 per cent in the past 15 years. At the recent sale of the late Robert Maxwell's collection, a dozen bottles of Latour 1982 sold for £800. Bidders paid around 20 per cent above the estimate, perhaps attracted by the notoriety of the cellar's previous owner. Andrew Lloyd-Webber's cellar, comprising 18,000 bottles, fetched £3¾m, that is more than £200 per bottle, when it was sold at auction by Sotheby's in May 1997. Serena Sutcliffe, head of Sotheby's international wine department, reportedly said on seeing the collection: 'If Bacchus had a cellar, this would be it. In terms of quality, choice and quantity, it represents the wine lover's dream.'.

Some specialists believe that wines can be restored. In one cited instance, a buyer paid £425 for a double magnum of 1865 Château Lafite in 1967. Fourteen years later the buyer took the bottles back to the chateau to have them topped up and new corks inserted. Sold at auction after a few months, the wine reached £12,000 per double magnum – that is, 25 per cent a year compound. The same connoisseur believed its value in mid-1990 would be about £48,500.

A sale of whisky fetched £98,000, including 14 bottles from the SS Politician, the ship which inspired the film classic 'Whisky Galore'. The bottles sold for £11,000.

19.2.7 Photographs

Photographic images do not come into existence primarily for exhibition and sale. Some, however, are so imaginative that they transcend the original purpose and make a photographer 'collectable'. There are two main kinds of collectable image: the 'vintage print' made for a magazine or other user at the time it was taken, sometimes marked up for publication; and modern prints made for sale or exhibition from the old negative, created with special care on fine paper and under the supervision of the photographer, who then signs the print. The Photographers Gallery in London specialises in the latter. In the gallery's early days, when it sold prints from its current exhibition displayed on a trestle table, a buyer could pick up a Bill Brandt for £50. Brandt made his name as a magazine photographer in Britain in the 1930s, famously recorded the devastation of London during the Blitz, and continued to capture historic images up to his death in 1983. Today the Gallery Print Room sells Brandt prints for between £900 and £3,000.

The cost of fine photographs no doubt discourages buyers; after all, the same image can often be snipped from books or magazines for a fraction of the cost. Nevertheless, top quality prints signed by photographers of the *Picture Post* era, for which prices start around £200, are among the Photographers Gallery's best sellers. Nostalgia is definitely 'in' with collectors. The amazing images of New York taken in 1926, just before the Wall Street crash, by Fred Zimmermann, the Hollywood film director (of 'High Noon', 'Oklahoma!'), sell for £325–600. In an attempt to attract new collectors the gallery has now introduced a plan for collectors called 'Prime Prints'. With every contemporary show it asks the photographer to prepare an edition of 50 prints of one successful image, which are marketed at £150 each. There is also a 'Patron Print Scheme' by which anyone signing up as a patron (which costs £200 and includes discounts, free publications and invitations to social events) receives one print free from a set of six specially made for the gallery by leading photographers.

By the end of the century beautifully printed photographs are likely to become a more prominent form of art exhibit, and the number of collectors in Britain will probably grow steadily. The UK has fallen behind North America. For example, New York has 32 galleries that are members of the Association of International Photography Art Dealers. Los Angeles, San Francisco, Chicago and Dallas have a dozen, but Britain only four. British members of the Photography Art Dealers' association are the Photographers' Gallery, Zelda Cheatle, Hamilton's, and Robert Herschkowitz. All sell more abroad than they do in the home market but maybe that will change, as the collecting of photographs gains in popularity.

19.2.8 Fishing tackle

The passion for collecting old fishing tackle is not confined to those countries in which angling is a prevalent sport. Buyers from around the world can drive up prices. Nonetheless, apart from some old reels, costs to collectors of entering the market for antique and old tackle are not generally prohibitive. For example, fishing rods remain at relatively low prices because they are hard to display, take up space, and buyers want to handle them. They also deteriorate, and older rods should not be used much, if at all.

Other fishing accessories are also highly collectable, particularly those which are not made today. Leather fishing creels, some of them as old as 250 years, are highly prized and are rare, as is the Layman Pneumatic Boat, an inflatable rubber tube which was secured around the angler's waist and enabled him to paddle about in deep water instead of using a boat. Today these bizarre objects have made a comeback in the US, where they are known as belly-boats. Other collectable objects are gaffs, particularly the 19th century models with telescopic brass handles, or handles of turned wood. And of course fly boxes, flies, guts, floats, lines, line-winders and driers, fly-wallets and reel cases of leather.

Fishing lures have also become popular with collectors. One keen angler comments: 'In the past five years, the number of people collecting lures has increased dramatically. People are beginning to collect for many different reasons, so the numbers are increasing.' The increase has stimulated the growth of an international organization, the National Fishing Lure Collection Club, with 4,000 members in seven countries. They are usually sportsmen who like to keep alive a part of history.

Connoisseurs among fishermen want their collections to include old lure boxes and other fishing memorabilia that preserve history. High-priced fishing tackle for collectors includes American lures that are both old and rare, like the Haskell Minnow made in Plainesville back in 1864. The best collectables look as if they are just out of the box. Enthusiasts prowl flea markets, antique shops and car boot sales to find rare items. In the US, the venerated and the venerable include a Heddon Vamp and an Arbogast Tin Liz, and collectors pursue sales in an area that covers Michigan to New York, and parts of Ohio within reach of the Canadian lakes. These anglers relied on spoons, spinners and plugs to catch fish in the wilderness north of the border.

Once a collector has built a reputation, and starts to display antique fishing lures at shows, he or she will receive calls from those in the know when they find a lure of possible interest. Of course, some who call have also begun collecting lures, enhancing values but increasing the competition for the best finds. American fishing tackle is attracting widespread interest. In 1978, the Fishing Lure Collectors' Club had about 60 members. It now has more than 7,000 members, and collectors from England and Japan attended last year's annual show in Little Rock, Arkansas. The next American lure show is in Dayton, 31 July 1997.

Collectors are generally keen anglers, but they also amass a large inventory of fishing gear, reel by reel, rod by rod, lure by lure. Typically, they segregate their purchases in hundreds of small wooden drawers, and display antique reels of unusual design in handsome glass cases. Twenty years ago, when today's leading collectors began their assemblies, virtually no-one bought collectable fishing gear. Now, lures routinely sell for £50–100, and the price of a reel can run as high as £1,250. Yet collecting is not about money or rarities; it is about dreams, about private museums that enthusiasts develop as they learn about the field. To improve their understanding, they study books and magazines, investigate the marketplace, attend events, and contact other collectors. Usually, they find it prudent to limit their interest. 'No one can possibly become knowledgeable about a very broad variety of collectables,' say the experts, 'and the risk is that the buyer ends up with junk; they pay cash for trash!'

Equally in this market, as in others, it is wise to avoid letting the marketplace dictate what to collect. Anyone can enjoy the thrill of buying low and selling high, but playing the collectables market is a reliable way to lose money. Sound advice is to join a collecting society before buying anything. Most such bodies publish newsletters and rosters of members with interests in common. These members usually know the reputable dealers and where they are, and can help to vet a purchase. Another judicious step is to attend specialist auctions. These events are often a good way to meet people who are knowledgeable, and to sharpen a collecting instinct. Cataloguing a collection is also sensible, even from the very beginning, after a few purchases. The records help to keep track of prices and sources. Insurance is another necessity to protect the investment, and most insurance companies demand a catalogue before they will issue a policy.

Fishing tackle can be relatively inexpensive compared with other areas of collecting, with one exception – angling art. Sporting art, and particularly angling art, has risen substantially in price in a few decades. Angling paintings show locations with an intrinsic charm; rivers, streams and still lakes of rustic tranquillity. Waterside angling, however, can seem less dramatic than hunting and shooting, where artists can capture electrifying moments. Fine angling artists whose works today command good prices include John Raphael Smith, Francis Barlow, Henry Alken, James Pollard, Ansdell, Hardie, Barrington-Browne, Rolfe, Rowlandson, and Walker. Some famous artists also executed many paintings with an angling theme, most notably Turner, but also Zoffany, Dadd and Cruikshank.

19.2.9 **Stamps**

For as long as stamps have served as a government license to post a letter, philately has been popular. with many devotees touring events around the country and abroad in a hunt for a rare find. Granted, Rowland Hill might not have imagined that, almost 160 years after he had the Penny Black printed, so many stamps would be issued worldwide each year. Earlier collectors had less difficulty in forming a basic international collection that reflected their interests. They have in common a curiosity about a time, place or a person that motivated them to collect stamps with a historical ambience. In these early days, philatelists collected stamps of particular periods or countries, of postal types such as airmails, postage dues and express mail stamps. With many early stamps now expensive, and a burgeoning of new issues from virtually every country, few can expect to create a comprehensive set. Collectors are therefore turning to thematic collecting – collecting stamps that illustrate a given topic, independent of time and place.

Thematic philately attracts many new collectors, who find it absorbing if not cost-free. A true thematic collection, whatever the topic, combines frustration, impatience, and eventual elation, when the components, like a puzzle, come together to illustrate a novel theme, and form a whole. Thematic collectors must think imaginatively, and show how apparently disparate items interrelate.

The topical approach has not long enjoyed respectability among serious philatelists. Of course, they now have a wider choice of themes: the beasts of the fields, the birds of the air, the fish of the sea, the people who possess fame and fortune, endorsed by provenance. One US collector has a franked Martin Luther King stamp, issued 1979, and has added to its value by persuading all the members of the King family to autograph the envelope. He also owns a stamp that shows the legendary jazz musician and composer Duke Ellington, first issued by the US Postal Service in 1986. Alongside the stamp are the autographs of all the members of his band.

Many countries no longer conform to the tradition that only people who are dead should appear on stamps. Postal authorities around the world have been eager to put stamps on sale featuring stars while people still remember them. Britain and the United States, however, retain the convention. British stamps depict no living person other than a member of the Royal Family. The literature of topical or thematic stamp collecting is also growing. The American Topical Association produces *Topical Time*. In Britain, Stanley Gibbons has several popular thematic catalogues. The British Thematic Association has the *Themescene* magazine and supports the yearly Thematica exhibition in London. Attendees include dedicated philatelists willing to research every item and write up the design of each stamp for an exhibition or a competition.

For research purposes, collectors often have many reference books, catalogues and magazines. They collect not only stamps, but envelopes, covers, post and meter marks, and stamped postcards. In the Internet era, stamp collecting is changing its image. Philatelists are moving into the computer age, and, to promote interest among young technocrats, the Royal Mail, alongside the British Philatelic Trust and the Philatelic Traders Society, has launched the Rowland Hill Awards.

The millennium will provide a spur to the producers and the connoisseurs of fine stamps. Plans are in hand for a large international exhibition in Britain in 2000. Also, new technology can help. 'CompuServe provides free demonstration disks and literature at our Stampex exhibitions. New technology such as e-mail won't threaten stamp collecting, as letters and e-mail seem to run in tandem. Also, many collectors buy new issues anyway. The Internet and CD-Roms will actually help,' according to Lindsay Towle of the Philatelic Traders Society.

Philatelic Software is a London-based firm which has launched StampMaster GB, costing £74.95. It is a CD-Rom database of all stamps issued by the British Post Office from 1840 to the end of 1995, with pictures and the official National Postal Museum history and description of each stamp. 'The system will help users to build catalogues of their own collections and work out which stamps they need to complete them,' says Angela Enoch for the firm. 'It can also be used with thematic collecting, as can our systems for dinosaur and ball sport stamp collections.'

Admittedly, stamps are not a standard item in portfolios. Like many alternative investments, they are risky and illiquid, and prudent advisers counsel stamp collectors never to rely on hard cash from their hobby. Yet returns can be worthwhile. In November 1996, for example, a rare stamp, an 1855 Yellow Treskilling from Sweden, sold for £1$\frac{1}{2}$m, a record price. That was £0.6m more than when it was on sale in 1990. Not long ago, an 1854 Bermuda cover – a stamp still on an envelope – sold for £230,000. In 1980, it went for £144,000.

'Globally, the stamp market is faring well, especially in Hong Kong and China,' said Robert Scott of Sotheby's stamp department. One reason for the steady rise is the influx of an aging generation into the pastime; another is the relative strength of the US and UK economies. 'A great many 40- to 50-year-olds who had stamp albums as kids are revisiting the hobby,' said Michael Laurence, the editor and publisher of *Linn's Stamp News*. According to the US Postal Service, about 20 million Americans keep stamps in sets. About 550,000 are serious collectors, who carefully research stamps and slowly build collections.

Price upswings now depend on collectors, in marked contrast with an artificial boom between 1979 and 1981, when investors fleeing high inflation pressed into the market. Prices soared. Then, in 1981, a new US federal law barred the inclusion of stamps and other tangible collectables in tax-deferred retirement accounts; they were thought too risky and difficult to value. With that change and a lessening of inflation, the market collapsed. By the end of 1991, the prices of American stamps had gone down by 56 per cent from their 1981 highs. Nonetheless, like gold, coins and other collectables, stamps can move out of phase with stocks and other financial instruments, and can help to hedge against losses in those assets.

Some people also like stamps for other reasons, including their portability. A person can put them in a pocket 'and cross a border with no questions asked,' one dealer emphasised. Profits from stamps can also be difficult for the Inland Revenue authorities to detect. Scott of Sotheby's stated that stamp collectors can enjoy 'a great deal of anonymity', a claim once made by tax haven banks. However, the required knowledge is a hurdle in the way of profit. The philatelist has to learn about individual stamps and postal history. Details such as the cancellation or the stamp gum can affect values. High markups are a factor too. 'People in the stock market pay a commission of 2 or 3 per cent on a buy-sell transaction,' one dealer revealed. 'In stamps, it can be 100 per cent or more. That's expensive, and it means you've got to hold for many years to cover the dealer charges.' Add the dangers of fraud and the illiquidity of this small market, and even a risk-prone investor might hesitate.

Defects can sharply increase a stamp's price. That Swedish Treskilling, for instance, was worth £1$\frac{1}{2}$m because it was wrongly printed in yellow, not the issue's standard green. In 1996, 32 cent Richard Nixon stamps had the former president's name printed upside down and his picture off-centre. One sold at Christie's for £10,000. The odds against such a find are long, but the collector will find the endeavour instructive.

19.2.10 Dolls and other pieces

For some collectors on the acquisitive trail, doll collecting is now preferred to coin and stamp collecting and, for a few, it has become an addiction. Specialist dealers see customers who come every week to see what new dolls have come on the market. At times, visits take on an air of secrecy. 'They may not all have spouses who condone their purchases,' a trader said. Another mentioned a customer who hides doll purchases under her bed until she can ease them into her collection. A few buy only with cash, so the sale will not show up on a credit card statement. In time, their collections reach a size where the family has to move to a larger house simply to accommodate the dolls.

Bought as an investment, dolls (other than antique dolls) are most valuable when in NRFB condition. Translated, that means 'Never Removed

From Box'. These dolls are meant to be kept in storage or posed prettily on a shelf, according to collectors. Their value has multiplied. Rare, mint-condition Barbies, for example, which sold for perhaps $2 when they were introduced in 1959, are valued at more than $1,000 today, according to American dealers.

Barbie, who made her debut in 1958, is rapidly approaching middle age, but she will queens collectables. The rarest Barbie dolls, so advisers believe, could be in demand among new century collectors, a view not limited to Barbies, or even to dolls. In 1996, a bidder paid £34,500 at auction for a puppet from the *Thunderbirds* science fiction series, the original Lady Penelope. In 1997, Levi Strauss paid $25,000 for an 1886 pair of jeans originally priced at $1.25, equivalent to annual compound interest of 10 per cent. Dealers and auction houses that promote this trade suggest that ephemeral products and packages could become collectors' 'desirables' in the twenty-first century, if they survive in their original condition. They might be worth more with the makers' signatures added.

Men sometimes enter this world of dolls, because their wives are doll collectors. Don Jensen, associate editor of *Doll News*, the quarterly magazine of the United Federation of Doll Clubs, is a doll collector and active member of the Lake County Doll Club of Illinois. He and his wife, Arlene, spread dolls through every room in their home, and display many in a floor-to-ceiling glassed cabinet that stretches over one full wall in one room of their house. Jensen was drawn into the hobby partly because of his wife's interest in dolls, and partly because of their shared pleasure in antiques.

In the US, any black doll is collectable, and nun dolls, which have appeal for certain collectors, come in at least 50 different habits. According to the experts, genuine antique dolls are better off left in the condition in which they were discovered.

Apart from dolls, the real gamblers bought the first national lottery scratch cards, but keep them in mint condition and unscratched. In 50 years, they could be worth more to the buyer, or his or her heirs, than the chances of a money prize plus interest. Less speculatively, museum and gallery shops trade in distinctive designs that promise to become tomorrow's antiques; and hoarders seize on children's books and toys, which they keep away from their offspring. The odds are that products handled by the young will not retain the untouched look and value of a fresh heirloom.

Some connoisseurs are confident that the largest demand in the next millennium will be for early technology and craft products. They are buying primitive calculators, contemporary packaging, and fine musical instruments. One antique dealer in the Cumbrian lakes is assembling a collection of high quality Steinway grand pianos, built from 1930 onwards and, in at least one instance, rebuilt by an expert. The dealer is confident that the pianos will appreciate hugely in value over the years. Another expert predicts that 'an early Sinclair adding machine costing £10 in 1996 could be worth £250 by 2006'. If he proves right, the rise in price would equal a 38 per cent annual compound rate of interest. Yet one more forecast is that a well-designed 1970s hi-fi stack, which a collector might pay £15 for at a car boot sale today, could sell for £1,500 by 2017, that is a 26 per cent a year compound rise in value.

19.2.11 Silver

Antique silver has already risen in value. For example, in America a pair of delicate eighteenth century wine coasters, estimated to be worth about $125,000 (£80,000) recently went to a private collector who paid $299,500 (£190,000). Fine old Tiffany silver is also popular. In the years after the American Civil War, Tiffany used mixed metals consisting of silver, copper and brass in crafting Japanesque pitchers, vases and trays, bizarrely engraved and encrusted with an assortment of reptiles, crustaceans and insect life. Europeans bought them at the 1876 Paris Exposition, and they have become valuable. A fine piece, bought for $1,000 (£625) or less in the 1970s, might easily be worth $25,000 (£15,500) today, up 17 per cent compound a year.

Buying silver also creates a need to keep it in good order. Cleaning sterling silver may be as simple as washing it with a little soap and water, then drying and buffing it with a suitable soft cloth. Professionals recommend buffing and polishing silver in the same direction as the manufacturer did. A magnifying glass will reveal the factory's polishing marks. Alternatively, a good way is to apply a jeweller's paste, liquid or foam. 'The art,' say antiques dealers, 'is using a polish that's relatively mild and a cloth that's very soft.' Cloths impregnated with polish can also be effective; but it is wise to avoid using the same cloth on more than one piece, because the residue from one will rub off on the next.

Stored silver is best kept behind glass, in flannel bags or in bags made from soft cloth, or wrapped in acid-free paper in acid-free, paper-lined drawers. It is imprudent to let rubber bands or plastic bags touch the collection: silver can be irrevocably harmed by contact with petroleum-based products, and plastic bags can do double damage by trapping moisture. Another golden rule of silver upkeep advocated by expert dealers is to bring it out of storage from time to time: 'The more you use it, the less frequently you have to polish it.'

19.2.12 **Prices for collectables**

Collectables generally escaped the worst effects of the recession in the arts and antiques market. However, prices did fall. Now, optimists and dealers see signs of recovery in trade buying, and highlight successful sales at which collectors paid spectacular prices. Nonetheless, these were exceptions. Watches, a favourite several years ago, have had variable results, and pop memorabilia have attracted less attention, with the exception of a recording by the late Beatle, John Lennon, singing with his first band, the Quarrymen, which sold for £78,500. On the other hand, rare books and coins, toys, glassware, ceramics, jewellery, basketball cards and Hollywood posters have continued to sustain interest, and rarity almost always excites bidders. In November 1996, a poster for the 1942 film, *Casablanca* sold at auction for £23,000, almost double the estimated price. In general, opulence, intricacy, ethnicity, authenticity, and the bizarre are likely to attract buyers.

Perfume bottles, biscuit tins, slot machines, costumes, dolls and typewriters are items cherished as never before. In the US, memorabilia related to slavery and American historical manuscripts have become favourites. Eighteenth century costumes are particularly sought after by both private buyers and museums. A hoard of Old Masterprints found inside a trunk that was home to a family of mice sold at Sotheby's for £587,952, more than twice their estimate.

Unusual early film posters have become highly collectable, and private deal prices in the US have reached £68,000, a threefold increase in three years. Dealers predict that unique posters will fetch $250,000 (£155,000) when released onto the open market. Hitherto, for British collectors, posters have meant Kitchener pointing, Toulouse-Lautrec, and British Railways. Also, paperweights have continued to climb in value during a period in which the value of other items has stagnated. A record $258,000 (£160,000) was paid at auction for a rare Clichy magnum basket weight. The market has been strong, with buyers attracted by artistry, craftsmanship and colours, much as with paintings.

Packaging has become another popular collectable item, and recent sales have featured biscuit tins produced from the 1870s to the 1930s, when British tin was popular. Shaped tins are the most prized. The best examples fetch more than £100 at auction. One, in the shape of an ocean liner, recently went for £880.

19.3 FUTURE DEVELOPMENTS

19.3.1 Potential areas for investment

Along with the recovery of property values in London, interest has revived at the top end of the classic car market. Quality vintage Edwardian and veteran cars may now increase in value from a reduced level. Apart from cars, collectors are currently displaying an interest in photographic equipment. An early Leica, with its mystique of Henri Cartier-Bresson, André Kertesz and 1920s Paris, may be worth thousands in mint condition. Even the humble box camera, the 'ordinary' Kodak which sold for £3 in the 1890s, can fetch £1,200 today.

Other collectables that *Antiques Roadshow* valuers favour include dolls, toys and the memorabilia of the early cinema. Dolls could fetch from £10 to £150,000; a 1939 German triplate Mickey Mouse £12,000; and film posters may reach between £35 and £70,000. A diversity of choice should suit the taste and pocket of the most eclectic of collectors. It might still be possible for a single enthusiast to create a sustainable market for a new collectable by writing the first textbook along the lines of Michael Bennett-Levy's work on pre-war television and Graham Turner's *Fishing Tackle: A Collector's Guide*, published six years ago.

However, spectacular record prices for a collectable do not necessarily reverberate in lower echelons of the market. Dinky toys are a good example. Although a unique Dinky Bentalls van made a record £12,700 at Christies' sale in Kensington three years ago, the common Dinky price is still only £30 each, compared with £20 in 1981, when the rarest Dinkies cost a mere £200–300. Top and bottom prices have polarised as buyers and markets have matured.

In the lottery of new collectables, Tibetan jewellery has an esoteric appeal. The jewellery is attractively chunky and skilfully made, often mixing vivid turquoise designs with gold, silver and coral. It is at its best in eye-catching pendants, earrings and necklaces, with prices from about £50 for a tiny item, a wide choice for less than £1,000, and more ambitious pieces up to £2,000. Designs often have a basis in traditional religious objects such as small boxes or belt pouches for holding prayers.

American publishers of trading cards have started issuing their own telephone cards as premium trading cards. One in every 36 nine-card packs of Baywatch trading cards includes a telephone card (or, more precisely, a pre-paid international 'remote memory' card that deducts the cost of calls from the user's account). Baywatch telephone cards are worth at least £10 to collectors, the price of ten packs of Baywatch cards. Cards autographed by Baywatch stars are issued in one in 432 packs. These are worth £25–40 each. Rare Batman cards the size of CDs are changing hands for £160.

Building society windfalls might also stimulate demand for fine quality furniture. The Antiques Collectors Club believes that the price of antique furniture could rise as a consequence by 20 per cent in 1997/98. The case was made powerfully by Antony Thorncroft in the *Financial Times*, 23 March 1997: 'The attraction of furniture is that, unlike paintings, it is practical. Since everyone needs tables, chairs and cabinets, why not buy antique examples, which are likely to appreciate in price compared with modern department store variants which steadily lose value?'

19.3.2 Far East markets

Economic changes in the 1980s and 1990s have created a cadre of affluent Chinese businessmen, who are becoming active at the art and antique auctions within the country and beyond its boundaries. China's growing class of rich entrepreneurs are spending their wealth on Mandarin and Cantonese antiques that they can appreciate, and believe will appreciate. Until these buyers came into the market, Chinese porcelain and jade, fine paintings and calligraphy had ebbed to the west and Japan in the backs of lorries, and the holds, boots and cases of smugglers, traders and collectors. The tide is beginning to turn. Local antique shops in Beijing and Shanghai are finding customers among the well-off, and Chinese auction houses are focusing on the local market. Sotheby's and Christie's have already opened offices in the two cities, though for the moment the authorities bar them from conducting auctions.

At a Beijing auction in 1996, a Chinese businessman paid 18m yuan (£1¼m) for a seven century old painting from the Northern Song dynasty. However, regulations and uncertainties currently constrain both traders in antiques and currency transfers, leaving the upper reaches of demand in the hands of Taiwanese and Hong Kong dealers and collectors. Also, it is difficult to assess how much of China's artistic heritage of calligraphy, paintings, porcelain, and jade stays hidden in private hands. Exporting these pieces would mean bypassing laws, with severe penalties, that are strict in the letter if not in their application. In auction catalogues, starring identifies pieces more than 200 years old to show that the regulations forbid their export. In reality, many that the local auctioneers do sell soon feature in auctions or dealers' showrooms outside China. This smuggling problem might lessen as local buyers increase their wealth, confidence and cosmopolitan ventures, and the authorities relax the regulations.

Partly in anticipation of such events, a stronger demand emerged in 1996 for Chinese artefacts at American and European auctions. Another factor is the size of the Chinese population outside China. The UK has about 170,000 Chinese, with 50,000 in London. The majority are from Hong Kong, with significant numbers from Malaysia, Vietnam and Korea.

Research published in April 1997 by the Policy Studies Institute shows that the Chinese are more likely than any other group in Britain, including whites, to earn £500 a week.

For some occidental collectors, furniture from China allows them 'to savour life of a cultivated genre'. Records reveal early Chinese furniture from the Shang Dynasty (sixteenth to eleventh centuries BC), which archaeologists found in tombs. Designs evolved from dynasty to dynasty, until styles matured in the era of Elizabeth I, when the furniture makers started to use central Asian hardwoods and shippers began to trade with China. These designs featured unique paints and woods. Experts esteem furniture made of 'light huanghuali or yellow rosewood, and the dark zitan or purple sandalwood'. In the 1930s, Sinophiles began to collect elegant pieces of Bauhaus simplicity, which remained in short supply until the 1980s, when the bootleggers increased their trade in Chinese art and antiques. Auction houses and dealers now expect to see a growing demand for these items in China and across the world.

Evidence of this demand emerged in a 1996 auction by Christie's New York, when all the lots in the sale of fine Ming furniture found buyers. The sum realised totalled US$11.24m (£7m). The auctioneers confirm that the revival of interest in classical Chinese furniture partly reflects increased demand from ethnic Chinese, who now have the disposable income to compete for antiques in world markets. At the New York auction, four of the most costly items went to Asian buyers.

Sales of Asian art increased generally in 1996, pointing the way to the future. An instance was an auction of Korean art where items from a private collection sold for US$18m (£11¼m). A rare 300-year-old dragon jar in this sale went to a bidder who paid US$8.4m (£5¼m). Successful Korean businessmen now pay high prices for pieces of good quality from their own culture – often national treasures that left Korea with diverse occupiers. A Christie's sale in Hong Kong during 1996 also recorded high prices for Chinese works of art, confirming the market's strength. For Asian collectors of Chinese antiques, Yuan, Ming and Qing ceramics and high-quality Imperial works of art attract the most interest. Jadeite jewellery (antique or new) is another important category for 1997/98.

The Chinese are also convinced that, by the end of the decade, coin and stamp prices will climb worldwide. Industrialisation is tilting the world's economic axis towards South-east Asia. British auctioneers predict that in China alone the demand for coins (and telephone cards) will rise 20-fold in the two decades. In the past five years, the number of Chinese stamp collectors has soared to 30 million. For investors seeking new collectables, the first question must now be: how much will they pay in South-East Asia? The region is dictating taste and forcing up prices.

The Chinese also want impressive coins from any nation and banknotes that were printed for China-based Dutch, German or French banks, or by the American Banknote Company or Britain's Bradbury Wilkinson, supplier of Hong Kong's paper money. Dealers predict that Chinese spending preferences will soon extend to stamps and coins of all nations. Sothebys expects China's most expensive stamp, an 1897 overprint, to double in value before the end of the century. It was worth only £1,200 twenty years ago. In May 1995, Sothebys sold one for £143,965 at its first Hong Kong stamp sale. Even in the west, where the stamp market has been at a low ebb since 1979, a stamp can fetch more than £1m (see **19.2.9**). Sothebys expects that South-East Asian stamp prices will continue to rise.

Western dealers hoping to become rich in South-East Asia are having to come to terms with the region's varying tastes. The Chinese are reluctant to buy excavated antiquities, second-hand jewellery or sapphires (blue is the colour of death). Unlike the Chinese, the Taiwanese buy western-style art, much of it, paradoxically, originating in Taiwan.

Japanese taste is the most westernised. Some western speculators have been dabbling in collectables abandoned by the Japanese, when recession struck their economy three years ago, in the hope that they will return to the same markets. These include posters by Toulouse-Lautrec, Paris school paintings, and Galle and Daum glass. Turkish money troubles have also aided speculators. Prices of the brilliant red, green and blue Iznik tiles of the 16th and 17th centuries, coveted by Turks, remain at bargain levels.

19.4 PURCHASING COLLECTABLES

19.4.1 Strategies

Collectors need to plan their strategies. Do they intend to become expert collectors, who gain thrill and pleasure out of the artefacts in which they invest? Or will they instead rely upon dealers to feed their hobbies or their alternative investment portfolios? If the latter, the player should realise that he or she will miss out on the social ambience of the market, which helps to keep real enthusiasts 'in the know'. According to a 1996 survey by the US Collectables and Platemakers Guild, 'New collectors are the key trend that industry executives see shaping the future', a trend that applies equally in Europe. 'Eighty percent of the industry executives surveyed expect company sales to increase next year, and new collectors coming into the marketplace are the primary reason for growth.'

However, the survey also refers to the 'greying' of many 'antiques categories and some collectables categories, as one of the major 1990s developments in the antiques marketplace'. Greying implies that most collectors in a category are over 55 years old. To sustain demand, the market will need enough entrants to replace collectors who lose interest or die. Equally, if collectors follow trends, and shift their loyalty to the next hot collecting craze, a category may decline in appeal, and pieces fall in value. At one time, collectors and dealers saw these shifts as part of the natural interplay of demand and supply in the antiques market. They did not worry, because they believed that everything would eventually recycle. Generally, it did – until the 1990s. The present decade has demonstrated that the recycling of a collecting category is no longer certain, at any rate in the medium term.

Nevertheless, the Guild's researchers conclude that 'Collecting is a hobby of the "empty-nesting" years, after children have left home. With the large "baby-boomer" generation reaching 50 years old, the total number of collectors could grow rapidly by 2000.' According to the specialists, the targeting of baby boomers by the 'desirables' industry depends largely on the appeal of nostalgia for the 1960s and later pieces, but means a decline in enthusiasm for 1940s and 1950s material, especially in the toy sector. Affordability is one reason. Many objects from this era are expensive. Another reason is the collecting base itself. New collectors in their fifties are seeking material from the late 1960s and 1970s.

In America, the 'collectables industry' expects to see extra sales through expanded and new channels of distribution. 'Electronic retailing, including TV shopping and computer shopping on the Internet's World Wide Web, and expansion of direct response marketing, including categories, direct mail, newsletters and other direct communications with collectors, are opening opportunities to build collections.'

19.4.2 Collectable cars

Intending purchasers of unique cars should probably buy through a private transaction after placing a classified advertisement in a car magazine, or from an enthusiast who belongs to a specialist automobile club. Some experts believe that, when buying cars, auctions can be particularly hazardous. They argue that there may be scant opportunity to inspect the car, and they suggest collectors need an iron will to avoid being swept away by the bidding excitement.

Another simple recommendation is not to buy a car unseen. It is advice that applies equally to many other alternative investments. Skilled salesmen may give 'cast-iron assurances that there will never be another chance to buy a car like this again, and urge the investor to send money without delay'. As a cynical commentator put it: 'Two weeks later, you will find a pile of rust on your doorstep. The chance of a lifetime comes along about once a week'.

Experts suggest that collectors should use a price guide and employ an appraiser to assess an intended purchase. 'Let someone else take a bath on the restoration,' says one cynic in the field. Buyers are also advised to check motoring publications on the availability of parts for an out-of-production vehicle. Costs in addition to the purchase price include, of course, storage, insurance and maintenance.

19.4.3 Predicting future collectables

Predicting which elements of a fickle, fast-changing culture will become the collectables of the future is a tricky exercise. Everyone was surprised by Swatch watches. Models from the 1980s now frequently fetch £20,000 upwards. 'Anything that was once popular will be of interest to someone,' says Catherine Higgins of Christie's in a reported interview. 'But that doesn't necessarily mean it will be worth a lot of money. Generally speaking, we'd be looking at things that were the first of their kind, the best of their kind, the rarest in the sense that either few were made or very few survive, or they are objects that in some way sum up the age that produced them.'

Paradoxically, in the design world, the objects that fetch the highest prices at auction are not necessarily the best. The real 'timeless classics' of the 20th century are never going to fetch high prices because they have remained in production. Design failures, on the other hand, especially fiascos such as the Sinclair C5, already have rarity and curiosity value. Should environmental awareness finally put paid to the combustion engine in the coming decades, collectors may even accord 'alternative' designs pioneer status. Perhaps society's very existence 50 years hence will depend on a revolution in energy consumption, in which case disposable goods such as throwaway cameras would become 'obsolete relics of a crazy age'.

Today's constant technology updates raise many questions when it comes to collecting computers. Will designs be coming out at such a rate that old models will be obsolete in the space of months? 'It's fairly safe to say that anything that's first of its kind will be of value – the first laptop computer of the early 1980s, for instance, or the first pocket-sized mobile phone' says John Stoddard, head of design at the international product design company IDEA, many of whose designs of the past decade are already in the permanent collection of the Design Museum. He believes that the future lies in information and communication technologies. 'The first machines will be as revolutionary as radio in the 1930s, with the same fusion of education, entertainment, work and information,' he enthuses. 'They will definitely be collectors' pieces.'

More advances in software, information, literature, music, and so on, will be coming into everyone's lives via a computer screen. So how, for example, will digital recording on CD-ROM affect collecting vinyl LPs and EPs? In an article in *Record Collector*, Ted Owen is adamant that vinyl is worth collecting, particularly rare or superior quality pressings: 'If you see a rare record, buy it, whatever the price, it's still an investment and is bound to go up in value.' Condition is always critical, so storage can be a problem, even with smaller items such as records. 'The general tendency is for people to want to get rid of something just when it's at its lowest value,' says the owner of Vinyl Exchange, a second-hand record shop in Manchester. 'We see it time and time again; troops of doleful, slightly balding men in their mid-30s whose wives have made them clear out their punk collection due to lack of space. If they could only hang on until there's no longer a glut, they might have something that other people want.'

19.5 TAXATION

19.5.1 Tax planning

If purchases can be justified as requirements of a business, for instance acquisitions of furniture or wall decorations for an office, investors paying high rates of tax may obtain benefits. They may be able to offset the costs of acquisitions as legitimate business expenses, but with a corresponding liability on disposal. If, on the other hand, the chattels which form the alternative investment portfolio are not regarded as income-producing, the owners will not normally be able to secure income tax relief in relation to insurance premiums or maintenance expenses.

19.5.2 VAT

A uniform system of VAT calculation for trade in second-hand goods took effect in the EU on 1 January 1995, when the Seventh VAT Directive came into force. Commercial transactions now carry VAT levied on the profit margin, while transactions between individuals are not liable to VAT. Second-hand cars are now defined as those more than six months old or with more than 6000 km mileage (twice the previous lower limits). The UK is allowed a transitional period up to 30 June 1999 at the latest, during which VAT will be charged at the reduced rate of 2.5 per cent. The changes to VAT explained in **18.7.5** also apply to collectors' items and second-hand goods. Collectors' items are defined as:

- Postage or revenue stamps, postmarks, first day covers, pre-stamped stationery and the like, franked, or if unfranked not being of legal tender and not being intended for use as legal tender.

- Collections and collectors' pieces of zoological, botanical, minerological, anatomical, historical, archaeological, palaeological, ethnographic or numismatic interest.

19.5.3 Sets of collectables

The investor may want to avoid acquiring 'a set of similar or complementary things' rather than a number of separate items which do not constitute a single set. The definition may affect future tax liabilities if the value of the set would exceed capital tax thresholds, whereas the individual items would be exempt. Thus the Inland Revenue is of the opinion that a collection of postage stamps per se constitutes a single set, although, in their view, the stamps of one definitive or commemorative issue would not necessarily do so.

An issue is whether the acquisition of a set or sets of collectables is a mere hobby or a bona fide investment. Implicit in the question is whether expenses will be deductible. On balance, if the collector buys strictly for investment and capital gains, and keeps accurate records including purchase dates, prices, provenance and current values, then it may be possible to make a case for deducting certain expenses (eg insurance, relevant publications, even travel to sales and auctions). In the majority of cases, however, the collector will be trying to create legal and tax history, in itself an expensive hobby.

When a collection is sold at auction, or after exhibition at a dealer's shop, the authorities may also be interested in the gains secured. In a case where someone has purchased collectables 'under the table', without a clean provenance, the Revenue may argue that the cost basis is zero. The gain would, therefore, be 100 per cent. The advantages of documented evidence are clear. Where the authorities take the view that efforts were being made to evade payment of tax, the legal penalties can be serious, even if the action was in truth innocent.

19.6 SUITABILITY AND MECHANICS

19.6.1 Risks

Snares await buyers. Markets may be thin. Collectables can be difficult to sell quickly, and meanwhile they pay no interest. Instead they can soak up steady outlays in insurance, storage, and maintenance. Repairs and restoration can also be expensive. To refurbish a good piano that a musician will want to play could cost £15,000. It might cost £60,000 to renovate a Ferrari, and only the reckless would drive it along the road.

The car has a hand-formed aluminium body. If a passer-by leans against the fender it can easily dent. Despite such costs and risks, enthusiasts still pay massive sums for rare vehicles. Two years ago, a 1936 Mercedes-Benz 500K Roadster, a stunning automobile, went at auction for £1.6m. It was not in first-class condition. According to one report, rats had eaten through the upholstery. A butcher had left it sitting in his shed, unused, for more than 30 years. Originality means a great deal with great cars.

19.6.2 Precautions

Independent advisers who specialise in collectables recommend that an investor should carefully check a dealer's reputation before deciding to employ his services. They suggest that enquiries should be pursued to find out how long the dealer has been in business, and to what professional organisations he belongs. In practice, it is also prudent to make sure that the collector fully understands what is being offered and promised.

To take coins, by way of illustration, questions might be asked about the grade of the coin, and the backing for any assurances. Does the dealer guarantee to buy back an investment? If so, at what price, and on what terms? Are there, for instance, any deductions affecting buy-back warranties? Is a service charge levied? With collectables of any value, it may be worth seeking a second opinion on quality and provenance, before confirming a decision to buy. Familiarity with sales and the publications in the field will also reveal whether an asking price is in line with the market, or well above it.

19.6.2 Other risks

Trading collectors' pieces over the Internet is gaining in popularity. The World Wide Web offers more information on alternative investment opportunities than ever before. However, the Internet is an unregulated market, and the new opportunities add to the risks. Investors should be as wary of offers on the Internet as they would be about any unsolicited mailshot.

The Securities and Investment Board has compared the Internet with 'a galactic car-boot sale: anyone from anywhere in the world can offer anything for sale'. As with any unregulated marketplace, those with established reputations will be pitching for business, with newcomers offering enticing deals. Investors will find false bargains, scams and frauds. Also, the Internet makes it easy, and will soon make it easier, to buy and pay for goods and services from foreign organisations, almost without being aware that they have their base abroad. So, before making a purchase, a buyer needs to know about the firm. Where is its base? Which authorities regulate it? Which country's laws will apply if a dispute occurs? Rights differ from place to place. For example, in some jurisdictions, when a firm fails, the liquidator holds clients' assets separately, and the firm's creditors do not have access to them. In other countries, the liquidator pools all the assets, and then shares out the proceeds between the owners and the creditors.

Crime adds to these risks. Sophisticated criminals are now targeting 1960s and 1970s collectables, according to the arts and antiques unit in New Scotland Yard. The unit's analyses suggest that burglars are taking pieces that, a decade ago, most people would have said were junk. The *Antiques Roadshow*'s experts have told the world, including breakers and enterers, that items that fell out of fashion years ago are now back in demand, and valuable. Auction houses have detected a similar market opportunity, and have opened outlets to deal with contemporary pieces. An example is Christie's Europa Gallery, which opened in London in Autumn 1996, and now handles designs from the 1960s, 1970s and even the 1980s.

The Metropolitan Police's unit enquires into art crime and manages a database of art and antiques reported stolen. Its *Bumblebee* imaging system came into operation in 1991, and now details thousands of stolen artefacts, worth from £100 to £½m that came to the unit's notice. Other European states have national art and antiques databases, and plans are in train to set up an EU system. Britain has still to integrate records of stolen art and antiques from police forces across the country. Yet law enforcement experts estimate that the purloining of paintings and other collectables represents a £5bn global industry, second only to narcotics in breadth and scale. In Britain alone, robbers make off with £½bn in such valuables each year.

In December 1996, the press reported a case where 200 people had paid £1.3m between them to a Mayfair company, James Devereaux Ltd. Their investment should have given them ownership of newly-distilled and semi-mature whisky, which they hoped would rise in value. However, the company ceased trading. The Department of Trade & Industry had been investigating the company; a spokesman for the DTI remarked that the trading by Devereaux 'was not in the public interest'.

The Department also petitioned the High Court to wind up the Napier Spirit Company, which offered immature whisky as an investment. In both instances, the official receiver is acting as liquidator, and hoping to trace the casks that the investors paid to buy. Jim Budd, who edits the Circle of Wine Writers' newsletter, *Circle Update*, believes that there are as many shady scams that promise spectacular returns from champagne as from whisky.

Readers of this chapter may seek to increase their wealth by buying rare stamps, fine wine, memorabilia, or other exotic objects. Many make worthwhile gains through these alternative investments; others lose a small fortune. Vast disparities can arise in risks. Firms that offer money-making opportunities of this kind may claim unrealistically high rates of return; businesses and advisers regulated by the Financial Services Act would find it difficult to make similar claims.

In alternative investment markets, highly speculative activities are usually unregulated. The prime movers are often individuals, with upper-class English, French or Scottish-sounding names. Their firms operate as unlicensed traders or brokers, ostensibly from prestigious addresses, but in reality from ramshackle buildings. This is the usual case in the UK, and means that:

- it is unlikely that anyone has vetted the people running the scheme to see if they are honest, competent and solvent;
- the firm does not have to follow the special rules and codes that apply to authorised firms, and help to ensure that they treat investors fairly;
- if a transaction goes wrong, no guarantees exist that anyone will look into complaints;
- if the firm fails, investors have no rights to claim compensation from authorised funds, and probably no access to any other compensation arrangements.

The first step for an alternative investor is therefore to make sure that a firm is legal. UK law generally requires authorisation of firms that formally run investment businesses. However, if such a firm has a current authorisation in another EU country, it may use its European passport to run an investment business lawfully in the UK. To operate an investment business without proper authorisation can be a criminal offence.

To check the status of a UK business, contact Financial Services Act regulators, and the Securities and Investment Board's Central Register (tel (0171) 929 3652). The SIB will advise enquirers to take full details of the salesperson, and to record his or her name, the firm's name, the full address, and the telephone and fax number. Equally, keeping all documents received is wise, including the envelope. If the firm is not authorised and should be, the SIB investigations' department would like to know about the matter.

When a firm can trade without authorisation, the investor must rely for protection on his or her own efforts, for example, by going through a checklist of commonsense questions. Usually, the greater the reward, the greater the risk. If the return is so much higher than is on offer elsewhere, why is the firm letting outsiders in on it?

Is the firm seeking money for a legitimate purpose? The scams are often ingenious, and sold by experts. Illegal operators know how to take advantage of weaknesses (including greed). They also know how to exploit vulnerability. If an investor sends money to illegal operators, he or she is unlikely to make a profit or ever recover the money. If the money goes out of the UK, restitution is even less likely. Many firms that operate illegally either collapse or the authorities put them out of business. In these cases, investors often find out too late that all their money has gone. Sometimes, the firm took the money in high management fees; often, the firm has lost or removed all the investors' money. In any event, the sums laid out have vanished at a cost, on occasion, of people's life savings, with scant hope of compensation.

If the value of a product, and the possibility of selling it at a high price, are based on rarity, will this scarcity continue? Can those behind the firm show evidence of the expertise they claim? What is the true level of risk, and is it acceptable? If the money is lost, what will be the effect on the investor's life style? What will happen to a guaranteed return, if the responsibility for delivering it lies with the firm and the firm fails? How long has it been, and will it be, in existence? The firm can only fulfil promises to buy something back if it and the money are still around.

19.7 CONCLUSION

In this field of alternative investments, the vital step is to decide whether to be an investor or a collector, or both. Those who take the trouble to understand a particular market well, and be a player, can gain the knowledge to be a specialist collector. In practice, only a limited number of people have the enthusiasm, dedication and resources to pursue the opportunities on a systematic basis. As indicated, any of these markets for collectables is also a social network. The participants derive much pleasure from being involved in this network. Keeping in touch with fellow devotees is rewarding in the interchanges and in the exchanges.

The investor will quickly learn that he or she has to spend time studying the subtle connotations of hallmarks on metalware, manufacturers' symbols on ceramics, makers' names on antique clocks, the marks of well-known furniture craftsmen and many thousands of other characteristics which influence the attribution of collectors' pieces. Those for whom time is scarce will quickly recognise that they need to specialise and to enlist the services of a specialist. The real collectors develop a burning fervour and could scarcely stop, even if they wanted to, or were forced to by circumstances. In essence, to be a mere investor is to miss out on the social rewards, and to enjoy only vicarious or second-hand advantages. But then collectables are after all second-hand.

SOURCES OF FURTHER INFORMATION

Bibliography (for Chapters 17–19)

Sponsoring the Art: New Business Strategies for the 1990s, The Economist Intelligence Unit (0171 830 1000)

Art Sales Index 1995–6 (28th edition), Art Sales Index Limited (01932 856426)

Art Market Bulletin, Art Sales Index Limited (01932 856426)

The Guide to the Antique Shops of Britain 1996–7, compiled by Carole Adams, Antique Collectors Club (01394 385501)

Guide Emer 1997–8 (bi-annual European guide), available from Mr G Gillingham, 62 Menelik Road, London NW2 3RH (0171 435 5644)

Antiquities Info (monthly European guide) (0171 435 5644)

Capital Taxation and the National Heritage, The Board of the Inland Revenue, London 1986 (amended 1988)

The Ephemerist (quarterly), Ephemera Society (0171 935 7305)

The Death Tax, Towry Law (01753 868244)

Works of Art: A Basic Guide to Capital Taxation and the National Heritage, Office of Arts and Libraries, 1982 (out of print)

Works of Art in Situ: Guidelines on In Situ Offers in Lieu of Capital Taxation, Department of National Heritage, 1984 (0171 270 3000) (out of print)

Gold to 2000, The Economist Intelligence Unit (0171 830 1000)

Diamonds: A Cartel and its future to 1996, The Economist Intelligence Unit (0171 830 1000)

Works of Art: Manuscripts and Archives. Basic information for Exemption from Capital Tax, Office of Arts & Libraries, 1991 (out of print)

Works of Art Private Treaty Sales: Guidelines from the Office of Arts and Libraries, Department of National Heritage, 1986 (0171 270 3000) (out of print)

Gold 1997, Goldfields Mineral Services, Greencoat House, Francis Street, London SW1P 1DH

Picture Guide to the UK Art Market 1997, Duncan Hislop, Art Sales Index Limited (01932 856426)

Official Review Antiques Price Guide 1996, Tony Curtis (ed), Lyle Publications

Millers Antique Price Guide 1996, Alison Starling (ed), Reed Consumer Books Ltd, Michelin House, 81 Fulham Road, London SW3 6RB

Art Newspaper, TG Scott Subscriber Services, 6 Bourne Enterprise Centre, Wrotham Road, Borough Green, Kent TN15 8DG (01732 884023)

Gold Demand Trends (quarterly), World Gold Council (0171 930 5171)

Platinum 1996, Johnson Matthey plc, New Garden House, 78 Hatton Garden, London EC1N 8JP (0171 269 8400)

Useful addresses

Arts Council of England
14 Great Peter Street
London
SW1P 3NQ

Tel: (0171) 333 0100.

Oriental Ceramic Society
30b Torrington Square
London
WC1E 7JL

Tel: (0171) 636 7985.

British Antique Dealers
    Association
20 Rutland Gate
London
SW7 1BD

Tel: (0171) 589 4128.

Royal Academy of Arts
Burlington House
Piccadilly
London
W1V 0DS

Tel: (0171) 439 7438.

Ephemera Society
8 Galveston Road
Putney
London SW15 2SA

Tel: (0171) 935 7305.

Royal Fine Art Commission
7 St James Square
London
SW1Y 4JU

Tel: (0171) 839 6537.

Incorporated Society of Valuers
    and Auctioneers
3 Cadogan Gate
London
SW1X 0AS

Tel: (0171) 235 2282.

Society of Antiquaries of London
Burlington House
Piccadilly
London
W1V 0HS

Tel: (0171) 734 0193.

Wine and Spirit Association of
    Great Britain (Inc)
Five Kings House International
1 Queens St Place
London
EC4R 1XX
Tel: (0171) 248 5377

Association of Professional
    Numismatists
11 Adelphi Terrace
London
WC2

London and Provincial Antique
    Dealers Association
535 Kings Road
London
SW10 0SZ

Tel: (0171) 823 3511.

The Standard Catalogue of UK
  Telephone Cards, from:
Kevin Baker
Pelennor Promotions
PO Box 12
Spalding
Lincolnshire
PE11 4HX

Tel: (01775) 821290
Fax: (01775) 821858.

The Telephone Card Catalogue
  Company
PO Box 1628
Largs
Ayrshire
KA30 8SU
BT Phone Card Direct: 0345
  697721.

British Antique Furniture
  Restorers' Association
The Old Rectory
Warmwell
Dorchester
Dorset
DT2 8HQ

Tel: (01305) 854822

Antiquarian Booksellers'
  Association
Sackville House
40 Piccadilly
London
W1V 9PA

Tel: (0171) 439 3118

British Art Market Federation
91 Jerym Street
London
SW1Y 6JB

Tel: (0171) 930 6137

Association of Art and Antique
  Dealers
535 Kings Road
Chelsea
London
SW10 0SZ

Tel: (0171) 823 3511

British Thematic Association
107 Charterhouse Street
London EC1M 6PT

Thesaurus Group Ltd
Mill Court
Furrlongs
Newport
Isle of Wight
PO30 2AA

Tel: (01983) 826000

Sotheby's
34–35 New Bond Street
London W1A 2AA

Tel: (0171) 493 8080

Christie's
8 King Street
St James's
London SW1Y 6QT

Tel: (0171) 839 9060
Fax: (0171) 839 1611

Phillips Fine Art Auctioneers
101 New Bond Street
London W1Y 0AS

Tel: (0171) 629 6602

20

TAX BENEFICIAL INVESTMENTS AND SAVINGS

MIKE WILKES

Pannell Kerr Forster, Chartered Accountants

20.1 INTRODUCTION

This chapter was completed prior to the election of the new government and the first Labour budget. It is possible that changes in legislation arising from the budget may materially affect some of the rules and reliefs outlined. Care should therefore be taken to ensure that the tax implications of any amendments are fully considered before proceeding with future investment.

The most important consideration of savings planning is to identify appropriate investments which offer good value; tax benefits and privileges represent only one aspect of this.

An investment which is appropriate for one person may not necessarily meet the needs of another in different circumstances. Some of the questions to ask are:

(1) How long can the savings be tied up?
(2) Are the savings for a particular purpose (school fees, daughter's wedding, retirement, etc)?
(3) When will the money be needed?
(4) Is income required?
(5) Will fluctuations in stock market and/or property prices be such a worry that the investments become unattractive?

You may also want to strike a balance. The criteria for investing the short-term part of the portfolio should be different from the method of investing in more volatile investments on a longer-term basis. Striking the right balance is one of the hardest aspects. If savings are fairly modest they may have to be invested on a conservative basis – and the return will reflect this. At the other extreme, a high net worth individual who has covered all his short-term requirements may deploy a proportion of his capital in more risky investments which offer the prospect of a very high return.

Once these decisions have been made, the next step is to identify investments which meet the specifications and offer good value. An investment may offer good value if the managers' charges are reasonable and the tax treatment is favourable.

This chapter starts by looking at tax privileged investments from the standpoint of the most cautious investor who may want access to capital at short notice and who is, therefore, not well disposed towards investments which may fall in value from time to time. Then a look is taken at tax privileged investments which involve a degree of risk arising from fluctuations in The Stock Exchange, etc. Finally consideration is given to bank deposits and 'near cash' investments, most of which involve little or no risk but do not have a privileged treatment. Many of these investments are provided by the government through the department of national savings or local authorities.

20.2 TAX PRIVILEGED INVESTMENTS

20.2.1 TESSAs

One of the government's more successful innovations are TESSAs (tax exempt special savings accounts). These are available to any individual who is resident in the UK and aged 18 or over.

The investment normally runs for five years. It offers a secure return since the money has to be deposited with an authorised bank or building society and the risk of capital loss is therefore remote. The investor can withdraw his capital within the five-year period but the tax benefits are forfeited if such withdrawals exceed certain limits. Subject to this, the benefit of having a TESSA is that the investor receives tax-free interest.

The maximum amount which may be withdrawn during the first five years without jeopardising the tax benefits is the interest credited to the account less the savings rate of tax of 20 per cent, which would have been deducted if the account had not enjoyed its special tax exempt status.

Example

Louise deposits £3,000 in a TESSA on 6 April 1997. In year one the bank credits interest of £195. The interest has not borne any tax. Louise can withdraw £195 less 20 per cent notional tax, ie £156.00, without affecting the exempt status of the account. The remaining £3,039.00 will continue to attract tax-free interest. However, if Louise withdraws £156.01 the bank will have to account to the Inland Revenue for the tax of £39.00 and the account will thereafter be treated as an ordinary deposit account. Once five years have elapsed, Louise can withdraw the entire amount with no tax consequences.

There are limits on the maximum amount which may be invested in a TESSA. An individual may invest up to £3,000 in the first year and up to £1,800 each year thereafter, subject to the total not exceeding £9,000. Alternatively, an individual can invest up to £150 per month.

To encourage reinvestment in a further TESSA account the limit of the first year deposit, for a second TESSA account, opened after a previous TESSA account has matured, is increased. Providing that the new TESSA account is opened within six months of the maturity of the previous account, the whole of the capital held in the matured account, excluding any interest element, up to a maximum of £9,000 can be invested in the new account in the first year. Individuals who invest less than £9,000 in the first year of their second TESSA account can continue saving over the next four years, within the usual limits for each year, subject to the overall limit of £9,000. If however the maximum is invested, no further investment is permitted.

An individual cannot have two TESSAs at any one time. However, the above limits apply separately for husband and wife. The terms under which banks and building societies accept deposits for TESSAs vary. The government regards it as a matter of choice of whether the deposit carries a rate of interest which is fixed for five years or a variable rate. TESSAs are 'portable' so an investor can transfer his savings from one financial institution to another without losing his tax benefits. However, the investor should check the level of any transfer penalty.

Uses of TESSAs

Older investor who needs income

The prime user of a TESSA is an older person who needs to take a regular income and who would rather avoid fluctuations in the value of his or her savings.

School fees provision

TESSAs are also suitable investments for individuals who wish to accumulate capital to cover school fees and similar costs – especially school fees payable in the medium term.

Quite sizeable sums can be accumulated. Thus if an individual makes the maximum deposits allowed, and interest is earned at a gross rate of 6.6 per cent, he accumulates a total of £11,319 at the end of five years (this assumes that interest is credited on an annual basis). Thus a married couple could accumulate just over £22,600 between them over five years. If we assume that they have put this aside to cover school fees payable when their son reaches 13, and the fees are currently £2,000 per term and likely to rise with inflation at 4 per cent per annum, they will still have covered the first three to four years' fees and this will allow other savings plans (such as PEPs – see **20.2.6**) to fund later years.

Why waste the tax exemption?

TESSAs may also be attractive to wealthy individuals who happen to have £10,000 on deposit and who may or may not keep it there for five years but would like to obtain the tax exemption if it is held for the full period (see also **2.3.15**).

20.2.2 National savings fixed interest certificates

These are another investment which provides a totally tax-free return. However, the yield reflects this and so TESSAs offer better value for most people.

National savings certificates are a five-year investment but they can be encashed early, although this involves surrendering a small amount of interest. The 43rd issue of national savings certificates is now available and if held to redemption (ie five years) give an overall net yield of 5.35 per cent.

Once certificates have matured, they attract tax-free interest at the national extension rate (currently 3.51 per cent) until they are redeemed.

Practical aspects

The certificates may be a suitable form of savings for children but children's bonus bonds are likely to be a far more attractive proposition for small savings. They are not, however, suitable for non-taxpayers or for short-term savings; but for the investor paying tax at the higher rate, the certificates may be attractive.

Application forms are available from most post offices and banks. Between £100 and £10,000 can be invested in the 43rd issue, plus up to £20,000 reinvestment of earlier issues which have matured.

Holdings should be reviewed from time to time, particularly since new issues may carry more attractive rates of capital appreciation than those already held. A review of holdings should certainly be made at the end of the specified period.

Any number of certificates can be cashed at one time, on at least eight working days' notice, and repayment forms are available at most post offices and banks.

20.2.3 Children's bonus bonds

As the name suggests, these bonds are specifically designed for children and are intended as longer-term savings, as the bondholder can retain the bonds up to the age of 21. The current issue (Issue H) has a guaranteed tax-free return of 6.75 per cent if held for five years. Anyone over 16 can purchase bonds for anyone under 16, and children under 16 who wish to purchase bonds for themselves will have to ask a parent or guardian to sign the application form. The maximum total holding in all issues of children's bonus bonds is £1,000 per child (excluding interest and bonuses) regardless of the number of donors, and can be purchased in £25 units. Shortly before each five-year period ends the next guaranteed interest rate and bonus is advised. No action is necessary unless it is decided to cash in the bond. Once the bondholder is over 16, the next offer of interest rates and bonus is for whatever length of time remains until he or she reaches 21. The bonds can be encashed at any time, with one month's notice, but there is a loss of interest unless this is at a five-year bonus date, or at age 21.

As with savings certificates, this investment is particularly suitable for parents, as the interest is not aggregated with their own income for tax purposes, even if the growth in value produces interest in excess of £100 per year.

20.2.4 National savings index-linked certificates

As with national savings certificates, these certificates are guaranteed by the government. They cannot be sold to third parties.

There is no lower age limit for holding these certificates, although encashment is not allowed until a child reaches the age of seven, except in special circumstances.

If a certificate is encashed within the first year, the purchase price only is repaid. If the certificates are held for more than a year, the redemption value is equal to the original purchase price, increased in proportion to the rise in the RPI between the month of purchase and the month of redemption. In the event of a fall in the RPI, the certificates can be encashed for the original purchase price. After the death of a holder, indexation can continue for a maximum of 12 months.

The latest issue (9th) guarantees a return above the rate of inflation for a five-year term by offering extra tax-free interest of 2.5 per cent as well as indexation. The amount of extra interest credited to the holding rises in each year of the life of the certificate and is itself inflation-proofed.

As with national savings certificates, capital appreciation is exempt from income tax and capital gains tax.

Certificates are suitable for individuals who do not need immediate income but are seeking protection in real terms for the amount invested.

Higher rate taxpayers in this category will find the certificates particularly attractive. The investment limit here is £10,000 with a minimum of £100, in addition to holdings of all other issues of savings certificates.

Application forms are obtainable from most post offices.

Comparison with TESSAs

There are circumstances where index-linked certificates could provide a better return than TESSAs. Interest rates are affected by a number of factors other than the rate of inflation. If you are pessimistic about the likely rate of inflation over the next five years index-linked certificates offer a low risk alternative.

20.2.5 Premium bonds

Premium bonds are guaranteed by the government. They cannot be sold to third parties.

Any person aged 16 or over can buy the bonds, and a parent or legal guardian may buy bonds on behalf of a child under 16. A bond cannot be held in the name of more than one person or in the name of a corporate body, society, club or other association of persons. Prizes won by bonds registered in the name of a child under the age of 16 are paid on behalf of the child to the parent or legal guardian.

The minimum purchase for a bondholder aged 16 or over is £100. Above this amount you can buy bonds in multiples of £10, up to a maximum of £20,000 per person.

No interest is paid, but a bond which has been held for one clear calendar month following the month in which it was purchased is eligible for inclusion in the regular draw for prizes from £50 to £1 million. Bonds can be encashed at any time, and all prizes are totally free of UK income tax and capital gains tax. Although the top prize may not compare favourably with potential National Lottery winnings, unlike the lottery the original stake will never be lost.

20.2.6 Personal equity plans

PEPs were introduced by the Chancellor of the Exchequer in the 1986 Finance Act to encourage wider share ownership by individuals in UK companies by offering investment tax incentives. Successive Finance Acts have introduced changes which make PEPs even more attractive.

Anyone who is over 18 years old and resident in the UK for tax purposes can take out a PEP. Crown employees working overseas are deemed to be resident for this purpose. Should a plan holder subsequently become non-resident, the plan can be maintained and its tax benefits preserved.

The tax benefits take the form of total exemption from capital gains tax and income tax on the appreciation and investment income earned from equities, unit trusts and investment trusts held within the plan. A plan can be terminated at any time and the funds withdrawn without loss of the tax benefits.

There are two distinct types of plan: general plans which have been available since the introduction of PEPs, and single company plans which were first introduced on 1 January 1992. Single company plans allow investment only in the shares of one designated company, and are subject to an additional condition that substantially the whole of the cash subscribed to the plan, or from the realisation of plan shares, must be reinvested in plan shares within 42 days.

There is no restriction on the investment switches that can be made within the fund and no liability to income tax or capital gains tax arises. A PEP can be transferred from one manager to another.

The maximum investment into a general plan is currently £6,000 per tax year and up to an additional £3,000 may be invested in a single company plan. Both husband and wife can invest this sum. The investment must generally be in the form of cash although shares acquired through a public offer may be transferred into a plan within 30 days. In addition, many managers offer share exchange schemes or reduce their normal charges for selling shares so that cash can be raised for investment in a PEP.

The cash held within the PEP can be held on deposit. The interest earned is paid gross and is exempt from tax provided that it is eventually invested in plan shares or units.

The full £6,000 may be invested in qualifying unit trusts or investment trusts which in turn invest at least 50 per cent of their funds in UK equities and shares quoted on EU stock exchanges. This range of investments is extended to include specified corporate bonds and convertibles of UK non-financial companies, and preference shares in UK and EU companies, providing they are quoted companies. As an alternative, up to £1,500 may be invested in a non-qualifying unit trust or investment trust, although at least one-half of the assets must consist of qualifying quoted securities.

Although no relief is available on the investment into the fund, the plan is virtually a gross fund in the same way as a pension fund. There is an important advantage over most pension funds in that all proceeds are tax free when drawn whereas at least part of what emerges from a pension scheme is taxable. It is therefore a useful addition for individuals to enhance retirement benefits. The fund can be used in the same way as a pension, ie tax-free cash can be taken or the fund could be used to purchase an annuity.

PEPs are not 'no risk' investments but in the past a combination/selection of unit/investment trusts and direct investment in bluechip or 'alpha' stocks have generally produced a reasonable return where the investment was kept for between three and five years (see also Chapter 3).

20.2.7 Insurance policies

Insurance policies are another type of tax privileged investment. Investors in qualifying policies are not subject to any tax on the maturity of the policy. For further discussion see Chapter 14.

20.2.8 Friendly society investments

Friendly societies issue qualifying insurance policies and there is no tax charge for investors when such policies mature. In this respect the position is no different from policies issued by insurance companies. The difference lies in the way that friendly societies are treated for tax purposes. Friendly societies are treated favourably as they are not normally subject to tax on life assurance business and this has generally enabled them to produce attractive returns.

Friendly society policies are, however, essentially a long-term investment since the surrender value can be very low where plans are cancelled or surrendered before the ten-year term has expired, as penalties tend to be heavy and frequently the charges on friendly society plans are high.

The maximum premiums are very low. The maximum annual limit is £270 but some societies do permit a lump sum investment to be made to cover the full ten-year plan. Policyholders must be between the ages of 18 and 70.

At least 50 per cent of the underlying fund of a friendly society must be invested in narrower range securities as defined in the Trustee Investment Act 1971. This could restrict the investment performance but on the other hand it offers a lower level of risk. All investment income and capital gains within the fund are free of all UK tax, which enhances the rate of return.

The Policyholder's Protection Act 1975 does not extend to friendly society plans and, unfortunately, there is no compensation scheme in the event of a friendly society having financial difficulties.

20.2.9 Pension policies

Personal pension policies and additional voluntary contributions to approved pension schemes are among the most favourably treated of all investments. Full tax relief is available for the individual's contributions and the fund enjoys total exemption from tax. This is discussed in Chapter 15.

20.2.10 Enterprise zone property trusts

These trusts are effectively collective schemes whereby an individual acquires an interest in a portfolio of properties located in one of the designated enterprise zones. The minimum investment is usually £5,000 but unlike the Enterprise Investment Scheme investments (see **13.5**) there is no maximum, and it is therefore possible for investors to shelter very large or exceptional income during a tax year. Investors are issued 'units' or 'shares' but in law they hold an interest in the properties as members of a syndicate.

The investment is allowable as a deduction from the investors' taxable income to the extent that the managers invest the cash raised by them to construct buildings or purchase newly constructed and unused buildings within an enterprise zone. There is usually a small part of the investment which attracts no tax relief representing the cost of purchasing the land on which the building has been constructed. Generally this is between 5 and 10 per cent of the total investment.

Example

> Stuart invests £100,000 in an enterprise property trust on 3 March 1997. He has income of £75,000 which is subject to the 40 per cent top rate.
>
> The managers of the trust invest all the money raised in qualifying property before 6 April 1997. The land element is 10 per cent. Stuart, therefore, gets a tax deduction of £100,000 × 90 per cent, ie £90,000. This deduction saves Stuart tax of £36,000 so the net cost of the investment is £64,000.

Current yields on such investments are between 6 and $7\frac{1}{2}$ per cent of the gross investment. The income is paid gross and is treated as rental income for the investor. The final investment return on such an investment is difficult to predict. Investors should expect to retain their units for a term of 25 years. A disposal within this term could give rise to a clawback of some or all of the income tax relief given in year one (although no such clawback need arise in the case of a gift).

The yield becomes more attractive when one compares it with the net cost of the investment, after tax relief. Thus if the trust yielded 6 per cent on the gross cost, the yield on Stuart's net cost becomes 9.7 per cent.

These investments are tax privileged because of the relief due to the investor when he makes the investment. However, they are not risk free as the investment produces income only if the properties are fully let. In practice this risk can be minimised.

The trust managers can generally secure rental guarantees of at least two years where they buy properties from developers. Sometimes the developer offers a further guarantee which in the short term provides effectively a guaranteed income. In many cases the managers buy enterprise properties which have been 'pre-let' and this means the investor is securing a guaranteed income, usually with upward only rent reviews for a 25-year period. If good rent reviews are achieved the capital value of the investment can be expected to appreciate.

Investors may also take a qualifying loan to acquire the units, the interest being set first against the rental income from the properties and any surplus is then available to be set off against any other Schedule A rental income for the same year. The balance of any unused interest relief is available to carry forward against rental income of future years.

In addition to the long-term nature of these investments, it is often difficult to dispose of the units as there is no established market through which units can be bought and sold. The managers do, however, offer to assist investors on a matched bargain basis.

Planning in later years

One planning possibility involving the use of these investments relies upon the fact that the clawback (or 'balancing charge') need not arise on a gift. Thus, Stuart might transfer the shares in the enterprise property trust to his wife if she is not subject to the 40 per cent rate. If she had no other income at all she would have only a small tax liability on the rents she received of £6,000 per annum.

20.3 CONCLUSION

Some of the tax benefit investments offer the prospect of outperforming inflation. The return on a TESSA might very well be 6.5 per cent or more per annum. PEP's invested in a range of equities should produce a comparable return over the medium to longer term. Index-linked national savings certificates are guaranteed to do so.

The return on some of the other privileged investments looks less attractive. Where savings certificates have matured the current rate of interest added (3.51 per cent) barely keeps pace with the current rate of inflation.

The various types of deposit schemes offer a poor long-term return to anyone who cannot enjoy the income gross. They are, therefore, sensible investments for married women with little or no other income, but less attractive for a person who is subject to tax at 40 per cent. That is not to say that these investments are not appropriate from time to time as a way of investing money short term or to secure a known commitment or liability.

INVESTOR PROTECTION

PETER HOWE, LLB

Barrister, Company Secretary, Allied Dunbar Assurance plc

21.1 INTRODUCTION

The Financial Services Act 1986 was enacted following widespread concern at the collapse of a number of investment firms in the early 1980s. The legislation is based on the recommendations of Professor Gower who, on behalf of the government, carried out an investigation which revealed a lack of consistency (and in some cases the absence of any controls) in the regulatory systems controlling different types of firm.

Professor Gower's approach was to recommend regulation only in so far as necessary for the protection of investors and that the regulatory structure should remain flexible so as not to impair market efficiency. The aim was to introduce a consistent regulatory structure which would produce a 'level playing field' (ie rules which do not put some firms at a competitive disadvantage compared with others). His view was that regulation should not try to do the impossible by protecting investors from their own folly but rather to prevent reasonable people from being deceived.

Finally, Professor Gower recommended self-regulation by the industry as preferable to the regulatory system in the US where the Securities Exchange Commission is a government agency. Although the UK system is backed up by statute, the day-to-day regulation of investment businesses is undertaken by self-regulatory organisations the boards and committees of which include practitioners drawn from the various types of investment business which operate in the market.

The Financial Services Bill was enacted in 1986 and brought into force by a number of Commencement Orders. The key provisions were implemented in 1988. A two-tier system of regulation was introduced with the creation of a Securities and Investments Board (SIB), responsible for several self-regulatory organisations (SROs) which are referred to in the paragraphs below. They each produced their own rules and determined their compliance and monitoring approach.

21.2 HIGHLIGHTS OF THE PREVIOUS YEAR

21.2.1 The Personal Investment Authority (PIA)

The PIA has almost completed the transfer of ex-FIMBRA and LAUTRO members. FIMBRA and LAUTRO have had their recognition orders revoked by the SIB although transitional provisions have been extended again to October 1997. Those few firms which obtained their authorisation from FIMBRA or LAUTRO but which have so far not been accepted into membership by PIA may continue to operate provided that they applied to PIA (or another regulator) by 1 October 1994. Any firms which failed to do this ceased to be authorised on that date.

The PIA Board is to reduce from 21 to 17 subject to members' agreement at the July 1997 annual general meeting. Two public interest directors and two practitioner directors will go, thereby maintaining the current balance.

A major discussion exercise, the Evolution Project, commenced in 1996 aimed at reviewing and if thought desirable changing the structure of regulation of the mass marketing of investment products in the UK, beginning with the selling process and moving on to consider the part rules play and the process of monitoring. The review is likely to involve a re-examination of such concepts as polarisation, standards of advice and disclosure. The hope is that developments in the area of training and competence, disclosure and consumer education might enable the regulator to regulate with a lighter touch in some areas.

A paper on the powers of the PIA Ombudsman proposes to increase the maximum award that he can make from £50,000 to £100,000 and removing the limit of £750 on the amount the Ombudsman can award for stress and inconvenience. These proposals have caused some concern, particularly the scrapping of the cap on stress and inconvenience payments which could result in firms being unable to obtain professional indemnity cover for such liabilities.

21.2.2 Disclosure

The PIA published its rules for disclosure for unit trusts and other non-life products. The rules follow those relating to life products and require projections at a specified rate of return. The rules came into effect on 1 May 1997.

21.2.3 Complaints and compensation

The SIB has proposed changes to the Investors' Compensation Scheme, aimed at strengthening the financial position of the scheme by introducing an element of pre-funding by investment firms' levies and the possible creation of a reserve fund which could be drawn on in emergencies. The PIA has already introduced rules which enable it to call on its members for pre-funding levies, but it has not so far acted on them and will not do so if the SIB proposals go ahead.

21.2.4 Pension transfers and opt-outs

Progress in completing case reviews and paying redress to those who suffered loss when they bought personal pensions has been much slower than the regulators had expected. Further guidance was given by the SIB in November 1996 to speed up the reviews with the threat of discipline for firms which do not comply. The new Labour Government's Economic Secretary to the Treasury, Helen Liddle, has taken a personal interest requiring the heads of insurance companies to update her on a regular basis.

21.2.5 Occupational pension schemes

The Pensions Act provisions are being brought into force. The new Occupational Pensions Regulatory Authority (OPRA) has been established, the role of the Pensions Ombudsman has been extended and a compensation scheme established. Other provisions giving scheme members the right to elect at least one-third of the trustees, providing for new minimum solvency requirements and tighter controls on the investment choices of trustees were introduced in April 1997.

21.2.6 OEICs

Regulations have been made by the Treasury and the SIB for the introduction of open-ended investment companies which will provide an alternative to investing in authorised unit trusts. It is likely that a number of existing unit trusts will be converted into OEICs, particularly where it is proposed to market these investments in the EEA.

21.2.7 Custody

The FSA was amended to make the business of the provision of custody services an activity requiring authorisation under the Act. This amendment was effective from 1 June 1997.

21.3 BASIC FRAMEWORK

The key provision in the Financial Services Act 1986 (FSA) makes it a criminal offence to carry on investment business in the UK unless the person concerned is authorised or exempt. Investment business is defined as carrying on certain activities, eg buying and selling, advising, arranging or managing 'things' which are investments under the FSA. The definition of investments includes most 'paper' securities such as stocks and shares, collective investment schemes, most life and pension policies, gilt-edged securities and futures and options. The definition excludes real property, bank and building society accounts or alternative investments such as antiques and works of art. Although most National Savings products satisfy the definition of investments they are specifically excluded.

The FSA has only minor application to the regulation of occupational pension schemes which are largely governed by trust law. Financial services regulation is only concerned with the investment management aspects. In particular the Act requires trustees to be authorised (see **21.3.1**) unless they have delegated day-to-day investment decisions to professional investment managers.

From 1 June 1997 the provision of custody services will require authorisation under the Act.

21.3.1 Authorisation

Firms carrying on investment business may obtain their authorisation from the SIB or more likely from one of the SROs which the SIB has recognised:

(1) the Securities and Futures Authority (SFA) which resulted from a merger, in April 1991, of The Securities Association (TSA) and the Association of Futures Brokers and Dealers (AFBD). TSA regulated the activities of those who deal in, advise on or manage securities whilst AFBD regulated those who advise on or deal in futures and options, including those handled by the commodity exchanges and the London International Financial Futures Exchange;

(2) the Investment Management Regulatory Organisation (IMRO) which regulates the managers of investments including the managers and trustees of collective investment schemes, eg unit trusts;

(3) the Life Assurance and Unit Trust Regulatory Organisation (LAUTRO) which regulates the marketing activities of life companies, friendly societies and collective investment scheme managers;

(4) the Financial Intermediaries Managers and Brokers Regulatory

Association (FIMBRA) which regulates the many intermediaries who advise and arrange deals in life and pension products, collective investment schemes and other investments.

(5) the Personal Investment Authority (PIA), which became operational in July 1994, effectively merges the regulatory activities of FIMBRA and LAUTRO as well as covering some of the non-stockbroking private investor responsibilities of IMRO and the SFA. LAUTRO and FIMBRA will cease to be recognised by the SIB as SROs once the process of transfer of membership to the PIA is completed.

Another way in which authorisation to carry on investment business can be obtained is through membership of a recognised professional body (RPB). Most solicitors and accountants obtain their authorisation from their respective professional bodies (eg The Law Society or one of the accountancy bodies) where their investment business is only a small proportion of their overall professional activities. The Insurance Brokers' Registration Council regulates insurance brokers whose main business is general insurance but who may undertake investment business so long as this does not exceed 49 per cent of their total business.

Finally, there are firms such as insurance companies and friendly societies which obtain their authorisation under separate legislation from the Department of Trade and Industry or the equivalent authorities in the EU member state in which the company's head office is situated, and the Registrar of Friendly Societies respectively. These firms do not need to seek additional authorisation under the FSA although their marketing activities are subject to regulation by LAUTRO/PIA or, in a very few cases, the SIB.

21.3.2 Exemptions

Some firms are exempted from the requirement to obtain authorisation under the FSA. These include the Bank of England, recognised exchanges and clearing houses, and members of Lloyd's.

An important category of exempt person is the appointed representative. This is an individual or firm which acts as the agent of an authorised person and for whose activities (within the limits of the authorised person's business activities) the authorised person takes legal responsibility. Although it is open to any firm which is authorised to appoint such representatives, the practice is most common in the case of insurance companies and firms that market life policies and collective investment schemes.

21.3.3 **The SIB Central Register**

The SIB is required under the FSA to maintain a public register of firms authorised to carry on investment business. This Central Register permits investors as well as firms to check on the authorisation status of firms including appointed representatives who trade under their own names and not that of the authorised firm which has appointed them. It will now be possible to check whether such an appointed representative is the agent of a particular company.

The Central Register can be contacted by telephoning 0171–929 3652 or by using New Prestel or Telecom Gold services.

21.3.4 **Authorisation criteria**

In deciding whether to authorise a firm the SIB, SROs or RPBs consider such matters as whether those involved in the business are fit and proper persons having the financial resources and competence to operate the business in a way which is unlikely to result in unreasonable risk to investors. In addition, the SIB has published ten Principles (see below) which it expects all firms to observe. The breach of any principle might call into question whether the firm was fit and proper to carry on investment business.

The Principles

(1) Integrity
A firm should observe high standards of integrity and fair dealing.

(2) Skill, care and diligence
A firm should act with due skill, care and diligence.

(3) Market practice
A firm should observe high standards of market conduct. It should also, to the extent endorsed for the purpose of this principle, comply with any code or standard as in force from time to time and as it applies to the firm either according to its terms or by rulings made under it.

(4) Information about customers
A firm should seek from customers it advises, or for whom it exercises discretion, any information about their circumstances and investment objectives which might reasonably be expected to be relevant in enabling it to fulfil its responsibilities to them.

(5) Information for customers
A firm should take reasonable steps to give a customer it advises, in a

comprehensible and timely way, any information needed to enable him to make a balanced and informed decision. A firm should similarly be ready to provide a customer with a full and fair account of the fulfilment of its responsibilities to him.

(6) Conflicts of interest

A firm should either avoid any conflict of interest arising or, where conflicts arise, should ensure fair treatment to all its customers by disclosure, internal rules of confidentiality, declining to act, or otherwise. A firm should not unfairly place its interests above those of its customers and, where a properly informed customer would reasonably expect that the firm would place his interests above its own, the firm should live up to that expectation.

(7) Customer assets

Where a firm has control of or is otherwise responsible for assets belonging to a customer which it is required to safeguard, it should arrange proper protection for them, by way of segregation and identification of those assets or otherwise, in accordance with the responsibility it has accepted.

(8) Financial resources

A firm should ensure that it maintains adequate financial resources to meet its investment business commitments and to withstand the risks to which its business is subject.

(9) Internal organisation

A firm should organise and control its internal affairs in a responsible manner, keeping proper records, and where the firm employs staff or is responsible for the conduct of investment business by others, should have adequate arrangements to ensure that they are suitable, adequately trained and properly supervised and that it has well-defined compliance procedures.

(10) Relations with regulators

A firm should deal with its regulator in an open and cooperative manner and keep the regulator promptly informed of anything concerning the firm which might reasonably be expected to be disclosed to it.

Source: *The Securities and Investments Board*

21.4 RULES AND REGULATIONS

The FSA contains only the bare framework of the total investor protection legislation. The detailed rules and regulations with which authorised firms are expected to comply are contained in rule books maintained and enforced by the SIB and the relevant SRO or RPB. The original rule books of individual SROs and RPBs were required to give investor protection which was equivalent to that given by the rules of the SIB itself. In an effort to avoid unnecessary duplication whilst preserving the ability of SROs and RPBs to make practitioner-based rules relevant to the particular business in which their members operate, some amendments have been made to the FSA. These amendments have allowed the SIB to make certain core rules which are directly applicable to all investment firms (except members of RPBs) whichever SRO they belong to. The designated core rules (of which there are 40) were intended to provide a degree of uniformity and common standards which the individual SROs could supplement by additional rules geared to the activities of the firms which they regulate. Instead of having to convince the SIB that their rule books are equivalent, the new arrangements require the SIB to agree that the rule books, together with the SRO's monitoring and compliance arrangements, provide adequate protection to investors. Since these amendments were made the SIB has had second thoughts about the need to designate core rules although most of them have been incorporated into the SRO's own rule books.

21.4.1 Business conduct

The detailed rules and regulations cover a number of areas relating to the conduct of investment business by authorised persons. These include:

(1) the way in which authorised firms and their appointed representatives seek new business;
(2) the ongoing relationships between authorised firms and their customers where such relationships exist;
(3) the way in which authorised firms must deal with complaints by investors.

21.4.2 Seeking business

There are detailed advertising rules which prohibit misleading advertisements and statements and claims which cannot be substantiated. For example, LAUTRO has required its member firms to submit their marketing material for with-profit bonds and guaranteed bonds which offer potential growth in line with a stock market index but with a guaranteed return of capital if performance is poor. Where potentially misleading advertising material was found LAUTRO required its member firms to check that investors had not been disadvantaged and to compensate any that had.

The PIA has issued a reminder that advertisements for unit trusts and

PEPs must give a fair indication of the nature of the investment. If an advertisement states there are 'no initial charges' or 'no entry or exit charges', it must take into account the difference between the buying and selling price, if a difference exists.

There are rules which require authorised firms to know their customer before making a recommendation or arranging an investment transaction and to make sure that any investment that is recommended or transacted is suitable, having regard to the investor's personal and financial requirements. Poor completion of 'fact finds' (the questionnaires which intermediaries normally use to get to know their customers) have been the subject of criticism by some SROs and the Insurance Ombudsman and has received significant attention in the proposals for training and competence.

In the case of packaged product investments such as life assurance, pension plans and collective investment schemes, the polarisation rule requires intermediaries to disclose in a Terms of Business letter (previously called a Buyer's Guide) and on business stationery whether they are independent from any particular product company, in which case the obligation is to recommend a suitable product from those available on the market or company representatives, who must recommend a suitable product from the product range of the particular company they represent.

Independent intermediaries and company representatives are permitted to make unsolicited calls (personal visits or oral communications other than at the investor's invitation) which cannot be made in relation to non-polarised investments. Investments which can be the subject of unsolicited calls normally give the investor cooling-off rights, enabling the investor to cancel an investment transaction within a reasonable period (normally 14 days) from entering into the contract. Detailed product disclosure rules are designed to provide sufficient information about the product to enable the investor to decide whether to continue with the contract.

From 1 January 1995 new product and commission disclosure rules for life companies have required a 'Key Features' document, setting out the essential elements of the product including charges and expenses, to be given to an investor before an application form is completed. The document must disclose the commission or other remuneration payable to the intermediary (whether independent or tied) and must give further important information, specific to the circumstances of the purchasing investor, about the product. The rules require life offices to use their own charges and not industry standard charges when preparing illustrations of future benefits and the clear disclosure to investors of the consequences of surrendering a policy before the end of its term or maturity. They also permit product providers to make charges which differ according to which distributor outlet is used to obtain the business. From 1 May 1997 these rules have applied to unit trusts and other non-life assurance packaged products (see **21.2.2**).

21.4.3 Customer agreements

The rules prescribe the terms of customer agreements between authorised firms and their customers including how such agreements are made, how instructions are to be communicated and how such agreements are terminated.

There are also rules requiring authorised firms to place client money in designated trust accounts to ensure that investors' money is kept separate from other money belonging to the firm. The rules provide for the payment of interest except in specified circumstances.

21.4.4 Complaints and compensation

There are rules requiring authorised firms to operate detailed monitoring and compliance procedures to ensure that the rules are obeyed and to have suitable procedures for dealing with complaints from investors. A breach of these rules may also result in a breach of SIB Principle 9 (see **21.3.4**).

Authorised firms are required to contribute a levy to a compensation scheme established by the SIB and administered by the Investors Compensation Scheme Limited under which, in the event of an authorised firm going into liquidation, investors may recover up to a maximum of £48,000 if the firm is unable to meet its liabilities.

21.5 COMPLAINTS AND REMEDIES

21.5.1 Basic procedures

If an investor has a complaint about an authorised firm, the investor should raise the matter initially with the firm's compliance officer who is usually an employee of the firm with responsibility for ensuring that the firm complies with the rules. If the firm does not handle the complaint to the investor's satisfaction, the investor may refer the matter to the relevant complaints body. The appropriate complaints body depends upon the arrangements which that firm's SRO or RPB has made. For example, nearly all life assurance companies and many unit trust companies are members of the PIA and it is the PIA Ombudsman that would deal with the investor's complaint. Disputes between members of IMRO and their customers are dealt with by the Investment Ombudsman. It is the authorised firm's responsibility to inform the investor of the appropriate complaints body. The complaints body has a range of sanctions which can be imposed including awarding appropriate compensation for any losses suffered by the investor.

Referring a complaint to one of the relevant complaints bodies does not normally prevent the investor from pursuing any other legal remedies. In addition to bringing civil actions for breach of contract or negligence, the private investor is given a right, under the FSA, to sue an authorised firm for any breach of the investor protection rules which causes the investor loss.

Individual SROs as well as the SIB have a range of intervention powers which can be used in the interests of investor protection. These include the SIB's power to prohibit the employment of persons considered to be unfit, to apply for an injunction or restitution order where a breach is threatened or where investors have suffered loss, to restrict the business of investment firms, to restrict any dealings with a firm's assets or even to vest those assets in a trustee. SROs have the power to discipline their members for misconduct and may impose fines.

21.6 OVERSEAS ASPECTS

Overseas firms are subject to the FSA if they carry on investment business in the UK. Unless an overseas company is authorised to carry on investment business in the UK, it is difficult for it to market its products and services to UK investors. It is possible for the overseas firm to promote its products and services in the UK through an authorised person.

If the investment is a recognised collective investment scheme or an insurance policy issued by a recognised insurer, which it may be if the scheme or insurer is authorised in another EU member state or in a territory designated by the Secretary of State for Trade and Industry (eg the Isle of Man, the Channel Islands), the authorised firm may market it freely within the UK. Although such a scheme may not be subject to the UK compensation scheme it is possible that it will be subject to a compensation scheme set up in the home country or territory concerned.

If the collective investment scheme or insurance policy is not a recognised scheme, there are severe restrictions on the extent to which it can be promoted in the UK. For example, an authorised person can promote such a scheme to established customers under the terms of a subsisting customer agreement but cannot market to investors generally.

21.7 PREVIEW OF THE YEAR AHEAD

The PIA will complete the process of vetting firms transferring from FIMBRA and LAUTRO after which the two SROs can be finally wound up. The PIA was created with the key aim that higher standards should be delivered in the retail sector and the PIA's performance will be closely watched.

The PIA and the SIB will closely monitor the progress of firms in implementing the pensions review, particularly in the light of the recent guidance. It is likely that a number of firms will be subject to disciplinary proceedings if they do not meet deadlines.

The new Labour government will introduce significant change in the current two-tier structure of regulation with the merger of all the current SROs into a single regulator.

It is likely that Long Term Care Insurance Products, which help people to meet the costs of nursing home care and other benefits in later life, will become regulated under the FSA.

The results of some of the discussions from the PIA's Evolution Project should become known, with the possibility of removing some of the more prescriptive rules, so long as this can be done without reducing standards of investor protection.

The Consumer Panel (an independent body set up to advise the PIA Board on the interests of private investors and the PIA effectiveness in protecting those interests) reported in October 1996 making several recommendations including that the PIA should investigate how effectively advisers explain the long-term nature of investments, and that mystery shopping should be introduced to check the quality of advice. It also recommended the PIA to investigate 'product bias' to see the extent to which commission influences the type of contract recommended by advisers. It will be interesting to see how these recommendations are taken forward in the coming year.

It is likely that an Investors' Compensation Directive will be introduced providing minimum standards throughout the EEA and thereby improving conditions for a common market in financial products.

Following some high-profile failures of management controls in some firms during 1996, the SIB have commissioned an independent analysis of current law and regulatory practice governing the responsibility of top management including the company law and fiduciary duties of directors. The results of this report will be awaited with interest and no doubt some uncomfortable anticipation in the boardrooms of banking and other financial services companies.

The SIB will be committing resource to the subject of investor education following the launch of the Personal Finance Education Group. This group is backed by Government and the industry and seeks to improve the public's understanding of life assurance, pensions and other financial products.

Mr Howard Davies will be the new SIB Chairman when Sir Andrew Large steps down in July 1997 after five years in the job.

21.8 CONCLUSION AND FUTURE DEVELOPMENTS

The FSA provides the framework for the most comprehensive investor protection system ever seen in the UK or elsewhere in Europe. In the past nine years considerable progress has been made by the SIB and the SROs in putting the flesh on the bare bones provided by the FSA.

Changing circumstances brought about by an innovative and competitive financial services industry as well as developments in Europe will require further adaptations of a system which needs to be responsive to such changes.

21.8.1 Future developments

Looking ahead, the scope for change and future development of the regulatory system is significant. The principle of self-regulation continues to be questioned and might not survive the recent election of a Labour government or a new major scandal affecting the industry. Indeed one conclusion of the final report of the House of Commons Treasury and Civil Service Committee, which looked at financial services regulation, was that: 'Whatever the Act says, and whatever the philosophy underlying the legislation, the SFA and the other SROs have now moved firmly towards acting as "Statutory regulators with practitioner involvement"'. Developments in Europe may also provide a focus for further questioning.

The implementation of the Third Life Insurance Directive will pave the way towards a workable investment protection system across member states. This process has accelerated from 1 January 1996 now that the Capital Adequacy Directive (setting minimum Community-wide levels of capital needed by investment firms) and the Investment Services Directive (enabling share dealers to operate throughout the European Economic Area with a single licence issued by their home country regulatory authority) have come into force. The adoption by member states of an investor's compensation directive will be a further step towards the creation of a regulated market in Europe.

Increasing resources will need to be expended on monitoring compliance, meeting the costs of the compensation scheme and financing the initial and ongoing costs of the training and competence proposals. These expenses, together with the cost of initiatives like the revised product disclosure regime and the setting up costs of the PIA for the retail sector, will add to the competitive pressures on investment firms. This is likely to produce an increasing number of mergers or take-overs and a search for more cost-effective methods of securing the distribution of financial products and services. Predictions have been made that the number of life companies will reduce substantially over the next few years and that the number of independent intermediaries will halve from 20,000 to 10,000 by 1997. New methods of distribution such as the sale of more products by telephone will occur. In this environment new challenges will be created for the regulators as well as for those regulated. It is possible that the regulators will focus their attention on minimising the risk of fraud and other market failures instead of concentrating on the improvement of the detailed standards of industry practice. This is a distinct possibility for regulators whose primary concern is not with the private investor since non-private investors should, arguably, be able to look after their own interests.

The FSA introduced a dynamic system capable of responding to change. There is little doubt that the system will be severely tested during the next few years.

SOURCES OF FURTHER INFORMATION

Useful addresses

PIA (Personal Investment
   Authority Limited)
1 Canada Square
Canary Wharf
London
E14 5AZ

Tel: (0171) 538 8860

LAUTRO (Life Assurance and
   Unit Trust Regulatory
   Organisation)
1 Canada Square
Canary Wharf
London
E14 5AZ

Tel: (0171) 538 8860

IMRO (Investment Management
  Regulatory Organisation Ltd)
5th Floor
Lloyd's Chambers
1 Portsoken Street
London E1 8BT

Tel: (0171) 390 5000

SIB (Securities and Investments
  Board)
Gavrelle House
2–14 Bunhill Row
London
EC1Y 8RA

Tel: (0171) 638 1240

FIMBRA (Financial
  Intermediaries, Managers
  and Brokers Regulatory
  Association)
1 Canada Square
Canary Wharf
London
E14 5AZ

Tel: (0171) 538 8860

Investors Compensation
  Scheme Limited
Gavrelle House
2–14 Bunhill Row
London
EC1Y 8RA

Tel: (0171) 638 1240

SFA (Securities and Futures
  Authority Limited)
Cottons Centre
Cottons Lane
London
SE1 2QB

Tel: (0171) 378 9000

The Law Society (of England
  and Wales)
The Law Society's Hall
113 Chancery Lane
London
WC2A 1PL

Tel: (0171) 242 1222

The Institute of Chartered
  Accountants (in England
  and Wales)
PO Box 433
Chartered Accountant's Hall
Moorgate Place
London
EC2P 2BJ

Tel: (0171) 920 8100

Insurance Brokers' Registration
  Council
63 St Mary's Axe
London
EC3A 8NB

Tel: (0171) 621 1061

The Insurance Ombudsman
  Bureau
City Gate One
135 Park Street
London
SE1 9EA

Tel: (0171) 928 7600

The Office of the Investment
  Ombudsman
Hertsmere House
Hertsmere Road
London
E14 4AB

Tel: (0171) 216 0016

Personal Investment Authority
  Ombudsman Bureau Ltd
3rd Floor
Centre Point
103 New Oxford Street
London
W1CA 1QH

Tel: (0171) 240 3838

The Pensions Ombudsman
11 Belgrave Road
London
SW1V 1RB

Tel: (0171) 834 9144

INDEX

Discount Offer to all Purchasers of the
Allied Dunbar Investment & Savings Handbook 1997/98

You can **save 10%** off any of the following Allied Dunbar Handbooks, if you purchase more than one book from the Allied Dunbar series.

Simply complete the following order form and return it to:
Justine Marsh, Pitman Publishing, FREEPOST, 128 Long Acre, London, WC2E 9BR, UK or fax your order on (0171) 836 4286 or telephone on (0171) 447 2010

ORDER FORM

Please send me:
No of copies

❏ Tax Handbook	Available Now	0273 62799 6	£25.99
❏ Pensions Handbook (6th edition)	Available now	0273 62506 3	£24.99
❏ Retirement Planning Handbook (6th edition)	Published Autumn '97	0273 62505 5	£25.99
❏ Expatriate Tax & Investment Handbook (6th edition)	Published Autumn '97	0273 62806 2	£25.99
❏ Business Tax & Law Handbook	Published Winter '97	0273 62807 0	£26.99

I have ordered more than one book, my 10% discount applies   ❏

PAYMENT (*Please complete*) Postage & Packing: Free of Charge

❏ I enclose a cheque payable to Pitman Publishing for _____ (total)
❏ Please debit my Access/Visa/Barclaycard/Mastercard/Amex/Switch/Diners
     for_____ (total)

Card Number

☐☐☐☐ ☐☐☐☐ ☐☐☐☐ ☐☐☐☐ ☐☐☐☐ ☐☐

Expiry Date _____ /9 ___

Issue No _____ (Switch Payments only)

Signature _____

Mr/Mrs/Miss/Ms _____ Initial _____   Surname _____

Job Title _____   Department_____

Company _____

Address _____

Town _____   Country _____

Postcode _____   Tel No _____

All prices quoted are in Sterling. Prices are subject to change without prior notification. Value Added Tax Number GB 213 6785 61. We occasionally make our customer lists available to companies whose products or service may be of interest. Anyone not wanting this free service should write 'exclude from other mailings' on this form. A division of Pearson Professional.